FORTY-SIX YEARS
IN THE ARMY

FORTY-SIX YEARS IN THE ARMY

BY
LIEUTENANT-GENERAL
JOHN M. SCHOFIELD

FOREWORD BY WILLIAM M. FERRARO

UNIVERSITY OF OKLAHOMA PRESS
NORMAN

THIS VOLUME IS DEDICATED TO THE YOUNG CITIZENS WHOSE PATRIOTISM, VALOR AND MILITARY SKILL MUST BE THE SAFE-GUARD OF THE INTERESTS, THE HONOR AND THE GLORY OF THE AMERICAN UNION

Library of Congress Cataloging-in-Publication Data

Schofield, John McAllister, 1831–1906.
    Forty-six years in the army / by John M. Schofield ; foreword by William M. Ferraro.
        p.   cm.
    Originally published: New York : Century Co., 1897.
    Includes bibliographical references and index.
    ISBN 0-8061-3080-6 (pbk. : alk. paper)
    1. Schofield, John McAllister, 1831–1906.
    2. Generals—United States—Biography.   3. United States. Army—Biography.   4. United States—History, Military—To 1900.   5. United States—History—Civil War, 1861–1865—Biography.   I. Title.
    E181.S34   1998
    355'.0092—dc21   98-23381
                                                            CIP

The paper in this book meets the guidelines for permanence and durability of the Committee on Production Guidelines for Book Longevity of the Council on Library Resources, Inc. ∞

Published by the University of Oklahoma Press, Norman, Publishing Division of the University. First published in 1897 by the Century Company. Foreword by William M. Ferraro copyright © 1998 by the University of Oklahoma Press. All rights reserved. Manufactured in the U.S.A. First printing of the University of Oklahoma Press edition, 1998.

1   2   3   4   5   6   7   8   9   10

TABLE OF CONTENTS

FOREWORD

ON November 1, 1895, shortly after retiring as commanding general of the United States Army, John M. Schofield expounded on his presidential aspirations with typical artfulness: "In all my army career I have never voted, nor have I at any time made known my politics, for I always felt that my allegiance was due to the President under whom I happened to serve. If the people desire that I shall be their president I shall not refuse, but I am now in private life, and shall make my home in Chicago. My leisure I shall devote to writing a book of reminiscences."[1] Schofield's presidential prospects quickly faded, but he fulfilled his promise to write his memoirs. Working through the winter of 1896–97, Schofield shaped notes and memoranda into a hefty volume that portrays his extraordinary Civil War experiences and equally remarkable postwar career involving army personalities, national politics, diplomacy, Indians, race relations, and labor unrest. Biographical tidbits and peevish assessments of military contemporaries give the memoirs a timelessness that outlives Schofield's explicit concern with abstract military lessons. Whether controversial, crotchety, or wise, Schofield consistently engages the reader.

Born on September 29, 1831, in upstate New York, Schofield came of age on the Illinois prairie in a devout Baptist family. He was blessed with intelligence and apparently never lacked for self-confidence, striking out on his own to survey land and teach a district school in

Wisconsin before reaching the age of eighteen. A determination to pursue law was cast aside when he received a congressional appointment to the United States Military Academy. Schofield entered West Point on June 1, 1849, and eventually graduated seventh out of fifty-two, but not before enduring dismissal and reinstatement. He had withheld information about improper cadet behavior, and his dismissal was upheld on review—with great irony given future events—by the rulings of George H. Thomas and Fitz-John Porter. Upset with this sour turn, Schofield appealed to Senator Stephen A. Douglass and secured reinstatement. Schofield's reflection on West Point is a cogent comment on his character: "The hardest lesson I had to learn was to submit my will and opinions to those of an accidental superior in rank who, I imagined, was my inferior in other things, and it took me many years to learn it. . . . What I needed to learn was not so much how to command as how to obey." (p. 6)

When President Abraham Lincoln called for volunteers on April 15, 1861, Schofield answered. He became major of the 1st Missouri and accepted Nathaniel Lyon's request to act as his adjutant general and chief of staff. Schofield served with credit under Lyon until the death of that ill-fated commander during the battle of Wilson's Creek on August 10, 1861. Schofield's official report on the Union defeat emphasized how the lack of supplies and logistical support had left Lyon and his fatigued and outnumbered troops in a predicament. In battle, Schofield earned praise for the "coolness and equanimity with which he moved from point to point carrying orders" and "the confidence his example inspired."[2]

Schofield's courage, nerve, and balance were tested repeatedly within the next three years of command in Missouri, Arkansas, and their troublesome border regions. He was caught in a factional crossfire between "radicals," who advocated immediate slave emancipation and aggressive military actions, and "conservatives," who pushed for restraint on both issues. Antagonistic relations with other generals and their political champions led to the Senate refusing to confirm Schofield's nomination as major general of volunteers. Deeply hurt by this public slight, Schofield remembers this period with much exasperation and expresses chagrin when a brief respite from command ended with Lincoln ordering him "back to the old scene of unsoldierly strife and turmoil in Missouri and Kansas." (p. 66) Schofield probably did as much as could be expected in that seething cauldron of political intrigue and animosity.

Partially in reward for enduring so many hardships, Lincoln eventually maneuvered the Senate into confirming Schofield as a major general of volunteers. With the support of Ulysses S. Grant, who had appreciated Schofield's compliance with a call for troops to assist in the campaign against Vicksburg, Schofield was assigned in January 1864 to command the Department and Army of the Ohio, fulfilling a wish "for purely military service in the field, free from political complications." (p. 106) Schofield assumed his new position and commenced preparations for William T. Sherman's campaign against Atlanta. Leading the smallest of three armies, Schofield and his troops performed competently in the series of actions that ended with the fall of Atlanta on September 2, 1864. His account of this campaign is significant because of its sustained criticism of Sherman's generalship, who he believed failed to balance the strength of the three armies, placed unwarranted reliance on the Army of the Tennessee, avoided combat too frequently, expected too much independent initiative from subordinate generals hamstrung by uneven resources and confusion over command hierarchy, and erred grievously by fixating on Atlanta while the Confederates regrouped to fight another day.[3] Schofield especially lamented the lost opportunity to crush the defeated foe and waxed sarcastic on this sore point: "So anxious was I that this be attempted that I offered to go with two corps, or even with one, and intercept Hood's retreat. . . . But more prudent counsels prevailed, and we remained quietly in our camps for five days, while Hood leisurely marched round us with all his baggage and Georgia militia, and collected his scattered fragments at Lovejoy's." (p. 159) The tactful Schofield published these criticisms—originally written upon reading Sherman's memoirs in 1876–77—only after the acclaimed general had been dead some six years.

Sherman's decision to "march to the sea" and leave behind an unconsolidated Union force to oppose the Confederate Army of the Tennessee occasioned additional caustic comments from Schofield, but it also gave the ambitious soldier his much-sought chance to exercise independent command. Schofield joined the army gathering under George H. Thomas, near Nashville, to contain John Bell Hood's Confederates, who were then lurking in the region bordering Georgia, Alabama, and Tennessee. Thomas worried that Hood would strike before he could organize the Union forces, and therefore he sent Schofield to Pulaski, Tennessee, with orders to delay Hood in every way possible short of risking destruction of his smaller army.

Schofield's account of the campaign resulting in the climactic battles at Franklin on November 30, 1864, and Nashville on December 15 and 16, is probably the most disingenuous of the entire memoirs. As was also the case in his official report written on December 31, Schofield portrays himself leading smartly, with sure responses to rapidly changing developments. "The 'fortune of war' was, upon the whole, always in my favor, in spite of adverse accidents; yet I have always acted upon the principle that the highest duty of a commander is to anticipate and provide for every possible contingency of war, so as to eliminate what is called chance." (p. 234) Problems resulted from the ineptness or jealousy of other Union generals, notably James H. Wilson, whose cavalry proved incapable of contending with Nathan B. Forrest's renowned Confederate troopers and failed to gather precise information about enemy movements and dispositions. Reviewing surviving evidence, modern scholars have presented a different Schofield, one who was groping, uncertain, and timid, who frenetically revised assessments, shifted tactical emphases, and disconcerted both subordinates and his superior Thomas. In this light, Schofield's army skirted disaster at Spring Hill and achieved a smashing victory at Franklin principally because of inexplicable luck and the woeful leadership of his counterpart Hood.[4]

Schofield's harshness toward Thomas for the commanding general's conduct during the Tennessee campaign surprised and angered contemporary reviewers, who read Schofield's opinion that "General Thomas did not possess in a high degree the activity of mind necessary to foresee and provide for all the exigencies of military operations." (p. 242) Schofield had been accused of undermining Thomas in order to see him dismissed and assume command himself, but later testimony proved this widespread notion false. Schofield's account of his support for the harassed Thomas in the apprehensive days before the Battle of Nashville can be regarded as truthful and sincere.

Unwilling to sit idly in what had become a secondary theater of the war, Schofield unofficially wrote Grant for transfer to more active duty in the east. Grant obliged, and Schofield went to North Carolina with the XXIII Corps for a brisk two months of marching and fighting. With his prior victory at Franklin and with Grant's steady backing, Schofield was promoted to the rank of brigadier general in the regular army. He connected with Sherman's army driving up from the southwest and was on hand in late April 1865 to help defuse the controversy that exploded following Sherman's overly generous surrender terms to Joseph E. Johnston's Confederate army. Many years later, Schofield offered this view of the conflict: "The great civil war was a contest of superior numbers and resources against an adversary inferior in both, and little better prepared at the commencement of the contest. The result was reached after a long, desperate, and exhausting struggle, characterized for the most part during the first half of its term by military failures, or imperfect successes, due entirely to lack of previous preparation."[5]

Schofield approached the reconstruction of the Southern states with trepidation. He never understood those who wanted to hurry uneducated freedmen into full political citizenship and prohibit educated whites who had been disloyal from participating in government. In his view, such a course would guarantee chaotic government and invidious racial hostility throughout the South. Nothing pained Schofield more than the failure to adopt the Fourteenth Amendment and the subsequent imposition of a punitive congressional reconstruction. As commander of the First Military District under the Reconstruction Acts, Schofield discouraged adoption of a state constitution in Virginia that attempted to disqualify from office all who had supported the Confederacy. Schofield had moved to another assignment before the final vote in 1869, but he firmly believed that the decision to follow his advice saved Virginia from the bloody racial violence and horrendous fraud that tormented citizens in other Southern states.[6]

A diplomatic mission to France provided Schofield with an interlude from contending with Reconstruction in North Carolina and Virginia. French troops in Mexico were threatening the U.S. border in 1865, and instead of pursuing military options, government leaders decided to send Schofield to France with directions to achieve a diplomatic solution. Progress proved painstakingly slow, and it was not until spring of 1866 that Schofield felt at liberty to return home.

The composure, mental acuity, and verbal deftness that led to Schofield's selection for this diplomatic task served likewise to commend him for an investigation in 1873 of the Hawaiian Islands' military usefulness.

The confidence contemporaries felt in Schofield brought his name forward in April 1868 as the man who could placate the politicians entangled in the impeachment of President Andrew Johnson. Schofield apparently listened with diffidence to overtures from Attorney General William M. Evarts to accept nomination as Secretary of War. He agreed to the arrangement after consulting with Grant and convincing himself that such a step was necessary to avert renewed civil strife in the country. Schofield's ten months as Secretary of War earned him the grudging respect of other cabinet members and precipitated a rather boastful observation that he had "the approbation of all for impartial discharge of duty." (p. 405)

Shortly after his inauguration as president in March 1869, Grant nominated Schofield for major general, a rank he held through an array of commands over the next quarter century. Schofield states that he regretted no command as much as the one he accepted at West Point in 1876. While there he tried to elevate the curriculum and public stature of the military academy, but incessant badgering from politicians and civilian officials as well as two sensational incidents understandably darkened Schofield's remembrance of his years at that post.

The first unpleasant episode involved Schofield's sitting as president of the court of inquiry to review Fitz-John Porter's cashiering for insubordination at Second Manassas in late August 1862. Porter's case exposed the cliquishness of professional officers, and because several officers implicated in the original affair and court-martial still held high position, Schofield's court of inquiry was forced to navigate the treacherous shoals of army politics. Convinced that Porter had been wronged, Schofield and his compatriots issued a thorough vindication, only to see their view of justice postponed a number of years by political vindictiveness.

Then came the case of Johnson C. Whittaker, the only black cadet then at the academy. He allegedly had been assaulted while sleeping in his room and was left unconscious. Schofield, who earlier had been solicitous of Whittaker when the latter had been troubled with studies, conducted what he deemed a thorough investigation and concluded that the black cadet's wounds had been self-inflicted in order to spare the likely ignominy of failing imminent examinations. Whittaker resolutely denied this conclusion and set off a newspaper frenzy that persisted through a turbulent court of inquiry and court-martial. Schofield steadfastly maintained that he was free of undue prejudice in his treatment of Whittaker and wrote indignantly in his official report for 1880:

He imagined that officers who had fought to make him free, and who were laboriously striving to teach him what he could not comprehend, were governed in their conduct toward him by "hate of the nigger," and that cadets who would neither touch him nor speak to him, could be believed to have tied his hands and feet and cut his hair and ears, and that so tenderly as not to hurt him. . . . The education and elevation of the newly enfranchised race is a work worthy of the united efforts of all good citizens. But that work cannot be advanced—it must rather be retarded—by forcing colored men into official positions for which they have not yet become duly qualified, or into social relations where they cannot be freely welcomed. The colored man cannot be truly free until he becomes independent of such extraneous aid, and the degree of freedom cannot be increased by depriving the white man of a portion of the liberty he has always enjoyed.[7]

Depending on one's perspective, such remarks and behavior either damn Schofield as a racist or absolve him from blame for a situation beyond his control.[8] In all events, Schofield was neither the first nor last public official to find the issue of racial prejudice utterly intractable and volatile.

Conflict between whites and Indians also vexed Schofield. He castigated those who treated Indians in unscrupulous or cruel fashion and certainly never subscribed to the simplistic creed that "the only good Indian is a dead Indian." As a military commander, however, it frequently became his responsibility to punish Indians for depredations on people or property, and he never shied from this duty. Realist enough to see that cultural patterns established through generations could not be reconfigured instantaneously, Schofield urged reforms—like recruiting Indians as soldiers—to hasten movement of the feared "savages" toward less-threatening habits and values. He worked throughout his long career for humane treatment of the Indians, and his surprise and regrets were real when Sioux unrest culminated in the bloody confrontation at Wounded Knee in late December 1890.

Labor discontent outpaced Indian outbreaks as a cause for concern as the nineteenth century came to a close. Widespread turmoil in economically depressed 1894 caused Schofield particular alarm: "[A]n infuriated mob in a single city was twice as formidable in numbers and capable of doing vastly greater injury to life and property than the most formidable combinations of Indian warriors that ever confronted the Army in this country."[9] Set in his views as to the proper ordering of society and quite comfortable at this stage of his life, Schofield penned cold and self-serving remarks about military intervention against insurgent workers in Chicago following the Pullman strike that summer. "The insurrection was promptly suppressed, and the authority of the Government everywhere enforced, and this without any unnecessary sacrifice of life in any case. . . . The people of the United States may well be proud of their little Army, so thoroughly devoted to the public interests."[10]

Schofield concludes his memoirs with grateful acknowledgment of promotion to the rank of lieutenant general, done as a special act of Congress out of appreciation for his distinguished career. In reaching this height, Schofield took scant notice of those at lower levels—common soldiers and common folk rarely appear in the memoirs. Other sources suggest that men in the ranks found Schofield willful, petty, and lacking in concern for their welfare—feelings captured in names like "Granny" and other disparaging remarks.[11] Schofield also reveals virtually nothing about his personal life. His brief mention of his first and second marriages (pp. 29, 489) provides no clues about the nature of these unions, especially no indication that the second marriage, in June 1891, was to a twenty-seven-year-old woman who had been his daughter's childhood friend and maid of honor at her wedding.[12]

The only book-length biographical study of Schofield published to date ends abruptly in 1868.[13] Astonishingly, after a century that has witnessed a torrent of books on seemingly every aspect of the Civil War, Schofield's scarce *Forty-Six Years in the Army* remains the only complete account of his important military career. It merits reissue, both for what it tells us about Schofield and his times and for what it tells us about ambition and persevering toward one's goals amid the challenges of any time or place.

WILLIAM M. FERRARO

Ulysses S. Grant Association
Southern Illinois University, Carbondale

NOTES

1. *New York Times*, 2 November 1895.

2. *The War of the Rebellion: A Compilation of the Official Records of the Union and Confederate Armies*, ser. 1 (Washington, 1880–1901), iii, 57–64, 69.

3. Modern historians have amplified Schofield's criticisms of Sherman. See especially Albert Castel, *Decision in the West: The Atlanta Campaign of 1864* (Lawrence: University Press of Kansas, 1992).

4. James L. McDonough and Thomas L. Connelly, *Five Tragic Hours: The Battle of Franklin* (Knoxville: University of Tennessee Press, 1983), 24–28, 95, 153–54; and Wiley Sword, *Embrace an Angry Wind: The Confederacy's Last Hurrah: Spring Hill, Franklin, and Nashville* (New York: HarperCollins, 1992), pp. 99–100, 103, 144–50, 159–61, 251, 273, 351–52, 386.

5. *House Executive Documents*, 53rd Cong., 3rd Sess., no. 1, pt. 2, I:62 (#3295).

6. John Y. Simon, ed., *Papers of Ulysses S. Grant* (Carbondale: Southern Illinois University Press, 1967–), 15:64–66, 18:8–9, 218–19, 222–23; James E. Sefton, ed., "Aristotle in Blue and Braid: General John M. Schofield's Essays on Reconstruction," *Civil War History* 17, no. 1 (March 1971): 45–57; and James L. McDonough, "John Schofield as Military Director of Reconstruction in Virginia," *Civil War History* 15, no. 3 (September 1969): 237–56.

7. *House Executive Documents*, 46th Cong., 3rd Sess., no. 1, pt. 2, I:229 (#1952); and letters from Schofield to Sherman between 11 April and 16 August 1880, William T. Sherman Papers, Library of Congress.

8. For a study that champions Whittaker and condemns Schofield, see John F. Marszalek, *Court-Martial: A Black Man in America* (New York: Scribner, 1972). See also Ari Hoogenboom, *Rutherford B. Hayes: Warrior and President* (Lawrence: University Press of Kansas, 1995), 425–27.

9. *House Executive Documents*, 53rd Cong., 3rd Sess., no. 1, pt. 2, I:57–59 (#3295).

10. Ibid., p. 58.

11. Nannie M. Tilley, ed., *Federals on the Frontier: The Diary of Benjamin F. McIntyre* (Austin: University of Texas Press, 1963), 87, 93, 133.

12. *New York Times*, 5, 6, 18, 19 June 1891.

13. James L. McDonough, *Schofield: Union General in the Civil War and Reconstruction* (Tallahassee: Florida State University Press, 1972).

PREFACE

MOST of the chapters constituting the contents of this volume, were written, from time to time, as soon as practicable after the events referred to, or after the publication of historical writings which seemed to me to require comment from the point of view of my personal knowledge. They were written entirely without reserve, and with the sole purpose of telling exactly what I thought and believed, not with any purpose of publication in my lifetime, but as my contribution to the materials which may be useful to the impartial historian of some future generation. These writings had been put away for safe-keeping, with "instructions for the guidance of my executors," in which I said:

"All the papers must be carefully revised, errors corrected if any are found, unimportant matter eliminated, and everything omitted which may seem, to a cool and impartial judge, to be unjust or unnecessarily harsh or severe toward the memory of any individual. I have aimed to be just, and not unkind. If I have failed in any case, it is my wish that my mistakes may be corrected, as far as possible. I have not attempted to write history, but simply to make a record of events personally known to me, and of my opinions upon such acts of others, and upon such important subjects, as have come under my special notice. It is my contribution to the materials from which the future historian must draw for his data for a truthful history of our time."

Now, in the winter of 1896–97, I have endeavored to

discharge, as far as I am able, the duty which I had imposed on my executors, and have decided to publish what I had written in past years, with corrections and comments, while many of the actors in the great drama of the Civil War are still living and can assist in correcting any errors into which I may have fallen.

After my chapters relating to the campaign of 1864 in Tennessee were in type, the monograph by General J. D. Cox, entitled "Franklin," was issued from the press of Charles Scribner's Sons. His work and mine are the results of independent analysis of the records, made without consultation with each other.

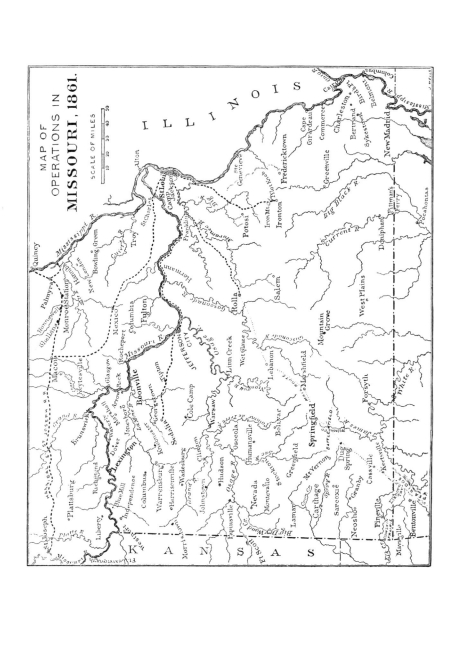

MAP OF
OPERATIONS IN
MISSOURI, 1861.

SCALE OF MILES
10 20 30 40 50

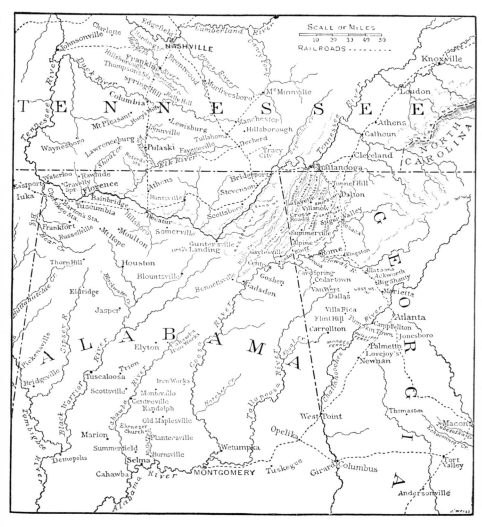

MAP OF OPERATIONS IN MIDDLE TENNESSEE AND NORTH ALABAMA, 1863-65.

FORTY-SIX YEARS
IN THE ARMY

FORTY-SIX YEARS
IN THE ARMY

CHAPTER I

PARENTAGE AND EARLY LIFE — APPOINTMENT TO WEST POINT — VIRGINIAN ROOM-MATES — ACQUAINTANCE WITH GENERAL WINFIELD SCOTT — CHARACTER OF THE WEST POINT TRAINING — IMPORTANCE OF LEARNING HOW TO OBEY — A TRIP TO NEW YORK ON A WAGER — THE WEST POINT BIBLE-CLASS — DISMISSED FROM THE ACADEMY WITHOUT TRIAL — INTERCESSION OF STEPHEN A. DOUGLAS — RESTORATION TO CADET DUTY — JAMES B. McPHERSON — JOHN B. HOOD — ROBERT E. LEE.

I WAS born in the town of Gerry, Chautauqua County, New York, September 29, 1831. My father was the Rev. James Schofield, who was then pastor of the Baptist Church in Sinclairville, and who was from 1843 to 1881 a "home missionary" engaged in organizing new churches, and building "meeting-houses," in Illinois, Iowa, and Missouri. My mother was Caroline McAllister, daughter of John McAllister of Gerry. We removed to Illinois in June, 1843, and, after a short stay in Bristol, my father made a new home for his family in Freeport, where he began his missionary work by founding the First Baptist Church of that place.

In all my childhood and youth I had what I regard as the best possible opportunities for education, in excellent public schools where the rudiments of English were taught with great thoroughness, in a fair amount of all kinds of manly sports, and in hard work, mainly on the farm and in building a new home, which left no time and little inclination for any kind of mischief. At sixteen years of age I spent three months in surveying public lands in the wilds of northern Wisconsin, and at seventeen taught district school in the little town of Oneco. By that time I had chosen the law as my profession, and was working hard to complete the preparatory studies at my own expense.

The winter school term in Oneco having closed early in the spring of 1849, I returned to Freeport and resumed my struggle with Latin. Then an unforeseen event turned the course of my life. The young man who had been appointed to West Point from our district only a year or two before had failed to continue his course in the Military Academy. Thus a vacancy occurred just at the close of Mr. Thomas J. Turner's term in Congress. There was no time for applications or for consultation. He must select another candidate to enter the following June, or leave the place to be filled by his successor. Fortunately for me, Mr. Turner, as one of the public-school directors, had been present at an examination where the subject with which I had to deal was mathematical; if he had caught me at Latin, the result must have been fatal to all my prospects. Besides, Mr. Turner had heard from his brother James of the stamina I had shown in the public land-surveying expedition; and also from my father of my determination to get a good education before beginning the study of law. So he brought me a cadet appointment when he came home, and said he believed a boy with that record could get through West Point, the training there being, in his opinion, a good preparation for the study of law.

The little savings from all my past work had been invested in a piece of land which was sold to fit me out for my journey to West Point, including some inexpensive visits en route. I reported at the Academy on June 1, 1849, with less than two dollars in my pocket, which I conscientiously deposited with the treasurer, as required by the regulations. My reception was of the most satisfactory character. William P. Carlin of the second class, and Hezekiah H. Garber of the third, both from Illinois, found me out very soon after I reported, took me under their protection in a brotherly way, and gave me some timely advice—not to take too seriously any little fun the "men" might make of my blue dress-coat and fancy gilt buttons, or anything like that; but I never experienced anything even approaching to hazing. My rather mature appearance may have had something to do with the respect generally paid me. It was true I was only seventeen years and nine months old, as recorded in the register, but my experience may have had some visible effect.

I was assigned to a room in the old South Barracks, which were demolished the next year. My room-mates were Henry H. Walker and John R. Chambiiss, two charming fellows from Virginia. We had hardly learned each other's names when one of them said something about the "blank Yankees"; but instantly, seeing something that might perhaps have appeared like Southern blood in my face, added, "*You* are not a *Yankee!*" I replied, "Yes; I am from Illinois." "Oh," said he, "we don't call Western men Yankees." In that remark I found my mission at West Point, as in after life, to be, as far as possible, a peacemaker between the hostile sections. If the great West could have been heard, and its more dispassionate voice heeded, possibly peace might have been preserved.

My experience at West Point did not differ in many particulars from the general average of cadet life, but a few incidents may be worthy of special mention. My experience in camp was comparatively limited. The first summer I was on guard only once. Then the corporal of the grand rounds tried to charge over my post without giving the countersign, because I had not challenged promptly. We crossed bayonets, but I proved too strong for him, and he gave it up, to the great indignation of the officer of the day, who had ordered him to charge, and who threatened to report me, but did not. That night I slept on the ground outside the guard tents, and caught cold, from which my eyes became badly inflamed, and I was laid up in the hospital during the remainder of the encampment. On that account I had a hard struggle with my studies the next year. While sitting on the east porch of the hospital in the afternoon, I attracted the kind attention of General Winfield Scott, who became from that time a real friend, and did me a great service some years later.

In our third-class encampment, when corporal of the guard, I had a little misunderstanding one night with the sentinel on post along Fort Clinton ditch, which was then nearly filled by a growth of bushes. The sentinel tore the breast of my shell-jacket with the point of his bayonet, and I tumbled him over backward into the ditch and ruined his musket. But I quickly helped him out, and gave him my musket in place of his, with ample apologies for my thoughtless act. We parted, as I thought, in the best of feeling; but many years later, a colonel in the army told me that story, as an illustration of the erroneous treatment sometimes accorded to sentinels in his time, and I was thus compelled to tell him I was that same corporal, to convince him that he had been mistaken as to the real character of the treatment he had received.

That third-class year I lived in the old North Barracks, four of us in one room. There, under the malign influence of two men who were afterward found deficient, I contracted the bad habit of fastening a blanket against the window after " taps," so that no one outside could see us " burning the midnight oil " over pipes and cards. The corps of cadets was not as much disciplined in our day as it is now. If it had been, I doubt if I should have graduated. As it was, I got 196 demerits out of a possible 200 one year. One more "smoking in quarters" would have been too much for me. I protest now, after this long experience, that nothing else at West Point was either so enjoyable or so beneficial to me as smoking. I knew little and cared less about the different corps of the army, or about the value of class standing. I became quite indignant when a distinguished friend rather reproved me for not trying to graduate higher — perhaps in part from a guilty conscience, for it occurred just after we had graduated. I devoted only a fraction of the study hours to the academic course — generally an hour, or one and a half, to each lesson. But I never intentionally neglected any of my studies. It simply seemed to me that a great part of my time could be better employed in getting the education I desired by the study of law, history, rhetoric, and general literature. Even now I think these latter studies have proved about as useful to me as what I learned of the art and science of war; and they are essential to a good general education, no less in the army than in civil life. I have long thought it would be a great improvement in the Military Academy if a much broader course could be given to those young men who come there with the necessary preparation, while not excluding those comparatively young boys who have only elementary education. There is too much of the " cast-iron " in this government of law under which we live, but "mild steel" will take its place in time, no doubt. The conditions and interests of so vast a country and people are too varied to be wisely subjected to rigid rules.

But I must not be misunderstood as disparaging the West Point education. As it was, and is now, there is,

I believe, nothing equal to it anywhere in this country.
Its methods of developing the reasoning faculties and
habits of independent thought are the best ever devised.
West Point *training* of the mind is practically perfect.
Its general discipline is excellent and indispensable in
the military service. Even in civil life something like it
would be highly beneficial. In my case that discipline
was even more needed than anything else. The hardest
lesson I had to learn was to submit my will and opinions
to those of an accidental superior in rank who, I imagined, was my inferior in other things, and it took me
many years to learn it. Nothing is more absolutely indispensable to a good soldier than perfect subordination
and zealous service to him whom the national will may
have made the official superior for the time being. I
now think it one of the most important lessons of my
own experience that, while I had no difficulty whatever
in securing perfect subordination and obedience in a
large public school when I was only seventeen years old,
or ever afterward in any body of troops, from a squad
of cadets up to an army of men, others did not find it by
any means so easy to discipline me. What I needed to
learn was not so much how to command as how to obey.

My observation of others has also taught much the
same lesson. Too early independence and exercise of
authority seem to beget some degree of disrespect for the
authority of others. I once knew a young major-general who, in his zeal to prevent what he believed to be
the improper application of some public funds, assumed
to himself the action which lawfully belonged to the Secretary of War. The question thus raised was considered
paramount to that of the proper use of the funds. The
young officer lost his point, and got a well-merited rebuke. But it is not to be expected that complete military education can be obtained without complete military
experience. The rules of subordination and obedience

in an army are so simple that everybody learns them with the utmost ease. But the relations between the army and its administrative head, and with the civil power, are by no means so simple. When a too confident soldier rubs up against them, he learns what "military" discipline really means. It sometimes takes a civilian to "teach a soldier his place" in the government of a republic. If a soldier desires that his own better judgment shall control military policy, he must take care not to let it become known that the judgment is his. If he can contrive to let that wise policy be invented by the more responsible head, it will surely be adopted. It should never be suspected by anybody that there is any difference of opinion between the soldier and his civil chief; and nobody, not even the chief, will ever find it out if the soldier does not tell it. The highest quality attributed to Von Moltke was his ability to make it clearly understood by the Emperor and by all the world that the Emperor himself commanded the German army.

My constitutional habit once led me into a very foolish exploit at West Point. A discussion arose as to the possibility of going to New York and back without danger of being caught, and I explained the plan I had worked out by which it could be done. (I will not explain what the plan was, lest some other foolish boy should try it.) I was promptly challenged to undertake it for a high wager, and that challenge overcame any scruple I may have had. I cared nothing for a brief visit to New York, and had only five dollars in money which Jerome N. Bonaparte loaned me to pay my way. But I went to the city and back, in perfect safety, between the two roll-calls I had to attend that day. Old Benny Havens of blessed memory rowed me across the river to Garrison's, and the Cold Spring ferryman back to the Point a few minutes before evening parade. I walked across the plain in full view of the crowd of officers and ladies, and appeared in

ranks at roll-call, as innocent as anybody. It is true my
up-train did not stop at Garrison's or Cold Spring, but
the conductor, upon a hint as to the necessity of the case,
kindly slacked the speed of the express so that I could
jump off from the rear platform. In due time I repaid
Bonaparte the borrowed five dollars, but the wager was
never paid. The only other bet I made at West Point was
on Buchanan's election; but that was in the interest of a
Yankee who was not on speaking terms with the South-
erner who offered the wager. I have never had any disposition to wager anything on chance, but have always
had an irresistible inclination to back my own skill whenever it has been challenged. The one thing most to be
condemned in war is the leaving to chance anything
which by due diligence might be foreseen. In the preparations for defense, especially, there is no longer any
need that anything be left to chance or uncertainty.

I attended the Bible-class regularly every Sunday after
I went to West Point, and rejoiced greatly in that opportunity to hear the Scriptures expounded by the learned
doctor of divinity of the Military Academy. I had never
doubted for a moment that every word of the Bible was
divinely inspired, for my father himself had told me it
was. But I always had a curious desire to know the
reason of things; and, more than that, some of my fellows
were inclined to be a little skeptical, and I wanted the
reasons with which I could overwhelm their unworthy
doubts. So I ventured to ask the professor one Sunday
what was the evidence of divine inspiration. He answered only what my father had before told me, that it
was "internal evidence"; but my youthful mind had not
yet perceived that very clearly. Hence I ventured very
modestly and timidly to indicate my need of some light
that would enable me to see. The learned doctor did
not vouchsafe a word in reply, but the look of amaze-
ment and scorn he gave me for my display of ignorance

sealed my lips on that subject forever. I have never since ventured to ask anybody any questions on that subject, but have studied it out for myself as well as I could. Soon after that the doctor preached a sermon in which he denounced skepticism in his own vigorous terms, and consigned to perdition all the great teachers of heresy, of whom he mentioned the names — before unheard, I am sure, by the great majority of cadets, though their works were to be found in the West Point and all other public libraries. I never looked into any of those books, though other cadets told me that they, at his suggestion, had sought there for the information the good doctor had refused to give us. I have never, even to this day, been willing to read or listen to what seemed to me irreverent words, even though they might be intended to convey ideas not very different from my own. It has seemed to me that a man ought to speak with reverence of the religion taught him in his childhood and believed by his fellow-men, or else keep his philosophical thoughts, however profound, to himself.

Another sermon of the good doctor of divinity, which I did not happen to hear, on the Mosaic history of creation, contained, as stated to me, a denunciation of the "God-hating geologists." That offended me, for I had, in common with all other cadets, learned greatly to admire and respect our professor of geology. So I did not go to the Bible-class any more. But the professor of ethics continued to drive his fine fast horse, much the best one on the Point, and I believe the best I had ever seen. Hence he continued to enjoy my esteem, though perhaps he did not know it.

Near the beginning of the last year of my cadet life an event occurred which very nearly proved fatal to my prospects, and I have often wondered that it did not have some effect on my hopes. But, singularly enough, I never had a moment's doubt or anxiety as to the final result. It was then the custom for candidates to report on June 1, or within the next few days. They were organized into sections, and placed under the instruction of cadets selected from the second class to prepare them, as far as possible, for examination about the middle of the month. I was given charge of a section in arithmetic, and have never in all my life discharged my duty with more conscientious fidelity than I drilled those boys in the subject with which I was familiar, and in teaching which I had had some experience. We had gone over the entire course upon which they were to be examined, and all were well prepared except two who seemed hopelessly deficient upon a few subjects which they had been unable to comprehend. Not willing to omit the last possible effort in behalf of those two boys, I took them to the blackboard and devoted the last fifteen or twenty minutes before the bugle-call to a final effort to prepare them for the ordeal they must face the next morning. While I was thus employed several of my classmates came into the room, and began talking to the other candidates. Though their presence annoyed me, it did not interfere with my work; so I kept on intently with the two young boys until the bugle sounded.

I then went to my quarters without paying any attention to the interruption, or knowing anything of the character of what had occurred. But one of the candidates, perhaps by way of excuse for his failure, wrote to his parents some account of the "deviltry" in which my classmates had indulged that day. That report found its way to the War Department, and was soon followed by an order to the commandant of cadets to investigate. The facts were found fully to exonerate me from any participation in or countenance of the deviltry, except that I did not stop it; and showed that I had faithfully done my duty in teaching the candidates. After this investigation was over, I was called upon to answer for my own conduct; and, the names of my guilty classmates being unknown to the candidates, I was also held responsible for their conduct. I answered by averring and showing, as I believed, my own innocence of all that had been done, except my neglect of duty in tolerating such a proceeding. My conscience was so clear of any intentional wrong that I had no anxiety about the result. But in due time came an order from the Secretary of War dismissing me from the academy without trial. That, I believe, shocked me a little; but the sense of injustice was too strong in my mind to permit of a doubt that it would be righted when the truth was known. I proposed to go straight to Washington and lay the facts before the government. Then I realized for the first time what it meant to have friends. All my classmates and many other cadets came forward with letters to their congressmen, and many of them to senators whom they happened to know, and other influential men in Washington. So I carried with me a great bundle of letters setting forth my virtues in terms which might have filled the breast of George Washington with pride.

There was no public man in Washington whom I had ever seen, and probably no one who had ever heard of me, except the few in the War Department who knew of my alleged bad conduct. The Secretary of War would not even see me until I was at last presented to him by an officer of the army. Then he offered me his forefinger to shake, but he could give me no encouragement whatever. This was after I had been in Washington several weeks. My congressman, Mr. Campbell, who had succeeded Mr. Turner, and several others received me kindly, read my letters, and promised to see the Secretary of War, which no doubt they did, though without any apparent effect. The only result was the impossible suggestion that if I would give the names of my guilty classmates I might be let off. I had made an early call upon the "Little Giant," Senator Douglas, to whom I had no letter, and whom I had never met; had introduced myself as a "citizen of Illinois" in trouble; and had told my story. He said he was not on good terms with that administration, and preferred not to go near the War Department if it could be avoided, but if it proved necessary to let him know. Hence, after all else failed, including my personal appeal, which I had waited so long to make, I told Mr. Douglas all that had occurred, and suggested that there was nothing left but to "put in the reserve," as the tacticians call it. He replied: "Come up in the morning, and we will go to see about it." On our way to the War Department the next morning, the senator said, "I don't know that I can do anything with this —— Whig administration"; but he assured me all should be made right in the next. That seemed to me the kind of man I had looked for in vain up to that time. I waited in the anteroom only a few minutes, when the great senator came out with a genial smile on his face, shook me warmly by the hand, and bade me good-by, saying: "It is all right. You can go back to West Point. The Secretary has given me his promise." I need not go into the details of the long and tedious formalities through which the Secretary's promise was finally fulfilled. It was enough for me that my powerful friend had secured the promise that, upon proof of the facts as I had stated them, I should be fully exonerated and restored to the academy. I returned to West Point, and went through the long forms of a court of inquiry, a court martial, and the waiting for the final action of the War Department, all occupying some five or six months, diligently attending to my military and academic duties, and trying hard to obey all the regulations (except as to smoking), never for a moment doubting the final result. That lesson taught me that innocence and justice sometimes need powerful backing. Implicit trust in Providence does not seem to justify any neglect to employ also the biggest battalions and the heaviest guns.

During all that time I continued to live with my old room-mate, James B. McPherson, in a tower room and an adjoining bedroom, which La Rhett L. Livingston also shared. I had been corporal, sergeant, and lieutenant up to the time of my dismissal; hence the duties of private were a little difficult, and I found it hard to avoid demerits; but with some help from our kind-hearted inspecting officer, Milton Cogswell,— bless his memory!— I contrived to get off with 196 demerits in a possible 200 that last year. In a mild way, McPherson was also a little under a cloud at that time. He had been first captain of the battalion and squad marcher of the class at engineering drill. In this latter capacity he also had committed the offense of not reporting some of the class for indulging in unauthorized sport. The offense was not so grave as mine, and, besides, his military record was very much better. So he was let off with a large demerit mark and a sort of honorable retirement to the office of quartermaster of the battalion. I still think, as I did then, that McPherson's punishment was the more appropriate. Livingston was one of those charming, amiable fellows with whom nobody could well find any fault, though I believe he did get a good many demerits. He also seemed to need the aid of tobacco in his studies. William P. Craighill, who succeeded McPherson as first captain, had no fault whatever, that I ever heard of, except one — that was, standing too high for his age. He was a beardless youth, only five feet high and sixteen years old when he entered the academy; yet he was so inconsiderate as to keep ahead of me all the time in everything but tactics, and that was of no consequence to him, for he was not destined to command troops in the field, while, as it turned out, I was. It has always seemed to me a little strange that the one branch which

I never expected to use afterward was the only study in which I graduated at the head. Perhaps McPherson and Craighill thought, as I did, that it made no difference where I stood in tactics.

Among all the tactical officers of our time, Lieutenant John M. Jones was esteemed the most accomplished soldier and tactician, and the most rigid but just and impartial disciplinarian. It had been my good fortune to enjoy his instruction while I was private, corporal, sergeant, and lieutenant, and I fully shared with others in the above high estimate of his character. I even flattered myself that my soldierly conduct in all that time had not escaped his favorable notice. When my case was before the court of inquiry in the summer of 1852, the professors who had been called to testify gave me a high character as a faithful, diligent student. When Lieutenant Jones was called to testify as to my character as a soldier, he replied that, in his opinion, it was very bad! While I was not a little surprised and disappointed at that revelation of the truth from the lips of the superior whom I so highly respected, and did not doubt for a moment his better judgment, I could not be unmindful of the fact that the other tactical officers did not know me so well, and had not so high a reputation as Lieutenant Jones in respect to discipline; and I felt at liberty to avail myself, in my own interest, of the opportunity suggested by this reflection. Hence, when, after my complete restoration to the academy in January, I found my demerits accumulating with alarming rapidity, I applied for and obtained a transfer to Company C, where I would be under Lieutenant Cogswell and Cadet Captain Vincent, my beloved classmate, who had cordially invited me to share his room in barracks.

John B. Hood was a jolly good fellow, a little discouraged at first by unexpected hard work; but he fought his way manfully to the end. He was not quite so talented as some of his great associates in the Confederate army, but he was a tremendous fighter when occasion offered. During that last period of our cadet life, Colonel Robert E. Lee was superintendent of the academy; he was the personification of dignity, justice, and kindness, and was respected and admired as the ideal of a commanding officer. Colonel Robert S. Garnett was commandant of cadets; he was a thorough soldier who meted out impartial justice with both hands. At our last parade I received "honorable mention" twice, both the personal judgment of the commandant himself. The one was for standing at the head of the class in tactics; the other, for "not carrying musket properly in ranks." Who can ever forget that last parade, when the entire class, officers and privates together, marched up in line and made their salute to the gallant commandant! To a West-Pointer no other emotion equals it, except that of victory in battle.

CHAPTER II

ON GRADUATING LEAVE — BREVET SECOND LIEUTENANT IN THE 2D ARTILLERY AT FORT MOULTRIE — AN OFFICER'S CREDIT BEFORE THE WAR — SECOND LIEUTENANT IN THE 1ST ARTILLERY — JOURNEY TO FORT CAPRON, FLORIDA — A RESERVATION AS TO WHISKY — A TRIP TO CHARLESTON AND A TROUBLESOME MONEY-BAG — AN "AFFAIR OF HONOR" — A FEW LAW-BOOKS — AN EXTEMPORIZED "MAP AND ITINERARY" — YELLOW FEVER — AT A. P. HILL'S HOME IN VIRGINIA — ASSIGNED TO DUTY IN THE DEPARTMENT OF PHILOSOPHY AT WEST POINT — INTEREST IN ASTRONOMY — MARRIAGE — A HINT FROM JEFFERSON DAVIS — LEAVE OF ABSENCE — PROFESSOR OF PHYSICS IN WASHINGTON UNIVERSITY.

AN old army colonel many years ago described a West Point graduate, when he first reported for duty after graduating leave, as a very young officer with a full supply of self-esteem, a four-story leather trunk filled with good clothes, and an empty pocket. To that must be added, in my case, a debt equal to the full value of trunk and clothes and a hundred dollars borrowed money. My "equipment fund" and much more had been expended in Washington and in journeys to and fro during the period of administrative uncertainty in respect to the demands of discipline at West Point. Still I had as good a time, that graduating leave, as any millionaire in the United States. My good father was evidently disturbed, and began to fear — for the first time, I think — that I was really going to the bad! His worst fears as to

16

the possible effects of a military education had, after all, been realized! When I showed him the first check from New York, covering my pay account for July, he said that it was enough to ruin any boy in the world. Indeed, I myself was conscious of the fact that I had not done a stroke of work all that month for those sixty-five and a half dollars; and in order that my father might be convinced of my determination not to let such unearned wealth lead me into dissipation, I at once offered to lend him fifty dollars to pay a debt due to somebody on the Freeport Baptist meeting-house. Confidence was thereby restored.

My first orders assigned me to duty at Fort Moultrie, South Carolina, as brevet second lieutenant in the 2d Artillery. The steamer landed me at Charleston, September 29, 1853, the day I became twenty-two years of age. The next morning I found myself without money enough to pay my hotel bill and take me over to Sullivan's Island, but pay was due me for September. Upon inquiry, I found that the paymaster was not in the city, but that he kept his public funds in the Bank of South Carolina. Being unacquainted with any of the good people of Charleston, the well-known rules of banks about identification seemed a serious obstacle. I presented my pay account at the bank, informing the cashier with a confident air that I was well aware of the fact that the major's money was there, but that the major himself was out of town. The accomplished cashier, after scrutinizing me for a time, handed me the money. My older brother officers at the fort had a good laugh at what they were pleased to call my " brass"; but I consoled myself with the reflection that I had found out that my face was good for something. It is an instructive fact that before the Civil War an officer of the army needed no indorser anywhere in this country. His check or his pay account was as good as gold. All that was

2

required was identification. It is lamentably true that such has not been the case since the war.

I found only one officer on duty with my battery at Fort Moultrie, and he was awaiting my arrival so that he might go on leave. He turned over the command with a manifestation of confidence which surprised me at the time, but which was fully explained the next day. In the morning the first sergeant reported to me, with the quarterly and monthly returns prepared for my signature, and made out more beautifully than anything in writing I had ever before seen, and explained to me in detail all the business affairs of the battery, as if he were reporting to an old captain who had just returned from a long leave of absence. Next to General Scott and Colonel Lee, with whom I had had the honor of some acquaintance, I was quite sure there stood before me the finest-looking and most accomplished soldier in the United States Army. What a hard time young officers of the army would sometimes have but for the old sergeants! I have pitied from the bottom of my heart volunteer officers whom I have seen starting out, even in the midst of war, with perfectly raw regiments, and not even one old sergeant to teach them anything. No country ought to be so cruel to its soldiers as that.

In September we had the usual artillery target practice, which was afterward recalled to my mind many times by the bombardment of Fort Sumter in 1861 by the same guns I had used in practice, and at the same range. Then came the change of stations of troops, which took the Moultrie garrison to Florida, and some of the 1st Artillery to their place. For a time the fort was left without garrison except a few officers who were awaiting the arrival of their regiment. I also was ordered to remain until I "got off my brevet" and was appointed "full second" in the 1st Artillery. It had been a yellow-fever summer, and the cottages on Sullivan's Island were even more fully occupied than usual, mostly by families of planters from the rice plantations of South Carolina. Hospitality was unbounded, and of the most charming character. Nothing I have experienced at home or in the great capitals of Europe has surpassed or dimmed the memory of that first introduction to Southern society.

In December, 1853, the order came announcing my appointment as second lieutenant, 1st Artillery, and directing me to join Battery D at Fort Capron, Indian River, Florida. A steamer took me to Palatka, stopping a short time at Jacksonville, which was then little more than a landing on the St. John's River. After a week's delay at Palatka, another little mail-steamer carried me and a few other passengers up the river to Lake Monroe, whence a mule served for transportation across to New Smyrna, on Mosquito Lagoon, opposite the inlet. It was a great day's sport going up the river. The banks seemed almost lined with alligators, and the water covered with water-fowl of all kinds, while an occasional deer or flock of turkeys near by would offer a chance shot. At New Smyrna Mrs. Sheldon provided excellent entertainment during the ten days' waiting for the mail-boat down Mosquito Lagoon and Indian River, while Mr. Sheldon's pack of hounds furnished sport. At length old Captain Davis took the mail and my baggage and me on board his sloop, bound for Fort Capron, opposite the mouth of Indian River. He divided his time fairly between carrying the United States mail and drinking whisky, but he never attempted to do both at the same time. I am not sure but it was the captain's example which first suggested to me the rule which I adopted when commanding an army in the field — to do no drinking till after the day's fighting was over. But, in fact, I never liked whisky, and never drank much, anyhow.

We arrived in twenty-five days from Charleston, which was regarded as a very satisfactory journey. At the fort I found Captain and Brevet-Major Joseph A. Haskin, commanding; First Lieutenant A. P. Hill, afterward lieutenant-general in the Confederate army; Dr. A. J. Foard, assistant surgeon; and my classmate Livingston, brevet second lieutenant; besides sixteen enlisted men — rather a close approximation to the ideal of that old colonel who once said the army would be delightful if it were not for the —— soldiers. But that was changed after a while by the arrival of recruits — enough in one batch to fill the battery full. The battery had recently come from the gulf coast, where yellow fever had done destructive work. I was told that there happened to be only one officer on duty with the battery — a Lieutenant somebody — when the fever broke out, and that he resigned and went home. If that is true, I trust he went into the Civil War and got killed in battle; for that was the only atonement he could possibly make for leaving his men in that way. But such cases have been exceedingly rare, while those of the opposite extreme have not been uncommon, where officers have remained with the sick and died there, instead of going with the main body of their men to a more healthy place. The proper place for a line officer is with the fighting force, to care for it and preserve its strength by every means in his power, for war may come to-morrow. The surgeons and their assistants must and do fully care for the sick and wounded.

Life at Fort Capron was not by any means monotonous. It was varied by sailing, fishing, and shooting, and even the continuity of sport was broken twice a month, generally, by the arrival of the mail-boat. But at length this diversion failed us. Some difference occurred between the United States Post-office Department and the mail-contractor on the St. John's River, and we got no mail for three months. Then the commanding officer ordered me to go to Charleston by the sloop that had brought us supplies, and bring back the mail by the regular route. I made the round trip in little more than a month. That same paymaster whom I had found away from his post on my first arrival in Charleston intrusted to me a carpet-bag full of gold and silver, to pay off the garrison for the past six months, with as much advance pay as the officers would consent to take, so that he would not have to make the trip down for a long time to come. I had to carry the money-bag and a revolver about with me for twenty-five days or more. I have never consented to handle Uncle Sam's money since that time.

It was during that short visit to Charleston that I became engaged, for the first and only time, in an "affair of honor." A young man who had been in my class at West Point, but had resigned before the class had graduated, came to me at the hotel, and asked me, as his "friend," to deliver a note he held in his hand. I replied: "Yes. If you will place yourself in my hands and do what I decide is honorable and right, I will be your friend. Tell me all about it." My condition was accepted without reserve. My friend, whose home was in a distant city, had been in Charleston some weeks, and had spent all the money he had and all he could borrow. He was on the eve of negotiating a further loan from a well-known banker when the son of that banker, who had met my friend about town, told his father the plain truth about my friend's habits and his probable value as a debtor. The negotiation was ended. My friend had become a stranger in a strange land, without the means to stay there any longer or to go home. It was a desperate case — one which could not be relieved by anything less than the blood of the young "villain" who had told his father that "infamous"—truth! I replied: "Yes, that is a bad case; we will have to fix that up. How are you off at

2*

home?" He said the "old man" had plenty of money, but had sent him enough to come home once or twice before, and would not send any more. Upon further inquiry, I found that my friend's hotel bill and expenses home would amount to a little less than the sum I had just drawn on my pay account up to date; so I handed him the money, saying that he could return it when convenient, and his "honor" was fully satisfied. I never afterward heard anything from him about that money, and my tailor had to wait a little longer for his pay; but I had done my duty, as I understood it, under the code of honor. I saw that friend once afterward. He went into the army in 1861, accidentally shot himself, and died miserably on the march, an old musket-barrel, placed there by my order, marking his grave by the wayside. It was not granted to him, poor fellow! to fight a battle for his country.

I took with me to Florida some law-books — Blackstone, Kent, and a few others: so few, indeed, that I learned them nearly all by heart; then, for want of anything better, I read over the entire code of the State of Florida. Several times in after years I found it necessary, in order to save time, to repeat to great lawyers the exact words of the Constitution of the United States; but their habit was much the better. It is seldom wise to burden the memory with those things which you have only to open a book to find out. I recollect well the answer once made by William M. Evarts, then attorney-general of the United States, to my inquiry whether he would give me, offhand, the law on a certain point, to save the time requisite for a formal application and answer in writing. He said if it was a question of statute law he would have to examine the books, but if only a question of common law he could make that as well as anybody. But I had nothing better to do for a time in Florida, and when I got out I did not find my memory half so much overloaded with law as my blood was with malarial poison. Luckily, I got rid of the poison after a while, but held on to the law, and I never found it did me any harm. In fact, I would advise all young officers to acquire as much of it as they can.

In the winter of 1853–4 there was an armed truce between the United States of America and the Seminole nation. A new policy was soon inaugurated, which had for its object to establish a complete line of posts across the State from Jupiter to Lake Okeechobee, and thence westward to the gulf, so as more securely to confine the Seminoles within the Everglade region, although, so far as I know, nobody then wanted the use of that more northern part of this vast territory. The first step was to reopen the old military road from the mouth of Indian River across to the Kissimmee River, and thence to Tampa. Being the second lieutenant of the single company, I was given the privilege of doing that work, and nine men and one wagon were assigned me for that purpose. I spent the larger part of my time, going and coming, in hunting on either the right or the left of the road, thereby obtaining all the deer and turkeys the command could consume, but paying very little attention to the road itself, in utter disregard of the usual military rule which requires that a sketch be made and an itinerary kept of all such marches. Hence I was a little puzzled when Acting-Inspector-General Canby, from Washington, wanted to go across from Indian River to Tampa, and called on me for a copy of my map and itinerary. But I had stood very high in drawing at West Point, and could not allow myself to be disturbed in any such way as that; so I unlocked what little recollection I had of the route and my general knowledge of the country, and prepared a very beautiful map and a quite elaborate itinerary, with which the inspector-general seemed greatly pleased. But I took great care, in addition, to send a man with him who had been with me, and who was a good guide, so I felt quite safe respecting any possible imperfections that the inspector-general might find in my work. I never heard anything more about that matter until General Sherman and I met General Canby at Portland in 1870. At that time we had a little laugh at my expense respecting the beauty of that map of mine, and the accuracy with which I had delineated the route. But as I was then a major-general, and Canby was a brigadier-general under my command, I was not subjected to the just criticism I deserved for having forgotten that map and itinerary at the time I made the march.

The next step in the strategical operations designed by the War Department for Florida was the occupation of Fort Jupiter, and the construction of a new post there, reopening the old military road of General Jesup and building a block-house on the bank of Lake Okeechobee, similar work to be undertaken from the other shore of the lake westward. The work was commenced about midwinter of 1854–5, and it was my privilege to do it. When the hot weather came on at Jupiter, fever began to break out among the troops. Jupiter Inlet had been closed for several years, and the water had become stagnant. Within a very few weeks, every man, woman, and child was down, or had been down, with fever. The mortality was such that there were hardly enough strong men remaining to bury the dead. As soon as I had sufficiently recovered to go in a boat to Fort Capron, the major sent me back with all the convalescents that were fit to be moved, and soon afterward broke up that pest-house at Jupiter and moved the command back to Capron. So far as I know, Fort Jupiter was never again occupied, and I think the block-house on Lake Okeechobee was never completed. At all events, as good luck would have it, I got through with my part of the work and was ordered out of Florida before the Seminoles found out what the plans of the War Department were. My old friend and companion George L. Hartsuff, who had like duty to perform on the west side of the lake, was attacked by the Indians and severely wounded, several of his men being killed. He and a few others made their escape. Hartsuff was one of the strongest, bravest, finest soldiers I ever knew, and one of my most intimate friends; but, unlike myself, he was always in bad luck. He got caught by the Seminoles in Florida; was shipwrecked on Lake Michigan; came very near dying of yellow fever; and after organizing the Twenty-third Army Corps and commanding it for a time, finally died of the wounds he had received in Florida.

I had a new and peculiar experience at Fort Capron during my convalescence. I had there twenty-five or thirty convalescent soldiers, and no doctor, but an intelligent hospital steward. I was like the lawyer who was asked to say grace at the table of one of his wealthy clients, and who was unwilling to admit, under such circumstances, that there was any one thing he could not do. So I had sick-call regularly every morning, carefully questioned every patient as to his symptoms, and told the steward what to give him, taking care not to prescribe anything which some doctor had not tried on me. All my patients got well. At length A. P. Hill came up from Jupiter, on his way home on sick-leave. At Capron he had a relapse, and was desperately ill. I had to send a barge to Jupiter for some medicine which he knew was necessary. Mr. Jones, the sutler, and some of the men helped me to nurse him night and day for a long time. At length he recovered so far as to continue his journey.

About the same time came orders promoting me to first lieutenant and detailing me for duty at West Point. So Hill and I came out of Florida together. On board the St. John's River steamer I had a relapse, and was very ill. Hill cared for me tenderly, kept me at Savannah awhile, and then some days at Charleston, where I became so much better that he ventured to leave me long enough to go over to Fort Moultrie to see some of our brother officers. While he was away I became so ill again that the doctor had to put me under the influence of chloroform. When Hill came back in the evening he cursed himself for all that was mean in the world for having left me even for an hour. That 's the kind of friends and comrades soldiers are! As soon as I was well enough to travel, Hill took me to his home at Culpeper Court-house in Virginia. There they kept me quite a long time. That dear old gentleman, his father, brought to my bedside every morning a brandy mint-julep, made with his own hand, to drink before I got up. Under its benign influence my recovery was very rapid. But let none of my young friends forget that the best gifts of Providence are those most liable to be abused. The wise Virginian never offered me too many of them. By the first of December Hill and I went together to West Point, I to report for duty, and he to visit his numerous warm friends at that delightful station. There we parted, in December, 1855, never to meet again. With the glad tidings from Virginia that peace was near, there came to me in North Carolina the report that Lieutenant-General A. P. Hill had been killed in the last battle at Petersburg. A keen pang shot through my heart, for he had not ceased to be esteemed as my kind friend and brother, though for four years numbered among the public enemy. His sense of duty, so false in my judgment, I yet knew to be sincere, because I knew the man. I wish all my fellow-citizens, North and South, East and West, could know each other as well as I knew A. P. Hill.

I was assigned to duty in the department of philosophy, under Professor W. H. C. Bartlett, one of the ablest, most highly esteemed, and most beloved of the great men who have placed the United States Military Academy among the foremost institutions of the world. At first it seemed a little strange to be called back, after the lapse of only two years, to an important duty at the place where my military record had been so " bad." But I soon found that at West Point, as elsewhere, the standard of merit depended somewhat upon the point of view of the judge. A master of "philosophy" could not afford to look too closely into past records in other subjects. Besides, philosophers know, if others do not, that philosophers are sure to profit by healthful experience. I never had any more trouble at West Point, though I did have much difficulty in helping younger men out. I had the great good fortune never to be compelled to report a cadet for any delinquency, nor to find one deficient in studies, though I did sometimes have, figuratively speaking, to beat them over the head with a cudgel to get in "phil" enough to pass the academic board.

I had then a strong impression, which has grown still stronger with time, that "equations A and B" need not be developed very far into the "mechanics of molecules" to qualify a gallant young fellow for the command of a squadron of cavalry; but this is, in fact, generally and perfectly well understood at West Point. The object there is to develop the mental, moral, and physical man to as high a degree as practicable, and to ascertain his best place in the public service. It is only the hopelessly incorrigible in some respect who fall by the way. Even they, if they have stayed there long enough, are the better for the training they have received.

In this congenial work and its natural sequence I formed for the first time the habit of earnest, hard mental work to the limit of my capacity for endurance, and sometimes a little beyond, which I have retained the greater part of my life. After the short time required to master the "Analytical Mechanics" which had been introduced as a text-book since I had graduated, and a short absence on account of my Florida debility, which had reduced me to 120 pounds in weight, I began to pursue physics into its more secret depths. I even indulged the ambition to work out the mathematical interpretation of all the phenomena of physical science, including electricity and magnetism. After three years of hard labor in this direction, I thought I could venture to publish a part of my work in book form, and thus submit it to the judgment of the able scientists whose acquaintance I had made at the meetings of the American Association for the Advancement of Science.[1]

While I was engaged in this work upon physics, a young gentleman named Drown came to West Point, and asked me to give him some private lessons in mechanics and astronomy, to perfect his qualifications as a teacher. I went over those subjects with him in about one hundred lessons, including a few in practical astronomy. He was the most ardent student I have ever known. Like, I doubt not, all the most earnest seekers for divine truth, in whatever way revealed to man, he would not be satisfied with his own perception of such truth unless he could feel it " burn in his brain." In that brief experience I became for the first time intensely interested in practical astronomy, about which I had thought little before, although I had had sole charge of the observatory for some time. I have always since given Professor Drown credit for teaching me practical astronomy by first leading me to the discovery that I had a natural taste and aptitude for such work, theretofore unsuspected. That new "lead" was followed with all possible zeal, day and night, for many months, until all the instruments in the observa-

---

[1] Much of my time in St. Louis during the winter preceding the Civil War was spent in revising this work, preparing illustrations, and getting it ready for the press. Then it was packed up in a box, and carefully stored away in the St. Louis Arsenal, to abide the results of war.

tory, fixed and movable, including the old mural circle, had gone through a season's work. Although my scientific experience has been very limited, I do not believe anything else in the broad domain of science can be half so fascinating as the study of the heavens. I have regretted many times that necessity limited my enjoyment of that great pleasure to a very few years instead of a lifetime.

In that West Point observatory I had one of the many opportunities of my life—one which I always enjoyed— of protecting the unfortunate from the stern decree of "justice." The old German custodian came to me one morning in great distress, saying that he had let the "astronomical chronometer" run down, and that the professor would kill him. I went with him to the transit tower, made an observation, and set the chronometer. The professor never knew the difference till I told him, after the lapse of time named in the military statute of limitations. Then he seemed to rejoice as much as I over the narrow escape of his faithful subordinate. The professor was not half as stern as he sometimes appeared to be.

I need hardly say that in the midst of these absorbing occupations I forgot all about the career I had chosen in my boyhood. The law had no longer any charms for me. Yet I found in after life far more use for the law than for physics and astronomy, and little less than for the art and science of war.

In June, 1857, I married Miss Harriet Bartlett, the second daughter of my chief in the department of philosophy. Five children were born to us, three of whom—two sons and one daughter—grew to maturity and survive their mother, who died in Washington soon after I was assigned to the command of the army, and was buried at West Point by the side of our first-born son, who had died in 1868, soon after I became Secretary of War.

In the summer of 1860 came the end of my term of

duty at West Point. My taste for service in the line
of the army, if I ever had any, was gone; and all hope of
promotion, if I ever had any, was still further away. I
had been for more than four years about nineteenth first
lieutenant in my regiment, without rising a single file. I
was a man of family, and had already become quite bald
"in the service of my country." There was no captaincy
in sight for me during the ordinary lifetime of man, so
I accepted the professorship of physics in Washington
University, St. Louis, Missouri. But Mr. Jefferson Davis,
an intimate friend of my father-in-law, gave me a timely
hint that promotion might be better in a year or two;
and his bitterest personal enemy, General Scott, gave me
a highly flattering indorsement which secured leave of
absence for a year. Thus I retained my commission.

As the period of the Civil War approached a very large
part of my time was occupied in reading and studying,
as coolly as possible, every phase of the momentous questions which I had been warned must probably be submitted to the decision of war. Hence, when the crisis
came I was not unprepared to decide for myself, without
prejudice or passion, where the path of duty lay, yet not
without some feeling of indulgence toward my brother
officers of the army who, as I believed, were led by the
influence of others so far astray. I took an early occasion to inform General Scott of my readiness to relinquish my leave of absence and return to duty whenever
my services might be required, and I had the high honor
of not being requested to renew my oath of allegiance.

My life in St. Louis during the eight months next preceding the Civil War was of great benefit to me in the
delicate and responsible duties which so soon devolved
upon me. My connection with Washington University
brought me into close relations with many of the most
patriotic, enlightened, and, above all, unselfish citizens
of Missouri. Some of them were of the Southern school

of politics, but the large majority were earnest Union men, though holding the various shades of opinion then common on the question of slavery. By long and intimate intercourse, in the joint prosecution of work of the highest philanthropy, such men had learned to respect the sincerity of each other's adverse convictions, and had become the exact exemplars of the many shades of honest, patriotic Unionism so clearly described in 1863 by President Lincoln in his letter to a delegation of partizans who had not learned that principle of charity which seems to have been born in the great martyr of freedom.

Would that I could do fitting honor to the names of those patriots, nearly all of whom have gone to their rest, including Dr. Elliot, President of Washington University. James E. Yeatman, President of the Sanitary Commission, still lives to honor his country and the great cause of humanity of which he was the faithful and efficient servant. I did not meet Hamilton R. Gamble until after he had become governor. I shall have occasion to say more of him later. He was the foremost champion of the Union cause in Missouri, and the most abused by those who were loudest in their professions of loyalty. Of the younger generation, I will mention only one, whose good deeds would otherwise never be known. While himself absent in the public service, wherein he was most efficient, he made me occupy his delightful residence near Lafayette Park, and consume all the products of his excellent garden. We knew each other then only as fellow-workers in the Union cause, but have been the most devoted friends from that day to this. The name of that dear friend of mine is Charles Gibson. Among the earliest and most active leaders in the Union cause in Missouri, I must not fail to mention the foremost — Frank P. Blair, Jr. His patriotism and courage were like a calcium light at the head of the Union column in the dark days and nights of the spring of 1861.

CHAPTER III

WHEN it became probable that military force would be required by the government to maintain its authority in the Southern States, I informed the War Department of my readiness to return to duty whenever my services might be required, and was instructed to await orders in St. Louis. Upon President Lincoln's first call for volunteers, I was detailed to muster in the troops required of the State of Missouri. With the order of detail was furnished a copy of the old instructions for mustering into service, etc., which required me to call upon the governor of Missouri for the regiments to be mustered, and to accept only fully organized regiments. It was well and publicly known that the executive of Missouri was disloyal to the United States, and that compliance with the President's demand for volunteers was not to be expected from the State government; yet my instructions authorized me to take no action which could be effective under such circumstances, and the then department commander, Brigadier-General William S. Harney, would not consent that any such action be taken without orders from Washington. I called upon Governor Jackson for his regiments, but received no reply.

In my visit to General Harney after the attack on Fort Sumter, I urged the necessity of prompt measures to protect the St. Louis Arsenal, with its large stores of arms and ammunition, then of priceless value, and called his attention to the rumor of an intended attack upon the arsenal by the secessionists then encamped near the city under the guise of State militia. In reply, the general denounced in his usual vigorous language the proposed attempt upon the arsenal; and, as if to clinch his characterization of such a " —— outrage," said: " Why, the State has not yet passed an ordinance of secession; she has not gone out of the Union." That did not indicate to me that General Harney's Union principles were quite up to the standard required by the situation, and I shared with many others a feeling of great relief when he was soon after relieved, and Captain Nathaniel Lyon succeeded to the command of the department. Yet I have no doubt General Harney was, from his own point of view, thoroughly loyal to the Union, though much imbued with the Southern doctrines which brought on secession and civil war. His appropriate place after that movement began was that of the honorable retirement in which he passed the remainder of his days, respected by all for his sterling character and many heroic services to his country.

Two days later, Captain Lyon, then commanding the St. Louis Arsenal, having received from the War Department authority to enroll and muster into the service the Missouri volunteers as they might present themselves, I reported to him and acted under his orders. Fortunately, a large number of the loyal citizens of St. Louis had, in anticipation of a call to take up arms in support

3

of the government, organized themselves into companies, and received some instruction in tactics at their places of secret nightly meeting in the city. On the other hand, the organized militia of the State, mostly disloyal, were in the city of St. Louis near the arsenal, which contained many thousand muskets, and which was defended by only a small body of regular troops. There was great danger that the arsenal would follow the fate of the public arsenals in the more Southern States. To avert this danger was the first great object.

Upon receipt of the necessary authority by Captain Lyon, I was called out of church on Sunday morning, April 21, and the loyal secret organizations were instructed to enter the arsenal at night, individually, each member being furnished with a pass for that purpose. The mustering officer employed himself all night and the following day in distributing arms and ammunition to the men as they arrived, and in stationing them along the arsenal walls. Thus the successful defense of the arsenal was secured, though its garrison was neither mustered into service nor organized into regiments, nor even enrolled. The organization of the volunteers now began, the mustering officer superintending the election of officers, enrolling the men, and perfecting the organization in conformity to the militia laws of the State.

On June 4 I transmitted to the adjutant-general " the muster-rolls of five regiments of infantry; of four rifle battalions of two companies each, attached to the 1st, 2d, 3d, and 4th regiments; of one artillery battalion of three companies; and of a company of pioneers "; also " the muster-roll of Brigadier-General Lyon's staff, mustered by himself." Accompanying the muster-rolls was a return showing the strength of each regiment and of the brigade.

Lyon had previously been elected brigadier-general of the brigade the regiments of which I had mustered in, but I had no authority to muster in a brigadier-general and staff.

The Missouri United States Reserve Corps, organized in St. Louis about the same time, consisting of five regiments, was mustered into service by General Lyon, under special authority from the War Department. Upon the cordial invitation of the officers of the 1st Regiment, I accepted the place of major of that regiment, mustered myself into service as such, and devoted all the time that could be spared from my mustering duties to instructing the officers in tactics and military administration — a labor which was abundantly repaid by the splendid record soon made by that regiment.

On June 24 I made a full report to the adjutant-general of the discharge of my duties as mustering officer, including three new regiments of three years' volunteers whose muster would be completed in a few days. With this report my connection with that service was terminated. On the following day I was relieved from mustering duty, and at General Lyon's request was ordered to report to him at Boonville, remaining with him as adjutant-general and chief of staff until his death at Wilson's Creek.

The foregoing account gives the organization (the strength was about 14,000) of the volunteer force with which the war in Missouri was begun. To this was added Lyon's company of the 2d Infantry, a detachment of regular recruits, about 180 strong, commanded by Lieutenant Lothrop, and Totten's battery of the 2d United States Artillery. Lyon, who, as described, had been elected brigadier-general of the militia, was on May 17 appointed by the President to the same grade in the United States volunteer forces; and when, on May 30, General Harney was relieved from the command of the Department of the West, General Lyon became the commander of that department.

General Lyon was a man of ability and scholarly attainments, an earnest patriot, keenly alive to the nature and magnitude of the struggle in which the country was about to engage, and eager to take the initiative as soon as he had at his command sufficient force to give promise of success. To his keen foresight the State militia at Camp Jackson, near St. Louis, though a lawful State organization engaged in its usual annual field exercises, was an incipient rebel army which ought to be crushed in the bud. This feeling was shared by the more earnest Union men of St. Louis, who had the confidence of the President and were in daily consultation with Lyon; while the more prudent or conservative, hoping to avoid actual conflict in the State, or at least in the city, advised forbearance. Subsequent events showed how illusive was the hope of averting hostilities in any of the border States, and how fortunate it was that active measures were adopted at once.

On May 10 General Lyon marched out with the force then organized, surrounded Camp Jackson, and demanded its surrender. The militia commander, Brigadier-General Daniel M. Frost, after protesting in vain against the " wrong and insult " to the State, seeing resistance hopeless, surrendered his command, about 1500 men, with their arms and munitions of war. After the surrender, and while preparations were making to conduct the prisoners to the arsenal, some shots were fired upon our troops from a crowd that had assembled round the campground. The fire was returned by some of the troops, in spite of all efforts of the officers to prevent it, and a number of persons, mostly inoffensive, were killed and wounded. In this affair I was designated by General Lyon to receive the surrender of the commander of Camp Jackson and his troops, and to take charge of the prisoners, conduct them to the arsenal, and the next day to parole them. I extended to the commander and other

officers the courtesy of permitting them to retain their
swords, and treated the prisoners in such a manner as
to soothe somewhat their intensely excited feelings. One
of the colonels, not anticipating such courteous treatment, had broken his sword and thrown the pieces upon
the ground, rather than surrender it to the hated Yankees.
The possession of St. Louis, and the supremacy of the
national authority therein, being now secured, General
Lyon directed his energies toward operations in the
interior of the State. On June 13 he moved up the Missouri River with the 1st Missouri Volunteers, Totten's
battery of the 2d United States Artillery, one company of the 2d United States Infantry, two companies
of regular recruits, and nine companies of the 2d Missouri Volunteers, and attacked the enemy under Sterling
Price on the 17th, near Boonville, and gained an easy
victory. The loss on our side was two killed and nine
wounded; that of the enemy, ten killed and a number
of prisoners.

I joined General Lyon at Boonville on June 26, and
began duty as his adjutant-general. Preparations were
now made as rapidly as possible to push operations into
the southwestern part of Missouri. A force consisting
of about 1500 infantry and one battery of four guns,
under Colonel Franz Sigel, was sent from St. Louis,
via Rolla, to Springfield; while a force of regular troops
under Major Samuel D. Sturgis, 1st Cavalry, consisting
of one company of the 2d Dragoons, four companies
of the 1st Cavalry, Du Bois's battery of four guns, three
companies of the 1st Infantry, two companies of the
2d Infantry, some regular recruits, the 1st and 2d
Kansas Infantry, and one company of Kansas Cavalry
Volunteers, was ordered from Fort Leavenworth to join
General Lyon's immediate command, en route to Springfield. General Lyon's march was begun on July 3, and
Major Sturgis joined him at Clinton, Mo., on the 4th.

The command reached Springfield on July 13, and there met Colonel Sigel's brigade, which we learned had pushed as far to the front as Newtonia, but, meeting a superior force of the enemy at Carthage on July 5, had fallen back to Springfield. General Lyon's intention was, upon effecting this junction with Sturgis and Sigel, to push forward and attack the enemy, if possible, while we were yet superior to him in strength. He had ordered supplies to be sent from St. Louis via Rolla, but they remained at Rolla, the railroad terminus, for want of wagon transportation. The troops had to live upon such supplies as could be obtained from the country, and many of them were without shoes. A continuous march of more than two or three days was impossible. General Lyon's force was rapidly diminishing, and would soon almost disappear by the discharge of the three months' men, while that of the enemy was as rapidly increasing and becoming more formidable by additions to its supplies of arms and ammunition. General Lyon made frequent appeals for reinforcements and for provisions, but received little encouragement, and soon became convinced that he must rely upon the resources then at his command. He was unwilling to abandon southwestern Missouri to the enemy without a struggle, even though almost hopeless of success, and determined to bring on a decisive battle, if possible, before his short-term volunteers were discharged. Learning that the enemy was slowly advancing from the southwest by two or three different roads, Lyon moved out, August 1, on the Cassville road, had a skirmish with the enemy's advanceguard at Dug Springs the next day, and the day following (the 3d) again at Curran Post-office. The enemy showed no great force, and offered but slight resistance to our advance. It was evident that a general engagement could not be brought on within the limits of time and distance to which we were confined by the state of our supplies. It was therefore determined to return to Springfield.

General Lyon was greatly depressed by the situation in which he was placed, the failure of expected reinforcements and supplies from St. Louis, and an evidently strong conviction that these failures were due to a plan to sacrifice him to the ambition of another, and by a morbid sensitiveness respecting the disaster to the Union people of southwestern Missouri, (who had relied upon him for protection) which must result from the retreat of his army. Lyon's personal feeling was so strongly enlisted in the Union cause, its friends were so emphatically his personal friends and its enemies his personal enemies, that he could not take the cool, soldierly view of the situation which should control the actions of the commander of a national army. If Lyon could have foreseen how many times the poor people of that section were destined to be overrun by the contending forces before the contest could be finally decided, his extreme solicitude at that moment would have disappeared. Or if he could have risen to an appreciation of the fact that his duty, as the commander in the field of one of the most important of the national armies, was not to protect a few loyal people from the inevitable hardships of war (loss of their cattle, grain, and fences), but to make as sure as possible the defeat of the hostile army, no matter whether to-day, to-morrow, or next month, the battle of Wilson's Creek would not have been fought.

On August 9 General Lyon received a letter from General John C. Frémont, then commanding the department, which had been forwarded to him from Rolla by Colonel John B. Wyman. The letter from General Frémont to Colonel Wyman inclosing that to General Lyon appears among the published papers submitted by Frémont to the Committee on the Conduct of the War in the early part of 1862, but the inclosure to Lyon is wanting. The original letter, with the records to which it belonged, must, it is presumed, have been deposited at the headquarters of the department in St. Louis when the Army of the West was disbanded, in the latter part of August, 1861. Neither the original letter nor any copy of it can now (July, 1897) be found. It can only be conjectured what motive caused General Frémont to omit a copy of the letter from the papers submitted to the committee, which were at the time strongly commented upon in Congress, or what caused to be removed from the official files the original, which had again come into his possession.

General Lyon's answer to this letter, given below, the original draft of which was prepared by me and is yet in my possession, shows that Frémont's letter to Lyon was dated August 6, and was received on the 9th. I am not able to recall even the substance of the greater part of that letter, but the purport of that part of it which was then of vital importance is still fresh in my memory. That purport was instructions to the effect that *if Lyon was not strong enough to maintain his position as far in advance as Springfield, he should fall back toward Rolla until reinforcements should meet him.*

It is difficult to see why General Frémont did not produce a copy of those instructions in his statement to the committee. It would have furnished him with the best defense he could possibly have made against the charge of having sacrificed Lyon and his command. But the opinion then seemed so strong and so nearly universal that Lyon's fight at Wilson's Creek was a necessity, and that Frémont ought to have reinforced him before that time at any cost, that perhaps Frémont had not the courage to do what was really best for his own defense, namely, to acknowledge and maintain that he had ordered Lyon to fall back, and that the latter should have obeyed that order.

At my suggestion, General Lyon instructed me to prepare an answer to General Frémont's letter on the morning of August 9. He altered the original draft, in his own hand, as is shown in the copy following; a fair copy of the letter as amended was then made, and he signed it.

SPRINGFIELD, Aug. 9, 1861.

GENERAL: I have just received your note of the 6th inst. by special messenger.

I retired to this place, as I have before informed you, reaching here on the 5th. The enemy followed to within ten miles of here. He has taken a strong position, and is recruiting his supplies of horses, mules, and provisions by forays into the surrounding country; his large force of mounted men enabling him to do this without annoyance from me.

I find my position extremely embarrassing, and am at present unable to determine whether I shall be able to maintain my ground or be forced to retire. I can resist any attack from the front, but if the enemy moves to surround me I must retire. I shall hold my ground as long as possible, [and not] *though I may without knowing how far* endanger the safety of my entire force with its valuable material, *being induced by the important considerations involved to take this step. The enemy yesterday made a show of force about five miles distant, and has doubtless a full purpose of making an attack upon me.*

Very respectfully your obedient servant,

N. LYON,

Brigadier-General Vols., Commanding.

MAJOR-GENERAL J. C. FRÉMONT,

Comdg. Western Department, St. Louis, Mo.

The words in my handwriting which were erased ("and not" in brackets), and those substituted by General Lyon, given in italics, clearly express the difference of opinion which then existed between us upon the momentous question which we had then been discussing for several days, namely: What action did the situation require of him as commander of that army?

I was then young and wholly inexperienced in war;

but I have never yet seen any reason to doubt the correctness of the views I then urged with even more persistence than my subordinate position would fully justify. And this, I doubt not, must be the judgment of history. The fruitless sacrifice at Wilson's Creek was wholly unnecessary, and, under the circumstances, wholly unjustifiable. Our retreat to Rolla was open and perfectly safe, even if begun as late as the night of the 9th. A few days or a few weeks at the most would have made us amply strong to defeat the enemy and drive him out of Missouri, without serious loss to ourselves. Although it is true that we barely failed winning a victory on August 10, that was, and could have been, hoped for only as a mere possibility. Lyon himself despaired of it before the battle was half over, and threw away his own life in desperation. In addition to the depressing effect of his wounds, he must probably have become convinced of the mistake he had made in hazarding an unnecessary battle on so unequal terms, and in opposition to both the advice of his subordinates and the instructions of his superior. But this is only an inference. After Lyon had with the aid of Sigel (as explained hereafter) decided to attack, and arranged the plan, not a word passed between him and me on the question whether an attack should be made, except my question: "Is Sigel willing to undertake this?" and Lyon's answer: "Yes; it is his plan."

We went forward together, slept under the same blanket while the column was halted, from about midnight till the dawn of day, and remained close together nearly all the time until his death. But he seemed greatly depressed, and except to give orders, hardly uttered a word save the few I have mentioned in this narrative.

He was still unwilling to abandon without a desperate struggle the country he had occupied, thought the importance of maintaining his position was not understood by his superior commander, and in his despondency believed, as above stated, that he was the intended victim of a deliberate sacrifice to another's ambition. He determined to fight a battle at whatever risk, and said: "I will gladly give my life for a victory."

The enemy had now concentrated his forces, and was encamped on Wilson's Creek, about ten miles from Springfield. There had been some skirmishing between our reconnoitering parties and those of the enemy during the past few days, and a general advance had been determined on for the night of August 8, but it was postponed on account of the fatigued condition of the troops, who had been employed that day in meeting a reconnaissance of the enemy. The attack was finally made at daylight on the morning of the eventful August 10.

The plan of battle was determined on the morning of the 9th, in a consultation between General Lyon and Colonel Sigel, no other officers being present. General Lyon said, "It is Sigel's plan," yet he seemed to have no hesitation in adopting it, notwithstanding its departure from accepted principles, having great confidence in Sigel's superior military ability and experience. Sigel's brigade, about 1200 strong, was to attack the enemy's right, while Lyon, with the main body, about 4000 strong, was to attack the enemy's left. The two columns were to advance by widely separated roads, and the points of attack were so distant that communication between the two columns was not even thought of. The attack was made, as intended, by both columns at nearly the same instant, and both drove the enemy from his advanced position, Sigel even occupying the enemy's camp. Here he was soon after assailed by a superior force, and driven from the field with the loss of his artillery and 292 men killed, wounded, and missing. He did not appear upon the scene again that day, and the result of his attack was unknown to any one in the other column until after the

close of the battle. The main body, under Lyon's immediate command, made no general advance from the position first gained, but maintained that position against
several fierce assaults. The enemy manifestly did not
make good use of his superior numbers. He attacked us
in front several times, but with a force not greatly superior to our own, and was invariably repulsed. Our men
fought extremely well for raw troops, maintaining their
ground, without any cover whatever, against repeated
assaults for six hours, and losing in killed and wounded
fully *one third of their number*. General Lyon received
two wounds, one in the leg and one in the head, about
the middle of the engagement; he then became more
despondent than before, apparently from the effects of
his wounds, for there appeared nothing in the state of
the battle to dishearten a man of such unbounded courage
as he undoubtedly possessed. A portion of our troops
had given away in some disorder. Lyon said: " Major, I
am afraid the day is lost." I looked at him in surprise,
saw the blood trickling down his face, and divining the
reason for his despondency, replied: " No, General; let us
try it again." He seemed reëncouraged, and we then
separated, rallied and led forward the only troops then
not in action—two regiments. Lyon was killed at the
head of one of these regiments while exposing himself
with utter recklessness to the enemy's fire.

When Lyon and I separated, he to lead the attack
in which he fell, I reformed the other regiment and
led it into action, giving the command " Charge!" as
soon as we came within plain view of the enemy, hoping to try conclusions with the bayonet, with which we
were much better supplied than they. That regiment
advanced in splendid style until it received the enemy's
fire, then the command " Charge!" was forgotten, and
the regiment halted and commenced firing. Thus I
found myself " between two fires." But the brave boys

in my rear could see me, and I don't believe I was in any danger from their muskets, yet I felt less " out of place " when I had passed around the flank of a company and stood in rear of the line. I there witnessed, for the only time in my experience, one of those remarkable instances of a man too brave to think of running away, and yet too much frightened to be able to fight. He was loading his musket and firing in the air with great rapidity. When I took hold of his arm and shook him, calling his attention to what he was doing, he seemed as if aroused from a trance, entirely unconscious of what had happened.

This circumstance recalls the familiar story of two comrades in the ranks, the one apparently unmoved, the other pale and trembling. The first said: " Why, you seem to be scared! " " Yes," replied the other; " if you were half as scared as I am, you would run away! "

A few minutes later I went toward the right to rejoin my chief, and found his lifeless body a few feet in rear of the line, in charge of his faithful orderly, Lehman, who was mourning bitterly and loudly the death of the great soldier whom he adored. At that supremely critical moment—for the fight was then raging with great fury—my only thought was the apprehension that the troops might be injuriously affected if they learned of the death of the commander who had so soon won their profound respect and confidence. I chided poor Lehman for his outcry, and ordered that the body be taken quietly to the rear, and that no one be told of the general's death.

Thus fell one of our bravest and truest soldiers and patriots, a man who had no fear of death, but who could not endure defeat. Upon Lyon's fall, Major Sturgis became the senior officer of military education and experience present. Several of the senior volunteer officers had been wounded and carried from the field. Who was the actual senior in rank on the ground was not easy to ascertain in the midst of a fierce engagement. It was no time to make experiments with untried military genius.

I captured a " secesh " horse found running loose,—for my own horse had been killed and I had been afoot quite a long time,—mounted him, and as soon as the state of the contest would permit, I rode to Major Sturgis, informed him of Lyon's death, and told him he must assume the command, which he accordingly did. It afterward appeared that there was one lieutenant-colonel of volunteers remaining on the field, but neither he nor any one else thought of questioning the propriety of Major Sturgis's taking the command. Soon after Lyon's death the enemy was repulsed, but then seemed to gather up all his remaining strength for a last effort. His final attack was heavier than any of the preceding, but it was more firmly met by our troops and completely repulsed. There is probably no room for doubt that the enemy was beaten if we had but known it; but the battle-field was covered with timber and underbrush, so that nothing could be seen beyond a few hundred yards. Our troops were nearly out of ammunition, and exhausted by a night march and by six hours' hard fighting without breakfast.

It did not seem possible to resist another such attack as the last, and there was no apparent assurance that another would not be made. Hence Major Sturgis decided to withdraw from the field while he was free to do so. The movement was effected without opposition, the wounded were brought off, and the command returned to Springfield in the afternoon. This retreat was undoubtedly an error, and the battle of Wilson's Creek must be classed as a defeat for the Union army. The error was a failure to estimate the effect that must have been produced upon the enemy as well as upon ourselves by so much hard fighting. It was only necessary to hold our ground, trusting to the pluck and endurance of our men, and the victory would have been ours. Had

Lyon, who was in front of the line of battle when wounded as well as when killed, appreciated this fact and acted upon it, instead of throwing his life away, it is safe to say he would have won a brilliant victory.

On the march from the battle-field the main body was joined by the remnant of Sigel's brigade, which had made a complete circuit in rear of the enemy's position. They were without brigade or regimental commanders, and were escorted by a troop of regular cavalry. On our arrival in Springfield it was found that Colonel Sigel and Colonel Salomon, commanding the 5th Missouri Regiment, of Sigel's brigade, had arrived in town some hours before. Major Sturgis then relinquished the command to Colonel Sigel, and it was determined to retreat toward Rolla next morning. Sigel's brigade was placed in advance, and Sturgis's brigade of regulars was assigned the important post of rear-guard. This order of march was continued during three days, and the march was so conducted that while the advance would reach camp at a reasonable hour and be able to get supper and rest, the rear-guard, and even the main body, would be kept in the road until late in the night, and then, unable to find their wagons, be compelled to lie down without food. The clamor for relief from this hardship became so general that Major Sturgis determined to resume the command, justifying this action upon the ground that Colonel Sigel, although mustered into the United States service, had no commission from any competent authority. Colonel Sigel protested against this assumption of Major Sturgis, but the latter was so manifestly sustained by the great majority of the officers of the army that Colonel Sigel quietly submitted.

One of Sigel's officers proposed that the question of title to the command be put to a vote of the assembled officers. Sturgis objected on the ground that the vote might possibly be in favor of Sigel. "Then," said

Sturgis, "some of you might refuse to obey my orders, and I should be under the necessity of shooting you."

The march was continued under Sturgis's command, and the column arrived at Rolla on August 19, nine days after the battle. Here the little Army of the West, after its short but eventful career, disappeared in the much larger army which Major-General Frémont was then organizing.[1]

My knowledge of the operations conducted by General Frémont in Missouri is so slight that I must confine myself to some account of those minor affairs with which I was personally connected.

My duties as assistant adjutant-general ceased when Major Sturgis resumed command on August 13. I then took command of my regiment, the 1st Missouri, the colonel and lieutenant-colonel being absent, the latter on account of wounds received at Wilson's Creek. Soon after our arrival at Rolla the regiment was ordered to St. Louis, to be converted into an artillery regiment. I was employed in the reorganization and equipment of batteries until September 16, when General Frémont ordered me to visit Cincinnati, Pittsburg, Washington, West Point, and such other places in the East as I might find necessary, to procure guns, harness, etc., to complete the equipment of the regiment.

While in St. Louis after the battle of Wilson's Creek, I learned much in confirmation of the opinion of the character and ability of General Frémont which had very generally been held in the army.

Immediately after my arrival Colonel Frank P. Blair, Jr., said he wanted me to go with him to see Frémont; so we went the next morning. The headquarters palace was surrounded by a numerous guard, and all ingress by the main entrance appeared to be completely barred. But Blair had some magic word or sign by which we

[1] My official report and others are published in the War Records, Vol. III.

passed the sentinels at the basement door. Ascending two flights of stairs, we found the commanding general with a single secretary or clerk occupying the suite of rooms extending from front to rear of the building. The general received me cordially, but, to my great surprise, no questions were asked, nor any mention made, of the bloody field from which I had just come, where Lyon had been killed, and his army, after a desperate battle, compelled to retreat. I was led at once to a large table on which maps were spread out, from which the general proceeded to explain at length the plans of the great campaign for which he was then preparing. Colonel Blair had, I believe, already been initiated, but I listened attentively for a long time, certainly more than an hour, to the elucidation of the project. In general outline the plan proposed a march of the main Army of the West through southwestern Missouri and northwestern Arkansas to the valley of the Arkansas River, and thence down that river to the Mississippi, thus turning all the Confederate defenses of the Mississippi River down to and below Memphis. As soon as the explanation was ended Colonel Blair and I took our leave, making our exit through the same basement door by which we had entered. We walked down the street for some time in silence. Then Blair turned to me and said: " Well, what do you think of him ? " I replied, in words rather too strong to repeat in print, to the effect that my opinion as to his wisdom was the same as it always had been. Blair said: " I have been suspecting that for some time."

It was a severe blow to the whole Blair family — the breaking, by the rude shock of war, of that idol they had so much helped to set up and make the commander of a great army. From that day forward there was no concealment of the opposition of the Blairs to Frémont.

4

I had another occasion at that time to learn something important as to Frémont's character. He had ordered me to convert the 1st Regiment of Missouri Volunteer Infantry into an artillery regiment. I had organized eight batteries and used all the field-guns I could get. There remained in the arsenal a battery of new rifled guns which Frémont had purchased in Europe. I applied to him personally for those guns, telling him I had a well-disciplined company of officers and men ready to man them. He gave me the order without hesitation, but when I went to the arsenal I found an order there countermanding the order he had given me. I returned to headquarters, and easily obtained a renewal of the order to issue the guns to me. Determining to get ahead this time, I took the quickest conveyance to the arsenal, but only to find that the telegraph had got ahead of me — the order was again countermanded. The next day I quietly inquired at headquarters about the secret of my repeated disappointment, and learned that some foreign adventurer had obtained permission to raise a company of artillery troops and wanted those new rifled guns. It was true the company had not been raised, but I thought that would probably make no difference, so I never mentioned the matter to the general again. Instead I planned a flank movement which proved far more successful than the direct attack could possibly have been. I explained to General Frémont the great need of field-guns and equipment for his army, and suggested that if ordered East I might by personal efforts obtain all he needed. He at once adopted my suggestion, bade me sit down at a desk in his room and write the necessary order, and he signed it without reading. I readily obtained twenty-four new rifled Parrott guns, and soon had them in service in the Western Department, in lieu of the six guns I had failed to get from the St. Louis Arsenal.

When I had accomplished this duty and returned to

St. Louis, where I arrived in the early part of October, 1861, General Frémont had taken the field in the central part of Missouri, with the main body of his army, in which were eight batteries of my regiment. I was instructed to remain in St. Louis and complete the organization and equipment of the regiment upon the arrival of guns and equipments procured in the East.

It was while waiting for the expected guns that a demand for artillery came from Colonel W. P. Carlin, commanding a brigade at Pilot Knob and threatened with an attack by a Confederate force under Jeff. Thompson. The latter had already made a raid in Carlin's rear, destroyed the railroad bridge across the Big River, and interfered seriously with the communication to St. Louis. In the nervous condition of the military as well as the public mind at that time, even St. Louis was regarded as in danger.

There was no organized battery in St. Louis, but there were officers and men enough belonging to the different batteries of the 1st Missouri, and recruits, to make a medium-sized company. They had been instructed in the school of the piece, but no more. I hastily put them upon the cars, with four old smooth-bore bronze guns, horses that had never been hitched to a piece, and harness that had not been fitted to the horses. Early next morning we arrived at Big River where the bridge had been burned, unloaded the battery and horses by the use of platforms extemporized from railroad ties, hitched up, and forded the river. On the other side we converted platform-cars into stock-cars, loaded up, and arrived at Pilot Knob the next morning (October 20). The enemy was understood to be at Fredericktown, about twenty miles distant, and Colonel Carlin determined to march that night and attack him at daylight the next morning. Carlin's command consisted of the 8th Wisconsin Volunteers, 21st Illinois Volunteers, parts of the 33d and 38th Illinois Volunteers, 350 of the 1st Indiana Cavalry, one company of Missouri Cavalry, and six pieces of artillery (including two old iron guns which he had managed to make available in addition to the four from St. Louis). His total force was about 3000 men. The enemy's strength was supposed to be about the same, but it turned out that he had only four old iron guns, so we had the advantage of him in artillery at least.

The head of our column reached the vicinity of Fredericktown some time before daylight, and the troops lay upon their arms until dawn. Upon entering the town in the morning, no enemy was found, and citizens reported that he had marched south the day before. The troops were ordered to rest in the village, and Colonel Carlin, who was not well, went to bed in the hotel. Some hours later, I think near noon, Colonel J. B. Plummer, with a brigade of infantry and two pieces of artillery from Cape Girardeau, arrived at Fredericktown. I am not aware whether this junction was expected by the respective commanders, or what orders they had received from department headquarters. Soon after Colonel Plummer arrived I was summoned to the presence of the two commanders and requested to decide a question of rank between them. It appeared that Colonel Carlin had the older date as colonel of volunteers, while Colonel Plummer was commanding, by special assignment of General Frémont, a brigade in which at least one of the colonels was senior, not only to him, but also to Colonel Carlin. It was clear enough that according to the Articles of War this senior colonel of the Cape Girardeau brigade should command the combined forces; but that would be in plain disregard of General Frémont's order, the authority for which nobody knew, but in comparison with which the Articles of War or the Army Regulations were at that time regarded as practically of trifling consequence. The question was settled, or rather avoided (for there was no satisfactory settlement of it), by the proposition that Colonel Plummer, who proposed to go in pursuit of the enemy, should take with him, besides his own brigade, such portion of Colonel Carlin's as he (Plummer) thought necessary, Colonel Carlin, who was sick, remaining behind with the remainder. Accordingly, early in the afternoon Plummer's column started in pursuit. It had hardly got well out of the village when the head of the column received a volley from the enemy drawn up in line of battle. How long the enemy had been in that position I have never learned; but it is certain that his presence there was not even suspected by our commander, who supposed him to be in full retreat. This mistake, however, did not seem to cost us anything, except perhaps the loss of a few men at the head of the column in the first volley. Colonel Plummer quickly formed his troops; Carlin jumped out of bed and galloped to the front, followed by those who had remained in town. The volunteers, who had not yet been in battle, threw off their knapsacks, blankets, and overcoats, and went into action most gallantly. The engagement was sharp for a few moments, and resulted in considerable loss on both sides; but the enemy soon gave way and retreated in disorder. The pursuit was continued several miles, and until near night, when a recall was ordered, and our troops returned to the town to pick up their trappings and get their supper.

The next morning Colonel Plummer continued his pursuit. I left my extemporized battery, under Captain Manter, with Colonel Carlin, and returned to St. Louis.[1]

1 For the official reports, see the War Records, Vol. III.

CHAPTER IV

HALLECK RELIEVES FRÉMONT OF THE COMMAND IN MIS-
SOURI — A SPECIAL STATE MILITIA — BRIGADIER-GENERAL
OF THE MISSOURI MILITIA — A HOSTILE COMMITTEE SENT
TO WASHINGTON — THE MISSOURI QUARREL OF 1862 —
IN COMMAND OF THE "ARMY OF THE FRONTIER" — AB-
SENT THROUGH ILLNESS — BATTLE OF PRAIRIE GROVE
— COMPELLED TO BE INACTIVE — TRANSFERRED TO TEN-
NESSEE — IN COMMAND OF THOMAS'S OLD DIVISION OF
THE FOURTEENTH CORPS — REAPPOINTED MAJOR-GEN-
ERAL — A HIBERNIAN "STRIKER."

ON November 19, 1861, Major-General H. W. Halleck
relieved Major-General Frémont of the command of
the Department of the Mississippi. On November 21 I
was appointed brigadier-general of volunteers, and reported to General Halleck for duty.

In the spring of 1861 a convention of the State of Missouri had assembled at St. Louis to consider the question
of secession, and had decided to adhere to the Union.
Nevertheless, the governor, Claiborne Fox Jackson, and
the executive officers had joined the rebellion and fled
from the State. The convention reassembled on July
20, and organized a provisional government. Hamilton
R. Gamble was chosen provisional governor, and intrusted with very large powers. He was a sterling patriot, a man of ability and of the highest character in
his public and private relations, much too conservative
on the questions of States' rights and slavery to suit the
"radical" loyalists of that time, but possessing probably

54

in a higher degree than any other citizen of Missouri the confidence of all classes of Union men in the State.

One of Governor Gamble's first important public acts was to seek and obtain from President Lincoln authority to raise a special force of State militia, to be employed only in defense of the State, but to be paid, equipped, and supplied in all respects by the United States. This force was to be organized in conformity with the militia laws of the State, was to include an adjutant-general, a quartermaster-general, and three aides-de-camp to the governor, one major-general and his staff, and a brigadier-general and staff for each brigade. The number of regiments, aggregate strength, and arms of service were not specified.

By the terms of this arrangement the force would remain subject to the governor's command; but at the suggestion of Major-General McClellan, then general-in-chief, to avoid possible conflict of command it was stipulated by the President that the commanding general of the department should be ex-officio major-general of the militia. And it is due to the memory of Governor Gamble to say that although partizan enemies often accused him of interfering with the operations of the militia in the interest of his supposed political views, there never was, while I was in command of the militia, the slightest foundation for such accusation. He never attempted to interfere in any manner with the legitimate exercise of the authority of the commanding general, but was, on the contrary, governed by the commander's views and opinions in the appointment and dismissal of officers and in other matters in which his own independent authority was unquestioned. This authority, given by the President, was subsequently confirmed by act of Congress, by which the force was limited to 10,000 men.

As stated above, I was appointed brigadier-general, to date from November 21, 1861; and on November 27 was assigned by General Halleck to the "command of all the militia of the State," and charged with the duty of raising, organizing, etc., the special force which had been authorized by the President.

The organization of the militia was not completed until about the middle of April, 1862, when the aggregate force was 13,800 men, consisting of fourteen regiments and two battalions of cavalry (mounted riflemen), one regiment of infantry, and one battery of artillery. But the troops were enrolled mainly in the districts where their services were required. As rapidly as companies were organized and equipped, they were put in the field with the United States troops then occupying the State, and thus rapidly acquired, by active service with older troops, the discipline and instruction necessary to efficiency, so that by the time the organization was completed this body of troops was an efficient and valuable force.

My official report, made on December 7, 1862,[1] to the department commander and the general-in-chief, gives a detailed account of the purely military operations of that period. But many matters less purely military which entered largely into the history of that time deserve more than a passing notice.

During the short administration of General Frémont in Missouri, the Union party had split into two factions, "radical" and "conservative," hardly less bitter in their hostility to each other than to the party of secession. The more advanced leaders of the radicals held that secession had abolished the constitution and all laws restraining the powers of the government over the people of the Confederate States, and even over disloyal citizens of States adhering to the Union. They advocated immediate emancipation of the slaves, and confiscation by military authority of all property of "rebels and rebel sym-

1 See War Records, Vol. XIII, p. 7.

pathizers "— that is to say, of all persons not of the radical party, for in their partizan heat they disdained to make any distinction between " conservatives," " copperheads," and "rebels." So powerful and persistent was the radical influence that even so able a lawyer as Edwin M. Stanton, then Secretary of War, was constrained to send an order to the commander of the District of Missouri, directing him to execute the act of Congress of July 17, 1862, relative to confiscation of property of persons engaged in the rebellion, although the law provided for its execution in the usual way by the judicial department of the government, and gave no shadow of authority for military action.

It is only necessary here to remark that the order was not, as it could not be lawfully, obeyed. Action under it was limited to the securing of property subject to confiscation, and liable to be removed or otherwise disposed of, and the collection of evidence for the use of the judicial officers. The following is Secretary Stanton's order sent by telegraph, September 5, 1862 :

It is represented that many disloyal persons residing at St. Louis and elsewhere in your command are subject to the provisions of the Confiscation Act, and that it would be expedient to enforce against them the provisions of that act. You are instructed to enforce that act within your command, and will please send directions for that purpose to your provost-marshal.

In compliance with the Secretary's instructions, I issued an order, on September 11, providing for the action above stated, and no further.

These instructions from the Secretary of War were subsequently repudiated by President Lincoln ; but in the meantime they produced serious evil under my successor, who fully enforced them by apparently committing the national administration to the extreme radical doctrine, and making the military commander in Missouri appear to be acting not in harmony with the President's views. So far as I know, this subject does not appear to have been submitted to the President until some time in 1863, after Major-General Curtis, as department commander, had for some months carried out the radical theory of military confiscation, and I, as his successor, had put a stop to it. Then an appeal was made to the President, and he, in his celebrated letter of instructions of October 1, 1863, directed the military to have nothing to do with the matter.

The State administration of Missouri, under its conservative governor, was of course sternly opposed to this radical policy, including the forced liberation of slaves, for which there was at that time no warrant of law or executive authority. A simple sense of duty compelled the military commander to act in these matters more in harmony with the State government than with the radical party, and in radical eyes he thus became identified with their enemies, the conservatives.

This gave rise on August 4, 1862, to a meeting of prominent citizens of St. Louis, who adopted resolutions, of the most important of which the following was reported to be a true copy:

> *Resolved*, That a committee of gentlemen be requested to go to Washington City to urge upon the President the appointment of a commander of the military forces of this State who will, under instructions, act with vigor in suppressing the guerrillas of this State, and with authority to enlist the militia of the State into the service of the United States.

The chair appointed, as the committee to go to Washington, Henry T. Blow, John C. Vogle, I. H. Sturgeon, and Thomas O'Reilley, and authorized Mr. Blow to add to this committee any other "true Union man" who would go. Who, if any, besides Messrs. Blow, Vogle, and O'Reilley actually composed the committee, I was never informed.

On August 10, Halleck, then general-in-chief, telegraphed me from Washington: "There is a deputation here from Colonel Blair and others asking for your removal on account of inefficiency."

Colonel Blair happened into my office a few minutes after the receipt of this despatch on the 11th, and I handed it to him. He at once said in substance, and with feeling: "That is not true. No one is authorized to ask in my name for your removal"; and he sent a despatch to that effect to General Halleck.

The next day (August 12) despatches were exchanged between General Halleck and Colonel Blair, of which the latter furnished me a copy, inclosed with the following note from himself:

St. Louis, Mo., August 13th, '62.

Brig.-Gen'l Schofield.

DEAR SCHOFIELD: I inclose you a copy of a despatch (marked "A") received yesterday from Major-General Halleck, and my answer thereto, marked "B."

Yours,

Frank P. Blair, Jr.

COPY "A."

To Hon. F. P. Blair,

August 12th, 1862.

(By telegraph from War Dep't.)

Washington, 12:50 p. m.

The committee from St. Louis — Henry T. Blow, John C. Vogle, and Thomas O'Reilley — told me, in presence of the President, that they were authorized by you to ask for Gen. Schofield's removal for inefficiency. The Postmaster-General has to-day sent to me a letter from Mr. ——, asking that you be put in Gen. Schofield's place. There has been no action in this or on the papers presented by the above-named committee.

H. W. Halleck,

General-in-chief.

COPY " B."

ST. LOUIS, MO., August 12th, 1862.

MAJOR-GENERAL HALLECK,

General-in-chief, Washington City, D. C. :

I despatched you yesterday, and wrote the Postmaster-General last week. Let the letter be submitted to you. Nobody is authorized to ask in my name for Gen'l Schofield's removal. I think the State military organization should be abandoned as soon as practicable, and a military commander, in this State, authorized to act without respect to Gov. Gamble. I do not want the place, but want the commander in the State to be instructed to act without any regard to the State authorities.

FRANK P. BLAIR, JR.

The foregoing gives, so far as I know it, the essence of the Missouri quarrel of 1862. I have never had the curiosity to attempt to ascertain how far the meeting of August 4 was hostile to me personally.

During the time, subsequent to General Halleck's departure for Washington, July 23, 1862, that the Department of the Mississippi was left without any immediate commander, there appears to have been a contest in Washington between the military and the political influence, relative to the disposition to be made of that important command. The following from General Halleck to me, dated September 9, 1862, indicates the situation at that time :

(Unofficial.)

MY DEAR GEN'L :

There has been a strong political pressure of outsiders to get certain parties put in command of new Dep'ts to be made out of the old Dep't of the Miss. The presence of the enemy and the danger of the capital have for the moment suspended these political intrigues, or rather prevented the accomplishment of their objects. If any one of our Western Gen'ls would do something creditable and brilliant in the present crisis, it would open the way to a new organization such as it should be.

From the position of St. Louis as the source of supplies, Missouri ought not to be separated from Arkansas and western Tennessee. What will be done in the matter I do not know.

Yours truly,

H. W. HALLECK.

None of "our Western generals" had then done anything very "creditable and brilliant." Even Grant was the object of grave charges and bitter attacks. Powerful influences were at work to supersede him in command of the army in west Tennessee. Had there been any available general at that time capable of commanding public confidence, the military idea would doubtless have prevailed, but in the absence of such a leader the politicians triumphed in part.

The old department, called Department of the Mississippi, was divided, and Major-General Samuel R. Curtis was assigned to command the new Department of the Missouri, composed of the territory west of the Mississippi River. For some months the radicals had it all their own way, and military confiscation was carried on without hindrance.

When this change occurred I was in the field in immediate command of the forces which I had assembled there for aggressive operations, and which General Curtis named the "Army of the Frontier." My official report of December 7, 1862, gave a full account of the operations of that army up to November 20, when sickness compelled me to relinquish the command.

As will be seen from that report and from my correspondence with General Curtis at the time, it was then well known that the enemy was concentrating in the Arkansas valley all the troops he could raise, and making preparations to return across the Boston Mountains and "dispute with us the possession of northwestern Arkansas and southwestern Missouri"; and I had placed my troops where they could live to a great extent on the country, and quickly concentrate to meet the enemy when he should advance. But General Curtis ordered me to move north and east with two divisions, leaving Blunt with one division to occupy that country. It was on this return march that I was overtaken by a severe attack of bilious fever.

As my official report of December 7, 1862, is published in Volume XIII of the War Records, I make no reference here to the operations covered by it. That able and impartial historian, the Comte de Paris, published a very accurate history of the operations in Missouri in the summer of 1862, in which he paid me the compliment, which a soldier values so highly, of saying that I was free from partizan passion.

It was during my absence through illness that Hindman made his expected advance. Blunt's division was encamped at Cane Hill, and Hindman crossed the mountains at Lee's Creek, aiming to reach Blunt's rear, cut off his retreat, and overwhelm him.

Fortunately, Blunt had received information in advance of the intended movement, and had called the two divisions from Missouri to his support. These two divisions, under General Herron, were encamped at Wilson's Creek, a distance of about 116 miles. On the morning of December 3 they began their march to join General Blunt. They had reached a point about six miles south of Fayetteville when, unexpectedly to both, Herron's and Hindman's heads of column met at Prairie Grove about seven o'clock in the morning of December 7, and the engagement commenced immediately. Blunt, hearing the sound of battle, moved rapidly toward Prairie Grove and attacked the enemy's left. The battle lasted all day, with heavy losses on both sides, and without any decided advantage to either side. At dark the enemy still held his position, but in the morning was found to be in full retreat across the mountains. A portion of our troops occupied the battle-field of Prairie Grove when I resumed command on December 29, and the remainder were making a raid to the Arkansas River, where they destroyed some property, and found that Hindman had retreated toward Little Rock. It was evident that the campaign in that part of the country for that season was ended. The question was " What next ? " I took it for granted that the large force under my command—nearly 16,000 men—was not to remain idle while Grant or some other commander was trying to open the Mississippi River; and I was confirmed in this assumption by General Curtis's previous order to march eastward with two divisions, which order, though premature when given, might now be renewed without danger. At once, therefore, I set to work to organize a suitable force, including the Indian regiments, to hold the country we had gained, and three good divisions to prosecute such operations as might be determined on, and at once commenced the march north and east toward the theater of future active operations.

Although I had at first esteemed General Blunt much more highly than he deserved, and had given him most liberal commendation in my official report for all he had done, I became satisfied that he was unfit in any respect for the command of a division of troops against a disciplined enemy. As was my plain duty, I suggested confidentially to General Curtis that the command of a division in the field was not General Blunt's true place, and that he be assigned to the District of Kansas, where I permitted him to go, at his own request, to look after his personal interests. General Curtis rebuked me for making such a suggestion, and betrayed my confidence by giving my despatch to James H. Lane, senator from Kansas, and others of Blunt's political friends, thus putting me before the President and the United States Senate in the light of unjust hostility to gallant officers who had just won a great victory over the enemy at Prairie Grove. The result of this, and of radical influence in general, was that my nomination as major-general of volunteers, then pending in the Senate, was not confirmed, while both Blunt and Herron were nominated and confirmed as major-generals!

Such as Lane and Blunt were the men who so long seemed to control the conduct of military affairs in the West, and whom I found much more formidable enemies than the hostile army in my front. Herron I esteemed a very different man from Blunt, and thought he would, with experience, make a good division commander. But circumstances occurred soon after which shook my confidence in his character as well as in that of General Curtis. Herron and some of his staff-officers were subpœnaed, through department headquarters, as material witnesses for the defense in the case of an officer on trial before a military commission. They failed to appear. Soon after, when Herron was assigned to command the Army of the Frontier, he "dissolved" the commission "for the present," adding: "The court will be reassembled by order from these headquarters in the field when witnesses not at present to be had can be brought forward." Upon learning this, after I assumed command of the department I ordered Herron to report for duty to General Grant before Vicksburg. In the meantime Herron wrote to the War Department protesting against serving under me as department commander, and got a sharp rebuke from the President through the Secretary of War. This brief explanation is all that seems necessary to show the connection between the several events as they appear in the official records.

After the battle of Prairie Grove, being then in St. Louis, I asked General Curtis to let me go down the Mississippi and join the expedition against Vicksburg, saying that as Blunt and Herron had won a battle in my absence, I did not wish to resume command over them. But Curtis would not consent to this; he said he wanted me to command the Army of the Frontier. He thus invited the confidence which he afterward betrayed, and for which he rebuked me. I felt outraged by this treatment, and thereafter did not feel or show toward General Curtis the respect or subordination which ought to characterize the relations of an officer toward his commander. This feeling was intensified by his conduct in the Herron affair, and by the determination gradually manifested not to permit me or my command to do anything. He for a long time kept up a pretense of wanting me to move east or west, or south, or somewhere, but negatived all my efforts actually to move. The situation seemed to me really unendurable : I was compelled to lie at Springfield all the latter part of winter, with a well-appointed army corps eager for active service, hundreds of miles from any hostile force, and where we were compelled to haul our own supplies, in wagons, over the worst of roads, 120 miles from the railroad terminus at Rolla. I could not get permission even to move nearer the railroad, much less toward the line on which the next advance must be made; and this while the whole country was looking with intense anxiety for the movement that was to open the Mississippi to the Gulf, and the government was straining every nerve to make that movement successful. Hence I wrote to General Halleck the letters of January 31, 1863, and February 3. These appear to have called forth some correspondence between Generals Halleck and Curtis, of which General Halleck's letter of February 18 was the only part that came into my possession.[1] This account was written several years before the War Records were published.

[1] The whole correspondence may be found in the War Records, Vol. XXII, part ii.

In my letter of January 31, I said:

Pardon me for suggesting that the forces under command of Davidson, Warren, and myself might be made available in the opening of the Mississippi, should that result not be accomplished quickly. . . .

The immediate result of this correspondence was that some troops were sent down the river, but none of my command, while two divisions of the latter were ordered toward the east. This march was in progress when Congress adjourned. The Senate not having confirmed my appointment as major-general, the time of my temporary humiliation arrived. But I had not relied wholly in vain upon General Halleck's personal knowledge of my character. He had not been able fully to sustain me against selfish intrigue in Kansas, Missouri, and Washington; but he could and did promptly respond to my request, and ordered me to Tennessee, where I could be associated with soldiers who were capable of appreciating soldierly qualities. One of the happiest days of my life was when I reported to Rosecrans and Thomas at Murfreesboro', received their cordial welcome, and was assigned to the command of Thomas's own old division of the Fourteenth Corps. One of the most agreeable parts of my whole military service was the thirty days in command of that division at Triune, and some of my strongest and most valued army attachments were formed there.

But that happy period of soldier life was brief. Early in May President Lincoln reappointed me major-general, with original date, November 29, 1862, and ordered me back to the old scene of unsoldierly strife and turmoil in Missouri and Kansas.

In 1861 and 1862 I had a Hibernian " striker " who had been a soldier in the old mounted rifles, and had been discharged on account of a wound received in an

Indian fight, but was yet well able to perform the duties of an officer's servant in the field. His care of his master's property, and sometimes of the master himself, was very remarkable. In the midst of the battle at Wilson's Creek the horse I was riding was killed, and I called in vain for my spare horse. From the best information obtained I concluded that both the horse and my faithful orderly had been killed, and I sincerely mourned my loss. But after the fight was over I found my man quietly riding the spare horse along with the troops, as if nothing unusual had happened. When I upbraided him for his conduct and demanded to know where he had been all that time, he replied: "Ah, Major, when I saw the one horse killed I thought I 'd better take the other to a place of safety!"

Where my efficient assistant obtained his supplies I never knew, but he would fill without delay any requisition I might make, from a shoe-string to a buffalo-robe. One day in 1862 I found in my camp trunk several pairs of shoulder-straps belonging to the grades of captain, major, and lieutenant-colonel. As I was then a brigadier-general, I inquired of my man why he kept those badges of inferior grades. He replied: " Ah, General, nobody can tell what may happen to you." When, only a few months later, after having been promoted to the rank of major-general I was again reduced to that of brigadier-general, I remembered the forethought of my Irish orderly.

CHAPTER V

IN COMMAND OF THE DEPARTMENT OF THE MISSOURI — TROOPS SENT TO GENERAL GRANT — SATISFACTION OF THE PRESIDENT — CONDITIONS ON WHICH GOVERNOR GAMBLE WOULD CONTINUE IN OFFICE — ANTI-SLAVERY VIEWS — LINCOLN ON EMANCIPATION IN MISSOURI — TROUBLE FOLLOWING THE LAWRENCE MASSACRE — A VISIT TO KANSAS, AND THE PARTY QUARREL THERE — MUTINY IN THE STATE MILITIA — REPRESSIVE MEASURES — A REVOLUTIONARY PLOT.

ON May 24, 1863, I relieved General Curtis in command of the Department of the Missouri. In his instructions of May 22, General Halleck said:

"You owe your present appointment entirely to the choice of the President himself. I have not, directly or indirectly, interfered in the matter. But I fully concur in the choice, and will give you all possible support and assistance in the performance of the arduous duties imposed upon you."

A few days later I received the following significant letter from the President:

EXECUTIVE MANSION, WASHINGTON, May 27, 1863.

GENERAL J. M. SCHOFIELD:

MY DEAR SIR: Having relieved General Curtis and assigned you to the command of the Department of the Missouri, I think it may be of some advantage for me to state to you why I did it.

I did not relieve General Curtis because of any full conviction that he had done wrong by commission or omission. I did it because of a conviction in my mind that the Union men of Missouri, constituting, when united, a vast majority of the whole people, have entered into a pestilent factional quarrel among themselves — General Curtis, perhaps not of choice, being the head of one faction, and Governor Gamble that of the other. After months of labor to reconcile the difficulty, it seemed to grow worse and worse, until I felt it my duty to break it up somehow; and as I could not remove Governor Gamble, I had to remove General Curtis.

Now that you are in the position, I wish you to undo nothing merely because General Curtis or Governor Gamble did it, but to exercise your own judgment and *do right* for the public interest.

Let your military measures be strong enough to repel the invader and keep the peace, and not so strong as to unnecessarily harass and persecute the people. It is a difficult rôle, and so much greater will be the honor if you perform it well. If both factions, or neither, shall abuse you, you will probably be about right. Beware of being assailed by one and praised by the other.   Yours truly,

A. LINCOLN.

In acknowledging the President's letter on June 1, I concluded by saying:

I have strong hopes that the Missouri State Convention, at its approaching session, will adopt such measures for the speedy emancipation of slaves as will secure the acquiescence of the large majority of Union men, though perhaps not quite satisfactory to either extreme. If this hope be realized, one of my most embarrassing difficulties will be removed, or at least greatly diminished.

The military problem in that department, as understood by me and by my superiors in Washington, was at that time a comparatively simple one, though my predecessor in command of the department entertained different views. With my views of the military situation, whether confined to my own department or extended to embrace the entire country, there was but one course to

5*

pursue, namely, to send all available force to assist in the capture of Vicksburg and the opening of the Mississippi to the gulf. After that I could easily operate from points on the Mississippi as a base, capture Little Rock and the line of the Arkansas, and then make that river the base of future operations.

Hence, in response to a request from General Halleck, I at once sent to General Grant and other commanders at the front all the troops I could possibly spare, saying at the same time that this would leave me very weak, but that I was " willing to risk it in view of the vast importance of Grant's success."

Thus I began my military operations by stripping the department of troops to the lowest possible defensive limit. But this was what I had so earnestly urged before, when in a subordinate position; and I was glad to do it when the responsibility rested upon me. My loan of troops to Grant was returned with interest as soon as practicable after Vicksburg had fallen, and I was then able to advance a large force, under General Steele, for the capture of Little Rock, resulting in holding the entire line of the Arkansas River from that time forward.

At that time I had met General Grant but once, and then for only a moment, and I have always assumed that the timely aid sent him at Vicksburg was the foundation for the kind and generous friendship and confidence which he ever afterward manifested toward me, and which, with the like manifestations of approval from President Lincoln, are to me the most cherished recollections of my official career.

The appreciation of my action in Washington was expressed by General Halleck in a letter dated July 7, 1863, in which he said : " The promptness with which you sent troops to General Grant gave great satisfaction here "; and by the President himself, in a letter to the " Hon. Charles D. Drake and others, committee," dated October

5, 1863, in which he wrote: "Few things have been so grateful to my anxious feelings as when, in June last, the local force in Missouri aided General Schofield to so promptly send a large general force to the relief of General Grant, then investing Vicksburg and menaced from without by General Johnston."

It would have been impossible for me to send away more than a small part of those troops if I had not been able to replace them by Missouri militia. This General Curtis had probably been unable to do because of the unfortunate antagonism between him and the State government; and perhaps this much ought to be said in explanation of his apparently selfish policy of retaining so many idle troops in Missouri. For my part, I could see neither necessity nor excuse for quarreling with the governor of Missouri, and thus depriving myself and the nation of his legitimate aid. Governor Gamble was perhaps "behind the times" in his views on the slavery question, although decidedly in favor of gradual emancipation; and he was utterly intolerant of those radical schemes for accomplishing ends by lawless means, then so loudly advocated. I thought at the time a more radical policy might possibly tend to harmonize the Union factions and allay the excitement, and frequently told Governor Gamble that it would be necessary to adopt a policy on the negro question more in harmony with the views of the administration and of the Northern people. To this the governor assented, and seemed desirous of going as far in that direction as he could carry the Union people of Missouri with him. From his seat in the State Convention at Jefferson City he made a speech advocating emancipation in a much shorter period than the convention could finally be prevailed upon to adopt, while I was using my personal influence with members to the same end.

But it soon became evident that nothing would satisfy

the radical leaders short of the overthrow of the existing State government; that a reconciliation of the quarrel between the "pestilent factions"[1] in Missouri, so much desired by Mr. Lincoln, was exactly what the radicals did not want and would not have. Satisfied of this and disgusted with the abuse heaped upon him by men who owed him warm and honest support, Governor Gamble tendered his resignation to the convention, then in session. His resignation was not accepted, and by a "majority of the convention and multitudes of private citizens" he was requested to withdraw it. In this request I united, for I could see no possibility of improvement under any governor that the convention — a very conservative body — might elect, while the result might be confusion worse confounded.

The governor submitted to me the following letter including conditions upon which he would consent to continue in office:

MAJOR-GENERAL SCHOFIELD.

GENERAL: For the purpose of restoring order and law and maintaining the authority of the Federal and State governments in the State of Missouri, it is necessary that we have an understanding as to the most important measures to be adopted.

I have tendered my resignation as governor, and have been requested to withdraw it on the ground that it is necessary to the peace and quiet of the State that I remain in office. In this request you have united with a majority of the convention and multitudes of private citizens. I am willing to accede to the request, and, if an ordinance of emancipation is passed, to remain in office, if on the part of the government I can be sure of its coöperation in my efforts to preserve the peace and remove all causes of dissension and dissatisfaction from among the people.

I think it necessary that the following measures be adopted by you as the commanding general of the department:

[1] The division of the Union party into radicals and conservatives, or "charcoals" and "claybanks," origi- nated during the administration of General Frémont.

First. That it be distinctly made known that the provisional government of the State is the government recognized by the government of the United States, and that any attempt, in any way, to interfere by violence, or by tumultuous assemblages, or in any other unlawful manner, will be suppressed by the power of the government of the United States.

Second. That the functions of the civil government of the State will be supported and upheld, and that the process of the State in civil and criminal matters may be executed in all posts and encampments of troops of the United States, and that resistance thereto by military persons shall be punished.

Third. That no recruiting of negroes within this State shall be recognized, unless the persons recruiting them shall be able to produce the written permission of the governor of the State; and that any person attempting to recruit without such permission, if he be in the military service shall be immediately prohibited from all such conduct, and if in civil life shall be proceeded against by the State authorities, without any interference by the military.

Fourth. That no countenance or encouragement shall be given to provost-marshals, or others in military authority, in any proceeding against the property of citizens, slaves included, upon the ground of its being liable to confiscation; but the confiscation shall be executed by the civil officers of the United States, as is directed by the authorities at Washington.

When we arrive at a perfect understanding between ourselves, I am willing to put myself in the same boat with you, and we will sink or swim together. If you should be censured or removed from this command because of what is done to carry these propositions into effect, I will abandon office immediately. . . .

To this I replied verbally that I could not enter into any agreement as to the policy to be pursued by me as commander of the department; that I must hold myself free to pursue such course as circumstances should from time to time indicate, or such as might be ordered by the President; my policy would be indicated from time to time by my general orders; in some respects it would doubtless conflict with that submitted by his Excellency. Nevertheless the governor finally consented to withdraw his resignation.

The convention at length passed an ordinance providing for the gradual extinction of slavery in the State, and adjourned. The feeling of bitterness between the opposing factions rather increased than diminished during its session.

The following letter to my friend Mr. Williams, which was published in the New York and St. Louis papers with my consent, made sufficiently clear the views I then entertained upon the slavery question, and left no reasonable ground for any emancipationist to quarrel with me on that subject, however much he may have been dissatisfied with the action of the convention,— just as my letter of June 1 to the President left him no room for doubt — if, indeed, he had entertained any before — upon the question then deemed so important:

HEADQUARTERS, DEP'T OF THE MISSOURI,

ST. LOUIS, June 1, 1863.

J. E. WILLIAMS, ESQ.,
Pres't Metropolitan Bank, New York.

MY DEAR SIR: Professor Bartlett has informed me of the interest you have manifested in my promotion and connection with this department, and, above all, that you have done me the kindness to assert my soundness on the important question of the day.

You are right in saying that I was an anti-slavery man, though not an abolitionist, before the war. These terms have greatly changed their relative meaning since the rebellion broke out. I regard universal emancipation as one of the necessary consequences of the rebellion, or rather as one of the means absolutely necessary to a complete restoration of the Union — and this because slavery was the great cause of the rebellion, and the only obstacle in the way of a perfect union. The perception of these important truths is spreading with almost astounding rapidity in this State. I have great hope that the State Convention, which meets on the 15th instant, will adopt some measure for the speedy emancipation of slaves. If so, our difficulties will be substantially at an end.

When the popular mind seizes a great principle and resolves to carry it into execution, it becomes impatient of the restraints imposed by existing laws, and in its haste to break down the barriers which stand in the way of its darling object, becomes regardless of all law, and anarchy is the result. This is our difficulty here. The people will have freedom for the slave. No law of the United States nor of Missouri, nor yet any order of the President, meets the case.

The loyal slave-owner demands that his rights *under the law* be protected. Let us have an ordinance of the State Convention which will satisfy the demands of the popular mind, and no loyal man will murmur.

You can imagine with what deep interest I look forward to the legal settlement of this question, so deeply involving the success of the great cause for the time being intrusted to my care.

In Arkansas and other States to which the President's proclamation applies, so far as I have observed, no such difficulty exists. The loyal people accept the decree without complaint, perfectly willing to give up all they have for the Union. So much the greater honor is due them for this cheerful sacrifice because they do not and cannot be expected to appreciate and understand the principle of freedom as it is impressed upon the loyal heart of the North.

Please accept my thanks for your kindness, and believe me,

Yours very truly,

(Signed) J. M. SCHOFIELD.

On June 20, I telegraphed to Mr. Lincoln:

The action of the Missouri State Convention upon the question of emancipation will depend very much upon whether they can be assured that their action will be sustained by the General Government and the people protected in their slave property during the short time that slavery is permitted to exist. Am I authorized in any manner, directly or indirectly, to pledge such support and protection?

This question is of such vital importance to the peace of Missouri that I deem it my duty to lay it before your Excellency.

The following reply from the President fairly illustrates the wisdom and justice of his views, and shows how perfectly I was in accord with him in my desire to do what was wisest and best for the peace of Missouri:

EXECUTIVE MANSION, WASHINGTON, June 22, 1863.

GENL. JOHN M. SCHOFIELD.

MY DEAR SIR: Your despatch, asking in substance whether, in case Missouri shall adopt gradual emancipation, the General Government will protect slave-owners in that species of property during the short time it shall be permitted by the State to exist within it, has been received.

Desirous as I am that emancipation shall be adopted by Missouri, and believing as I do that *gradual* can be made better than *immediate*, for both black and white, except when military necessity changes the case, my impulse is to say that such protection would be given. I cannot know exactly what shape an act of emancipation may take. If the period from the initiation to the final end should be comparatively short, and the act should prevent persons being sold during that period into more lasting slavery, the whole would be easier. I do not wish to pledge the General Government to the affirmative support of even temporary slavery, beyond what can be fairly claimed under the Constitution. I suppose, however, this is not desired; but that it is desired for the military force of the United States, while in Missouri, to not be used in subverting the temporarily reserved legal rights in slaves during the progress of emancipation. This I would desire also. I have very earnestly urged the slave States to adopt emancipation; and it ought to be, and is, an object with me not to overthrow or thwart what any of them may in good faith do to that end. You are therefore authorized to act in the spirit of this letter, in conjunction with what may appear to be the military necessities of your department.

Although this letter will become public at some time, it is not intended to be made so now.   Yours truly,

A. LINCOLN.

My impression is that the nature of this quarrel in Missouri was not fully understood at the time in Washington, as General Halleck wrote me that neither of the factions was regarded as really friendly to the President. But my belief is that they were then, as they subsequently proved to be, divided on the Presidential question as well as in State politics; that the conservatives were sincere in their friendship and support of Mr. Lincoln, and desired his renomination, while the radicals were intriguing for Mr. Chase or some other more radical man.

This struggle between extreme radicalism and conservatism among the Union people of Missouri was long and bitter, but I have nothing to do with its history beyond the period of my command in that department. It resulted, as is now well known, in the triumph of radicalism in the Republican party, and the consequent final loss of power by that party in the State. Such extremes could not fail to produce a popular revulsion, and it required no great foresight to predict the final result.

The factions in Missouri gave the military commander trouble enough in 1863; but to that was added the similar and hardly less troublesome party quarrel in Kansas. I cannot give a more accurate account of the complicated situation there than by quoting from my correspondence and journal of that period. On August 28 I wrote to President Lincoln as follows:

In reply to your telegram of the 27th, transmitting copy of one received from two influential citizens of Kansas, I beg leave to state some of the facts connected with the horrible massacre at Lawrence, and also relative to the assaults made upon me by a certain class of influential politicians.

Since the capture of Vicksburg, a considerable portion of the rebel army in the Mississippi valley has disbanded, and large numbers of men have come back to Missouri, many of them doubtless in the hope of being permitted to remain at their former homes in peace, while some have come under instructions to carry on a guerrilla warfare, and others, men of the worst character, become marauders on their own account, caring nothing for the Union, nor for the rebellion, except as the latter affords them a cloak for their brigandage.

Under instructions from the rebel authorities, as I am informed and believe, considerable bands, called " Border Guards," were organized in the counties of Missouri bordering on Kansas, for the ostensible purpose of protecting those counties from inroads from Kansas, and preventing the slaves of rebels from escaping from Missouri into Kansas. These bands were unquestionably encouraged, fed, and harbored by a very considerable portion of the people of those border counties. Many of those people were in fact the families of these " bushwhackers," who are brigands of the worst type.

Upon the representation of General Ewing and others familiar with the facts, I became satisfied there could be no cure for this evil short of the removal from those counties of all slaves entitled to their freedom, and of the families of all men known to belong to these bands, and others who were known to sympathize with them. Accordingly I directed General Ewing to adopt and carry out the policy he had indicated, warning him, however, of the retaliation which might be attempted, and that he must be fully prepared to prevent it before commencing such severe measures.

Almost immediately after it became known that such policy had been adopted, Quantrill secretly assembled from several of the border counties of Missouri about 300 of his men. They met at a preconcerted place of rendezvous near the Kansas line, at about sunset, and immediately marched for Lawrence, which place they reached at daylight the next morning. They sacked and burned the town and murdered the citizens in the most barbarous manner.

It is easy to see that any unguarded town in a country where such a number of outlaws can be assembled is liable to a similar fate, if the villains are willing to risk the retribution which must follow. In this case 100 of them have already been slain, and the remainder are hotly pursued in all directions. If there was any fault on the part of General Ewing, it appears to have been in not guarding Lawrence. But of this it was not my purpose to speak. General Ewing and the governor of

Kansas have asked for a court of inquiry, and I have sent to the War Department a request that one may be appointed, and I do not wish to anticipate the result of a full investigation. . . . I am officially informed that a large meeting has been held at Leavenworth, in which a resolution was adopted to the effect that the people would assemble at a certain place on the border, on September 8, for the purpose of entering Missouri to search for their stolen property. Efforts have been made by the mayor of Leavenworth to get possession of the ferry at that place, for the purpose of crossing armed parties of citizens into north Missouri.

I have strong reasons for believing that the authors of the telegram to you are among those who introduced and obtained the adoption of the Leavenworth resolution, and who are endeavoring to organize a force for the purpose of general retaliation upon Missouri. Those who so deplore my "imbecility" and "incapacity" are the very men who are endeavoring to bring about a collision between the people of Kansas and the troops under General Ewing's command.

I have not the "capacity" to see the wisdom or justice of permitting an irresponsible mob to enter Missouri for the purpose of retaliation, even for so grievous a wrong as that which Lawrence has suffered.

I have increased the force upon the border as far as possible, and no effort has been, or will be, spared to punish the invaders of Kansas, and to prevent such acts in the future. The force there has been all the time far larger than in any other portion of my department, except on the advanced line in Arkansas and the Indian Territory. . . .

P. S. Since writing the above I have received the "Daily Times" newspaper, published at Leavenworth, containing an account of the meeting referred to, and Senator Lane's speech, which I have the honor to inclose herewith for your information.

In a letter of that same date (August 28), Governor Carney informed me, among other things, that "after the fearful disaster at Lawrence and on the return of our troops who had pursued Quantrill and his murderous band, General Ewing and General James H. Lane met at Morristown and spent the night together. The latter re-

turned to Lawrence and called a mass meeting, at which
he defended General Ewing and made an intensely bitter
speech against you. Yesterday he arrived in this city,
and soon after caused to be issued a placard stating he
would address the citizens on war matters. There are
two parties here—one for and the other against Ewing.
That against him is headed by Mr. Wilder, member of
Congress, and by Mr. Anthony, mayor of this city. This
division put General Lane in this dilemma here, that he
could not defend Ewing as he had done in Lawrence, and
hence he devoted his whole attention to you. The more
violent of the men opposing you are for independent raids
into Missouri. How far General Lane encouraged this
class you must judge from the facts I have stated and
from the inclosed speech. To give tone and distinction
to the meeting, General Lane offered a resolution calling
upon the President to relieve you, affirming that there
could be no safety in Kansas, no help for Kansas, unless
this was done. . . . You will judge from the facts stated,
from the course pursued by General Lane at Lawrence,
and from his speech here, how far General Ewing is your
friend or fit to command this district."

On August 31, I started for the scene of the agitation.
The following extracts from my journal reveal the
situation:

Sept. 2.— Reached Leavenworth at five o'clock A. M. Stopped at the Planters' Hotel; was called upon by Governor Carney and several of his political friends. Discussed at much
length the condition of affairs in the District of the Border.
Carney is an aspirant for the United States Senate. Intends to
run against Lane. Desires to kill off Ewing, considering him
a formidable rival, or at least a supporter of Lane. Ewing has
determined not to be a candidate at the next election, and will
not commit himself in support of either Carney or Lane. Desires to keep on good terms with Lane because he thinks Lane
will probably be reëlected. Carney understands Ewing as sup-

porting Lane, or at least as having withdrawn in Lane's favor. In fact, Ewing refuses an alliance with Carney. Carney therefore desires to kill Ewing. Lane finds it to his interest to sustain Ewing so long as Schofield commands the department. Ewing is a better man for Lane than any other Schofield would be likely to give him. Lane's desire is to remove Schofield and get in his place a general who would place Kansas under command of one of Lane's tools, or a man who could be made one by Lane; therefore Lane defends Ewing and concentrates his attack upon Schofield. . . .

Asked and obtained a long private interview with Lane. Went over the whole ground of his hostility to Genl. S. during the past year. Showed him the injustice he had done Genl. S., and how foolish and unprofitable to himself his hostility had been. He stated with apparent candor that he had bent the whole energies of his soul to the destruction of Genl. S.; had never labored harder to accomplish any object in his life. Said he had been evidently mistaken in the character and principles of Genl. S., and that no man was more ready than he to atone for a fault. We then approached the subject of the invasion of Missouri by people of Kansas. Genl. Lane still adheres to his design of collecting the people at Paola and leading them on an expedition " for the purpose of searching for their stolen property." He professes his ability to control the people; that he would be answerable, and offered to pledge himself to Genl. S. and the government that they should do nothing beyond that which he declares as the object of the expedition. . . .

Lane was informed that Genl. S. would go to Kansas City the next day, and Lane replied that he intended to go also. It was agreed that both should go the next morning and converse with Genl. Ewing on the subject. The same evening Genl. Lane made a public speech in Leavenworth, in which he urged the people to meet at Paola, and assured them that the department and district commanders would not interfere with the proposed expedition; on the contrary, that both would countenance and coöperate with it. He also proclaimed the object to be to lay waste the border counties of Missouri and exterminate the disloyal people. This statement, following an interview on that subject, was calculated to mislead a large number of well-disposed people who would not for a moment think of acting in opposition to military rules, and to greatly increase the number

6

of people who would assemble at Paola, and seriously complicate the difficulty.

In the evening had another interview with Gov. Carney and some of his friends. My main object was to secure the full co-operation of the State government in preventing the invasion of Missouri. For this purpose I had to consult to a considerable degree the political views and aims of the governor and his friends. Their object was, of course, to make out of Lane's project as much capital as possible against him. It was held by many of them that Lane had no serious design of entering Missouri; that he expected, of course, that the military authorities would forbid it; and that he would yield as a military necessity, and thus gain with his people additional ground for condemnation of the department commander, while he had the credit of having done all he possibly could to enable them to "recover their stolen property." . . . Viewing matters in this light, the governor and his advisers were strongly inclined to the opinion that the surest way of making capital for themselves out of Lane's move was to let him go on with it, without any interference on their part, confident that it would turn out a grand humbug. . . . After reaching Kansas City and talking with Genl. Ewing, I replied to the governor, accepting the services of as many of his troops as he and Genl. Ewing should deem necessary for the protection of all the towns in Kansas near the border, stating that with Kansas so protected, Genl. Ewing would not only carry out his order for the expulsion of disloyal persons, but also in a short time drive out the guerrillas from his district and restore peace. In addition to this, I wrote the governor a private letter urging him to issue his proclamation discouraging the Paola meeting and warning his people against any attempt to go into Missouri, and informing him I would issue an order forbidding armed men not in the regular military service from crossing the line.

Sept. 4.—I received the governor's reply that he would issue his proclamation as requested, and also asking permission to publish a letter which I had written him on August 29, in reply to one from him regarding these matters. This permission was granted.

My order was also published declaring that the militia of Kansas and Missouri would be used only for the defense of their respective States; that they should not pass from one State into the other without express orders from the district commander;

that armed bodies of men *not* belonging to the United States troops, or to the militia placed under the orders of the department commander by the governors of their respective States, should not, under any pretext whatever, pass from one State into the other.

In the evening of the 3d I sent a despatch to the general-in-chief [Halleck], informing him that the Paola movement was under the control and guidance of Lane, and that I should not permit them to enter Missouri; that Lane said he would appeal to the President; that I did not apprehend a hostile collision; but that a despatch from the President or the Secretary of War (to Lane) would aid me much in preventing difficulty.

If such despatch should be sent, I requested to be informed of its purport. No reply received from the general-in-chief up to this time (1 P. M., Sept. 5). . . .

Sept. 6.—Lane failed to meet me at Kansas City, according to agreement. My correspondence with Governor Carney relative to the Lawrence massacre and the Paola movement appeared in the Leavenworth papers of yesterday; also my order forbidding armed citizens from crossing into Missouri.

The governor's proclamation did not appear according to promise; probably he may have decided to defer it until after the Paola meeting, as a means of making capital against Lane.

A private letter from one of Governor Carney's advisers was received yesterday (5th), dated the 3d, but evidently written in the evening of the 4th or morning of the 5th, which indicated that Carney does not intend to publish a proclamation, for the reason that Lane desires to force him to do it. . . .

Went to Westport yesterday. Met several of the leading loyal citizens; all agree that Genl. Ewing's order No. 11 is wise and just—in fact a necessity. I have yet to find the first loyal man in the border counties who condemns it. They are also warm in their support of Genl. Ewing, and deprecate his removal. I am satisfied he is acting wisely and efficiently. . . .

The radicals in Missouri condemn him (Ewing) as one of my friends; the conservatives, because he is a Kansas man, and more especially because of his order No. 11, and similar reasons and radical measures. For a time this will weaken me very much, and possibly may cause my overthrow. This risk I must take, because I am satisfied I am doing the best for the public good, and acting according to my instructions from the President. I seem in a fair way to reach one of the positions referred to in the President's letter of instructions, viz.: that in which both factions will abuse me. According to the President's standard, this is the only evidence that I will ever have that I am right. It is hardly possible that I will ever reach a point where both will commend me. . . .

Sept. 8.—Went to Independence yesterday, in company with Genl. Ewing; . . . made a few remarks to quite a large assemblage of people, which were well received; was followed by Genl. Ewing in an appropriate speech, which produced a good effect.

Have determined to modify General Ewing's order, or rather he will modify it at my suggestion, so that no property shall be destroyed. I deem the destruction of property unnecessary and useless. The chief evil has resulted from the aid given to guerrillas in the way of information conveyed by disloyal people, and by preparing their food for them. This evil is now removed. Forage and grain cannot be destroyed or carried away to such extent as materially to cripple them. I will as far as possible preserve the property of all loyal people, with the view of permitting them to return as soon as the guerrillas shall be driven out. Property of known rebels will be appropriated as far as possible to the use of the army and loyal people who are made destitute. None will be destroyed.

Had a long interview this morning with Mayor Anthony of Leavenworth and a number of influential citizens of that place. Anthony was arrested and sent to this place yesterday by a detective in the employ of Genl. Ewing. The arrest was without authority, and Genl. Ewing promptly discharged the mayor. The object of the citizens was to obtain a revocation of martial law in Leavenworth, and come to a correct understanding as to the relation between the military and civil authorities in that town, so as to prevent difficulty in future. The whole matter was satisfactorily arranged. . . .

So far as can be learned, no people have gone from Leavenworth to the Paola meeting, and it is probable the whole affair will amount to nothing. Believing that the trouble here is substantially over, I propose to start for St. Louis to-morrow morning.

A regiment of enrolled militia ordered to New Madrid to relieve the 25th Missouri, in order that the latter might go to reinforce General Steele in Arkansas, mutinied after they had gone on board the steamer, brought the boat ashore, and went to their homes. The provost guard of St. Louis was sent to arrest them. News having come of the capture of Little Rock, the two enrolled militia regiments in St. Louis were dismissed, except the mutineers, who were kept at hard labor for some time, and the leaders tried for mutiny.

This mutiny was caused by the efforts of the radical papers and politicians, who had for some time openly opposed the organization of the provisional regiments, and encouraged the men to mutiny.

I published an order enforcing martial law against all who should incite mutiny among the troops, and through General Halleck obtained the President's approval of this order, but did not find it necessary to make that approval public until it was made known by the President himself.

In writing to General Halleck on September 20, I said:

I inclose herewith a copy of an order which I have found it necessary to publish and enforce. The revolutionary faction which has so long been striving to gain the ascendancy in Missouri, particularly in St. Louis, to overthrow the present State government and change the policy of the national administration, has at length succeeded so far as to produce open mutiny of one of the militia regiments and serious difficulties in others.

I inclose a number of slips from papers published in Missouri, to show the extent to which this factious opposition to the government has been carried. The effect already produced is but natural, and the ultimate effect will be disastrous in the extreme, unless a strong remedy be applied speedily.

Out of consideration for popular opinion and the well-known wishes of the President relative to freedom of speech and of the press, I have forborne until, in my belief, further forbearance would lead to disastrous results. I am thoroughly convinced of the necessity for prompt and decided measures to put down this revolutionary scheme, and my sense of duty will not permit me to delay it longer. It is barely possible that I may not have to enforce the order against the public press. They may yield without the application of force; but I do not expect it. The tone of some of their articles since the publication of the order indicates a determination to wage the war which they have begun to the bitter end. This determination is based upon the belief that the President will not sustain me in any such measures as those contemplated in the order. A distinct approval by the President of my proposed action, and a knowledge of the fact here, would end the whole matter at once. I desire, if possible, to have such approval before taking action in any individual case. Indeed, I believe such approval would prevent the necessity for the use of force. It is difficult, I am aware, for any one at a distance to believe that such measures can be necessary against men and papers who claim to be "radically loyal." The fact is, they are "loyal" only to their "radical" theories, and are so "radical" that they cannot possibly be "loyal" to the government. . . .

These men were styled "revolutionists," not without sufficient cause. It was currently reported that they had in 1861 conceived the elevation of Frémont to a dictatorship. In 1862, and again in 1863, they invented a scheme for the violent overthrow of the provisional State government and the existing national administration in Missouri. The first act of the program was to seize and imprison Governor Gamble and me. In 1862 some of them committed the indiscretion of confiding their plans to General Frank P. Blair, Jr., who at once warned me of it, but refused to give me the names of his informers or of the leaders. He said he could not do so without breach of confidence, but that he had informed them that he should give me warning and expose the individuals if any further steps were taken. Here the matter ended.

In 1863 I received warning through the guard stationed at my residence in the suburbs of the city, with which the revolutionists had the folly to tamper in their efforts to spread disaffection among my troops. This discovery, and the premature mutiny of the regiment ordered to New Madrid, nipped the plot in the bud. I refer to the circumstances now only to show that I was not unjust in my denunciation of the "revolutionary faction" in Missouri. In General Halleck's letter of September 26, inclosing the President's written approval of my general order, he said:

. . . Neither faction in Missouri is really friendly to the President and administration; but each is striving to destroy the other, regardless of all other considerations. In their mutual hatred they seem to have lost all sense of the perils of the country and all sentiment of national patriotism. Every possible effort should be made to allay this bitter party strife in that State.

In reply, September 30, I expressed the following opinion:

. . . I feel compelled to say that I believe you are not altogether right in your information about the factions in Missouri. If the so-called "claybank" faction are not altogether friendly to the President and administration, I have not been able to discover it. The men who now sustain me are the same who rallied round Lyon and sustained the government in the dark days of 1861, while the leaders of the present "charcoal" faction stood back until the danger was past. I believe I have carried out my instructions as literally as possible, yet I have received a reasonable support from one faction and the most violent opposition from the other. I am willing to pledge my official position that those who support me now will support me in the execution of any policy the President may order. They are the real friends of the government. It is impossible for me to be blind to this fact, notwithstanding the existence, to some extent, of the factional feeling to which you allude.

The improvement produced by the order was so decided that publication of the President's approval was thought unnecessary. It only became public through his letter of October 1, 1863, of which he gave a copy to the radical delegation.

In September the governor of Missouri placed all the militia of the State, including those not in active service, under my command. I published orders intended to control their action and prevent interference with political meetings; also to secure freedom of voting at the coming election in November. Several militia officers guilty of such interference were dismissed, which produced a wholesome effect.

CHAPTER VI

A MEMORANDUM FOR MR. LINCOLN — THE PRESIDENT'S IN-
STRUCTIONS — HIS REPLY TO THE RADICAL DELEGATION
— THE MATTER OF COLORED ENLISTMENTS — MODIFICA-
TION OF THE ORDER RESPECTING ELECTIONS REFUSED
— A LETTER TO THE PRESIDENT ON THE CONDITION OF
MISSOURI — FORMER CONFEDERATES IN UNION MILITIA
REGIMENTS — SUMMONED TO WASHINGTON BY MR. LIN-
COLN — OFFERED THE COMMAND OF THE ARMY OF THE
OHIO — ANECDOTE OF GENERAL GRANT.

ON October 1, 1863, I furnished the following memorandum to the Hon. James S. Rollins, M. C., for the
information of the President. It was doubtless seen by
the President before the date of his letter to the radical
delegation, quoted further on.

The radicals urge as evidence of Genl. Schofield's misrule
that Missouri is in a worse condition than at any time since the
rebellion; that he has failed to use the troops at his disposal
to put down the rebellion. This charge is false, unless it be admitted that the radicals are rebels. It is true that the State is
in a bad condition, and it is equally true that this condition is
directly brought about by professed Union men — radicals.

There has been no time since the beginning of the war when
there were so few armed rebels or guerrillas in Missouri as at
the present time. The only trouble at all worth mentioning in
comparison with what the State has suffered heretofore is the
lawless acts of radicals in their efforts to exterminate or drive
out all who differ from them in political sentiment. This lawlessness is instigated, encouraged, and applauded by the radical
press and leaders. Every effort to put down this lawlessness is

denounced by the radicals as persecution of loyal men. When Genl. Curtis relinquished command he had in Missouri and Kansas 43,000 men; Genl. Schofield retained in these States only 23,000. Of the remaining 20,000, he sent some reinforcements to Genl. Rosecrans and a large force to Genl. Grant, to assist in the capture of Vicksburg; and with the remainder and a force equivalent to the one sent to Genl. Grant, returned by him after the fall of Vicksburg, he has reclaimed all Arkansas and the Indian Territory.

The radicals denounce Genl. Schofield because of his relations to the State government. It is true that those relations have been most cordial, but it is not true that his policy has been controlled or materially influenced by Gov. Gamble. Gov. Gamble has not sought to exercise any such control. He, without hesitation, placed all the militia in active service under Genl. S.'s command, and yielded to him the control of all military operations. As an example to illustrate the truth of this statement: Genl. S. required the militia to obey the 102d Article of War; although they were not in the service of the United States, and although they constituted the only force in the State capable of arresting fugitive slaves with any certainty, no complaint was made by the State government. No military force is used in this department for the return of fugitives. All assertions to the contrary are false. On the contrary, it has been invariably held by Genl. Schofield and Col. Broadhead that free papers given under Genl. Curtis were to be held valid, even though wrongfully given, the negroes having been the slaves of loyal men. So also when the slaves of loyal men have, by mistake or otherwise, been enlisted in colored regiments, Genl. Schofield has invariably held that they have been made free by their enlistment, and cannot be returned to their masters or discharged from the service.

It cannot be denied that Genl. Schofield's whole influence has been in favor of emancipation. He did all in his power to secure the passage of an ordinance of emancipation by the late State Convention. The leaders of the present "charcoal" faction, who now war on Genl. Schofield, are not the men who sustained the government at the beginning of the war. The men who now support Genl. S. are the identical ones who stood around Lyon and sustained the government in the dark days of 1861. They are the true friends of the government; men who stand between the rebels on one side and the radical revolutionists on the other; the men who maintain the Constitution, uphold the laws, and advocate justice to all men. If sustained by the President, they will rally to their standard all the best men of the State, of all parties.

Secession is dead in Missouri. As a party the secessionists are utterly without influence. The degree of support which they will hereafter give to the government will depend upon its policy. If the radicals triumph, the enemies of the government will be increased both in numbers and bitterness. If a wise and just policy be pursued, every respectable man in the State will soon be an active supporter of the government, and Missouri will be the most loyal State in the Union.

This, in fact, is the cause of the present fierce action of the radicals. They know they must get the power at once, or there will soon be an overwhelming loyal party opposed to them. The "claybank" leaders control all the conservative elements in the State, and give to Genl. S., as the representative of the President, an honest support. They will continue to support him in the execution of any policy the President may order to be carried out. They sustain him, and will sustain him in future, although they may not approve all his acts, because it is their duty to the government.

About the last of September a radical delegation of about one hundred members from Missouri and Kansas went to Washington to urge my removal from command in Missouri. The President sent me the following instructions, and made a reply to the delegation, also given below:

EXECUTIVE MANSION, WASHINGTON, D. C., Oct. 1, 1863.

GENERAL JOHN M. SCHOFIELD.

SIR: There is no organized military force in avowed opposition to the General Government now in Missouri; and if any such shall reappear, your duty in regard to it will be too plain to require any special instructions. Still, the condition of things both there and elsewhere is such as to render it indispensable to maintain for a time the United States military establishment in that State, as well as to rely upon it for a fair contribution of support to the establishment generally. Your immediate duty in regard to Missouri now is to advance the efficiency of that establishment, and to use it, as far as practicable, to compel the excited people there to leave one another alone.

Under your recent order, which I have approved, you will only arrest individuals, and suppress assemblies or newspapers, when they may be working palpable injury to the military in your charge; and in no other case will you interfere with the expression of opinion in any form, or allow it to be interfered with violently by others. In this you have a discretion to exercise with great caution, calmness, and forbearance.

With the matters of removing the inhabitants of certain counties *en masse*, and of removing certain individuals from time to time, who are supposed to be mischievous, I am not now interfering, but am leaving to your own discretion.

Nor am I interfering with what may still seem to you to be necessary restrictions upon trade and intercourse.

I think proper, however, to enjoin upon you the following: Allow no part of the military under your command to be engaged in either returning fugitive slaves, or in forcing or enticing slaves from their homes; and, so far as practicable, enforce the same forbearance upon the people.

Report to me your opinion upon the availability for good of the enrolled militia of the State.

Allow no one to enlist colored troops, except upon orders from you, or from here through you.

Allow no one to assume the functions of confiscating property, under the law of Congress or otherwise, except upon orders from here.

At elections see that those, and only those, are allowed to vote who are entitled to do so by the laws of Missouri, including, as of those laws, the restriction laid by the Missouri Convention upon those who may have participated in the rebellion.

So far as practicable, you will, by means of your military force, expel guerrillas, marauders, and murderers, and all who are known to harbor, aid, or abet them. But, in like manner, you will repress assumptions of unauthorized individuals to perform the same service, because, under pretense of doing this, they become marauders and murderers themselves.

To now restore peace, let the military obey orders, and those not of the military leave each other alone, thus not breaking the peace themselves.

In giving the above directions, it is not intended to restrain you in other expedient and necessary matters not falling within their range.   Your obt. servt.,   A. LINCOLN.

I wrote in my journal, under date of October 2:

Colonel Du Bois, Captain Benham, and Captain Howard, who were sent to inspect in Genl. Ewing's and Genl. Blunt's districts, have returned. They report affairs in Blunt's district in a disgraceful condition. I have determined to relieve Blunt, and propose to send McNeil to Fort Smith. I telegraphed my intentions to Genl. Halleck this morning, and asked for a general officer to command one of the two districts. Soon after I received a despatch from the President saying Genl. Halleck had shown him my despatch, and adding: "If possible, you better allow me to get through with a certain matter here before adding to the difficulties of it. Meantime supply me with the particulars of Maj.-Genl. Blunt's case."

I replied: "I will forward the papers in Genl. Blunt's case, and defer action until I know your pleasure regarding it. I desire, if possible, to diminish and not increase your difficulties. This is one reason why I informed Genl. Halleck what I thought it necessary to do." Have since received a despatch from Genl. Halleck saying that he had ordered Brig.-Genl. J. B. Sanborn from Vicksburg to report to me for duty.

Have received a letter from Atty.-Genl. Bates, dated Sept. 29, saying I need have no fear of the result of the efforts of the radical delegation.

On Sept. 30 I received a despatch from the President transmitting the false report from Leavenworth that Col. Moss, of the militia, was driving out Union families from Platt and Union counties. After full inquiry from Col. Guitar, Genl. Ewing, and Col. Williams at St. Joseph, have replied to the President, informing him the report is false, and a base attempt of my enemies to influence his action.

Under date of October 4, I wrote in my journal:

The address presented to the President by the radical delegation from Missouri was published in the "Democrat" last evening. I telegraphed the President last night that "so much of it as relates to me is not only untrue in spirit, but most of it is literally false. If an answer or explanation is on any account desirable, I shall be glad to make it." To-day I received from the President a despatch saying: "Think you will not have just cause to complain of my action. . . ."

The next day the President made this reply to the radical delegation:

EXECUTIVE MANSION, WASHINGTON, D. C., October 5, 1863.

HON. CHARLES D. DRAKE AND OTHERS, Committee.

GENTLEMEN: Your original address, presented on the 30th ultimo, and the four supplementary ones, presented on the 3d inst., have been carefully considered. I hope you will regard the other duties claiming my attention, together with the great length and importance of the documents, as constituting a sufficient apology for my not having responded sooner.

These papers, framed for a common object, consist of the things demanded, and the reasons for demanding them.

The things demanded are:

First. That General Schofield shall be relieved and General Butler be appointed as commander of the Military Department of Missouri.

Second. That the system of enrolled militia in Missouri may be broken up, and national forces be substituted for it; and,

Third. That at elections persons may not be allowed to vote who are not entitled by law to do so.

Among the reasons given, enough of suffering and wrong to Union men is certainly, and I suppose truly, stated. Yet the whole case as presented fails to convince me that General Schofield, or the enrolled militia, is responsible for that suffering and wrong. The whole can be explained on a more charitable and, as I think, a more rational hypothesis.

We are in civil war. In such cases there always is a main question; but in this case that question is a perplexing compound — Union and slavery. It thus becomes a question not of two sides merely, but of at least four sides, even among those who are for the Union, saying nothing of those who are against it. Thus, those who are for the Union *with*, but not *without*, slavery; those for it *without*, but not *with*; those for it *with* or *without*, but prefer it *with*; and those for it *with* or *without*, but prefer it *without*. Among these again is a subdivision of those who are for *gradual*, but not for *immediate*, and those who are for *immediate*, but not for *gradual*, extinction of slavery. It is easy to conceive that all these shades of opinion, and even more, may be sincerely entertained by honest and truthful men; yet all being for the Union, by reason of these differences each will prefer a different way of sustaining the Union. At once sincerity is questioned and motives are assailed; actual war coming, blood grows hot and blood is spilled. Thought is forced from old channels into confusion; deception breeds and thrives; confidence dies, and universal suspicion reigns. Each man feels an impulse to kill his neighbor, lest he be first killed by him. Revenge and retaliation follow, and all this, as before said, may be among honest men only. But this is not all. Every foul bird comes abroad, and every dirty reptile rises up. These add crime to confusion. Strong measures deemed indispensable, but harsh at best, such men make worse by maladministration. Murders for old grudges and murders for pelf proceed under any cloak that will best cover for the occasion.

These causes amply account for what has occurred in Missouri, without ascribing it to the weakness or wickedness of any general. The newspaper files — those chronicles of current events — will show that the evils now complained of were quite as prevalent under Frémont, Hunter, Halleck, and Curtis as under Schofield.

If the former had greater force opposed to them, they had also greater forces with which to meet it. When the organized rebel army left the State, the main Federal force had to go also, leaving the department commander at home relatively no stronger than before.

Without disparaging any, I affirm with confidence that no commander of that department has, in proportion to his means, done better than General Schofield.

The first specific charge against General Schofield is that the enrolled militia was placed under his command, when it had not been placed under the command of General Curtis.

That, I believe, is true; but you do not point out, nor can I conceive, how that did or could injure loyal men or the Union cause.

You charge that upon General Curtis being superseded by General Schofield, Franklin A. Dick was superseded by James O. Broadhead as provost-marshal-general. No very specific showing is made as to how this did or could injure the Union cause. It recalls, however, the condition of things, as presented to me, which led to a change of commanders for the department.

To restrain contraband intelligence and trade, a system of searches, seizures, permits, and passes had been introduced by General Frémont. When General Halleck came, he found and continued the system, and added an order, applicable to some parts of the State, to levy and collect contributions from noted rebels to compensate losses and relieve destitution caused by the rebellion. The action of General Frémont and General Halleck, as stated, constituted a sort of system which General Curtis found in full operation when he took command of the department. That there was a necessity for something of the sort was clear; but that it could only be justified by stern necessity, and that it was liable to great abuse in administration, was equally clear. Agents to execute it, contrary to the great prayer, were led into temptation. Some might, while others would not, resist that temptation. It was not possible to hold any to a very strict accountability; and those yielding to the temptation would sell permits and passes to those who would pay most, and most readily, for them, and would seize property and collect levies in the aptest way to fill their own pockets; money being the object, the man having money, whether loyal or disloyal, would be a victim. This practice doubtless existed to some extent, and it was a real additional evil that it could be, and was, plausibly charged to exist in greater extent than it did.

When General Curtis took command of the department, Mr. Dick, against whom I never knew anything to allege, had general charge of this system. A controversy in regard to it rapidly grew into almost unmanageable proportions. One side ignored the necessity and magnified the evils of the system, while the other ignored the evils and magnified the necessity, and each bitterly assailed the motives of the other. I could not fail to see that the controversy enlarged in the same proportion as the professed Union men there distinctly took sides in two opposing political parties. I exhausted my wits, and very nearly my patience also, in efforts to convince both that the evils they charged on each other were inherent in the case, and could not be cured by giving either party a victory over the other. Plainly the irritating system was not to be perpetual, and it was plausibly urged that it could be modified at once with advantage. The case could scarcely be worse; and whether it could be made better, could only be determined by a trial. In this view, and not to ban or brand General Curtis, or to give a victory to any party, I made the change of commander for the department. I now learn that soon after this change Mr. Dick was removed, and that Mr. Broadhead, a gentleman of no less good character, was put in the place. The mere fact of this change is more distinctly complained of than is any conduct of the new officer, or other consequences of the change.

I gave the new commander no instructions as to the administration of the system mentioned, beyond what is contained in the private letter, afterward surreptitiously published,[1] in which I directed him to act solely for the public good, and independently of both parties. Neither anything you have presented me, nor anything I have otherwise learned, has convinced me that he has been unfaithful to this charge.

Imbecility is urged as one cause for removing General Schofield; and the late massacre at Lawrence, Kansas, is pressed as evidence of that imbecility. To my mind that fact scarcely tends to prove the proposition. That massacre is only an example of what Grierson, John Morgan, and many others might have repeatedly done on their respective raids, had they chosen to incur the personal hazard and possessed the fiendish hearts to do it.

The charge is made that General Schofield, on purpose to protect the Lawrence murderers, would not allow them to be pursued into Missouri. While no punishment could be too sudden or too severe for those murderers, I am well satisfied that the preventing of the remedial raid into Missouri was the only safe way to avoid an indiscriminate massacre there, including probably more innocent than guilty. Instead of condemning, I therefore approve what I understand General Schofield did in that respect.

The charges that General Schofield has purposely withheld protection from loyal people, and purposely facilitated the objects of the disloyal, are altogether beyond my power of be-

---

[1] By a radical newspaper.

lief. I do not arraign the veracity of gentlemen as to the facts complained of, but I do more than question the judgment which would infer that those facts occurred in accordance with the *purposes* of General Schofield.

With my present views, I must decline to remove General Schofield. In this I decide nothing against General Butler. I sincerely wish it were convenient to assign him a suitable command.

In order to meet some existing evils, I have addressed a letter of instructions to General Schofield, a copy of which I inclose to you.

As to the " enrolled militia," I shall endeavor to ascertain better than I now know what is its exact value. Let me say now, however, that your proposal to substitute national forces for the enrolled militia implies that in your judgment the latter is doing something which needs to be done, and if so, the proposition to throw that force away, and supply its place by bringing other forces from the field, where they are urgently needed, seems to me very extraordinary. Whence shall they come? Shall they be withdrawn from Banks, or Grant, or Steele, or Rosecrans?

Few things have been so grateful to my anxious feelings as when, in June last, the local force in Missouri aided General Schofield to so promptly send a large general force to the relief of General Grant, then investing Vicksburg and menaced from without by General Johnston. Was this all wrong? Should the enrolled militia then have been broken up, and General Herron kept from Grant to police Missouri? So far from finding cause to object, I confess to a sympathy for whatever relieves our general force in Missouri, and allows it to serve elsewhere. I, therefore, as at present advised, cannot attempt the destruction of the enrolled militia of Missouri. I may add that, the force being under the national military control, it is also within the proclamation in regard to the *habeas corpus.*

I concur in the propriety of your request in regard to elections, and have, as you see, directed General Schofield accordingly. I do not feel justified to enter upon the broad field you present in regard to the political differences between radicals and conservatives. From time to time I have done and said what appeared to me proper to do and say. The public knows it all. It obliges nobody to follow me, and I trust it obliges me to follow nobody. The radicals and conservatives each agree with me in some things and disagree in others. I could wish both to agree with me in all things; for then they would agree with each other, and would be too strong for any foe from any quarter. They, however, choose to do otherwise, and I do not question their right; I, too, shall do what seems to be my duty. I hold whoever commands in Missouri, or elsewhere, responsible to me, and not to either radicals or conservatives. It is my duty to hear all; but at last, I must, within my sphere, judge what to do and what to forbear.   Your obt. servt.,

A. LINCOLN.

On October 13, I wrote in my journal:

The radical delegation has returned from Washington very much crestfallen. It is generally conceded that they have accomplished nothing. Nothing official is yet known on the subject. . . .

Lane spoke at Turner's Hall last evening; no disturbance; was silent on the subject of the department commander. He informed me yesterday, through Major Vaughan, that he had stopped the war upon me, and intended hereafter not to oppose me unless circumstances rendered it necessary. Said the President told him that whoever made war on General Schofield, under the present state of affairs, made war on him—the President. Said he never had made war on General S., "except incidentally."

Oct. 14.—Received yesterday an order from Genl. [Lorenzo] Thomas appointing officers for the 1st Regt. Mo. Volunteers, of African descent, and directing that they be detailed to raise the regiment.

Have telegraphed to the War Department for instructions as to the mode of raising these troops, referring to a letter I wrote to Col. Townsend on the subject on the 29th of September. In that letter I explained the difficulty of raising such troops in Missouri, unless it be done without regard to the claims of loyal slave-owners. I also recommended that all able-bodied negroes be enlisted, receipts given as a basis for payment to loyal owners, and suggested that those of unquestioned loyalty might be paid at once from the substitute fund. No answer has been received to that letter.

Some months ago I wrote to the Secretary of War, asking instructions about the negro question. No answer. The Hon.

Secretary seems determined to make me deal with that question on my own responsibility. It is very natural, but hardly just to me.

I had issued an order respecting elections, in accordance with the President's instructions. A personal request was made to me for a modification of the order. The following letter was written in reply to that request:

HEADQRS., DEPARTMENT OF THE MISSOURI,
ST. LOUIS, Oct. 24th, 1863.
HON. C. DRAKE, St. Louis.

SIR: After full consideration of the subject of our conversation this morning, I am of the opinion that no further orders upon the subject of the election are necessary. The law which provides the manner in which soldiers shall vote, and directs how the judges of election shall be appointed, is as binding upon all persons to whom it relates as any order would be.

Genl. Order No. 120 also alludes to the subject of soldiers voting, I think, in sufficiently strong terms, although it is taken for granted in that order that officers will do their duty under the law in appointing judges of election and in giving their men an opportunity to vote. Moreover, any failure on their part to do their whole duty in this regard would be a clear violation of Genl. Order 101. I believe there is no ground for apprehension that officers will neglect their duty regarding the election. If anything is needed, it is that the troops be given full information through the daily papers, which they all read, of their duties and privileges under the laws.

From the short examination I have been able to give, I am of the opinion that the Act of the General Assembly changing the mode of voting does not apply to soldiers voting at the company polls; that the ordinance of the convention remains unrepealed.

This, however, is a question which I will not presume to decide or to refer to even in an order.

I return herewith the copy of Laws of Missouri which you were so kind as to lend me.

Very respectfully your obt. servt.,

J. M. SCHOFIELD, Major-Genl.

On October 25 I wrote to Mr. Lincoln in regard to a reorganization of the militia of northwestern Missouri which had been made for the purpose of suppressing the lawlessness that had prevailed there under the name of "loyalty," saying:

I take the liberty of sending you a letter which I have this day received from Hon. Willard P. Hall, Lieut.-Governor of Missouri.

It may be of interest to you, as showing the good effect of the stringent measures which I felt compelled to adopt in some portions of Missouri, and of the firm support you have given me.

The immediate effect, as might have been expected, was a terrible storm, but it has passed away, I hope never to return.

The State is now in far better condition than it has been at any time during the war.

I have issued an election order in compliance with your instructions, with which all parties express themselves well satisfied. It seems I have at last succeeded in doing one thing which nobody can find fault with.

Shelby's raid has terminated with a loss of about one half of the men with which he entered the State, and *he received no recruits* except the robbers under Quantrill and Jackman. These left the State with him. This fact is gratifying as showing that the rebel power in Missouri is completely broken.

Whatever may be the secret feelings of the former secessionists of Missouri, their influence now, so far as it is exerted at all, is for peace and submission to the national authority. All that is now necessary to secure peace to Missouri, with the possible exception of occasional raids from Arkansas, is union among the loyal people. I shall spare no effort to reconcile their differences as far as possible, or at least to restrain their quarrel within peaceable limits. The additional strength your support has given me will enable me to do this far better than before. My radical friends now exhibit some disposition to stop their war upon me, and I shall certainly not give them any good reason for continuing it. The honest enthusiasts on the subject of liberty, who compose the respectable portion of this party, are already well disgusted with their lawless brethren who have brought such odium upon them, and now begin to realize the necessity of sustaining me in enforcing the laws.

Whatever may be the result of the pending election, I believe the most serious danger is already past.

I shall not fail to exercise great forbearance in enforcing restrictions upon speech and the press. I have enforced my order in only one case, and that so clear that the offender fully confessed and asked pardon on any terms. It will not probably be necessary for me to exercise any control over the press hereafter.

Your accurate appreciation of the real difficulty here, and the strong and generous manner in which you have sustained me, will do more good in Missouri than to have doubled the troops under my command. This I hope soon to show you by sending additional forces to the front.

With the above letter to the President I inclosed the following:

ST. JOSEPH, MO., Oct. 21st, 1863.

GENERAL: It is with very great pleasure that I can inform you of the satisfactory condition of things in this section of Missouri. There is more security for men and property in northwestern Missouri than there has been since the rebellion began. There is not a spark of rebellious feeling left here, and all citizens seem to be, and I believe are, ready to discharge all the duties of loyal men.

The people are truly grateful to you for your efforts to protect them, and you may rest assured will never fail you in any emergency. Yours truly,

WILLARD P. HALL.

MAJOR-GENL. SCHOFIELD, etc.

The following was written by me, November 1, 1863, to Mr. James L. Thomas of St. Louis, in answer to what was understood to be an attempt to obtain some expression of partizan preference as between the " pestilent factions ":

In reply to your letter of Oct. 30th, I will state that in some important particulars you entirely misapprehended my remarks made during our conversation on the 29th. I spoke of the law-less acts committed in some portions of Missouri by men claim-ing to be radicals and acting in the name of radicalism; and asserted that leading men and papers of the party had failed to do their duty by disavowing and frowning down this lawless-ness; that in this course they had been guilty of great folly, and had brought odium upon their party in Missouri and throughout the country; that they had injured rather than advanced the cause of emancipation. I made no remarks rela-tive to the radical party, nor to radicals as a party or class of citizens. I spoke of those men and papers who by tolerating and encouraging lawlessness in the name of radicalism had done so much towards producing trouble in the State.

It is perhaps natural that any honest man should feel, as you propose, to disown a party in which such abuses are tolerated, but I cannot see the propriety of so doing. Would it not be much wiser and more patriotic to endeavor to purify the party, to bring it back to the high principles upon which it was founded, and to rid it of the elements whch have disgraced those principles?

Our conversation on the 29th was regarded by me as con-fidential, and I still desire it to be so regarded by you, and also this letter. No possible good can result from a public discus-sion by me of such matters.

You are aware that as department commander I have no-thing to do with politics, nor with offenders as members of any party. I shall unquestionably, upon proper proof, punish all who have been, or may hereafter be, guilty of the crimes you mention, without regard to the party they may belong to; but I do not propose to condemn any party or class of men because of the guilt of one or any number of its members. When I find men acting wrongfully or unwisely to the prejudice of the Union cause, I endeavor, within my proper sphere, to correct or restrain them by appropriate means according to circum-stances. Whether my influence thus exerted inures to the benefit of one party or another is a question which I cannot take into consideration.

My dealing is with individuals, not with parties. Officially I know nothing of radicals or conservatives. The question with me is simply what individuals obey the laws and what violate them; who are for the government and who against it. The measures of the President are my measures; his orders, my rule of action. Whether a particular party gains strength or loses it by my action must depend upon the party, and not upon me.

At this time occurred the following exchange of letters with the President:

(Private and confidential.)

EXECUTIVE MANSION, WASHINGTON, Oct. 28th, 1863.

GENERAL JOHN M. SCHOFIELD: There have recently reached the War Department, and thence been laid before me, from Missouri, three communications, all similar in import and identical in object. One of them, addressed to nobody, and without place or date, but having the signature of (apparently) the writer, is a letter of eight closely written foolscap pages. The other two are written by a different person at St. Joseph, Mo., and of the date, respectively, October 12th and 13th, and each inclosing a large number of affidavits.

The general statements of the whole are that the Federal and State authorities are arming the disloyal and disarming the loyal, and that the latter will all be killed or driven out of the State unless there shall be a change.

In particular, no loyal man who has been disarmed is named, but the affidavits show, by name, forty-two persons as disloyal who have been armed. They are as follows: [Names omitted.]

A majority of these are shown to have been in the rebel service. I believe it could be shown that the government here has deliberately armed more than ten times as many captured at Gettysburg, to say nothing of similar operations in East Tennessee. These papers contain altogether thirty-one manuscript pages, and one newspaper in extenso; and yet I do not find it anywhere charged in them that any loyal man has been harmed by reason of being disarmed, or that any disloyal one has harmed anybody by reason of being armed by the Federal or State government.

Of course I have not had time to carefully examine all; but I have had most of them examined and briefed by others, and the result is as stated. The remarkable fact that the actual evil is yet only anticipated—inferred—induces me to suppose I understand the case. But I do not state my impression, because I might be mistaken, and because your duty and mine is plain in any event.

The locality of nearly all this seems to be St. Joseph and Buchanan County. I wish you to give special attention to this region, particularly on Election day. Prevent violence, from whatever quarter, and see that the soldiers themselves do no wrong. Yours truly,

A. LINCOLN.

HDQRS., DEPT. OF THE MISSOURI,
ST. LOUIS, Nov. 9th, 1863.

MR. PRESIDENT: I have the honor to acknowledge the receipt of your confidential letter dated Oct. 28th, and containing the names of men enlisted in the militia of northwest Missouri who are said to have been disloyal.

On my visit to Kansas and northwest Missouri during the troubles there in September last, I examined personally into the difficulties in Platte, Buchanan, and other western counties, and learned fully their nature and origin. I at once ordered the reorganization of the militia, which created so much commotion for a time, but which has restored that portion of the State to a condition of profound peace.

I have watched the progress of affairs there closely, and have kept myself fully advised of all the facts. It is true that about twice as many former rebels as were named by your informants are in the militia organization, amounting to from five to ten per cent. of the whole. It is also true that a very much larger number of returned Missouri rebels have enlisted in the Kansas Volunteers, and, so far as I know, are faithful, good soldiers.

The rule I established for the militia organization in northwest Missouri was that the officers should be of undoubted loyalty, original Union men, and that both officers and privates, as far as possible, should be men of wealth and respectability, whose all depended upon the preservation of peace.

The former sufferings of these men from the lawlessness which has so long existed on the border made them willing to do military duty to save from destruction or loss what property they had left. I have yet to hear the first report of a murder, robbery, or arson in that whole region since this new organization was made. The late election was conducted in perfect peace and good order. There is not the slightest pretense from any source of any interference or other misconduct on the part of any of the troops. I have not deemed it necessary to be very particular about the antecedents of troops that are producing such good results. If I can make a repentant rebel of more service to the government than a man who never had any political sins to repent of, I see no reason for not doing so. Indeed, I take no little satisfaction in making these men guard the property of their more loyal neighbors, and in holding their own property responsible for their fidelity.

I have the satisfaction of reporting to you that the late election in all parts of the State passed off in perfect quiet and good order. I have heard of no disturbance of any kind anywhere. The aggregate vote, I think, shows that the purity of the ballot-box was preserved in a remarkable degree. If the loyal people all voted, few or no rebels did.

The prospects of future peace in this State are highly encouraging.

I am very respectfully your obt. servt.,

J. M. SCHOFIELD, Maj.-Genl.

To the President.

I had abundant reason to be satisfied with the result of this controversy, so far as it concerned me, and with the condition of the department when it terminated, near midwinter. Yet I was satisfied some change was impending, and cared not how soon it might come, now that my administration had been fully vindicated. In fact, such a command was not at all to my taste, and I had always longed for purely military service in the field, free from political complications. It was therefore with sincere pleasure that I received, in December, a summons from the President to come to Washington.

But before relating the circumstances of my visit to the President, I must refer to an incident which occurred a short time before I left St. Louis, and which I was afterward led to suspect was the immediate cause of the President's desire to see me.

The Missouri legislature was in session and balloting for a United States senator. The legislature was divided into three parties — radicals, conservative Republicans, and Democrats, or " copperheads," neither strong enough to elect without a fusion with one of the others. A union of the radicals and the conservatives was, of course, most desired by the administration ; but their bitterness had become so great that either would prefer a bargain with the Democrats rather than with the other. The Hon. E. B. Washburne, representative in Congress from Illinois, made an opportune visit to St. Louis about this time, procured an interview with me at the house of a common friend, and led me into a frank conversation relative to this political question. I told him candidly that in my opinion the desired union of radicals and conservatives was impossible, for they were more bitterly opposed to each other than either was to the Democrats. Mr. Washburne went to Washington, and reported to the President that I was opposed to the much-desired radical and conservative union in Missouri, and was using my influence to prevent it. So opposite was this to the truth that I had even written a letter to my friend Colonel J. O. Broadhead, the conservative candidate, asking him to withdraw in favor of the radical candidate, as a means of bringing about the harmony so much desired by the President. This letter was not sent, because the telegraphic reports from Jefferson City showed that it was too late to do any good; but it was handed to Colonel Broadhead on his return to show him my wishes in the matter.

Upon my first visit to the President, he repeated to me this Washburne story, without, however, intimating that he attached much weight to it. I at once replied by giving him the simple facts about my conversation with Washburne, and what my true position was on that question. Mr. Lincoln promptly dismissed the subject with the words: "I believe you, Schofield; those fellows have been lying to me again."

Mr. Lincoln undoubtedly referred here to a previous incident which was related to me by the Hon. James S. Rollins, member of Congress from Missouri, one of the truest and most truthful men in the world, as having occurred in his presence. Some men from Missouri had prevailed upon Mr. Rollins to introduce them to the President, to whom they wished to represent the condition of affairs in Missouri as viewed from their standpoint. After listening to their story, the President opened the little right-hand drawer of his desk, took out a letter from me, and read it to them. He then said: "*That* is the truth about the matter; you fellows are lying to me."

Determined to leave no room for doubt in the President's mind, I telegraphed to St. Louis and got the Broadhead letter; but by the time it arrived I had become so satisfied of Mr. Lincoln's confidence that I did not think it worth while to show it to him.

I remained at the capital several weeks, and had full conversations with the President on public affairs. The political situation was a perplexing one. The state of parties in the West seemed that of inextricable confusion, which Mr. Lincoln and his friends were anxious to unravel, if possible, before the next Presidential nomination. In Missouri the faction which had been friendly to me was also a supporter of Mr. Lincoln, while the radicals were opposed to him. In Kansas, on the contrary, the so-called Lane and Carney factions, while vying with each other in professions of radicalism, were divided in the opposite manner. The former supported the President, but was bitterly hostile to me, while the latter was friendly to me and opposed to Mr. Lincoln. I frankly told the President that it was impossible for me to reconcile those differences — indeed, that I did not believe any general in the army could, as department commander, satisfy the Union people of both Kansas and Missouri; neither the man nor the policy that would suit the one would be at all satisfactory to the other. Mr. Lincoln had evidently already arrived at much the same conclusion, and soon determined to divide the old Department of the Missouri into three departments, and try to assign to each a commander suited to its peculiarities. But Mr. Lincoln declared decidedly to me, and to my friends in the Senate, that he would make no change until the Senate united with him in vindicating me by confirming my nomination as major-general, then in the hands of the Military Committee of the Senate, and that he would then give me a more important command.

A large majority—indeed, all but some half-dozen—of the Senate were known to be favorable to the confirmation; but this small minority had control of the Military Committee, and were consequently able to delay any report of the case to the Senate, and thus to thwart the President's wishes.

The matter stood thus for nearly a month, and seemed no nearer solution than at first, when a despatch was received in Washington from General Grant, then commanding the Military Division of the Mississippi, saying it was necessary to relieve General Foster, on account of ill-health, from the command of the Department and Army of the Ohio, and to appoint a successor. Upon being asked whom he wanted for that command, Grant replied: "Either McPherson or Schofield."

Among the changes then known in Washington to be in the near future was Grant's elevation to the command of "all the armies," to be naturally followed by Sherman's succession to that of the Division of the Mississippi, and McPherson's to that of the Army of the Tennessee. But Grant alone, perhaps, had no right to anticipate those changes, hence he gave his just preference to my senior, McPherson.

Halleck handed me Grant's despatch, and asked me how I would like that. I replied: "That is exactly what I want; nothing in the world could be better." He then told me to take the despatch to the President, which I immediately did, and in handing it to him said: "If you want to give me that, I will gladly take all chances for the future, whether in the Senate or elsewhere." Mr. Lincoln replied in his characteristic way: "Why, Schofield, that cuts the knot, don't it? Tell Halleck to come over here, and we will fix it right away." I bade the President adieu, and started at once for St. Louis, to turn over my command and proceed to my new field of duty.

I saw Mr. Lincoln only once after that time. That was when, just a year later, I was passing through Washington with the Twenty-third Corps, and called merely to pay my respects. The President greeted me with the words: "Well, Schofield, I have n't heard anything against you for a year." Apparently, the great trouble to him with which I had been so closely connected, if not the cause, was uppermost in his mind.

With Mr. Lincoln I had no personal acquaintance, having met him but once, previous to the visit above described. But in assigning me to the command in Missouri he had, contrary to the usual custom, written for me his own instructions, thus inviting my fullest confidence. I had availed myself of this to tell him everything without reserve, and he appeared never to doubt the exact truth of my statements.

My personal acquaintance with General Grant was equally limited — we having met but once, and for only a moment. He knew me only by reputation. I never had any conversation or correspondence with him on the subject, but presume he knew something about the trouble I was in, had not forgotten the aid I sent him at Vicksburg, and believed I would do what was right to the best of my ability. I have had abundant reasons for believing that he never felt disappointed in his trust and confidence.

General Halleck knew me much better, having been my immediate commander in Missouri in 1861 and 1862. Although on one or two occasions he seemed a little harsh in respect to unimportant matters, he was uniformly kind, considerate, and unwavering in his personal and official support.

The Secretary of War, Mr. Stanton, expressed his confidence and approval; said he was opposed to any change; that it was the President's affair, with which he had nothing to do. I got the impression that he regarded the whole scheme as a political one, in which he took no interest, and with which he felt no sympathy.

In St. Louis I met General Grant, who was then so soon to be assigned to the command of "all the armies of the United States," and for the first time really became acquainted with him. We were together much of the time for several days and nights. The citizens of St. Louis entertained the general in a most magnificent manner. At a grand banquet given in his honor, at which I sat on his right, he did not even touch one of the many glasses of wine placed by the side of his plate. At length I ventured to remark that he had not tasted his wine. He replied: "I dare not touch it. Sometimes I can drink freely without any unpleasant effect; at others I cannot take even a single glass of light wine." A strong man, indeed, who could thus know and govern his own weakness! In reply to the toast in his honor, he merely arose and bowed without saying a word. Then turning to me, he said it was simply impossible for him to utter a word when on his feet. As is well known, the great general finally overcame his reserve.

It was very difficult for me to comprehend the political necessity which compelled Mr. Lincoln to give his official countenance to such men as Lane and Blunt in

Kansas, but such necessity was thought to exist. I suppose a great statesman should use in the best way he can the worst materials as well as the best that are within his reach, and, if possible, make them all subserve the great purposes he has to accomplish.

The old department was cut up, the Lane faction in Kansas was given the man of its choice — General Curtis; Missouri was placed alone under General Rosecrans — not Butler, as the radicals had asked; Arkansas, having no voice in the matter, was left under the soldier, General Steele, then in command there; and I left them all without regret and with buoyant hopes of more satisfactory service in a purely military field.

CHAPTER VII

CONDITION OF THE TROOPS AT KNOXVILLE — EFFECT OF
THE PROMOTION OF GRANT AND SHERMAN — LETTER TO
SENATOR HENDERSON — A VISIT FROM GENERAL SHER-
MAN — UNITED WITH HIS OTHER ARMIES FOR THE AT-
LANTA CAMPAIGN — COMMENTS ON SHERMAN'S "ME-
MOIRS" — FAULTY ORGANIZATION OF SHERMAN'S ARMY
— MᶜPHERSON'S TASK AT RESACA — MᶜPHERSON'S CHAR-
ACTER — EXAMPLE OF THE WORKING OF A FAULTY
SYSTEM.

I ARRIVED at Knoxville, Tennessee, on February 8,
1864, and the next day relieved General John G.
Foster. The troops then about Knoxville were the Ninth
Corps, two divisions of the Twenty-third, and about one
thousand cavalry and two divisions of the Fourth Corps;
the latter belonged to the Department of the Cumberland, but had been left with General Burnside after the
siege of Knoxville was raised by General Sherman.

The Ninth and Twenty-third Corps were reduced in
effective strength to mere skeletons, the former reporting present for duty equipped only 2800 men, and the
latter 3000 men; and these had for a long time been living on half rations or less, and were generally far less
than half clad, many of them being entirely without
shoes. The remainder of these troops were disabled by
wounds, sickness, lack of food or clothing, or were employed in the care of the sick or on extra duty.

Many thousands of dead horses and mules were scattered round the town, while the few remaining alive were

reduced to skeletons. Of about 30,000 animals with which General Burnside had gone into East Tennessee, scarcely 1000 remained fit for service; while his army of over 25,000 men had been reduced to not more than 7000 fit for duty and effective for service in the field. Such was the result of the siege of Knoxville, and such the Army of the Ohio when I became its commander.

But the splendid victory gained a short time before at Chattanooga had raised the blockade upon our line of supply, and the railroad to Chattanooga and Nashville was soon opened, so that our starving and naked troops could begin to get supplies of food and clothing. The movement of the first train of cars was reported by telegraph from every station, and was eagerly awaited by the entire army. When the locomotive whistle announced its approach, everybody turned out to welcome it with shouts of joy. It proved to consist of ten car-loads of horse and mule shoes for the dead animals which strewed the plains! Fortunately the disgust produced by this disappointment was not of long duration. The next train, which followed very soon, contained coffee, sugar, and other articles to gladden the hearts of hungry soldiers.

The Confederate army under Longstreet still remained in East Tennessee. A movement had recently been made by our troops, under the immediate command of General John G. Parke (General Foster being too lame to take the field in person), to drive Longstreet out. But the movement had failed, the troops returning to Knoxville with the loss of considerable material. In consequence of this, much anxiety was felt in Washington regarding the situation in East Tennessee. It was even apprehended that Knoxville might be in danger; and an advance of Longstreet's force to Strawberry Plains, where he laid a bridge over the Holston and crossed a part of his troops, seemed to give some ground for such apprehensions.

The miserable condition of our troops, the season of the year, the almost total lack of means of transportation for supplies and of a pontoon bridge to cross the river, rendered any considerable movement on our part impossible. But to relieve the existing apprehension, I determined to assume the offensive at once, and to maintain it as far as possible.

Early in February General Grant had proposed to give me 10,000 additional troops from General Thomas's army at Chattanooga, and to let me begin the campaign against Longstreet at once. But on February 16 he informed me that the movement would have to be delayed because of some operations in which General Thomas was to engage. Nevertheless, I advanced on the 24th with what force I had, at the same time sending a reconnaissance south of the French Broad River to ascertain the nature of a hostile movement reported in that direction.

Upon our advance, Longstreet's troops withdrew across the Holston and French Broad and retreated toward Morristown. His advance had evidently been intended only to cover an attempted cavalry raid upon our rear, which the high water in the Little Tennessee rendered impracticable.

We now occupied Strawberry Plains, rebuilt the railroad bridge, pushed forward the construction of a bateau bridge which had been commenced, in the meantime using the bateaux already constructed to ferry the troops across the river. In this manner we were able to advance as far as Morristown by February 29 with sufficient force to reconnoiter Longstreet's position. This reconnaissance demonstrated that the enemy held Bull's Gap, and that his entire force was grouped about that strong position. The object of this movement having been accomplished without loss, our troops retired to New Market to await the arrival of the troops to be sent by General Thomas, the completion of the railroad bridge, and other necessary preparations for the expected campaign.

On March 12 another reconnaissance was made as far as Bull's Gap, which was found to be still occupied by the enemy, although reliable information indicated that Longstreet was preparing for, and had perhaps already begun, his movement toward Virginia. Although his force, if concentrated, was much superior to mine, I determined to endeavor to take advantage of his movement to attack his rear. My advance held Morristown; all the troops were ordered forward to that place, and preparations made for an attack, when, on the 15th, orders came from General Grant to send the Ninth Corps to the Army of the Potomac.

Such a reduction of my command, instead of the expected reinforcement, left me wholly unable to do more than observe Longstreet as he leisurely withdrew from Tennessee and joined Lee in Virginia, and prepare for the campaign of the coming summer, the nature of which I could then only conjecture.

This entire change of program doubtless resulted from the promotion of General Grant to lieutenant-general and commander-in-chief, and General Sherman to his place in command of the Military Division of the Mississippi, which occurred at that time. The change of plans was undoubtedly wise. The Confederate government could not afford to leave Longstreet's force in East Tennessee during the summer. He must join Lee or Johnston before the opening of the summer campaign. It was not worth while for us to expend time and strength in driving him out, which ought to be devoted to preparations for vastly more important work. I felt disappointed at the time in not having an opportunity of doing something that would silence my enemies in Washington, who were not slow to avail themselves of any pretext for hostile action against me. It was not difficult to manufacture one out of the public reports of what had been done, or not done, in East Tennessee, and the Military Committee of the Senate reported against the confirmation of my appointment as major-general. Of this I was informed by my friend Senator J. B. Henderson, in a letter urging me to "whip somebody anyhow." This information and advice elicited a long reply, from which the following are extracts, which expressed pretty fully my views and feelings on that subject, and which, with events that soon followed, ended all trouble I ever had with that august body, the United States Senate.

I recollect in this connection a very pertinent remark made by General Grant soon after he became President. My nomination as major-general in the regular army, with those of Sherman and Sheridan as general and lieutenant-general, had been sent to the Senate and returned approved so promptly as to occasion comment. I remarked that it had on one occasion taken me a year and a half to get through the Senate. President Grant, as he handed me my commission, replied: "Yes; and if your conduct then had been such as to avoid that difficulty with the Senate, you would probably never have received this commission at all." I have no doubt he was right. To have pleased the radical politicians of that day would have been enough to ruin any soldier.

HEADQUARTERS, ARMY OF THE OHIO,
KNOXVILLE, TENN., April 15, 1864.

DEAR SENATOR: I have just received your letter of the 7th informing me that the Military Committee has reported against my nomination, and urging me to "whip somebody anyhow." I am fully aware of the importance to me personally of gaining a victory. No doubt I might easily get up a little "claptrap" on which to manufacture newspaper notoriety, and convince the Senate of the United States that I had won a great victory, and secure my confirmation by acclamation. Such things have been done, alas! too frequently during this war. But such is not my theory of a soldier's duties. I have an idea that my military superiors are the proper judges of my character and conduct, and that their testimony ought to be considered satisfactory as to my *military qualities.* I have the approval and support of the President, the Secretary of War, General Halleck, General Grant, and General Sherman. I am willing to abide the decision of any one or all of them, and I would not give a copper for the weight of anybody's or everybody's opinion in addition to, or in opposition to, theirs. If the Senate is not satisfied with such testimony, I can't help it. I never have and never will resort to "buncombe" for the purpose of securing my own advancement. If I cannot gain promotion by legitimate means, I do not want it at all. . . . In all this time I have yet to hear the first word of disapproval, from my superior officer, of any one of my military operations (unless I except Curtis, who disapproved of my pursuing Hindman so far into Arkansas), and in general have received high commendation from my superiors, both for my military operations and administration. I would rather have this record without a major-general's commission, than to gain the commission by adding to my reputation one grain of falsehood. . . .

Grant was here in the winter, and Sherman only a few days ago. They are fully acquainted with the condition of affairs. I have been acting all the time under their instructions, and I believe with their entire approval. They are generally understood to be men whose opinions on military matters are entitled to respect. I cannot do more or better than refer the Senate to them.

One thing is certain: I shall not be influenced one grain in the discharge of my duty by any question as to what action the Senate may take on my nomination. . . . If the Senate is not satisfied as to my past services, why not wait until they can know more? I am tired enough of this suspense, but still am perfectly willing to wait. In fact, I have become, in spite of myself, very indifferent on the subject. I am pretty thoroughly convinced that a major-general's commission is not worth half the trouble I and my friends have had about mine, and I feel very little inclination to trouble them, or even myself, any more about it.

The Senate has its duty to perform in this matter, as well as myself and my superior officers. If senators are not willing to act upon the concurrent testimony of all my superior officers as to what services I have rendered, I shall not condescend to humbug them into the belief that I have done something which I really have not.

You ask me what are the prospects of putting down the rebellion. I answer unhesitatingly that when the management of military matters is left to military men, the rebellion will be put down very quickly, and not before. I regard it as having been fully demonstrated that neither the Senate, nor the House of Representatives, nor the newspapers, nor the people of the United States, nor even all of them together, can command an army. I rather think if you let Grant alone, and let him have his own way, he will end the war this year. At all events, the next ninety days will show whether he will or not.

I find this letter is both too long and too ill-natured. I feel too much as if I would like to "whip somebody anyhow," so I will stop where I am. Let me hear from you again soon.

Yours very truly,

J. M. SCHOFIELD.

HON. J. B. HENDERSON,
U. S. Senate, Washington, D. C.

Of course I knew the advice of my friend Senator Henderson was not intended to be taken seriously, but only as expressing his view, much the same as my own, of the then existing situation in the Senate. But it gave me, all the same, the opportunity I wanted to give his brother senators, through him, " a piece of my mind."

General Sherman, on a visit to Knoxville about the end of March, a few days before the date of the foregoing letter, disclosed to me his general plans for the coming campaign, and the part I was expected to take in it.

It would be difficult to give an adequate conception of the feeling of eager expectation and enthusiasm with which, having given my final salutation to my " friends " in the Senate, I entered upon the preparations for this campaign. Of its possible results to the country there was room in my mind only for confidence. But for myself, it was to decide my fate, and that speedily. My reputation and rank as a soldier, so long held in the political balance, were at length to be settled. The long-hoped-for opportunity had come, and that under a general whose character and ability were already established, and of the justice of whose judgment and action regarding his subordinates there could be no reason for doubt in my mind. My command was to be mostly of veteran troops, and not too large for my experience. Its comparative smallness was a source of satisfaction to me at that time, rather than anything like jealousy of my senior brother commanders of the Cumberland and Tennessee.

My first care was to provide my men with all necessary equipment for the campaign, and to fill up the ranks by calling in all absentees. It was a refreshing sight to see the changed aspect and feeling of the gallant little army as it marched with full ranks and complete equipment, newly clad, from Knoxville toward Dalton.

My next thought was to win the respect and confidence of my men. An opportunity to do this was speedily afforded in the delicate operations in front of Dalton. The result may perhaps be fairly expressed in the words of an old soldier who was overheard to say as I passed his regiment that day under fire: "It is all right, boys; I like the way the old man chaws his tobacco." From that day forward I felt that the Twenty-third Corps confided in me as I did in them. I never had any doubt they would do just what I expected them to do, and would take it for granted that it was "all right."

It is with the greatest pleasure that I record here the just tribute paid to that splendid body of men by General Sherman about the close of the Atlanta campaign: "The Twenty-third Corps never failed to do all that was expected of it."

And it is with equal pleasure that I record the just

and generous treatment shown by General Sherman toward me from the beginning of that campaign. Although much my senior in years, experience, and reputation, he never showed that he was aware of it, but always treated me as his peer. In his official reports and his memoirs he has never been unkind or unjust, though it has never been his habit to bestow much praise on individuals, or to think much of the rewards due his subordinates, generally giving credit as justly due to troops rather than to commanders. It would be impossible for me not to cherish feelings of strong affection for my old commander, as well as the profound respect due his character as a man and soldier, and his brilliant genius.

If anything I may say in criticism of General Sherman's acts or words shall seem unkind or be considered unjust, I can only disclaim any such feeling, and freely admit that it would be wholly unworthy of the relations that always existed between us. I write not for the present, but for the future, and my only wish is to represent the truth as it appears to me. If I fail to see it clearly, I do but condemn myself. History will do impartial justice. Having been in a subordinate position in the campaigns of 1864 in Georgia and Tennessee, I shall not attempt to write a full account of those campaigns, but shall limit myself to such comments as seem to me to be called for upon the already published histories of those campaigns.

In estimating the merits of Sherman's " Memoirs,"[1] it should be remembered that he does not, and does not claim to, occupy the position of a disinterested, impartial historian. He writes, not for the purpose of doing equal and exact justice to all actors in a great historical drama, but for the purpose of elucidating his own acts and motives, and vindicating himself against the harsh criticism

[1] The following was written in 1875, soon after the appearance of the first edition.

and censure which have followed some of his most important transactions. However unconscious General Sherman himself may have been of the influence of such motives, their existence was natural, even inevitable, and they have manifestly given their coloring to all of the memoirs. This should not occasion surprise, nor even regret, much less be held to justify unkind criticism. It is desirable for the future historian to have the view of the chief actor in any portion of history taken from his own standpoint. It is only by a critical, laborious and honest comparison of this view with those of other actors and eye-witnesses that impartial history may ultimately be written.

My present purpose is simply to direct attention to some points in the history of those campaigns of General Sherman in which I was one of his principal subordinates, upon which the views of others were at the time, or have since been, different from his own. In what I have to say the motive of self-vindication can have little or no influence; for, with some unimportant exceptions, General Sherman does relatively full justice to me and to the little army which I had the honor to command. I shall speak mainly of the acts of others, especially the noble dead.

I must preface my remarks by observing that the organization of Sherman's army during the Atlanta campaign was extremely faulty, in that the three grand divisions were very unequal in strength, the Army of the Cumberland having nearly *five times* the infantry strength of the Army of the Ohio, and more than twice that of the Army of the Tennessee, even after the junction of Blair's corps. The cavalry, of which two divisions belonged to the Army of the Ohio, always acted either under the direct orders of General Sherman or of the nearest army commander, according to the flank on which it was operating. This inequality resulted from the fact that Sherman's army was composed of three separate armies, or such portions of them as could be spared from their several departments, united for that campaign. General Thomas was, naturally enough, disinclined to part with any of his troops, and the troops did not wish to be separated from the old army in which they had won so much honor, nor from the commander whom they revered. Besides, General Thomas had had much greater experience in the command of troops in the field than I, and General Sherman, if he thought of it at all, may well have doubted the wisdom of diminishing the command of the one to increase that of the other. I do not know whether this matter was discussed at all before the opening of the campaign, certainly not by me, who would have been restrained by motives of delicacy, if by no other, from mentioning it. But in fact my ambition was then limited to fighting well and successfully with the single corps under my command. It was only after experience had drawn attention more pointedly to the evils resulting from faulty organization, and success had inspired legitimate confidence, that this subject became matter of much thought and some discussion.

But this faulty organization continued to the end of the Atlanta campaign, and was, as I think will clearly appear, one of the causes of many of the partial failures or imperfect successes that characterized our operations. General Thomas's command often proved unwieldy and slow from being larger than one man could handle in a rough and in many places densely wooded country, while the others were frequently too small for the work to be done. It was often attempted to remedy this defect by ordering a division or corps of the Army of the Cumberland to "coöperate with" or "support" one of the others in making an attack; but military experience has shown that "coöperate" and "support" mean, in general, to do nothing effective. The corps commanders, generally, not being in the habit of acting independently, and not being in direct communication with the general-in-chief, and hence not familiar with his plans and views, would not act with the necessary promptness or vigor; and not regarding themselves as absolutely under the orders of the general they were directed to support, they would not obey his orders or requests unless they were in accord with their own views; while one of these corps commanders, General Sherman says, manifested an ambition to get one of the separate armies under his command and win a victory on his "own hook." But General Sherman fails to state that he encouraged all this by his own now well-known erroneous opinion upon the question of the relative rank of army and corps commanders; that this vital question was evaded until its decision in a special case—that of Stanley and Schofield—became absolutely necessary, and was then decided erroneously, the error resulting in failure and great disappointment to Sherman. Had this question been decided at an early day according to the plain import of the law, as was afterward done by the War Department, and orders given to corps commanders to obey instead of "coöperate" or "support," much trouble would have been avoided.

First among the most important events of the Atlanta campaign were the operations about Dalton and Resaca. Here I have always thought General Sherman committed the mistake, so common in war (and, as I believe, not infrequently afterward committed by himself and others in the Union armies), of assigning to too small a force the main attack upon the vital point of an enemy's position. McPherson had only about 22,000 infantry, while Sherman estimated Johnston's force at about 60,000. Thomas's position in front of Rocky-face Ridge was virtually as unassailable as that of Johnston behind it. The only weak point of our position was that of two divisions of the Twenty-third Corps on our left, north of Dalton. Had these divisions been attacked, as Sherman apprehended, they might have suffered severely, but would have drawn off force enough from the enemy to increase largely the probabilities of success in the attack in Johnston's rear. One half of Sherman's infantry was ample for the demonstration in front of Dalton. At least one half should have been sent through Snake Creek Gap to strike the enemy's rear. There was no necessity to attack Resaca at all, and experience has shown what terrible losses a small force in a strongly fortified position may inflict upon a very large attacking force. Two or three brigades could have invested Resaca, with the garrison it then held, while a force large enough to hold its ground against Johnston's whole army could have been put upon the railroad between Resaca and Dalton. The result would then, in all probability, have been what Sherman expected. Indeed, the fate of Johnston's army might perhaps have been decided then and there.

Sherman certainly cannot be suspected of wishing to do injustice to the memory of McPherson, for he loved and respected him most highly, and mourned his death with evident sincerity. But I think he is in error in saying that "at the critical moment McPherson seems to have been a little timid." I believe the error was Sherman's, not McPherson's; that McPherson was correct in his judgment, which certainly was mine (after passing over the same ground and fighting the battle of Resaca), that his force was entirely too small for the work assigned it. I had not the same opportunity General Sherman had of judging of McPherson's qualities as a commander; but I knew him well and intimately, having sat upon the same bench with him at West Point for four years, and been his room-mate for a year and a half. His was the most completely balanced mind and character with which

I have ever been intimately acquainted, although he did not possess in a very high degree the power of invention or originality of thought. His personal courage seemed to amount to unconsciousness of danger, while his care of his troops cannot, I believe, be justly characterized otherwise than as wise prudence. I consider this to be only a just tribute to the memory of the nearest and dearest friend of my youth.

If McPherson had commanded one third of the army, he might, with a corps of Thomas's army in close support, have felt strong enough to occupy and hold a position between Dalton and Resaca. As it was, Thomas should have followed close upon his rear through Snake Creek Gap, with two corps. The distance between the two wings of the army would have been so short and the ground between them so impassable to the enemy as to give us practically a continuous line of battle, and Thomas's two corps in the valley of the Connasauga near Tilton would have been in far better position to strike the retreating enemy when he was compelled to let go of Dalton, than they were in front of Rocky-face Ridge. Impartial history must, I believe, hold Sherman himself mainly responsible for the failure to realize his expectations in the first movement against Johnston.

It seems at least probable that at the beginning of the movement against Dalton, Sherman did not fully understand the character of the enemy's position; for his plan clearly appears to have been to make the main attack in front at the moment Johnston should be compelled to let go from his stronghold by reason of McPherson's operations in his rear; while McPherson, after breaking the railroad and then falling back for security to the Gap, should strike Johnston in flank during the confusion of retreat.

The nature of the position rendered this plan impracticable for producing any important result. Had McPherson broken the road ever so "good" and then fallen back to the Gap as ordered, Johnston could have moved his main army to Resaca that night, and at daylight the next morning Sherman would have found in the enemy's trenches at Dalton only a skirmish-line which would have leisurely retreated before him to the new position at Resaca. The result would have been essentially the same as that which was actually accomplished.

Indeed, as it now seems clearly to appear to General Sherman, the only possible mode of striking an effective blow at Dalton was to capture Resaca or seize and hold a point on the road in rear of Dalton, and *not* to break the road and fall back as McPherson was ordered to do. If Sherman had seen this clearly at the time, it is inconceivable that he would have sent less than one fourth of his army to execute the all-important part of the plan. And he now judges McPherson as manifesting timidity[1] because he did not at the critical moment attempt to accomplish, with his comparatively small force, what Sherman should have ordered to be done by a much larger force.

A very bold, independent commander might have attempted, whether successful or not, what Sherman thinks McPherson ought to have done at Resaca; and, as Sherman says, such an opportunity does not occur twice in the life of any man. But McPherson was a subordinate in spirit as well as in fact, and cannot fairly be charged with timidity for not attempting what he was not ordered to do, and what, in fact, was no part of the plans of his superior so far as they were indicated in his orders.

If McPherson had assaulted Resaca, it is possible, but only possible, that he might have succeeded. There were some cases during the Civil War where intrenchments hastily constructed and imperfectly defended were car-

[1] In the revised edition, Vol. II, p. 34, General Sherman substitutes "cautious" for "timid."

ried by assault; many more where the assault failed; and, I believe, not one case where intrenchments carefully prepared in advance, with obstructions in front, and defended by a force commensurate with the extent of the line, like those at Resaca, were successfully assaulted.

It is true that McPherson's force was vastly superior to the single brigade that held Resaca that day, but that practically amounts to nothing. A single division would have been as good for such an assault as two corps. Beyond a reasonable proportion, say of three or four to one, numbers amount to nothing in making such an assault. It would be physically possible for numbers to succeed in such a case if their immediate commander was willing to sacrifice them and they *were willing to be sacrificed*. But considering the general unwillingness among commanders and men to sacrifice or to be sacrificed beyond what seems to them a reasonable expenditure of life for the object to be gained, success is *morally* impossible, or very nearly so, in an assault such as would have been required to capture Resaca on May 9, 1864. Clearly, such an assault should not be attempted except as the only chance of victory; and then the subordinate officers and men should be clearly informed precisely what they are expected to do, and made to understand the necessity for so great and unusual a sacrifice. In that case brave and true men will make the sacrifice required, provided their pluck holds out long enough; and that no man is wise enough to predict, even of himself, much less of a large number of men.

The only chance of success was to invest Resaca on the west and north, and put between the investing line and Dalton troops enough to hold their ground against the main body of Johnston's army; and this must have been done in a single day, starting from the débouché of Snake Creek Gap, the troops moving by a single, common country road. Johnston's whole army, except a small rear-guard, would by the use of three roads have been in position to attack McPherson at dawn of day the next morning, while the main body of Sherman's army was far away on the other side of Rocky-face. Or if McPherson had not held the entire natural position as far east as the Connasauga River, Johnston could have passed round him in the night. It seems to me certain that McPherson's force was too small to have taken and held that position. Indeed it does not seem at all certain that, however large his force might have been, he could have put troops enough in position before night to accomplish the object of cutting off Johnston's retreat. The case was analogous to that of Hood's crossing Duck River in November of that year, and trying to cut off our retreat at Spring Hill. There was simply not time enough to do it in that one day, and if not done in one day it could not be done at all.

So that it does not seem at all certain that this, which was " Thomas's plan " to throw the entire Army of the Cumberland on the road in Johnston's rear and thus cut off his retreat, would have succeeded any better than Sherman's, yet it gave greater promise of success, and therefore ought to have been tried. It is at least probable that Johnston's view of the case (see his "Narrative," pages 15, 16, 17) is the correct one : that, with his thorough knowledge of the ground, ample roads, and means of early information, together with our ignorance of the ground and our extremely deficient roads, he could have defeated any possible attempt to cut him off from Resaca.

To illustrate the faulty system of organization and command which characterized the Atlanta campaign, I will now refer to an incident of the operations about Dallas, it being next in order of date of those I wish to consider. General Sherman does not allude to it at all in his " Memoirs."

Near the close of the operations about Dallas, the Twenty-third Corps was moved to our left, under instructions from General Sherman to endeavor to strike the enemy's right flank. A division of the Army of the Cumberland was ordered to "support" the Twenty-third Corps. There were no roads available, and the country was in the main densely wooded. The head of the column was directed by the compass toward a point where our maps, the general topography of the country, and the enemy's known position indicated that his right must probably rest. After a laborious march through dense undergrowth, during which our skirmish-line was lost in the woods and another deployed to replace it, we struck an intrenched line strongly held, and a sharp action ensued. The Twenty-third Corps was deployed as far to the left as possible, and the skirmishers reported that they had reached the extremity of the enemy's intrenched line, but could not overlap it. At this moment the division of the Army of the Cumberland came up in splendid style, and *massed* immediately in rear of our left, in "close supporting distance," and under a pretty heavy fire. I first sent a staff officer and then went myself to the division commander, explained the situation, and asked him to put in a brigade on my left and turn the enemy's flank so as to give us a footing beyond his parapet. He replied that he was ordered by General Thomas only to "support" me, and that he would do no more. The day was already far advanced, and before I could bring troops from another part of my line darkness came on, and the action ended for the day. By the next morning I had brought another division of the Twenty-third Corps to the flank, and General Sherman arrived on the ground. By his personal orders this division was pushed straight through the woods to a point in the enemy's rear, on the road leading from Dallas to Acworth, which point it reached without any opposition, and there intrenched.

That night Johnston abandoned his lines. An inspection of the enemy's intrenchments demonstrated that our skirmishers were right, and that a single brigade on our left would have been ample to turn the enemy's flank and open the way to victory. The above facts were immediately reported to Sherman and Thomas. I do not know what action, if any, was taken upon them.

I refer to this incident, not as especially affecting the military reputation of any officer one way or the other, but to illustrate the working of a faulty system. Under proper organization and discipline, any division commander could hardly have failed with that fine division to do all that was desired of him that day. I believe that division commander's commission as major-general of volunteers was anterior in date to mine, and he, no doubt, with General Sherman and some others, thought he was not subject to my orders.

CHAPTER VIII

SHERMAN'S DISPLEASURE WITH HOOKER GROWING OUT OF
THE AFFAIR AT KOLB'S FARM — HOOKER'S DESPATCH
EVIDENTLY MISINTERPRETED — A CONVERSATION WITH
JAMES B. MᶜPHERSON OVER THE QUESTION OF RELATIVE
RANK — ENCOURAGING JOHN B. HOOD TO BECOME A
SOLDIER — VISIT TO THE CAMP OF FRANK P. BLAIR, JR.
— ANECDOTE OF SHERMAN AND HOOKER UNDER FIRE —
THE ASSAULT ON KENESAW — TENDENCY OF VETERAN
TROOPS — THE DEATH OF MᶜPHERSON BEFORE ATLANTA
— SHERMAN'S ERROR IN A QUESTION OF RELATIVE RANK.

IN the affair at Kolb's Farm, on June 22, Hascall's division of the Twenty-third Corps was abreast of and connecting with Hooker's right, while his advance-guard was many yards in advance of the line, when the enemy's attack at the Kolb House began. The first attack fell upon this advance-guard, the 14th Kentucky Volunteers, which gallantly held its ground until twice ordered to retire and join the main line. In the meantime Hascall's line had been formed in prolongation of Hooker's and covered with the usual hastily constructed parapets, and three brigades of Cox's division had been ordered forward to protect Hascall's right. The attack was repulsed with ease, and there was no ground for apprehension about the safety of my immediate flank, much less of Hooker's, after the arrival of Cox's division, which occurred before the hour of Hooker's signal-despatch to Sherman expressing anxiety about our extreme right. On the following morning we reoccupied the ground held by the 14th Kentucky at the opening of the engagement, and not only did I offer to show General Sherman that the dead of my "advance division were lying farther out than any of Hooker's," but he actually rode with me over the ground, and saw the dead of the 14th Kentucky lying in advance of Hooker's picket-line.

My impression is that Hooker, in his signal-despatch of 5:30 P. M., saying, "We have repulsed two heavy attacks, and feel confident, our only apprehension being for our extreme right flank. Three entire corps are in front of us,"[1] meant by "our extreme right flank" not his own right, but mine—that is, the *extreme* right of the entire line; for at the time of that despatch nearly my whole corps was strongly posted on Hooker's right, and was well "refused," forming a strong right flank. This General Hooker well knew. But the Sandtown Road leading to our rear, on which Cox's division had been posted until Johnston's attack made it necessary to close him up on Hascall, was now less strongly guarded. I believe that General Hooker had conceived the idea, as indicated by his despatch to Sherman, that Johnston had drawn his main force from around Kenesaw, and was about to strike our extreme right. I recollect that I was all the time on the watch for such a blow, but relied upon my cavalry to give me some warning of it, and made it a rule to be always as well prepared for it as I could. Being habitually on the flank, I had got used to that sort of thing, while Hooker, having been habitually in the center with his flanks well protected, was more nervous about having them exposed. At all events, I did not regard the situation at the Kolb House as anything unusual, and did not think of mentioning it in such a light to General Sherman; while General Hooker, with a sort of paternal feeling of seniority, may have thought it his duty to take care of the whole right wing of the

[1] War Records, Vol. XXXVIII, part iv, p. 558.

army, and to advise the general-in-chief of the supposed danger to our " extreme right flank."

There occurred on that occasion one of those little and seemingly trifling incidents which never escape the memory, and are always a source of pride, especially to those who are comparatively young. When Sherman read Hooker's despatch, which he interpreted as meaning that my corps was not in position to protect Hooker's flank, he said in substance, if not literally, and with great emphasis: " That is not true. I sent Schofield an order to be there. I know he received the order, for his initials, in his own hand, are on the envelop which the orderly brought back, and I know he is there. Hooker's statement is false." What a delight it was to execute the orders of a chief who manifested such confidence !

I do not remember that I was " very angry " about Hooker's despatch, as General Sherman says (Vol. II, page 59), though I think Sherman was. Indeed, he had more reason to be angry than I; for the fact, and evidence of it, were so plain that the Twenty-third Corps had done its duty as ordered, that if Hooker's despatch was meant to imply the contrary, which I doubt, that was a cause of anger to the general-in-chief, whom he had unnecessarily alarmed, rather than to me, who had no apprehension of being suspected by the general-in-chief of having failed in my duty.

In fact, I do not recollect having seen Hooker's despatch at all until I saw it quoted in Sherman's " Memoirs." My recollection is that Sherman told me, on his visiting us the next day, that he had received during the battle a despatch from Hooker to the effect that his flank was unprotected. In reply to this I explained to General Sherman where my troops had been during the engagement, and showed him the dead of the 14th Kentucky lying on the advanced ground they had held while Hascall's division was forming. I believe that if I had seen Hooker's despatch at the time, I should have interpreted it then, as I do now, as referring, not to his immediate right, but to the extreme right of the line. I do not recollect any words, "pretty sharp" or otherwise, between General Hooker and myself on that subject, and do not believe it was ever mentioned between us. In short, I do not think I was present at the interview in the "little church" described by General Sherman (Sherman's "Memoirs," Vol. II, page 59). I have an impression that General Hascall was there, and that it is to him General Sherman refers. I believe the Kolb House difficulty was almost entirely a misapprehension between General Sherman and General Hooker. Why this mistake was not explained at the time or afterward I do not know, unless it was that the feelings of those two gentlemen toward each other were unfavorable to any such explanation.

I will add that General Hooker and I were together both before and after the opening of the Kolb House engagement. He knew perfectly well where my troops were, and what they were doing, and it seems to me utterly impossible that he can have meant by his despatch what General Sherman understood it to mean.

My despatches of that date to Sherman show that I had no special apprehension even in respect to our extreme right flank, and that I doubted the report that one whole corps was in our front.

My orders on that day[1] show that Hascall was up with Hooker at the intersection of the Marietta and Powder Spring roads, near the Kolb House, as early as 3 P. M., and that Cox was ordered up with three brigades at 4:15 P. M., *before the assault began.* Cox arrived with the head of his column during the enemy's attack, and was directed by me in person where and how to put his troops in position. Hence I think I must be right in the inference that in Hooker's despatch to Sherman of 5:30 P. M., the

1 War Records, Vol. XXXVII, part iv, pp. 566 and 568.

words "our extreme right flank" must have been intended to refer to *my* extreme right, and not *his.* He was simply unduly apprehensive for the safety of the extreme right flank of the army, not of his own corps in particular. My report to General Sherman at 9 p. m. simply shows that I did not share that apprehension; that, instead of believing there were "three entire corps in front of us," I doubted whether there was even all of Hood's corps.

General Hooker's habit of swinging off from the rest of General Thomas's army, and getting possession of roads designated for McPherson or for me, was a common subject of remark between Sherman, Thomas, McPherson, and myself; and his motive was understood to be, as General Sherman states, to get command of one of the armies, in the event of battle, by virtue of his senior commission. But the subject was never mentioned between General Hooker and me, and he never even approximated to giving me an order. No doubt he entertained the opinion that he would have a right to give orders to either General McPherson or myself under certain circumstances likely to arise, for General Sherman entertained the same opinion. What General Thomas thought on the question I never knew. My own opinion and McPherson's were decidedly the contrary.

In the final movement which resulted in the withdrawal of Johnston's army from Kenesaw, the Army of the Tennessee passed by the right flank of my infantry line along the famous Sandtown Road. While this was going on, McPherson and I sat on our horses together a long time, observing the movement and renewing the familiar intercourse of our youth. We had a long and free conversation on a great variety of subjects — a rare opportunity for commanders, even in the same army, where their troops were generally from ten to twenty miles apart in line of battle. One of the first subjects that came up was that question of relative rank; for our troops had "met" and were then "doing duty together," in the language of the old article of war. But the subject was quickly dismissed with the remark, made almost simultaneously by both, that such a question could not possibly cause any difficulty between us. McPherson had the senior commission of major-general, and I the senior assignment as army commander. Perhaps it would have puzzled even Halleck to frame a satisfactory decision in that peculiar case. I had long before determined what my decision would be if that question ever became a practical one between McPherson and myself on the field of battle. I would have said, in substance at least: "Mac, just tell me what you want me to do."

As we sat together that day, McPherson confided to me the secret of his marriage engagement, for the purpose, as he stated, of inquiring whether, in my opinion, he could before long find a chance to go home and get married. I told him I thought that after the capture of Altanta operations would be suspended long enough for that. But my dear and noble friend was killed in the next great battle. After Atlanta had fallen I went home, as McPherson would doubtless have done if he had lived; but our common friend and classmate Hood cut the visit so short that there would have been little time for marriage festivities.

McPherson, among other high qualities, was one of the most generous men I ever knew. He was remarkably skilful in topographical drawing, etching, lettering, and all other uses of the pen. Although at the head of the class and a most conscientious student whose time was very valuable to himself, he would spend a very large part of that precious time in "lettering" problems for classmates who needed such help. For this reason and others he was, by common consent of all the classes, the most popular man in the corps. I could not compete with "Mac" at all in the lettering business, but I tried to follow his good example, in my own way, by helping the boys over knotty points in "math" and "phil." I had taught district school one winter before going to West Point, and hence had acquired the knack of explaining things.

Hood was not well up in mathematics. The first part of the course especially he found very hard—so much so that he became discouraged. After the unauthorized festivities of Christmas, particularly, he seemed much depressed. On the 26th he asked me which I would prefer to be, "an officer of the army or a farmer in Kentucky?" I replied in a way which aroused his ambition to accomplish what he had set out to do in coming to West Point, without regard to preference between farming and soldiering. He went to work in good earnest, and passed the January examination, though by a very narrow margin. From that time on he did not seem to have so much difficulty. When we were fighting each other so desperately, fifteen years later, I wondered whether Hood remembered the encouragement I had given him to become a soldier, and came very near thinking once or twice that perhaps I had made a mistake. But I do not believe that public enmity ever diminished my personal regard for my old friend and classmate.

In thinking of McPherson, I recall an interesting incident connected with Frank P. Blair, Jr.'s arrival with his corps about June 9, referred to by General Sherman (Vol. II, page 24). For some reason we had an afternoon's rest the day after Blair arrived; so I rode over to his camp — seven or eight miles, perhaps — to greet my old friend. McPherson, to whose army Blair's corps belonged, and other officers were there. To our immense surprise, Blair had brought along great hogsheads of ice and numerous baskets of champagne, as if to increase the warmth of our welcome. Of course we did not disdain such an unusual treat in the enemy's country.   About sunset McPherson invited me to visit his camp, and we started off at full gallop, which we kept up all the way, yet it was some time after dark when we reached the headquarters of the Army of the Tennessee.   A good camp supper was awaiting us, with jolly young officers to make it merry.   It was not until supper was ended that I began to realize the necessity of a night's march to get back to my own camp.   As our infantry line was twenty miles long, and the cavalry stretched it out on either flank as many more, my single orderly was quite sufficient protection from any attack from the enemy; but the Georgia bushes, brambles, and mud, combined with the absence of any known road, constituted an enemy hard to overcome.   However, by the aid of the compass which I have always carried in my head since I used to hunt in the wilds of the West, I got back to camp, and went to bed, taking care not to observe the time of night by my watch.

As I have said, I was often much annoyed by General Hooker's corps getting possession of roads which had been designated for mine to advance upon, thus greatly delaying my movements.   But it is but just to say that this is susceptible of an explanation much more creditable to General Hooker than that given by General Sherman. General Thomas's army was so large that he could never get his three corps into position as soon as expected by the use of the roads designated for him.   Hence, when Hooker was not in advance he would "switch off" and hunt for another road to the right or left, and thus sometimes strike in ahead of McPherson or me, and leave us no road at all to move on.   In fact, the army was so large and the roads were so few that our movements were often painfully slow and tedious, and General Hooker's motive may have been only to get ahead and bring his corps into action or to the position assigned to it in whatever way he could.

The first time I ever saw General Sherman and General Hooker together, or got even a suspicion that their personal relations were other than the most satisfactory, was at Resaca. Cox's division had gained possession of some portions of the enemy's outer works, so that from a bald hill just in rear of our line some parts of the main line of defense could be distinctly seen. Upon my informing General Sherman of this, he soon appeared on the ground, accompanied or closely followed by a large number of general and staff officers. Besides Sherman, Thomas, Hooker, and Newton, a score of others were there, all eager to see what they could of the now famous stronghold which McPherson had refrained from assaulting. I led them to the hill, on which a few dead trees were still standing, and from which the much-desired view could be obtained. Of course all were on foot, yet they were too numerous not to attract the attention of the enemy. Very soon the sound of musketry in front, then not very heavy, was varied by the sharp explosion of a shell overhead, and fragments of branches of dead trees came falling all around. A general " scatteration " occurred in all directions save one. Newton and I, who were conversing at the time, quietly stepped aside a few paces out of the line of fire, where we were much safer than we would have been in full retreat, and then turned round to see what had become of our companions. All save two had disappeared, even Thomas having abandoned the field, probably for the first and only time in his life. But still there, on the bald hill, in full view of the hostile artillery, were the two already highly distinguished generals, Sherman and Hooker, both alike famous for supreme courage, striding round the ground, appearing to look at nothing in particular and not conversing with each other, but seeming at least a foot taller than usual, each waiting for the other to lead off in retreat. After quite a long continuance of this little drama, which greatly entertained Newton and me, the two great soldiers, as if by some mysterious impulse,—for they did not speak a word,—simultaneously and slowly strode to the rear, where their horses were held. I cheerfully give the "Johnny Rebs" credit for the courtesy of not firing another shot after they saw the effect of the first, which I doubt not was intended only as a gentle hint that such impudence in Yankees was not to be tolerated. Yet a single shell from the same direction,—probably from the same battery,—when we were moving into action that morning, exploded near my head, and killed the aide who was riding behind me.[1] My too numerous staff and escort had attracted attention. I had at Dalton a few days before forbade the staff and escort to follow me into action, unless specially ordered to do so; but they had not so soon learned the lesson which the sad casualty at Resaca taught them. It was then early in the campaign. Later, both generals and orderlies had learned to restrain somewhat their curiosity and their too thoughtless bravery. The perfect old soldier has learned to economize the life and strength of men, including his own, with somewhat the same care that he does those of artillery horses and transportation mules. It is only the young soldier who does not know the difference between husbanding the national resources and showing cowardice in face of the enemy.

At Wilson's Creek, where the brave Lyon was killed in August. 1861, and where the gallant volunteers on both sides had fought with almost unexampled courage, standing up to their work all the time, until one third of their numbers were killed or wounded, and their forty rounds

---

[1] Captain A. H. Engle, who was killed at Resaca, was a most charming and talented youth, only twenty years of age. That was his first battle. He was caterer of the headquarters mess. That morning, before leaving camp, Captain Engle made out all his accounts and handed them, with the money for which he was responsible, to another staff officer, saying he was going to be killed that day.

of ammunition gone, the little companies of old, regular Indian-fighters had been deployed as skirmishers in close order, behind trees and bushes and hillocks, and had suffered comparatively small losses. The following colloquy occurred between one of them and a volunteer whose cartridge-box, as he was proud to show, was empty. Volunteer: "How many shots did *you* fire?" Old soldier (looking into his cartridge-box): "I fired just nineteen." Volunteer: "And how many rebs do you think you killed?" Old soldier: "I guess I killed about nineteen."

One beautiful, quiet Sunday afternoon, in front of Atlanta, when even the pickets were respecting the Sabbath day, my headquarters band, which had been playing selections of sacred music, easily heard on the other side of the lines, struck up a favorite Southern air of quite a different character. Quickly came a shell crashing through the trees far over our heads. The band as quickly took the hint and changed the tune. Such little "courtesies" from our "friends the enemy" were not at all uncommon in the short intervals of rest from deadly work.

General Sherman says in Vol. II, page 60, of his "Memoirs":

During the 24th and 25th of June, General Schofield extended his right as far as prudent, so as to compel the enemy to thin out his lines correspondingly, with the intention to make two strong assaults at points where success would give us the greatest advantage. I had consulted Generals Thomas, McPherson, and Schofield, and we all agreed that we could not with prudence stretch out any more, and therefore there was no alternative but to attack "fortified lines"—a thing carefully avoided up to that time.

The first sentence literally means that I extended my right "with the intention," *on my part,* "to make two strong assaults," etc. But that is a mere verbal error. General Sherman, of course, meant to say that the intention was his.

The second sentence is, perhaps, ambiguous. At least it has been construed to mean more than the truth. It is undoubtedly true that " we all agreed that we could not with prudence stretch out any more," but we did not agree in the conclusion " and therefore there was no alternative," etc.

Indeed, such conclusion was extremely illogical, as was demonstrated a few days later, when one of the other " alternatives" was adopted with success. This successful movement was essentially the same as that which had been previously made to dislodge the enemy from Dalton, and that by which Sherman's army had been transferred from New Hope Church to the railroad in front of Allatoona, as well as that by which Atlanta was afterward captured. Hence the existence of this " alternative" could not have been unthought of by any of us at the time of the assault on Kenesaw.

But there was another alternative in this and similar cases, which was much discussed at various times during the campaign. Its practicability can be judged of only upon general principles, for it was never tried. It was to detach two or three corps, nearly half our army (which was about double the strength of the enemy), make a detour wide enough to avoid his fortifications, and strike directly at his flank and rear. Such a movement, it was urged, at Dalton, Kenesaw, or Atlanta would have compelled Johnston to fight a battle on equal terms with one half of Sherman's army, while he had to hold his parapets against the other half. Whatever else may be said of this proposed movement, it would undoubtedly have been more hazardous and much more decisive, one way or the other, than any of the plans actually adopted. It certainly promised success proportionate to the cost, instead of a costly failure, which the assault of fortified lines had almost invariably proved to be.

I did not see Thomas or McPherson for some days before the assault, but I believe their judgment, like mine, was opposed to it. Undoubtedly it was generally opposed, though deferentially as became subordinates toward the commanding general. The responsibility was entirely Sherman's, as he afterward frankly stated; and I presume he did not mean to imply otherwise by the language used in his "Memoirs" above quoted (Vol. II, page 60). General Sherman's orders, issued on June 24 (Special Field Orders, No. 28), directed each of the three armies to make an attack (under the word "assault" for Thomas and "attack" for McPherson and me). I had made all preparations to carry out the order on my part. Being visited by General Sherman a day or two before the date named for the execution of the order (June 27), I explained to him what I had done, and how little hope there was of success, on account of the smallness of my reserve to push the advantage even if we should break the line, when he at once replied that it was not intended that I should make an attack in front, but to make a strong demonstration in my front, and gain what advantage I could on the enemy's flank. During the day Cox's division forced the passage of Olley's Creek and secured a position on the head of Nickajack, which was spoken of by Sherman as the only success of the day.

There were doubtless many occasions in the Atlanta campaign when the enemy's intrenchments could have been assaulted with success. These were when the position had been but recently occupied and the fortifications were very slight. After several days' occupation, as at the points attacked by Thomas and McPherson, the lines became impregnable. Frequent efforts were made, and by none more earnestly than by General Sherman, to press the troops to a vigorous assault of the enemy's position under the favorable circumstances above referred to. But the general feeling of the army, including not only privates, but officers of nearly all grades, was undoubtedly opposed to such attacks. The notion was very prevalent that there was no necessity of fighting the enemy on unequal terms. When attacked, either with or without cover, the troops would fight with the most determined valor, and almost invariably with success. So when attacking the enemy in open ground there was no lack of energy or pluck. But we lose one of the most important lessons of the war if we fail to remember and appreciate the fact that our veteran troops are very loath to make an attack where they believe they have not a fair chance of success. This feeling must be attributed, not to a lack of high soldierly qualities, but to intelligence and good sense. The veteran American soldier fights very much as he has been accustomed to work his farm or run his sawmill: he wants to see a fair prospect that it is "going to pay." His loyalty, discipline, and pluck will not allow him under any circumstances to retreat without orders, much less to run away; but if he encounters a resistance which he thinks he cannot overcome, or which he thinks it would "cost too much" to overcome, he will lie down, cover himself with a little parapet, and hold his ground against any force that may attempt to drive him back. This feeling of the soldier is an element in the problem of war which cannot be ignored. The general who, with such an army, would win the full measure of success due to greatly superior numbers, must manœuver so as to compel the enemy to fight him on approximately equal terms, instead of assaulting fortifications where, against modern weapons, numbers are of little or no avail. In the days of the bayonet successful tactics consisted in massing a superior force upon some vital point, and breaking the enemy's line. Now it is the fire of the musket, not the bayonet, that decides

10

the battle. To mass troops against the fire of a covered line is simply to devote them to destruction. The greater the mass, the greater the loss—that is all. A large mass has no more chance of success than a small one. That this is absolutely true since the introduction of breech-loaders is probably not doubted by any one; and it was very nearly true with the muzzle-loading rifles used during our late war, as was abundantly demonstrated on many occasions.

I have always believed that the true tactics of our late war, whenever our force was double that of the enemy (as it sometimes was and always should have been at all points where decisive movements were to be made), were to throw one half the force upon the enemy's rear, so as to compel him to attack that force or else retreat by side roads with loss of trains and artillery. This would doubtless have been a bold departure from the ancient tactics, which had not yet been proved obsolete. Yet I always thought it strange that our leading generals were unwilling to attempt it. Had Sherman divided his army in such a way, and struck at Hood's rear, he might have found a chance to destroy that army as well as the railroads in Georgia.

The death of McPherson, on July 22, was felt by all to be an irreparable loss, and by none more so than by General Sherman, who manifested deep feeling when the body was brought to the Howard House, east of Atlanta. I recollect well his remark to the effect that the whole of the Confederacy could not atone for the sacrifice of one such life.

My recollection of some of the incidents of that day differs in some respects from that of General Sherman. As soon as it was known that the Army of the Tennessee was heavily engaged I drew out of line the larger part of my troops, leaving the picket-line in position, with strong reserves behind the parapets, and massed them near my left, ready to send reinforcements to the Army of the Tennessee if necessary, or to form a temporary left flank if the line on my left should be broken, as it was late in the day, as described by General Sherman.[1] When that break was made in the line immediately to the left of mine, I had a rare opportunity of witnessing Sherman's splendid conduct as a simple soldier, the occasion for which occurs so rarely to the general-in-chief of a great army. Sherman at once sent to me for *all my artillery*, which responded to his call at a full gallop. He led the batteries in person to some high, open ground *in front of our line* near the Howard House, placed them in position, and directed their fire, which from that advanced position enfiladed the parapets from which our troops had been driven, and which the enemy then occupied. With the aid of that terrible raking fire, the division of Union troops very quickly regained the intrenchments they had lost. General Sherman, on page 81, Vol. II, gives me the credit due to himself for that soldierly conduct as an artillery commander. I was occupied in forming my infantry reserve to meet the enemy if Logan's troops did not drive them back. Only my artillery was used in restoring this broken line, because Logan's infantry proved sufficient without further aid. This action of mine was taken with General Sherman's knowledge and approval, and was the correct thing to do, for the reason that the ground in my front was such as to make both my position and that of the enemy practically unassailable. I had no apprehension of an attack in my front, and there was no question of my attempting to "make a lodgment in Atlanta" that day, as stated by Sherman in Vol. II, page 80.

It was proposed by me that my reserve and Thomas's should go to the assistance of the Army of the Tennessee, either directly or, better still, by making a counter-

[1] Vol. II, pp. 80, 81.

attack in front of the right of that army, which, if successful, would cut off the hostile force then attacking its
left. Sherman replied, as I recollect, that he had asked
Thomas to send some troops to the left, and the latter
had replied that he had none to spare. Without these the
proposition to make a counter-attack could not be entertained. But my memory is only that of conversations
with General Sherman during the day, and he ought to
be much better informed than I concerning what passed
between General Thomas and himself. I recollect that
General Sherman during the day expressed something
like a wish to "let the Army of the Tennessee fight its
own battle," but in his statement of motive for so doing
I think he does that army injustice. My impression
was, and is, that they would have been very glad of assistance, and that timely help would have increased the
fraternal feeling between the armies, instead of creating
unworthy jealousy.

I cannot but believe, as I then thought, that we were
losing a great opportunity that day. A large force of
the enemy had made a wide circuit from his defenses
about Atlanta and attacked our left several miles distant. We there had a chance to fight him on equal
terms. I thought, and still think, we ought to have concentrated a large part of Thomas's force and mine near
the Howard House, and made a strong counter-attack
upon this attacking column of the enemy, with the hope
of cutting it off from Atlanta. Instead of this, Thomas
spent the day in efforts to "make a lodgment in Atlanta" over well-prepared fortifications which the Georgia militia could hold against him about as well as the
veteran Confederate troops.

The movement of August 4 and 5 was designed to be
substantially what had been frequently suggested, but
which I have heretofore referred to as having never
been tried, with the exception that the attacking force

was not to sever its connection with the main body, and hence might not reach far enough to strike an exposed flank of the enemy. But even with this modification I thought the movement ought to have a fair chance of success. That movement was not suggested by me in any way, and, so far as I know, not by General Thomas. I believe it originated entirely with General Sherman. I never heard of it until I received his orders. There was no "argument" by me of the question of relative rank, as suggested by General Sherman (Vol. II, page 99).

The positions of the troops when the order for the movement was made rendered it convenient that the Twenty-third Corps be put in first,— that is, next to the right of General Thomas's troops then in position,— while the Fourteenth Corps, commanded by General John M. Palmer, was relied upon to develop rapidly to our right and endeavor to strike the enemy's flank before he could extend his intrenched line far enough to meet and resist our attack. It was not until some time after my orders for this movement had been issued and should have been in process of vigorous execution that I received the first intimation that the question of rank had been raised, as stated by General Sherman, and that my orders had simply been transmitted to the division commanders of the Fourteenth Corps.

It cannot for a moment be admitted that any share of the blame for that failure attaches to the Fourteenth Corps, as such. Nor do I believe with General Sherman that its slowness on that occasion was due to anything "imbibed" from General Thomas.

My own view of military duty was different from that entertained by the commander of the Fourteenth Corps, as was shown in my subsequent action, hereinafter referred to, when I was ordered to report to and act under the orders of General Stanley. But if the distinguished statesman who then commanded the Fourteenth Corps fell into error at that time, he has doubtless since regretted it far more than any other man could possibly do; and he has many times atoned for that error by the great services to the country which he has continued to render up to the present time.

The primary and principal cause of this and all similar difficulties during the Atlanta campaign was the grave error of opinion which disregarded the special rank of army and department commanders given them by the President's assignment under the law, and the still graver error of judgment in leaving such an important question open until the eve of battle, in the "hope that there would be no necessity for making this decision." This error seems incomprehensible when it is considered that it in effect nullified the President's selection of army and department commanders at the most important of all moments, the crisis of battle, by making these commanders subject to the orders of any general of older commission whose troops happened to be adjacent to theirs.

In the midst of battle, when the orders of a common superior cannot be obtained in time to meet an emergency, the highest commander present must give the necessary orders and must be obeyed. This is probably the gravest responsibility of war. Yet Sherman's opinion and decision would have placed this responsibility, not upon the army commander who had been selected by the President, upon the advice of the general-in-chief, under an act of Congress passed especially for the purpose, but upon some one who through political influence or otherwise had got an earlier commission of major-general. So many of the latter had proved to be unqualified for responsible command that Congress had enacted a special law authorizing the President to supersede such prior commissions and assign commanders of armies or army corps in the field and in any department whom he deemed competent.[1] Palpable as this fallacy seems, yet it was adhered to until overruled by the War Department.

It is proper for me to add that I had at that time but a very slight personal acquaintance with General Palmer. However, I knew him well by reputation, and esteemed him highly. General Thomas, especially, had given me a high estimate of his character and abilities. If there was any cause of jealousy or ill-feeling between us, I never suspected it.

[1] Reference is made here to the 122d Article of War, and the resolution of Congress especially intended to modify it in respect to command in any "field or department," approved April 4, 1862.

CHAPTER IX

THE FINAL BLOW AT ATLANTA — JOHNSTON'S UNTRIED PLAN
OF RESISTANCE — HOOD'S FAULTY MOVE — HOLDING THE
PIVOT OF THE POSITION — ANECDOTES OF THE MEN IN
THE RANKS — DEFERRING TO GENERAL STANLEY IN A
QUESTION OF RELATIVE RANK — THE FAILURE AT JONES-
BORO' — THE CAPTURE OF ATLANTA — ABSENT FROM THE
ARMY — HOOD'S OPERATIONS IN SHERMAN'S REAR — SENT
BACK TO THOMAS'S AID — FAULTY INSTRUCTIONS TO OP-
POSE HOOD AT PULASKI — AT COLUMBIA — REASON OF
THE DELAY IN EXCHANGING MESSAGES.

WHEN all our efforts to accomplish decisive results
by partial operations upon the flanks had failed,
this question was much discussed: What more decisive
movement shall next be made for the capture of Atlanta?
There were practically but two propositions to be considered: that of General Sherman, which was adopted with
success; and that heretofore referred to as having never
been tried, to detach two or more corps to make a lodgment on the railroad at or below East Point, and thus
compel the enemy to come out of Atlanta and endeavor
to regain control of his only line of supply, or abandon
that city altogether. General Sherman thought it too
hazardous to detach two corps, though he was willing for
me to undertake it with one. In fact, this feeling marked
General Sherman's action throughout the campaign. He
had no hesitation in detaching a small force, the loss of
which would still leave him greatly superior in numbers
to the enemy, or a very large force under his own com-

mand, leaving the enemy to the care of the smaller part, as in his march to Savannah. General Thomas, on the contrary, thought the movement proposed by General Sherman "extra hazardous," as Sherman says in his "Memoirs" (Vol. II, page 106). I did not regard either of them as very hazardous, and upon consideration rather preferred General Sherman's, because I thought it could not fail to be decisive of the capture of Atlanta, while the other might fail if not executed with promptness and vigor, and this, experience had warned us, we could not be quite sure of.

Some time after the war, that very able commander General Joseph E. Johnston told me that in his judgment Sherman's operations in Hood's rear ought not to have caused the evacuation of Atlanta; that he (Johnston), when in command, had anticipated such a movement, and had prepared, or intended to prepare, to oppose it by constructing artillery redoubts at all suitable points in the rear of Atlanta, as well as in front, which redoubts could be very speedily connected by infantry intrench-ments whenever necessary; that he aimed to keep on hand in Atlanta at all times supplies enough to last him longer than Sherman's army could subsist on the con-tents of their wagons and haversacks; and that Sherman could not possibly hold all the railroads leading into At-lanta *at the same time*, nor destroy any one of them so thoroughly that it could not be repaired in time to re-plenish Johnston's supplies in Atlanta.

Here is presented a question well worthy of the careful study of military critics. Whatever may be the final judgment upon that question, it seems perfectly clear that Johnston's plan of defense ought at least to have been tried by his successor. If Hood had kept all his troops in compact order about Atlanta, he would have been in the best possible condition to resist Sherman if the latter turned back from Jonesboro' and attacked Atlanta from the rear, or to strike Sherman's rear or flank in full force if he made any other movement. The division of Hood's forces at that time, one part holding on to Atlanta while the other went to *head off* Sherman, was the worst disposition that could have been made.

As related to me personally by General Sheridan,—for I have not yet studied the Virginia campaigns so thoroughly as to justify me in speaking from the records,—it was a similar mistake on the part of the Confederate cavalry commander General J. E. B. Stuart, in trying to get between Sheridan and Richmond, which gave Sheridan the advantage and led to Stuart's defeat. Stuart had ridden hard all night, and got between Sheridan and Richmond, his men and horses exhausted, while Sheridan had been resting and feeding his men and animals. In the morning Sheridan "rode over" his exhausted antagonist. These are among the many cases where exaggerated ideas of the importance of places have led to the defeat of armies. I knew Stuart well at West Point, he having been in the class next to mine. He then gave promise of his future brilliant career as a cavalry leader.

The only specially hazardous part of Sherman's movement was that which would fall to my lot — namely, to hold the "pivot" against a possible attack of Hood's whole army while Thomas and Howard should swing round it, and then draw out and join them after the swing was made. Upon my reporting that I was perfectly willing to undertake this task, and had no doubt of the ability of my corps to accomplish it, all question about making the movement appeared to be settled, and it was at once ordered. Hood did not avail himself of his opportunity to attack me when alone, either in position or in motion, hence my part of the movement proved easiest of all.

I had placed my corps in a completely inclosed fieldwork, large enough to contain all my trains, and strong enough to resist any attack from a greatly superior force until Sherman's movement could be accomplished.

I recollect even to this day a little incident of that time which was, at least to me, both amusing and instructive. After receiving Sherman's orders, which meant " suspend aggressive work and go to fortifying," I was directing the laying out of the new work at the most important part of the line, and the men had been ordered to commence digging, when I heard an old volunteer, as he laid aside his gun and put off his accoutrements with manifest reluctance, say, *sotto voce:* " Well, if digging is the way to put down the rebellion, I guess we will have to do it." Our old soldiers had a "mind of their own," and were not afraid to let their commanders know it ; yet they were essentially as thoroughly subordinate and reliable as any troops any general ever had the honor to command.

I now recall another incident which occurred a few days earlier, in which a young Indiana volunteer was somewhat less respectful, though he had no idea whom he was addressing, nor, probably, any thought whatever about " relative rank." I had come out from my tent, before sunrise in the morning, and was performing my morning ablutions in the ordinary camp basin, preparatory to putting on my outer clothing. None of my " people" were yet up, and the night sentinel of my camp was a little way off. There came up a weary, belated soldier who had, perhaps, been trudging along much of the night, trying to overtake his regiment. I heard him ask in a loud voice : " Where is the 128th Indiana ? " Not supposing the question was addressed to me, I did not look up. Then came in still louder tones and in an amended form which left no room for doubt as to whom it was addressed : " I mean you old fellow there with the red shirt ! Where is the 128th Indiana ? "

If from lapse of time my memory may not be exact as to the number of the regiment, I am sure no apology is necessary to the gallant 128th. It was, anyhow, one of those very high-numbered new Indiana regiments which had recently joined the army. The young soldier was sent to the headquarters escort, given his breakfast, and carried along until his regiment was overtaken.

The Twenty-third Corps reached the railroad about the close of day on August 31, having time to do no more than intrench our positions. The orders that day and night were urgent to make the destruction of the railroad thorough and extensive. This was evidently General Sherman's primary object, showing a doubt in his mind whether the effect of his movement would be the speedy abandonment of Atlanta, or whether he would have to trust to his destruction of the railroad to accomplish that object.

Late in the night of the 31st, after General Stanley and I, who were encamped near together, had gone to sleep, we received despatches from General Sherman stating in effect that as we were too far from the main body of the army to receive orders from him or General Thomas, our two corps must act on the morrow under the orders of the highest commander present, and that General Stanley, having the older commission, was that highest commander. I was therefore directed to report to General Stanley and act under his orders. I replied to General Sherman that while I differed from him in opinion upon the question of relative rank, I would for the present cheerfully abide his decision and execute his orders. Early the next morning, before I had time to report to General Stanley, he appeared at my camp, evidently much disturbed by the orders he had received. He said General Sherman was wrong; that he was not entitled to the command and did not want it; and urged me to accept the chief command, and let him act under my orders. I replied that General Sherman's order was imperative, and I could not relieve him (General Stanley) from the responsibility of executing it. It was all wrong, but there was no present remedy, and he must do the best he could. The position of his corps on the right made it necessary that it should have the advance in the day's movement, while I would follow close after and support him under all circumstances.

So we started early in the morning to execute Sherman's orders — thoroughly to destroy the railroad, and close down on Thomas toward Jonesboro'. That morning, as Sherman says (Vol. II, page 107), "Howard found an intrenched foe (Hardee's corps) covering Jonesboro'," and "orders were sent to Generals Thomas and Schofield to turn straight for Jonesboro', tearing up the railroad track as they advanced." But of course, as General Sherman had anticipated the night before, such orders could not reach me in time to do any good. They were not received until after the affair at Jonesboro' was ended. But hearing the sound of battle in our front, I rode rapidly forward to the head of Stanley's column, which was then not advancing, made inquiries for that officer, and was informed that he was trying to find General Thomas to get orders. I immediately brought my infantry of the Twenty-third Corps out of the road occupied by Stanley's corps, moved it to the front through woods and fields, and endeavored to find a way by which I could reach the enemy's flank or rear, riding so far ahead with a few staff officers and orderlies that I escaped very narrowly being captured by the enemy. Finally, near dark, General Stanley's troops began to deploy and attack the enemy; and as there were more troops on the ground than could possibly be used that day, I could do no more than stand and watch their movements, as I did with intense interest until my medical director, Dr. Hewit, one of the bravest and coolest men I ever knew, called my attention to the fact that the place was much too hot for a general and his staff who had nothing to do there. I believe if General Sherman had been in our place he would have thought it "more than a skirmish-line" (Vol. II, page 108) in Stanley's front that gave us that fire both of musketry and artillery which my staff officers have frequently spoken of as one of the ugliest they ever experienced. General Stanley's fault was, not that he deployed his troops, but that he did not put them in at once when he arrived on the ground, instead of waiting for orders. But General Stanley, whose gallantry was never questioned, was a subordinate in experience. He had but recently risen to the command of a corps, and had been little accustomed to act on his own responsibility. Feeling overburdened with the responsibility wrongfully thrust upon him that day, he naturally sought relief from it by reporting for orders to General Thomas as soon as his corps was reunited to the main army.

The failure at Jonesboro', as at so many other places, was due to that erroneous interpretation of the law that threw the supreme responsibility at the crisis of battle upon untried and (in this case) unwilling shoulders, or else left the lawful commander without recognized authority, to beg in vain of others to "coöperate" with him.

During the night of August 31 others besides General Sherman were too restless and impatient to sleep (Vol. II, page 108). The sounds of explosion in Atlanta were distinctly heard, and the flashes of light distinctly seen. With the compass for direction and the watch for intervals of time between flash and sound, there was no difficulty in locating their origin at Atlanta. An untutored farmer may well have thought "these sounds were just like those of a battle," but a practised ear could not have failed to note the difference. First there would come an explosion louder than and unlike the report of one or several guns, and this would be followed by numerous smaller, sharper, and perfectly distinct reports, quite unlike that of musketry, which could not be mistaken for anything but the explosion of shells. There could be no room for doubt that these lights and sounds meant the destruction in Atlanta of magazines or carloads of fixed ammunition, and hence that Hood was abandoning that place. I reported my observations and conclusion to General Sherman, but he "still remained in doubt." The doubt was to me incomprehensible; but perhaps that was because I had no doubt from the start, whether I was right or wrong, what the result would be. My period of elation was when we got firm hold of the railroad at Rough and Ready. Hood having failed to attack our exposed flank during the movement, the fall of Atlanta was already an accomplished fact with me when Sherman was still in doubt, as well as when Thomas thought the news "too good to be true." But the above is worthy of noting only as a necessary introduction to something far more important.

Hood's army was now divided and scattered over a distance of thirty miles, one corps below Jonesboro' being just driven from its ground with considerable loss and in retreat to Lovejoy's, the main body leaving Atlanta and stretched along the road toward McDonough ; while Sherman's whole army, except Slocum's corps, was in compact order about Jonesboro', nearly in a straight line between Atlanta and Lovejoy's. This seemed exactly the opportunity to destroy Hood's army, if that was the objective of the campaign. So anxious was I that this be attempted that I offered to go with two corps, or even with one, and intercept Hood's retreat on the McDonough road, and hold him until Sherman could dispose of Hardee or interpose his army between him and Hood. But more prudent counsels prevailed, and we remained quietly in our camps for five days, while Hood leisurely marched round us with all his baggage and Georgia militia, and collected his scattered fragments at Lovejoy's.

Atlanta had become, like Richmond, in popular estimation the real objective of military operations. The
public lost sight of the fact that it was armies in the
field, and not fortified places, which gave strength to
the rebellion; and apparently even prominent generals, if
they did not share the popular delusion, at least recognized its value. The capture of Atlanta was enough to
meet the "political necessity," make "the election of Mr.
Lincoln certain," and win rejoicings and congratulations
from all parts of the North! It was not worth while to
run any risk of trying to do more at that time! It had
to be left for two of Sherman's corps, after the other
four had gone on "the march to the sea," to fight Hood
at Columbia and Spring Hill, hurl him back from Franklin, and then, with reinforcements not equal to half what
Sherman had taken away, to overwhelm him at Nashville. Why was not this done with a much larger force
under Sherman at Atlanta? This is one of the questions
for the future historian to discuss.

During our rest near Lovejoy's, General Sherman requested me to give him a statement in writing of my
dissent from his decision upon the question of relative
rank, which I did. This he submitted to the War Department for decision, as a "question of rank that had
arisen between Generals Schofield and Stanley." At this
General Stanley was very indignant, as well as at General Sherman's censure of his conduct on September 1;
for the reason that no question of rank had been raised
by us, and the command was thrust upon him in opposition to his wish and in violation of the law as he understood it. In due time came the decision of the War
Department, written by General Halleck, sustaining the
view of the law Stanley and I had taken, and reversing
that of General Sherman; also kindly commending my
action in waiving the question during active operations.

It was by virtue of the above decision of the War Department that I, instead of General Stanley, had command of the force that in the following November, 1864, opposed Hood's advance from the Tennessee River and repulsed his fierce assault at Franklin.

As I was absent from the army on business connected with my department during most of Hood's raid upon the railroad in the rear of Atlanta (Sherman having announced his purpose to let his army rest during that time), I have little to say in respect to the operations resulting therefrom. But some things in Sherman's account seem to require a little elucidation.

Being informed by General Sherman of Hood's movement, I hurried to the front and tried to reach the army by a special train with a small guard from Cleveland, Tenn., but met, October 13, the head of Hood's column at Dalton, where several trains of cars with supplies and men without arms returning from furlough on their way to Sherman had been stopped by the reported approach of Hood. I ordered all back to Cleveland, and we barely had time to escape capture by Hood's cavalry. On arriving at Cleveland, I reported by telegraph to General Thomas, then at Nashville; and he desired me to go to Chattanooga, take command of the troops there, and prepare to defend that place, which it was thought Hood might attempt to take by a *coup de main*, or to coöperate with Sherman. As General Sherman says (Vol. II, page 156), "Hood had broken up the telegraph, and thus had prevented quick communication"; but through my own scouts and spies I was able to keep track of Hood's movements. As soon as he turned westward I determined to move with the troops, when no longer necessary to the defense of Chattanooga, rapidly to Trenton and Valley Head, seize the passes through the Lookout range, and prevent Hood's escape in that direction, presuming that Sherman would intercept his retreat down the Chattanooga valley. I sent a courier to General Sherman informing him of my purpose, and informed General Thomas by telegraph. But the latter disapproved my plan, and directed me to move to defend Caperton's Ferry. This is what General Sherman refers to in his despatch of October 16: "Your first move on Trenton and Valley Head was right; the move to defend Caperton's Ferry is wrong. Notify General Thomas of these, my views." But the difference between right and wrong proved immaterial, since Hood was left free to escape down the Chattanooga valley. Why this was done, or why Sherman did not want to force the enemy east, by Spring Place, into the barren mountains, where Johnston would have been compelled to go if McPherson's move on Resaca in May had been successful, seems a mystery. The explanation is probably to be found in Sherman's wish that Hood would go where he would not be compelled to follow, and thus would leave him (Sherman) a clear road for his march to the sea. Indeed the conviction seems irresistible that Sherman and Hood could hardly have acted in more perfect concert if they had been under the same commander. The one did exactly what the other wanted, and the other took care not to interfere with his movement.

At the close of the Atlanta campaign, I promised General Sherman that I would, as soon as I should be able to do so, write a full critical history of that campaign as a text-book for military students. I have not yet found time to fulfil that promise. The foregoing pages were intended, when written, as only a very partial fulfilment of that task, and that almost entirely of one side of it—far the most difficult side. The other side is so easy, comparatively, and is already so familiar to military students, that further elucidation now seems hardly necessary. Yet I hope, as a labor of love, if for no other reason, to present my impressions of those grand tactical evolutions of a compact army of one hundred thousand men, as I witnessed them with the intense interest of a young commander and student of the great art which has so often in the history of the world determined the destinies of nations.

After the capture of Atlanta, in September, 1864, General Sherman proposed to give his army rest for a month while he perfected his plans and preparations for a change of base to some point on the Atlantic or the gulf, in pursuance of the general plan outlined by General Grant before the Atlanta campaign was opened in May. But the Confederate commander took the initiative, about September 20, by moving his army around Sherman's right, striking his railroad about Allatoona and toward Chattanooga, doing some damage, and then marching off westward with the design of transferring the theater of war from Georgia to Alabama, Mississippi, or Tennessee.

Sherman very promptly decided not to accept that challenge to meet Hood upon a field chosen by the latter, but to continue substantially the original plan for his own operations, having in view also new ulterior plans opened to him by this erratic movement of his adversary. An essential modification of the original plan, to meet the unexpected movement of Hood, was to send back into Tennessee force enough, in addition to the troops then there and others to be assembled from the rear, to cope with Hood in the event of his attempting the invasion of Tennessee and Kentucky, or to pursue and occupy his attention if he should attempt to follow Sherman. General George H. Thomas, commanding the Department of the Cumberland, whose headquarters were at Nashville, was already at that place, and was directed by General Sherman to assume command of all the troops in the three departments under Sherman's command, except those with the latter in Georgia, and to direct the operations against Hood.

Thomas had in his department at that time only the garrisons and railroad guards which had been deemed essential during the preceding operations in Georgia; and many of those were soon to be discharged by expiration of their terms of enlistment, their places to be supplied by new regiments coming from the rear. General A. J. Smith's corps, then in Missouri, about ten thousand strong, was ordered to Tennessee, and Sherman also ordered Stanley, with the Fourth Corps, about twelve thousand men, to return from Georgia to Tennessee and report to Thomas. Stanley had started by rail to Tullahoma, and was to march, as he did, from the latter point to Pulaski, Tennessee, which had been selected as the point of concentration for Thomas's forces. This was the situation when I returned to the army and reported in person to General Sherman.

Under Sherman's promise of a month's rest for his army, I had gone back to attend to the business of my department, as General Thomas had also done, and hence was in the rear when Hood made his raid upon Sherman's railroad. Upon reporting to General Sherman near the end of October, I learned for the first time his purpose to march to Savannah, and what troops he had provided for Thomas in Tennessee. I told Sherman, with that perfect candor which he always invited, that in my opinion Thomas's force was much too small; that Hood evidently intended to invade Tennessee; and that he would not be diverted from his purpose by Sherman's march in the opposite direction, but would, on the contrary, be encouraged thereby to pursue his own plan. Hence I requested Sherman to send me back with the Twenty-third Corps to join Thomas. Sherman at first appeared to understand my suggestion as a desire to be left in Tennessee instead of Thomas, the latter to go with Sherman. But I explained to him emphatically that such was not my thought. I took it for granted that Thomas was to command the army in Tennessee, and I wanted only to go back and help him because he would, in my opinion, have to do the fighting while Sherman's march would be unopposed. Sherman then replied that he must have three grand divisions, under Slocum, Howard, and myself, to make his army complete, and that he could not spare me; and he gave no indication of concurrence in my opinion that he ought to send back more troops.

After leaving General Sherman that afternoon and returning to my own camp, I wrote him a letter giving a special reason why my corps, rather than any other, should be sent back to Tennessee in order that it might be filled up by new regiments which had been ordered from the North. No answer came to these suggestions until I had made three days' march toward Atlanta, *en route* for Savannah. Then I received an order, October 30, to march to the nearest point on the railroad, and report by telegraph to General Thomas for orders.

At first General Thomas ordered me to move by rail to Tullahoma, and then march across to Pulaski, as Stanley was doing. But just then Forrest with his cavalry appeared at Johnsonville, on the Tennessee River west of Nashville, and destroyed a great quantity of property, General Thomas not having sufficient force available to oppose him; hence on November 3 Thomas ordered me to come at once by rail to Nashville with my corps, where I reported to him with the advance of my troops on November 5. He then ordered me to go at once with some of my troops to Johnsonville and dispose of the Confederate cavalry there, and then to return to Nashville and proceed to Pulaski, to take command of all the troops in the field, which would then include the Fourth Corps, my own Twenty-third, except the detachment left at Johnsonville, and the cavalry watching Hood toward Florence. My duty at Johnsonville, where I left two brigades, was soon disposed of; and I then returned to Nashville, and went at once by rail to Pulaski, arriving at that place in the evening of November 13.

Some so-called histories of the Tennessee campaign have been based upon the theory that I was marching from Georgia to Tennessee, to unite my corps with General Thomas's army at Nashville, when I encountered Hood at Franklin, and after a sharp contest managed to elude him and continue my march and unite with the Army of the Cumberland at Nashville. Hence I wish to point out clearly that I had been with the entire Twenty-third Corps to Nashville, with a part of it to Johnsonville and back to Nashville, and thence to Columbia and near Pulaski, all by rail; that all of the Army of the Cumberland then in Tennessee was the Fourth Corps and the cavalry at and near Pulaski; that General Thomas placed those troops under my command, and that they remained so until after the battle of Franklin, November 30, and the retreat to Nashville that night; and that General Thomas did not have an army at Nashville until December 1. I had united with Thomas's troops two weeks before the battle of Franklin, and was commanding his army in the field as well as my own during that time. If the historians had read the records [1] they could not possibly have fallen into such a mistake.

Before reaching Pulaski I was furnished with an order from General Thomas's headquarters assigning me to the command in the field, by virtue of my rank as a department commander, and a copy of instructions which had already been telegraphed to General Stanley at Pulaski. I assumed command in the morning of November 14. The moment I met Stanley at Pulaski, in the evening of November 13, he called my attention to the faulty position of the troops and to an error in General Thomas's instructions, about which I then knew nothing because I

[1] War Records, Vol. XLV.

was unacquainted with the geography of the surrounding country. Upon Stanley's statement, I halted Cox's division of the Twenty-third Corps a few miles north of Pulaski so that the troops might be the more readily placed as the situation required when I had time to consider it. No part of the Twenty-third Corps actually went to Pulaski, although that was the place to which General Thomas had ordered it.

On the 19th General Thomas repeated to me the same orders he had sent to General Stanley, in these words: "If the enemy advances in force, as General Hatch believes, have everything in readiness either to fight him at Pulaski if he advances on that place, or cover the railroad and concentrate at Columbia, should he attempt to turn your right flank. . . ."[1] I then telegraphed General Thomas, November 20, pointing out the faulty nature of the position selected by him for the troops at Pulaski, and the danger that must be incurred in attempting to carry out his instructions to fight Hood at Pulaski if he should advance upon that place; also suggesting what seemed to be the best way to avoid that difficulty. General Thomas very promptly approved these suggestions, and thus ended the embarrassment occasioned by the faulty instructions. But his official report on that point has made it necessary for me to comment upon it more fully later.

The season of Hood's invasion of Tennessee was extremely unfavorable for aggressive operations, and hence correspondingly favorable for the defense. The ordinary country roads were almost impassable, while the turnpikes were in good condition. As we held the crossing of the Tennessee River at Decatur, Hood was compelled to cross at the Shoals below, and to advance over those very bad roads; hence we had ample time in which to make the necessary dispositions to oppose him.

[1] War Records, Vol. XLV, part i, p. 944.

Our cavalry gave us accurate information that the enemy was advancing on the 21st, when Cox, with Wagner in support, was ordered to interpose between the enemy's cavalry and Columbia; while Stanley, with two divisions of the Fourth Corps, marched from Pulaski to that place, and our cavalry moved on the enemy's right to cover the turnpike and railroad. The whole army was in position at Columbia, November 24, and began to intrench. Hood's infantry did not appear in sight until the 26th. Cox had a brush with the enemy's cavalry, which had driven in one of our cavalry brigades. That action was magnified at the time, and afterward, into evidence of a race between our troops and the enemy for the possession of Columbia. In fact, Ruger's troops at Columbia were quite capable of holding that place against Forrest, and Hood's infantry was not within a day's march of either Cox or Stanley until after both had reached Columbia.

We held our intrenched position in front of Columbia until the evening of November 27, inviting an attack, and hoping that Thomas would arrive with, or send, reinforcements in time to assume the offensive from Columbia; but reinforcements did not come, and the enemy did not attack. It became evident that Hood's intention was not to attack that position, but to turn it by crossing Duck River above; hence the army was moved to the north bank of the river in the night of the 27th. It was still hoped that the line of Duck River might be held until reinforcements could arrive. General Thomas was very urgent that this should be done, if possible, as the arrival of General A. J. Smith's corps from Missouri had been expected daily for some time, when General Thomas intended, as it was understood, to come to the front in person with that corps and all the other troops he could assemble in his department, take command, and move against the enemy.

About that time was disclosed one of those contrivances by which the non-military agencies of government interfere with the operations of armies. The War Department telegraph corps alone was intrusted with the cipher in which General Thomas and I could communicate with each other by telegraph. Neither he, nor I, nor any of our staff officers were permitted to know the telegraph code. The work was so badly done that from eight to forty-eight hours were occupied in sending and delivering a despatch. Finally the cipher-operator attached to my headquarters in the field deserted his post and went to Franklin, so that the time required for a messenger to ride from Franklin to my position in the field was added to the delay caused by deciphering despatches. From all this it resulted that my superior at Nashville was able to give me little assistance during the critical days of that campaign. It has been generally supposed that I was all that time acting under orders or instructions from General Thomas, and his numerous despatches have been quoted in " histories " as evidence in support of that supposition. The fact is that I was not only without any appropriate orders or instructions nearly all the time, but also without any timely information from General Thomas to guide my action.

This fact appears to have been fully recognized by General Thomas in his official report, wherein he made no mention of any orders or instructions given by him during the progress of those operations, but referred only to " instructions already given " before I went to Pulaski, and said: " My plans and wishes were fully explained to General Schofield, and, as subsequent events will show, properly appreciated and executed by him." [1]

[1] War Records, Vol. XXXIX, part i, p. 590.

CHAPTER X

HOOD FORCES THE CROSSING OF DUCK RIVER — IMPOR-
TANCE OF GAINING TIME FOR THOMAS TO CONCEN-
TRATE REINFORCEMENTS AT NASHVILLE — THE AFFAIR
AT SPRING HILL — INCIDENTS OF THE NIGHT RETREAT
— THOMAS'S REPLY TO THE REQUEST THAT A BRIDGE
BE LAID OVER THE HARPETH — THE NECESSITY OF
STANDING GROUND AT FRANKLIN — HOOD'S FORMIDABLE
ATTACK — SERIOUS ERROR OF TWO BRIGADES OF THE
REAR-GUARD — BRILLIANT SERVICES OF THE RESERVE —
YELLOW FEVER AVERTED — HOOD'S ASSAULTS REPULSED
— JOHNSTON'S CRITICISM OF HOOD — THE ADVANTAGE
OF CONTINUING THE RETREAT TO NASHVILLE.

IN the afternoon of November 28 I received information
that the enemy's cavalry had forced the crossing of
Duck River above Columbia, and driven our cavalry back;
and, about two o'clock that night, that prisoners reported
the enemy laying pontoon bridges, and that Hood's infantry would begin to cross that morning. The army was
ready to march at a moment's notice. It could have retired to Spring Hill or to Franklin without molestation or
delay, but that would have given the enemy the crossing
of Duck River at Columbia and the turnpike road for his
advance with his artillery and trains. There was no
assurance that Thomas had assembled any of his expected
reinforcements at Nashville or elsewhere. It was known
that orders had been given some days before looking to
concentration of some of the troops in his department
somewhere, but what had been accomplished I was not

informed. About A. J. Smith I was in a like state of
uncertainty. Only one thing was clear, and that was that
I must hold Hood back, if possible, until informed that
Thomas had concentrated his troops; for if I failed in
that, Hood would not only force me back upon Nashville
before Thomas was ready to meet him there, but would
get possession of the Chattanooga Railroad, and thus cut
off the troops coming to Nashville from that direction.
After considering the matter some time in the night, I
decided to hold on at least until morning. Early in the
morning a brigade of infantry was sent up the river to
reconnoiter and watch the enemy's movements; at the
same time Stanley was ordered, with two divisions of his
corps, back to Spring Hill, to occupy and intrench a position there covering the roads and the trains, which were
ordered to be parked at that place, and General Thomas
H. Ruger was ordered to join him.

About 8 A. M. on the 29th came a despatch from Thomas,
dated 8 P. M. of the day before, conveying the information
that Smith had not arrived, and saying nothing about any
other reinforcements, but expressing the wish that the
Duck River position be held until Smith arrived; and
another despatch designating Franklin, behind the Harpeth River, as the place to which I would have to retire if
it became necessary to fall back from Duck River. I then
decided to hold on to the crossing of Duck River until the
night of the 29th, thus gaining twenty-four hours more
for Thomas to concentrate his troops. I did not apprehend any serious danger at Spring Hill; for Hood's infantry could not reach that place over a wretched country
road much before night, and Stanley, with one division
and our cavalry, could easily beat off Forrest. Hence I
retained Ruger's division and one of Stanley's, and disposed all the troops to resist any attempt Hood might
make, by marching directly from his bridges upon my
position on the north bank of Duck River, to dislodge me

from that position. That was his best chance of success, but he did not try it.

Stanley arrived at Spring Hill in time to beat off Forrest and protect our trains. Then he intrenched a good position in which to meet Hood's column when it should arrive, which it did late in the afternoon. They had a hard fight which lasted until about dark. Much bitter controversy arose between Hood and some of his subordinates because of their failure to dislodge Stanley's division and get possession of the turnpike at Spring Hill. While I have no wish to take any part in that discussion, I must say that I think the mistake was Hood's. I think he attempted a little longer march, over a very bad road, than could be made in so short a time. The 29th of November is a very short day, and the march of troops across pontoon bridges and through deep mud is very slow. If Hood had turned down the north bank of Duck River, across the fields, which were no worse than his road, he could have got into a fight about noon; but he thought, according to his own account in " Advance and Retreat," that he was deceiving me by his thundering demonstrations at Columbia, and that I did not know he was marching to Spring Hill. He thought he was going to " catch me napping," after the tactics of Stonewall Jackson, while in fact I was watching him all day. Besides, Hood went to bed that night, while I was in the saddle all night, directing in person all the important movements of my troops. Perhaps that is enough to account for the difference between success and failure, without censuring subordinate commanders. Mine did all I could have asked anybody to do that night.

As soon as I was satisfied that Hood was gone to Spring Hill and would not attack me on the bank of Duck River, I took the head of my troops — Ruger's division — and marched rapidly to Spring Hill, leaving staff officers to give orders to the other division commanders to follow immediately in proper order as then formed in line. These orders were somehow misunderstood. The order of march was reversed, and the troops, except Ruger's, and Whitaker's brigade of Kimball's division, did not move at once. But the delay did no harm, and I did not know of the mistake until several days afterward. If Hood had only known of that mistake, he might have troubled me no little, perhaps, by pushing a column across from his camp, south of Whitaker's right flank at Spring Hill, until it reached the Columbia turnpike. But I had prepared even for that, as well as I could, by sending a company of infantry to occupy the only cross-road I could see near Spring Hill as we approached that place. I ordered the captain of that company to hold that road at all hazards until he was relieved by my orders! Some of Hood's troops "relieved" him next morning! We have to do cruel things sometimes in war. On arriving at Spring Hill, Whitaker's brigade was put in line on the right of the troops then in position, so as to cover the turnpike on which we were marching. This was about dark. In a few minutes the Confederate camp-fires were lighted a few hundred yards in front of that brigade. It was a very interesting sight, but I don't think any of Whitaker's men cared to give the Confederates a similar view of them.

After stopping to see Stanley a few minutes, and learning that some of Forrest's troopers had been seen at Thompson's Station, three miles farther north, about dusk, I went with Ruger's division to drive them off and clear the way to Franklin. To my great surprise, I found only smoldering fires — no cavalry. This was where our men passed so close to the "bivouac" that they "lighted their pipes by the enemy's camp-fires"; and that is the way romance is woven into history! But I took it for granted that the famous Forrest must be on my road somewhere; for he was there in the afternoon, and I had no cavalry anywhere near to drive him away. I could not take time to go with or send infantry to find out where he was. But I had with me my headquarters troop and as gallant an aide — Captain William J. Twining — as ever wore spur. Twining was the same gallant and accomplished aide and officer of the corps of engineers, now dead, who afterward made the famous ride of one hundred and ten miles, through the enemy's country in North Carolina, to carry a despatch from me to Sherman. He was a commissioner of the District of Columbia at the time of his death. I ordered them to go at full gallop down the pike to Franklin, and to ride over whatever might be found in their way. I sat motionless on my horse at Thompson's Station until the clatter of hoofs on that hard road died out in the distance, and I knew the road was clear. I did not tell the brave Twining the object of that ride, but simply to report the situation to General Thomas by telegraph from Franklin, and if any troops were at that place, as had been reported, to order them forward at once. I had not yet determined whether I could continue the retreat that night, or whether it might be necessary to fight Hood at Spring Hill the next day. In either case the troops at Franklin, if any were there, might be useful.

Upon returning to Spring Hill near midnight, I found my column from Duck River there in compact order. As the road was clear and the Confederates all sound asleep, while the Union forces were all wide awake, there was no apparent reason for not continuing the march that night. A column of artillery and wagons, and another of infantry, moved side by side along the broad turnpike, so that if the redoubtable Forrest should wake up and make his appearance anywhere, he would be quickly brushed away. It was reported that he did attack somewhere in the night, but I heard nothing of it at the time, perhaps because I was sleeping quietly on my horse as we marched along!

I arrived at Franklin with the head of my column a short time before the dawn of day, November 30; indicated to General J. D. Cox, commanding the Twenty-third Corps, the line upon which the troops were to be formed; and intrusted to him the formation, as the several divisions of both corps should arrive, General Stanley being in the rear directing the operations of the rear-guard. The Twenty-third Corps occupied the center of the line crossing the Columbia turnpike, and extended to the river on the left, while the Fourth Corps was to extend the line to the river on the right. Fortunately the natural position was such that Kimball's division of the Fourth Corps was sufficient, leaving both Wood's and Wagner's in reserve. I then gave my undivided attention to the means of crossing the Harpeth River.

Two days before I had telegraphed to General Thomas suggesting that he have a pontoon bridge laid at Franklin, to which he replied: "You can send some of the pontoons you used at Columbia to Franklin to lay a bridge there."[1] General Thomas or his staff should have known that it was utterly impossible for me to use the pontoons which I had at Columbia. Those pontoons were heavy wooden bateaux, and there were no wagons to transport them, the train that brought them there having been taken away, it is presumed by his order, certainly not by mine. Hence I was compelled to burn that pontoon bridge as well as the railroad bridge (partially) when my troops retreated from Ducktown. But even if this were not all true, Thomas knew the enemy was already crossing Duck River on my flank, and that I must speedily take up a new position behind the Harpeth, and that I desired him to provide the means for my army to cross that river. It was a reasonable inference that I should not have asked him to send another bridge if I already had one that I could use. Besides, I

[1] War Records, Vol. XLV, part i, p. 1108.

was commanding General Thomas's army, operating in his department, wherein I had no control of anything in rear of the troops under my charge. It was his duty to foresee and provide for all the necessities that might arise in the rear of the army in the field. I telegraphed him again for a bridge at the Harpeth on the 29th, when I found that retreat was inevitable, but he apparently did not get that despatch. He nevertheless sent bridge material by rail to Franklin, where it arrived on the morning of November 30, too late for the pontoons to be used, though the flooring was useful in covering the railroad bridge and the burned wagon-bridge. I found also on the south side of the river a very large park of wagons belonging to the Department of the Cumberland, which, as well as my own trains and artillery, must be crossed over before I could withdraw my troops to the north side. The troops were very much fatigued by their long night march, rendering considerable rest indispensable. Hence there could not be much time in which to prepare defensive works with such obstructions as to insure successful defense against a very heavy assault. But, much more serious, Hood might cross the river above Franklin with a considerable force of infantry, as well as with all his cavalry, before I could get my materials over and troops enough to meet him on the north side. The situation at Franklin had become vastly more serious than that at Columbia or Spring Hill, and solely because of the neglect of so simple a thing as to provide the bridge I had asked for across the Harpeth. If that had been done, my trains could have passed over at once, and the entire army could have crossed before Hood reached Franklin.

To meet this greatest danger, Wood's division of the Fourth Corps was crossed to the north side to support the cavalry in holding the fords above, if that should become necessary; while Wagner's division, which had acted as rear-guard from Spring Hill, was ordered to remain far enough in front of the line to compel Hood to disclose his intention to attack in front or to turn the position, and was to retire and take its position in reserve at the proper time, if the enemy formed for attack. Only one of those three brigades—Opdycke's— came in at the proper time and took its appropriate place; and that, it was asserted, no doubt truly, was by the brigade commander's own volition, he having been soldier enough to know his duty in such a case, without the necessity for any orders. The other two brigades remained in their advanced position until they were run over by the enemy. Much idle controversy was indulged in among officers of the Fourth Corps and others in respect to the action of those two brigades. The only proper way to settle such a question was by a court-martial. As the corps passed from my command the next morning, and had been under my orders only a few days, I have never made any effort to fix, even in my own mind, the responsibility for that blunder.

By great exertion on the part of the engineers, the means of crossing the river were at length provided. The supports of the burned wagon-bridge were still standing at a level with the surface of the water. They were timbered and planked over, and the railroad bridge was also covered with planking, thus giving us two passable bridges. The trains had all been crossed over, and a part of the artillery. Orders had been issued for the troops to begin crossing at dark, when Hood disclosed his purpose to attack. The artillery was ordered back to its position in the line, and General Stanley and I, who were then together on the north side of the river, rode rapidly to our posts, he to his corps on the south side, and I to the high redoubt on the north bank, overlooking the entire field.

There I witnessed the grandest display possible in war.

Every battalion and battery of the Union army in line was distinctly seen. The corps of the Confederate army which were advancing or forming for the attack could also be seen, though less clearly on account of their greater distance, while the Confederate cavalry could be dimly discerned moving to the fords of the river above Franklin. Only a momentary view was permitted of this scene of indescribable grandeur when it was changed to one of most tragic interest and anxiety. The guns of the redoubt on the parapet of which I stood with two or three staff officers had fired only a few shots over the heads of our troops at the advancing enemy when his heavy line overwhelmed Wagner's two brigades and rapidly followed their fragments in a confused mass over our light intrenchments. The charging ranks of the enemy, the flying remnants of our broken troops, and the double ranks of our first line of defense, coming back from the trenches together, produced the momentary impression of an overwhelming mass of the enemy passing over our parapets.

It is hardly necessary to say that for a moment my "heart sank within me." But instantly Opdycke's brigade and the 12th and 16th Kentucky sprang forward, and steadily advanced to the breach. Up to this moment there had been but little firing at that point, because of our own troops and the enemy coming in pellmell; hence there was not much smoke, and the whole could be seen. But now all became enveloped in a dense mass of smoke, and not a man was visible except the fragments of the broken brigades and others, afterward known to be prisoners, flocking to the rear. A few seconds of suspense and intense anxiety followed, then the space in the rear of our line became clear of fugitives, and the steady roar of musketry and artillery and the dense volume of smoke rising along the entire line told me that "the breach is restored, the victory won"! That scene, and the emotion of that one moment, were worth all the losses and dangers of a soldier's lifetime.

It would hardly be possible to frame language that would do more than justice to the magnificent conduct of Emerson Opdycke's brigade and Laurence H. Rousseau's 12th Kentucky and John S. White's 16th Kentucky, which were also in reserve, and their commanders, in that battle. Their action was beyond all praise, and nothing that can justly be said in respect to the battle can detract one iota from their proud fame. Yet the light in which the part acted by Opdycke's brigade (the others not being mentioned) is presented by some "historians," to the prejudice, relatively, of other portions of the army and of their commanders, is essentially false. It is represented as something purely spontaneous, out of the ordinary course, not contemplated in the dispositions made for battle, unforeseen and unexpected; in short, something more—yes, vastly more—than the reasonable duty of the brigade; or, "beyond all power of generalship to mold the battle or control its issue, the simple charge of Opdycke's brigade stands in boldest relief." The same might be said with equal truth of the action of any brigade upon which devolves the assault or defense of the key of a military position. The success or failure of "generalship to mold the battle or control its issue" depends absolutely upon the action of such brigades, their doing, or failure to do, the duty belonging to the position to which they are assigned. Every soldier in the army knew what his duty was in such a case— knew for what he had been placed in that position. It would have been strange indeed if the gallant commander of that brigade had waited for orders from some higher officer to move "forward to the lines." As well might the commander of a brigade in the line wait for orders from the general-in-chief before commencing to fire on the advancing enemy.

The highest tribute that can be paid to Opdycke's brigade is the just and true one, that it did exactly the duty assigned it in the plan of battle, and did that duty nobly and with complete success. That other brigades did the same is sufficiently shown by the fact that twenty battle-flags were captured by a single brigade of the Twenty-third Corps on the same part of the line, and that the 12th and 16th Kentucky regiments relatively suffered equally heavy losses in killed and wounded with those of Opdycke.[1]

As before stated, the dispositions for defense contemplated the whole of Wagner's division as the reserve to support the center, that being the only part of the line upon which the enemy would have time to make a heavy assault that day. This provision for an ample reserve had been made after full consideration and before Wood's division was ordered to the north side of the river, which was after the day was well advanced and the enemy's cavalry had begun to threaten the crossing above. The blunder respecting the two brigades of Wagner's division came near being disastrous, and the repulse of the assault in spite of that blunder makes it highly probable that if the dispositions ordered had been properly made, the repulse of the enemy would have been easy beyond reasonable doubt. Yet it would be difficult to find a fairer chance of success in a direct assault upon troops in position. Our intrenchments were of the slightest kind, and without any considerable obstructions in front to interfere seriously with the assault. The attack, no less than the defense, was characterized by incomparable valor, and the secret of its failure is to be found in one of the principles taught by all military experience—the great superiority in strength of a fresh body of troops in perfect

[1] War Records, Vol. XLV, part i, pp. 241 and 413. The loss at Franklin of Opdycke's six regiments was 205, while the 12th and 16th Kentucky regiments lost 106 men.

order over another in the state of disorder which necessarily results from even the most successful assault. There was really no comparison, in effective strength, between Opdycke's orderly and compact brigade and the confused mass of Confederates that were crossing over our parapet. The result was nothing extraordinary or at all unprecedented. It was but one of the numerous proofs afforded by military history of the value of that prudent maxim in the art of war which dictates the placing of a suitable reserve in close support of that portion of a defensive line which is liable to heavy assault.

The surprising conduct of the commanders of the two brigades of Wagner's division which were run over by the enemy, and of the division commander himself, whatever may be true as to the conflicting statements published in respect to their action, is one of the strongest possible illustrations of the necessity of the higher military education, and of the folly of intrusting high commands to men without such education, which, fortunately for the country and the army, is rarely learned by experience, but must be acquired by laborious study of the rules and principles laid down by standard authors as derived from the practice and teachings of the great masters of the art of war in all ages. A well-educated officer, either as brigade or division commander, would not have needed orders from any source to tell him what to do in that emergency. He would have known so surely what his duty was that he would have retired at the proper time behind the main line, without ever thinking whether or not he had orders to do so. As well might I have waited for orders from General Thomas to retire across the Harpeth after my duty on the south side of that river had been accomplished. The cases are closely parallel. Any unofficial discussion of the question of responsibility for the sacrifice of those two brigades is idle. According to the established rules of war, those three commanders ought to have been tried by court, martial, and, if found guilty, shot or cashiered, for sacrificing their own men and endangering the army. One example of such punishment would do much to deter ignorant and incompetent men from seeking high commands in the field. But the discipline of the volunteer army of a republic must, it appears, inevitably be, especially in respect to officers of high rank, quite imperfect, although it may become in respect to the great mass of the troops, as ours certainly did, exceedingly efficient.

In the Atlanta campaign I sent a division commander to the rear in permanent disgrace for sacrificing his men in a hopeless assault upon a fortified line, contrary to the general orders and instructions which General Sherman had published before the opening of the campaign. But I never heard of another similar case of even approximate justice to an officer of high rank. It is a striking proof of the evil effect of war upon the minds and passions of men, not only of those who are engaged in it, but even more upon those who see it from a distance, that commanders are often severely condemned for prudent care of the lives of men under their command, who have no choice but to march blindly to death when ordered, while the idiotic sacrifice of the bravest and noblest of patriotic soldiers is loudly applauded as a grand exhibition of "gallantry" in action. If George H. Thomas had had no other title to honor or fame, he would have deserved the profound gratitude of the American people, and a very high place among the country's patriots and heroes, for the reason that while he never yielded ground to an attacking foe, he never uselessly sacrificed the life of a soldier.

It is a sin for a soldier to throw away his own life. It is not his, but belongs to his country. How much greater sin and crime in an officer to throw away the lives of a thousand men! If he threw away a thousand dollars, he would be court-martialed and cashiered Are not the soldiers of a republic worth even a dollar apiece! Patriotism and courage exist in great abundance in the breasts of young Americans. All they need is instruction, discipline, a little experience, such as our greatest soldier said he himself needed at first, and, above all, intelligent leadership, which can be acquired only by military education, to make them the best soldiers the world has ever known.

When I joined my company as second lieutenant in Florida in the winter of 1853-4, I found the company had been reduced to one lance-sergeant, two lance-corporals, and thirteen privates. Yellow fever had done its deadly work. But that lesson was not lost. In later years, upon the approach of that enemy, which could not be conquered even by the highest science then known or practised, the troops were marched a few miles into the pure air of the piney woods, where the dreaded fever could not reach them. At the close of the epidemic season which occurred when I had the honor to command the army, I had the great satisfaction of reporting that not a single soldier had been killed by that most dreaded of all enemies, and the even greater satisfaction of reporting that those bravest of the brave, the surgeons who volunteered to go into the very midst of the camp of the enemy that does not respect even the red cross, to minister to those who had been stricken down and to study the nature of the disease for the future benefit of the army and of mankind, had also been unharmed. As chief of those I do not hesitate to name the present surgeon-general of the army, George M. Sternberg. Yet how many of the noblest soldiers of humanity have given their lives in that cause!

Hood's assault at Franklin has been severely criticized. Even so able a man as General J. E. Johnston characterizes it as a "useless butchery." These criticisms are founded upon a misapprehension of the facts, and are essentially erroneous. Hood must have been fully aware of our relative weakness in numbers at Franklin, and of the probable, if not certain, concentration of large reinforcements at Nashville. He could not hope to have at any future time anything like so great an advantage in that respect. The army at Franklin and the troops at Nashville were within one night's march of each other; Hood must therefore attack on November 30, or lose the advantage of greatly superior numbers. It was impossible, after the pursuit from Spring Hill, in a short day to turn our position or make any other attack but a direct one in front. Besides, our position, with the river in our rear, gave him the chance of vastly greater results, if his assault were successful, than could be hoped for by any attack he could make after we had crossed the Harpeth. Still more, there was no unusual obstacle to a successful assault at Franklin. The defenses were of the slightest character, and it was not possible to make them formidable during the short time our troops were in position, after the previous exhausting operations of both day and night, which had rendered some rest on the 30th absolutely necessary.

The Confederate cause had reached a condition closely verging on desperation, and Hood's commander-in-chief had called upon him to undertake operations which he thought appropriate to such an emergency. Franklin was the last opportunity he could expect to have to reap the results hoped for in his aggressive movement. He must strike there, as best he could, or give up his cause as lost. I believe, therefore, that there can be no room for doubt that Hood's assault was entirely justifiable. It may have been faulty in execution, in not having been sufficiently supported by a powerful reserve at the moment of first success. I have not the means of knowing the actual facts in this regard; but the result seems to render such a hypothesis at least probable, and the rapidity and impetuosity of Hood's advance and assault add to that probability.

It is interesting to consider what would probably have been the march of events if we had retreated from Duck River in the night of November 28, upon first learning that Hood had forced the crossing of that river. We would have reached Franklin early on the 29th, could have rebuilt the bridges and crossed the Harpeth that day and night, and Hood could not have got up in time to make any serious attack that day. So far as our little army was concerned, for the moment all would have been well. But Hood would have been in front of Franklin, with his whole army, artillery, and ammunition-trains, by dawn of day on the 30th; he could have forced the crossing of the Harpeth above Franklin early that day, compelled us to retire to Nashville, and interposed his cavalry between Nashville and Murfreesboro' that night or early on December 1. Thus Thomas's remaining reinforcements from the south and east would have been cut off, and he might have been attacked in Nashville, not later than December 2, with several thousand fewer men than he finally had there, a large part of his army — A. J. Smith's three divisions — not fully ready for battle, and with fewer effective cavalry; while Hood would have had his whole army, fresh and spirited, without the losses and depression caused by its defeat at Franklin, ready to attack an inferior force at Nashville or to cross the Cumberland and invade Kentucky. In short, the day gained at Duck River and Spring Hill was indispensable to Thomas's success. The time gained by that "temerity" made success *possible*. The additional time and relative strength gained by Hood's disastrous repulse at Franklin made final success easy and certain. A retreat at any time before nine o'clock A. M. on the 29th would have led to substantially the same result as if begun at 2 A. M.

If the plan adopted and ordered early in the morning of

November 29 had been carried out, by which the line of Duck River would have been abandoned in the middle of that day, the head of the column from Spring Hill would have arrived at Franklin about midnight, expecting to cross the Harpeth without delay; but, under the conditions actually found to exist at Franklin, not much progress toward providing the means of crossing the Harpeth could have been made before daylight in the morning; therefore our condition for battle at Franklin would not have been materially different, in time or otherwise, from what it actually was. Hood's artillery, as well as his infantry, could have reached Spring Hill before daylight on the 30th, and would have had practically a clear road to Franklin; for the enemy's superior cavalry having been interposed between our cavalry and infantry, it was necessary for our infantry, artillery, and trains to retreat from Spring Hill to Franklin in one compact column. A small force could not have been left at Spring Hill, as had been suggested, to delay Hood's advance, because of the imminent danger that it would be attacked in flank and rear by the enemy's cavalry, and thus cut off and captured; hence Hood could have made his attack at Franklin about noon, instead of at 4:30 P. M., and with a large force of artillery as well as of infantry. Such an attack would, of course, have been far more formidable than that which was actually made; whether it could have been successfully resisted from noon until dark can only be conjectured. It is sufficient here to note that the delay of Hood's advance very greatly diminished the force of his attack at Franklin, besides making his arrival before that place so late that he could not turn that position that day by crossing the Harpeth above. The tenacity with which the crossing of Duck River at Columbia was held was well rewarded at Franklin.

The question has been raised whether we ought not to have held our position in front of Franklin after having repulsed Hood's attack and inflicted such heavy losses upon his troops. General Sherman himself impliedly made this suggestion when he expressed the opinion that Thomas ought to have turned on Hood after his repulse at Franklin; and General Jacob D. Cox, who had been in the thickest of the fight all the time, with high soldierly instinct sent me, by one of my staff officers, the suggestion that we stay there and finish the fight the next day. A fight to a finish, then and there, might quite probably have given us the prize. But the reasons for declining that tempting opportunity for complete victory will, I believe, seem perfectly clear when fully stated.

In anticipation of orders from General Thomas to fall back to Nashville that night, the trains had been ordered to the rear before the battle began, so as to clear the way for the march of our troops, and to render impossible any interference by the enemy's cavalry. Our ammunition had been well-nigh exhausted in the battle at Franklin, as is shown by my telegram to General Thomas to send a million rounds to Brentwood, thinking he might want me to hold Hood there until he could get A. J. Smith's troops in position and supplied with ammunition. If I had needed any such warning, that given me by the general in his despatch,[1] "But you must look out that the enemy does not still persist," would have been sufficient to deter me from fighting him the next day with my "back to the river." Besides, it is not easy to estimate at midnight exactly the results of a desperate battle then just terminated. But all this is insignificant when compared with the controlling reason. I had then fully accomplished the object (and I could not then know how much more) for which the command in the field had for a time been intrusted to me. My junction with reinforcements at Nashville was assured, as also the future

[1] War Records, Vol. XLV, part i, p. 1171.

success of the army under my superior in command. Why run any further risk ? If it had been possible for me, at that moment of supreme satisfaction, to have had any thought of self, I might perhaps have considered the project of turning upon my adversary at dawn the next morning, in the hope of routing his dispirited army. But if any man thinks such a thought possible under such circumstances, he knows nothing about the character of a patriotic soldier. If the troops I then had at Franklin had been the sole reliance for ultimate success in the campaign, nothing could have been clearer than my duty to turn and strike with all my might at dawn the next day.

(A copy of all the correspondence between General Thomas and myself, with annotations showing the time of receipt of the several despatches from General Thomas, thereby showing their influence upon my actions, has been placed on file at the War Department. These copies of despatches, with annotations, are intended mainly for the military student who may care to make a close and critical study of such military operations. The original records of such correspondence are often worse than useless, for the reason that the exact time of sending and receipt of a despatch is so often omitted. All sent or received the same day are frequently printed in the records indiscriminately, so that the last is as likely to come first as otherwise; and, sometimes, historians have used despatches as if they had been received at the time they were sent, though in fact many hours or some days had elapsed. My annotations were made in 1882–3, at Black Point, San Francisco, California, with the assistance of my ever faithful and efficient aide, Colonel William M. Wherry, now lieutenant-colonel of the 2d United States Infantry, and were attached to the copies of the records in 1886.)

CHAPTER XI

I WILL now add to the foregoing sketch what seems
to me necessary to a full understanding of the operations preceding and immediately following the battle
of Franklin, referring briefly, as necessary to an exact understanding of some things that occurred, to the relation
in which I stood to General Thomas. He was my senior
by thirteen years as a graduate of the Military Academy,
where I had known him well as my highly respected
instructor. He had won high distinction in Mexico, and
had been twice brevetted for gallant services in that
war. He had seen far more service in the field than
I had, and in much larger commands, though almost
always under the immediate command of a superior—
Buell, Rosecrans, and Sherman. Even in the Atlanta
campaign, then recently ended, his command was nearly
five times as large as mine. In 1864 he had already become a brigadier-general in the regular army, having
risen to that rank by regular stages, while I was only a
captain thirty-three years of age. It will also be neces-

sary for the reader to realize that when I asked for and received orders to report with the Twenty-third Corps to General Thomas in Tennessee, I felt in the fullest degree all the deference and respect which were due to his seniority in years and rank and services. When I went back to Tennessee my only anxiety respecting the situation, so far as General Thomas's personality affected it, was on account of his constitutional habit of very deliberate action. I was apprehensive that, in some emergency created by the action of the daring and reckless, though not over-talented, antagonist he would have to meet, General Thomas might not be able to determine and act quickly enough to save from defeat his army, then understood to be so far inferior to the enemy in numerical strength. I had far too high an opinion of his capacity as a general to doubt for a moment that with sufficient time in which to mature his plans to resist Hood's invasion and to execute those plans so far as was in his power, he would do all that the wisest generalship could suggest.

I will also refer to the official returns of that period, which show what troops General Thomas had elsewhere in his department and available for service, as well as the effective strength of the force then under my immediate command in the field, and that of General A. J. Smith's three divisions, which had been ordered from Missouri to join the forces of General Thomas. In his entire department, excluding the Fourth and Twenty-third corps in the field, the infantry and artillery force, present for duty equipped, officers and men, November 20, 1864, amounted to 29,322; the two corps in the field, to 24,265; and A. J. Smith's corps, to about 10,000. The entire cavalry force, mounted and equipped, was about 4800; that unmounted, about 6700.

It is necessary to exclude from this statement of troops available for service in middle Tennessee those in Kentucky and East Tennessee, belonging to the Department of the Ohio, for the reason that just at that time unusual demand was made upon those troops for service in East Tennessee, where some of the State forces had met with disaster. This probably accounts in part for the discrepancies in General Sherman's estimates referred to later.

Hood's forces were then understood by General Thomas to consist of from 40,000 to 45,000 infantry and artillery, and 10,000 to 12,000 cavalry, including Forrest's command. I find from General Sherman's despatch to Thomas, dated October 19, that his estimate of Hood's strength, October 19, 1864, was about 40,000 men of all arms.

I do not find in General Thomas's report or despatches any exact statement of his own estimate; but the following language in his official report of January 20, 1865, seems quite sufficiently explicit on that point: " Two divisions of infantry, under Major-General A. J. Smith, were reported on their way to join me from Missouri, which, with several one-year regiments then arriving in the department, and detachments collected from points of minor importance, would swell my command, when concentrated, to an army nearly as large as that of the enemy. Had the enemy delayed his advance a week or ten days longer, I would have been ready to meet him at some point south of Duck River. . . ."

This must of course be accepted as General Thomas's own estimate of the enemy's strength, on which his own action was based. And it should be remembered that military operations must be based upon the information then in possession of the commander, and just criticism must also be based upon his action upon that information, and not upon any afterward obtained.

General Sherman estimated the force left with Thomas[1] at about 45,000 (exclusive of the Fourth and Twenty-

[1] See his "Memoirs," Vol. II, pp. 162, 163.

third corps, and Smith's corps coming from Missouri), in which he included about 8000 or 10,000 new troops at Nashville, and the same number of civil employees of the quartermaster's department. The Fourth and Twenty-third corps he estimated at 27,000 men, and Smith's at 10,000, and the cavalry in the field at 7700. All this was sufficiently accurate if no account were taken of men unfit for duty or not equipped. But the official returns show that the number of officers and men present for duty equipped amounted to 29,322 in the department, and in the two corps in the field to 24,265, and in the cavalry in the field, to 4800. There were therefore the following discrepancies in Sherman's estimate, due in part to the discharge of men whose terms had expired, as well as to the usual number of men not equipped for duty in the ranks: in the troops in the department, a discrepancy of 8000; in the army corps in the field, 2735; in the cavalry in the field, 2900 [1] — a total discrepancy of 13,635. That is to say, Sherman's own estimate was in excess of Thomas's actual strength by a force greater than either of the two army corps he sent back to help Thomas. If he had sent back another large corps,— say the Fourteenth, 13,000 strong, having besides the moral strength due to the fact that it was Thomas's old corps,— the discrepancy in his own estimate would doubtless have been sufficiently overcome, and the line of Duck River at least, if not that of the Tennessee, as Sherman had assured Grant, would have been securely held until A. J. Smith arrived and Thomas could assume the offensive.

Hood's force was ready to invade Tennessee in one

[1] It appears from General Thomas's report that he did have in his department, by November 29, the mounted cavalry force stated by General Sherman — viz., 7700; but only 4800 of that force joined the army in the field before the enemy forced the crossing of Duck River. The remaining 2900 were not available for service in the field until after the crisis of the campaign was passed so far as the cavalry could affect it.

compact army, while Thomas then had in the field ready
to oppose it a decidedly inferior force, even admitting
the lowest estimate made of that hostile army.

The superiority of the enemy's cavalry made it necessary that the garrisons of all essential posts and the
guards of important railroad bridges should be strong
enough to resist attack from a large force of dismounted
cavalry and light artillery, so long as Thomas was compelled to remain on the defensive. The records of that
time indicate that Thomas then appreciated, what mature
consideration now confirms, that if Hood's advance had
induced him (Thomas) to draw off sufficient troops from
garrisons and railroad guards to enable him to give battle on equal terms to Hood at Pulaski or Columbia, a
raid by Hood's cavalry would probably have resulted in
the destruction or capture of nearly everything in the
rear, not only in Tennessee, but also in Kentucky, except perhaps Nashville and Chattanooga. It was only
wise forethought which suggested that such might be
the nature of Hood's plans, especially in view of the
season of the year and the condition of the roads, which
made aggressive operations of a large army, where all the
hard roads were held by the opposing forces, extremely
difficult. The official returns, now published in the War
Records,[1] show that the troops were sufficient only for the
purpose of garrisons and guards and defensive action in
the field until after the arrival of A. J. Smith; and this
is true even if Hood's cavalry force was no larger than
that which now appears from Forrest's report — 5000; for
Forrest might easily have got a day or two the start of
his pursuer at any time, as had often been done on
both sides during the war.

It is true that Sherman's instructions to Thomas appear to have contemplated the possibility, at least, that
Thomas might be reduced to the extreme necessity of

---

[1] See Vol. XLV, parts i and ii.

13

holding Nashville, Chattanooga, and Decatur defensively, even during a long siege, and of abandoning all points of less importance than the three named, so that all the garrisons of such minor points and all the railroad guards might be concentrated with the garrisons of those three important strategic points, for their defense during a siege. This must of course have referred to the defensive period of the campaign only, for the moment that Thomas's reinforcements should enable him to assume the offensive all the necessities above referred to must have disappeared. It must, I think, be admitted as beyond question that, in view of his daily expectation of the arrival of A. J. Smith's troops from Missouri, Thomas was perfectly right in not acting upon Sherman's suggestion of extreme defensive action, and thus abandoning his railroads to destruction.

If, on the other hand, Thomas's reinforcements had arrived in time to enable him to take the initiative by moving against Hood from Pulaski or Columbia, then he might have drawn quite largely from his garrisons in the rear to reinforce his army in the field, since his "active offensive" operations would have fully occupied Hood's cavalry, and thus have prevented a raid in Thomas's rear. But until he was strong enough to advance, unless forced to the extreme necessity of defending Nashville, Chattanooga, and Decatur, and abandoning all else, Thomas could not prudently have reduced his garrisons or guards.

I knew nothing at that time of Sherman's instructions to Thomas, and little about the actual strength of Thomas's garrisons and railroad guards. But I was under the impression that some reinforcements must be available from his own department, and felt a little impatient about the long delay in their arrival, and hence telegraphed General Thomas, November 24, suggesting the concentration of R. S. Granger's troops and those along the railroad. The despatches to me at that time,

to be found in the War Records,[1] fully show the earnest
determination of General Thomas to send forward reinforcements as soon as possible, and even in detail, and
to fight Hood at or near Columbia. Indeed, those despatches misled me somewhat as to what I might expect.

Notwithstanding this earnest desire, General Thomas
does not appear to have realized the existence of a force
available for the purpose he had in view. The railroad
guards from Atlanta to Chattanooga or Dalton, withdrawn after Sherman started on his march, and convalescents, men returning from furlough and others going
to the front, but failing to reach Sherman's army in time,
all assembled at Chattanooga, made a surplus force at
that point of about 7000 men.[2] Some of these troops
had been sent to East Tennessee, as well as all the
mounted troops available in Kentucky, for the purpose
of retrieving the disaster which had befallen the Tennessee military governor's troops there, under Gillem. But
all sent from Chattanooga had been returned by November 21, about the time when Hood's advance from Florence had become certainly known. Yet it does not
appear that General Thomas even inquired what force
was available at Chattanooga until November 25, when,
in reply to a telegram, he learned that Steedman could
raise 5000 men (in fact, 7000), in addition to all necessary
garrisons and guards, "to threaten enemy in rear," in case
he should "get on Chattanooga railroad." It may then
(November 25) have been too late to send those 5000 or
7000 men to the line of Duck River, or perhaps even to
Franklin. They were sent to Nashville, reaching there
after the battle of Franklin. If they had been ordered
to Columbia by rail, via Nashville, as soon as Hood's advance was known to General Thomas, they must have
reached Duck River some time before Hood attempted

[1] See Vols. XXXIX and XLV.
[2] See General Thomas's report: War Records, Vol. XLV, part i, p. 33.

to cross that stream. This addition to the Fourth and Twenty-third corps would have raised the infantry in the field to nearly an equality with that of Hood in fact, though not nearly to˜ what Hood's force was then supposed to be. That increased force would doubtless have made it possible to prevent Hood from crossing Duck River anywhere near Columbia for several days, and perhaps to force him to select some other line of operations, or to content himself with sending his cavalry on another raid. In any case, the arrival of A. J. Smith a few days later would have enabled Thomas to assume the aggressive before Hood could have struck a serious blow at Thomas's army in the field. In view of the earnest desire of General Thomas to reinforce the army in the field at Columbia, there does not appear to be any rational explanation of the fact that he did not send those 7000 men from Chattanooga to Columbia. His own report states the fact about those " 7000 men belonging to his [General Sherman's] column," but does not give any reason why they were not used in his " measures to act on the defensive." As General Thomas says: " These men had been organized into brigades, to be made available at such points as they might be needed." At what other point could they possibly be so much needed as that where the two corps were trying to oppose the advance of the enemy long enough for Thomas to get up his other reinforcements ?

General Thomas appears to have been puzzled by doubt whether Hood would aim for Nashville or some point on the Nashville and Chattanooga Railroad, and not to have realized that his own plan should have been to concentrate all his available active force into one army, so as to move against the enemy with the greatest possible force, no matter what the enemy might do. With the exception of those 7000 men belonging to Sherman's column, Thomas had for necessary garrisons and railroad guards essentially the same number of men as had been employed in that service all the preceding summer,— no more and no less,— and the necessity for that service had not been very much diminished, except at and about Decatur, Stevenson, and Tullahoma, which Hood's advance from Florence had rendered of no further consequence at that time. But the 7000 men available at Chattanooga ought unquestionably to have been sent to Columbia, or at least moved up to Nashville or Franklin, where they could "join the main force," as suggested in my despatch of November 24 to Thomas,[1] instead of being left at Chattanooga "to threaten enemy in rear."[2] As suggested in my despatch of November 24, R. S. Granger's force and others along the railroad south of Duck River, as well as Steedman's, might have joined the main force at Columbia, if orders had been given in time, thus increasing the army in the field by fully 10,000 men.

If R. S. Granger's force had been left at Decatur, it would have drawn off from Hood's invading army at least an equal force to guard his bridges at Florence, or else would have destroyed those bridges and cut off his retreat after the battle of Nashville. This was practically what had been suggested by Sherman in his instructions to Thomas. But the withdrawal of Granger's troops and their detention at Murfreesboro', instead of sending them to "join the main force," served no good purpose at the time, and prevented their use in the capture of Hood's defeated and retreating troops. The failure to make this timely concentration was the one great fault in Thomas's action, instead of his delay in attacking at Nashville, for which he was so much criticized. But Hood's repulse at Franklin had made this previous mistake a matter of past history, and hence it was lost sight

---

[1] War Records, Vol. XLV, part i, p. 1017.
[2] Thomas to Steedman, November 25: War Records, Vol. XLV, part i, p.1050.

of in view of the imminent danger afterward supposed to exist at Nashville, just as the brilliant victory at Nashville was accepted as demonstrating the wisdom of all that had gone before, even including Sherman's division of his army between himself and Thomas before his march to the sea. Such is the logic of contemporaneous military history!

In my long conversations with General Grant on the steamer *Rhode Island* in January, 1865, I explained to him fully the error into which he had been led in respect to Thomas's action or non-action at Nashville in December, and he seemed to be perfectly satisfied on that point. But he did not ask me anything about what had occurred before the battle of Franklin, and hence I did not tell him anything.

In connection with the action of General Thomas previous to the battle of Franklin, the following instructions from General Sherman on October 31 are important: "You must unite all your men into one army, and abandon all minor points, if you expect to defeat Hood General Schofield is marching to-day from here. . . ." [1] Again, on the same date, he telegraphed: "Bear in mind my instructions as to concentration, and not let Hood catch you in detail." [2]

Sherman thus gave the most emphatic warning against the mistake which Thomas nevertheless made by failing to concentrate all his own available troops until it was too late to meet Hood's advance, thus leaving two corps to bear the entire brunt of battle until the crisis of the campaign was passed at Franklin.

The following correspondence relating to the command of the army in the field, to increasing the Fourth and Twenty-third corps, and to the use to be made of R. S. Granger's troops, and the reason why Thomas should assume the offensive as soon as possible, is also important,

[1] War Records, Vol. XXXIX, part iii, p. 535.   [2] *Ibid.*, p. 536.

especially as showing that Sherman expected the two corps to be increased to 50,000 men, and that Thomas should command in person:

KINGSTON, November 7, 1864, 10 A. M.

MAJOR-GENERAL THOMAS: Despatch of 12:30 P. M. yesterday received. General Schofield is entitled to the command [over Stanley] by virtue of a recent decision of the War Department. I would advise you to add to those corps new regiments until they number 25,000 men each. If Beauregard advances from Corinth, it will be better for you to command in person. Your presence alone will give confidence. Granger should continue all the time to threaten the rear, and as soon as possible some demonstration should be made from the direction of Vicksburg against the Mobile and Ohio Railroad. Also I want you to assume the offensive as quick as possible, as I have reason to believe all of Beauregard's army is not there, but that he has also divided his forces.

W. T. SHERMAN, Major-General.[1]

On the same day Thomas telegraphed to Sherman in reply to the above:

It is, and always has been, my intention to command the troops with me in person. My object in giving the preference to General Schofield [over Stanley] was merely that he should exercise command should accidental circumstances prevent my presence.[2]

Sherman and Thomas were equally right — Sherman in saying, " It will be better for you to command in person. Your presence alone will give confidence"; and Thomas in replying, " It is, and always has been, my intention to command the troops with me in person." The proper place for a general-in-chief is with his army in the field, where battles are to be fought, and not in the rear, where there is little to do but to assemble reinforcements, which his chief of staff could do as well as he. Thomas could have reached the army at Columbia by rail in two

[1] War Records, Vol. XXXIX, part iii, p. 685.   [2] Ibid.

hours, and at Franklin in one hour; yet he left a subordinate to fight against a superior force, while he remained in Nashville until he had collected there an army superior to that of his adversary. But General Thomas must have had some reason which seemed to him good and sufficient for his absence from the field. He was the last man in the world to shrink from his duty in battle.

Before the above correspondence between General Sherman and General Thomas was known to me I had written the following: "The relations existing between General Thomas and me, and the confidence he had shown in all his despatches, commencing with those received at Pulaski, left little room for hesitation or doubt about doing, in every emergency, what my own judgment dictated, as if I had been in chief command, confident of the approval which he so fully expressed after the events. Yet my experience then, as always, led me to the opinion that it is better for the general-in-chief, in all operations of a critical nature, to be present with the troops in the field, if possible; he must be able to act with more confidence than any subordinate can possibly feel. He was the sole judge as to the necessity of his remaining in Nashville, and no good reason could now be given for questioning the correctness of his judgment. It is only intended as an expression of a general rule for the consideration of military students."

General Thomas's orders to General D. S. Stanley upon his being sent to Pulaski, and his subsequent orders to me, dated November 19, to fight the enemy at Pulaski if he advanced against that place, were, as shown in the following despatch from me, quite inapplicable to the then existing situation:

PULASKI, November 20, 1864.

MAJOR-GENERAL THOMAS: After full consideration I am of the opinion that this is not the best position for the main body of our troops, at least so long as we are inferior in strength to the enemy. If Hood advances, whether his design be to strike this place or Columbia, he must move via Lawrenceburg on account of the difficulty of crossing Shoal Creek. Under cover of his cavalry, he can probably reach Lawrenceburg without our knowledge, and move his forces a day's march from that point toward Columbia before we could learn his designs, and thus reach that point ahead of us; or he might move upon this place, and while demonstrating against it throw his forces on to the pike north of us, and thus cut us off from Columbia and from our reinforcements. Lynnville would be free from these objections as a point of concentration for our forces. On the other hand, a force at this point covers the Nashville and Chattanooga Railroad to the best advantage; but a brigade in the inclosed works at this place could hold out against any force until relieved, while the main force at Lynnville would be sure of concentrating with the troops still in rear. I respectfully submit these views for your consideration.

J. M. SCHOFIELD, Major-General.

To this General Thomas replied at once:

NASHVILLE, November 20, 1864.

GENERAL SCHOFIELD: Your despatch of 2 P. M. this day just received. Two other despatches of to-day were received previous to this one. Do you mean that one brigade in the intrenchments at Pulaski could hold out for a week? The reason I ask is, General Smith cannot get here before next Friday. If one brigade can hold the fortifications of Pulaski for a week or ten days, you are authorized to leave a brigade or a division there, and concentrate the rest of your force at Lynnville preparatory to support Hatch, or fall back on Columbia, whichever may be necessary. Part of Ruger's troops will start for Columbia to-night, the remainder at two o'clock to-morrow, and the railroad superintendent says he will have them at Columbia by to-morrow night. The very moment Smith's troops arrive I will start them for Columbia. In any event, all surplus transportation should be sent to Columbia. I have just received General Hatch's of this P. M., and it seems from it that Hood is advancing. His movements will indicate to you what disposition you should make — whether to concentrate at Columbia or remain at Lynnville. If Hood's entire army should advance, you must use your own discretion as to holding the fortifications at Pulaski or withdrawing the troops.

GEO. H. THOMAS, Major-General.

General Thomas thus gave me the full freedom of action demanded by the situation in which I was placed, in lieu of his previous embarrassing orders about fighting the enemy at Pulaski.

The following correspondence,[1] with the above, shows the situation as reported by me to General Thomas, and his " plans and wishes" as then explained to me immediately before and after Hood began his advance:

THOMAS TO SCHOFIELD.

November 24, 1864.

. . . Have the fords above Columbia as well guarded as you can, and I think you will then have checked the advance of Hood, and we shall have time to get up our reinforcements.

SCHOFIELD TO THOMAS.

November 24, 1864, 1:39 P. M.

Do you think it important to hold Columbia? My force is not large enough to cover the town and railroad bridge. I can hold a shorter line covering the railroad bridge, leaving the town and railroad depot outside; but in any case the enemy can turn the position by crossing above or below, and render my withdrawal to the north bank very difficult. Please give me your views soon.

THOMAS TO SCHOFIELD.

November 24, 1864.

If you cannot hold Columbia, you had better withdraw to the north bank of the river. From the description given I supposed the line was sufficiently short to enable you and Stanley to hold it securely and have a reserve. But it is better, of course, to substantially check the enemy than to run the risk of defeat by risking too much. Where is Stanley? Is he with you?

[1] War Records, Vol. XLV, part i.

SCHOFIELD TO THOMAS.

COLUMBIA, November 24, 1864, 8:30 P. M.

I have examined the ground and considered the situation carefully. My troops are in position on the outer line, covering the railroad depot and bridge, and pretty well intrenched. The line is too long; yet if Hood wishes to fight me on it to-morrow, I am willing. I think he will attack to-morrow, if at all. If he does not, I must prepare to meet any attempt to cross Duck River above or below. For this purpose I am preparing an interior line covering the railroad bridge, which can be held by about seven thousand men, which I propose to occupy, and put the rest of my troops and material on the north bank of the river, ready to move as may be necessary. With the fords guarded, as will then be practicable, I think Hood cannot get the start of me. I think it best not to risk much now; for a few days' delay, if we concentrate rapidly, will make us strong enough to drive Hood back. My theory is that he will operate against the Chattanooga Railroad, and I do not see how we can save it from some damage at least. But if we concentrate Granger's troops and those along the road promptly, so that they can join the main force, there can be no doubt of the final result. Please inform me whether my proposed arrangements meet with your approval.

THOMAS TO SCHOFIELD.

NASHVILLE, November 24, 1864.

. . . Can you not cover the pontoon bridge with a bridge-head, and hold it so as to preserve the bridge for crossing whenever we get ready to advance? General Rousseau informed me that the blockhouses protecting the railroad bridge cannot be reached by the enemy's artillery; therefore the enemy could not get near enough to the bridge to destroy it if the blockhouses are held. . . .

As stated in my official report, I did prepare and hold a bridge-head covering both the railroad and the pontoon bridges over Duck River at the same time, for which purpose I floated the pontoons down the river to a point near the railroad bridge, having found that the blockhouses referred to by General Rousseau could not be made available for the protection of the pontoon bridge where it before was — at the crossing of the turnpike. I abandoned that bridge-head on the night of November 27, upon receipt of information leading me to believe that Hood intended to cross Duck River above Columbia.

On November 25 General Thomas telegraphed me, in the following terms, his approval of the dispositions I had made, and the information that he had already ordered the concentration of troops which I suggested in my despatch of the 24th:

Your cipher despatch of 8:30 P. M. is just received; some difficulty in transmission the cause. Your arrangements are judicious and approved. I gave orders two days ago to make the concentration you suggest, and hope it will be nearly or quite completed to-day. Will telegraph you further this morning.

This despatch was more than twelve hours in transmission.

Again, November 26, I reported the situation at Columbia, and my action, as follows; also suggesting that infantry be sent forward at once:

The enemy has kept up a strong demonstration with dismounted cavalry since yesterday morning. He now shows a column of infantry on the Mount Pleasant pike, about three miles distant. I cannot yet tell how great the force. I have drawn my force in the interior line, and will fight him there. If you have any infantry available, I think it should be sent forward at once.

Yet no infantry reinforcements were sent, although the "7000 men" at Chattanooga could easily have reached Columbia before that time.

At 8 A. M. the next day General Thomas replied as follows:

Your despatch of 10 A. M. yesterday received. I will send you all the available infantry force I can raise. I expect some of Smith's command here to-day, and will send it forward as rapidly as possible. Sent you two regiments of cavalry day before yesterday, two yesterday, and will send another to-day. If you can hold Hood in check until I can get Smith up, we can whip him.

Thus it appears that even as late as November 27 General Thomas had not thought of sending the 7000 men at Chattanooga to "join the main force," although so anxious that I should hold Hood in check until he could get Smith up. He was still relying entirely upon A. J. Smith, whose advance, so surely expected on the 25th, was still expected on the 27th. It seems incredible that General Thomas had not thought of sending Steedman's troops from Chattanooga, instead of waiting for the uncertain arrival of A. J. Smith.

On November 27 I received an important despatch from General Thomas, dated November 25. It was written under the apprehension that Hood's design might be to move upon the Nashville and Chattanooga Railroad, as I had suggested to Thomas on the 24th, and informed me fully of his plans and instructions to meet such a movement, requesting me to give him my views in reply. In that despatch General Thomas said:

In case you have to move to the north bank of Duck River, I wish you to keep some cavalry on the south side to observe and delay Hood's advance on the Chattanooga Railroad as much as possible. I hope to have five regiments of Granger's troops in Murfreesboro' to-day. Have made arrangements for Milroy to fall back to Murfreesboro' or this side of Duck River also, if the enemy advances. The cavalry on the south side of Duck River should cover the approaches to Shelbyville, and cross at that place, and hold the bridge in case of an advance in force. I have asked General Steedman how large a force he can raise to threaten the enemy's rear, should he get on the Chattanooga road, and expect an answer soon. About 1000 of Hatch's cavalry have arrived here from Memphis, dismounted, but they will be mounted here as soon as possible and sent to the front; three regiments should start to-day, making about 1000 men. I have not heard from any of Smith's troops yet; some of them will surely be here to-day. If Hood moves on the Chattanooga road, I will send Smith to Murfreesboro', as we shall be enabled thereby to concentrate more rapidly. If you can hold Hood on the south side of Duck River, I think we shall be able to drive him back easily after concentrating. Answer, giving your views.

Although that despatch of the 25th was not deciphered so as to be read by me until the 27th, forty-eight hours after it was sent, nevertheless it gave me timely information that Thomas had concentrated all his available troops (except Steedman's, which he appears to have overlooked until the 25th, and about which I had no knowledge) at Murfreesboro', from which place they could "join the main force," as I had suggested, in a few hours, either by rail or by wagon-road, as circumstances might indicate. I was also led to infer from Thomas's language on the 25th — "Some of them [A. J. Smith's troops] will surely be here to-day" — that on the 27th Smith's corps was already at Nashville, and that Thomas was only waiting for information respecting the enemy's designs to select his point of concentration and order all his available troops to join the army in the field at that point. And it was still expected on the 27th that this junction might be effected on the north bank of Duck River, opposite Columbia. Hence I telegraphed General Thomas, November 27, at 12:30 p. m.:

The enemy has made no real attack, and I am satisfied he does not intend to attack. My information, though not very satisfactory, leads me to believe that Hood intends to cross Duck River above Columbia, and as near it as he can. I shall withdraw to the north bank to-night and endeavor to prevent him from crossing. Wilson is operating mainly on my left, with a portion of his command south of the river. I have no late information from him. I have succeeded in getting your cipher of the 25th translated. I believe your dispositions are wise.

It appears from his despatch of November 25 that Thomas hoped we might be able to hold the line of Duck River from Columbia as far east as Shelbyville, as well as west to the Tennessee River. Although this proved to be impracticable on account of the enemy's superiority in cavalry at that time, the point (Murfreesboro') which Thomas had selected for his concentration was far enough in the rear of that line (Duck River) to make the concentration certain if orders were given in due time.

I learned in the afternoon of November 27, by General Thomas's despatch of 8 A. M., already quoted, that A. J. Smith's troops were not, as I had supposed, already in Nashville, but that some of them were expected there that day, and would come forward to join me at once.

In the morning of November 28, at 8:45, I reported my withdrawal to the north side of the river, saying:

My troops and material are all on the north side of Duck River. The withdrawal was completed at daylight this morning without serious difficulty. Cox holds the ford in front of Columbia, and Ruger the railroad bridge, which I partially destroyed. Stanley is going into position a short distance in rear of Cox. I think I can now stop Hood's advance by any line near this, and meet in time any distant movement to turn my position. I regret extremely the necessity of withdrawing from Columbia, but believe it was absolute. I will explain fully in time. Reinforcements will have to march from Spring Hill or Thompson's Station. Supplies should be sent to Thompson's Station.

After withdrawing to the north bank of Duck River I telegraphed on the morning of November 28:

I am in doubt whether it is advisable, with reference to future operations, to hold this position or to retire to some point from which we can move offensively. Of course we cannot recross the river here. I could easily have held the bridge-head at the railroad, but it would have been useless, as we could not possibly advance from that point. Please give me your views and wishes.

This was answered by General Thomas at "8 P. M.," the answer being received by me next morning, November 29.

It is thus seen that up to the morning of November 28 I was still hoping for reinforcements on the line of Duck River, and thought I could stop Hood's advance by any line near the Columbia and Franklin pike, which I then held, as well as meet in good time any distant movement to turn my position. Accordingly, at 9:10 A. M. that day I telegraphed General Thomas:

I have all the fords above and below this place well watched and guarded as far as possible. Wilson is operating with his main force on my left. The enemy does not appear to have moved in that direction yet to any considerable distance. I will probably be able to give you pretty full information this evening. Do you not think the infantry at the distant crossings below here should now be withdrawn and cavalry substituted? I do not think we can prevent the crossing of even the enemy's cavalry, because the places are so numerous. I think the best we can do is to hold the crossings near us and watch the distant ones.

But I learned soon after noon of the same day that our cavalry found the fords so numerous that they could hardly watch them all, much less guard any of them securely; and a little later I learned that the enemy's cavalry had forced a crossing at some point only a few miles above, between Huey's Mill and the Lewisburg-Franklin pike. At 2:30 P. M. I telegraphed General Thomas:

The enemy was crossing in force a short distance this side of the Lewisburg pike at noon to-day, and had driven our cavalry back across the river on the pike at the same time. The force is reported to be infantry, but I do not regard it as being probable. Wilson has gone with his main force to learn the facts, and drive the enemy back, if practicable.

In the appendix to General Thomas's report the date of the above despatch is given as "3:30 A. M." It was answered by General Thomas at "10:30 P. M." and his answer was received by me November 29 (no hour mentioned in the records). The Department of the Ohio records say that I sent it at "2:30 P. M." The appendix to my report mentions the date "November 29," but does not give the hour. My official report, as published, also says this information was received "about 2 A. M. on the 29th"; but this is evidently a clerical error: clearly the report should read, "about 2 P. M. on the 28th."

But our cavalry was unable to drive that of the enemy back, and hence Hood was free to lay his pontoon bridge and cross his infantry and artillery at any point above Columbia. We had not been able to hold even the crossings near us.

The same day, November 28, at 4 P. M., I telegraphed:

If Hood advances on the Lewisburg and Franklin pike, where do you propose to fight him? I have all the force that is necessary here, and General Smith's troops should be placed with reference to the proposed point of concentration.

And again, at 6 P. M.:

The enemy's cavalry in force has crossed the river on the Lewisburg pike, and is now in possession of Rally Hill.

Wilson is trying to get on to the Franklin road ahead of them. He thinks the enemy may swing around in between him and me, and strike Spring Hill, and wants Hammond's brigade to halt there. Please give it orders if you know where it is. Also, I think it would be well to send A. J. Smith's force to that place.

14

In the night of November 28-9, about 2 A. M., I received the report of the cavalry commander, conveying the information given him by prisoners that the enemy had commenced to bridge the river near Huey's Mill, and urging the necessity of immediate retreat to Franklin.[1] The staff officer who handed me the despatch called my attention especially to the words urging immediate action, and I considered the subject quite a long time. But there did not seem to me to be any necessity for such haste. The enemy could not accomplish much before morning. It would then be early enough to decide what must be done. Besides, it was not yet certain that Hood was attempting to cross his infantry at Huey's Mill. The vigorous action of his cavalry might be intended only to induce me to fall back, and thus give him the use of the crossing at Columbia, and of the turnpike from that place, for the movement of his infantry, artillery, and trains.

In the morning, November 29, I sent a brigade of infantry toward Huey's Mill to reconnoiter and report the enemy's movements. At the same time Stanley was ordered to Spring Hill, with two divisions of his corps, to occupy and intrench a good position commanding the roads at that place and protecting the trains and reserve artillery which had been ordered to be parked there. Ruger's division of the Twenty-third Corps, except one regiment, was ordered to follow Stanley. The army was ready to occupy Spring Hill in full force, and in ample time to meet any possible movement of the enemy either on that place or, by the Lewisburg pike, on Franklin.

In my orders to Ruger, dated 8 A. M., directing him to move at once to Spring Hill, he was ordered to leave one regiment to guard the river until dark and then join him at Spring Hill. It was then intended, in any event, to hold Spring Hill until the morning of November 30.

[1] War Records, Vol. XLV, part i, p. 1143.

At the same time Ruger was directed to order his troops guarding the river below to march at once for Franklin. But very soon after those orders were issued—that is, soon after 8 A. M.—a courier from Franklin brought me the two following despatches from General Thomas:

FRANKLIN, November 28, 1864.
(By telegraph from Nashville. 9 P. M.)

To MAJOR-GENERAL SCHOFIELD:

If you are confident you can hold your present position, I wish you to do so until I can get General Smith here. After his arrival we can withdraw gradually and invite Hood across Duck River, and fall upon him with our whole force, or wait until Wilson can organize his entire cavalry force, and then withdraw from your present position. Should Hood then cross river, we can surely ruin him. You may have fords at Centreville, Bean's [Beard's] Ferry, Gordon's Ferry, and Williamsport thoroughly obstructed by filling up all the roads leading from them with trees, and then replace your infantry by cavalry. Send an intelligent staff officer to see that the work is properly done. As soon as relieved, concentrate your infantry; the cavalry will be able to retard, if not prevent, Hood's crossing, after the roads are thoroughly obstructed, if they do their duty. The road leading from Centreville to Nashville should be thoroughly obstructed. I am not sure but it would be a good plan to invite Hood across Duck River if we can get him to move toward Clarksville. Is there no convenience for unloading beyond Thompson's Station?

GEO. H. THOMAS, Major-General, Commanding.[1]

The published records give this despatch as having been sent at "8 P. M." The Department of the Cumberland records say that it was telegraphed in cipher to Franklin at 9 P. M., and there deciphered and sent by courier to my position near Columbia. The records do not show the hour of receipt by me; but my reply to General Thomas of 8:30 A. M., November 29, and my orders to Ruger of 8 and 8:45 A. M., and to Stanley be-

---

[1] War Records, Vol. XLV, part i, p. 1108.

fore and after 8 A. M., and my despatch to Wilson of 8:15
A. M., fix the time of the receipt by me of this despatch
from General Thomas at a few minutes after 8 A. M.,
November 29.

The other despatch was as follows:

(U. S. Military Telegraph.)

FRANKLIN, TENN., November 28, 1864.

(By telegraph from Nashville. 9:30 P. M.)

To MAJOR-GENERAL SCHOFIELD:
  Your despatch of 3:30 [2:30] P. M. just received. If Wilson
cannot succeed in driving back the enemy, should it prove true
that he has crossed the river, you will necessarily have to make
preparation to take up a new position at Franklin, behind Harpeth, [while] immediately, if it become necessary to fall back.

(Signed) GEO. H. THOMAS, Major-General, Commanding.

The records of the Department of the Cumberland
merely state that this despatch was sent in " cipher."
The appendix to my report gives the hour "9:30 P. M."
The appendix to General Thomas's report fixes it at "10:30
P. M." The despatch from General Thomas to General Halleck of 10 P. M., November 28, forwarding my despatch
of " 8:45 A. M.," indicates that at 10 P. M. Thomas had not
received my report of " 2:30 P. M." Hence " 10:30 P. M.,"
as given by General Thomas, must be the correct hour
of the above despatch. It was answered by me, together
with the preceding telegram, at 8:30 A. M., November 29;
and was probably received by me at the same time as
the previous despatch,— very soon after 8 A. M.,— as indicated by my despatch to Wilson of 8:15 A. M.

I thus learned, a short time after eight o'clock on the
morning of the 29th, that A. J. Smith had not yet arrived at Nashville, and that the position behind the Harpeth River at Franklin was that to which I must retire
when compelled to fall back.

(Another despatch from Thomas, dated November 28, 10 A. M., appears in the records, in which he said: "... General Smith will certainly be here in three days. ..." But when that despatch reached my headquarters in the field, the cipher-operator had left his post and gone to Franklin. Hence the despatch could not be read by me in time to be of any service. The records do not show when I received it.)

I was then confronted with the grave question, How long might it be possible to hold Hood back, and thus gain time for Thomas to get up his reinforcements? By holding on to the crossing of Duck River at Columbia until dark that night, and thus preventing Hood from using the turnpike for the movement of his artillery and trains until the next day, we would practically gain twenty-four hours; for he could not move them readily over his mud road from Huey's Mill. To do this, I must not only head Hood off at Spring Hill, but defeat any attempt he might make to dislodge me from the north bank of Duck River.

Early on November 29, I sent the following brief despatch in reply to both of those which had been received a few minutes before from General Thomas:

The enemy's cavalry has crossed in force on the Lewisburg pike, and General Wilson reports the infantry crossing above Huey's Mill, about five miles from this place. I have sent an infantry reconnoissance to learn the facts. If it proves true, I will act according to your instructions received this morning. Please send orders to General Cooper,[1] via Johnsonville. It may be doubtful whether my messenger from here will reach him.

The appendix to General Thomas's report says that I sent this despatch at "8:30 A. M." The appendix to my report says "8:20 A. M." This despatch was evidently in

[1] Cooper commanded the brigade guarding the river below Columbia.

answer to those from General Thomas of 8 P. M. and 10:30 P. M., November 28, as indicated by my orders to Stanley and Ruger, and my despatch of 8:15 A. M. to Wilson. Soon after 10 A. M., November 29, the first report from the brigade sent toward Huey's Mill showed that the enemy's infantry was crossing the river at that place. That report is not found in the records, and I do not recollect its words. But it did not produce the impression upon my mind that Hood's movement was so rapid or energetic as to prevent me from doing what seemed of such vital importance. Therefore I decided not to yield my position unless compelled by force to do so. While considering this question I had detained one of Stanley's two divisions (Kimball's), and had suspended the orders for Ruger's division to march to Spring Hill. When the decision was reached, I put Kimball's and Wood's divisions in position between Duck River and Rutherford's Creek, and Ruger's north of that creek, to resist any attempt the enemy might make upon our position. I then sent the following to Stanley at Spring Hill:

NEAR COLUMBIA, TENN., November 29, 1864, 10:45 A. M.

MAJOR-GENERAL STANLEY, Commanding Fourth Army Corps.

GENERAL: General Wood's reconnoissance shows a considerable force, at least, on this side of the river. I have halted Kimball's division this side of the creek and put it in position. I will try to hold the enemy until dark, and then draw back. Select a good position at Spring Hill, covering the approaches, and send out parties to reconnoiter on all roads leading east and southeast. Try to communicate with Wilson on the Lewisburg pike. Tell him to cover Franklin and Spring Hill, and try not to let the enemy get between us.

Very respectfully,

J. M. SCHOFIELD, Major-General.

The situation early in the morning had been a very simple one, free from any embarrassment or unusual danger. If the plan then decided on and ordered had been carried out, three divisions of infantry and nearly all the artillery of the army would have been in position at Spring Hill and well intrenched long before the head of Hood's infantry column, without any artillery, came in sight of that place late in the afternoon. That position would have been secured beyond doubt until the next morning. The other two divisions (Cox's and Wood's) would have withdrawn from Duck River and marched to Spring Hill early in the afternoon, before the enemy could seriously interfere with them. Ruger's one regiment, without impedimenta, was directed to march along the railway track to Spring Hill, and thus avoid any interference from the enemy. The army would have marched to Franklin early in the night of the 29th, instead of after midnight as it actually did. That would have given the enemy the afternoon and night in which to lay his pontoons and cross his artillery and trains at Columbia. But that would not have been a serious matter, in view of the situation as it was understood by me up to about 8 A. M. of the 29th; for the information I had received up to that hour justified the belief that both A. J. Smith's troops and those concentrated at Murfreesboro' would meet me at Franklin, or perhaps at Spring Hill, where we would be able to give battle to the enemy on equal terms.

But in view of the information received by me after eight o'clock that morning, and the altered plan decided on soon after ten o'clock, the situation became very materially different. Under this plan the army must be ready to encounter a formidable enemy either in the position then occupied on Duck River, or at some point on the road between that place and Spring Hill. Hence I determined to keep the main body of the troops together, and trust to Stanley's one division to hold Spring Hill until the army should reach that point. That is to say, I decided to take the chances of a pitched battle at any point the enemy might select between Duck River and Spring Hill, as well as that of holding the latter place with one division against any hostile force which might reach it before dark.

There was no anxiety in my mind about what might happen at Spring Hill after dark. The danger which actually developed there between dark and midnight —of which I knew nothing until several days afterward — resulted entirely from faulty execution of my orders.

I arrived at Spring Hill at dusk with the head of the main column, having ordered all the troops to follow in close order, and (except Ruger's troops, which I took to Thompson's) to form line on the right of Stanley's division at Spring Hill, covering the pike back toward Columbia. Cox's division, being the last, was to form our extreme right. In that contemplated position, if Hood had attacked at any time in the night we would have had decidedly the advantage of him. I had no anxiety on that point. When informed, about midnight, that Cox had arrived, I understood that my orders had been exactly executed, and then ordered Cox to take the lead and the other divisions to follow, from the right by the rear, in the march to Franklin.

But it happened that only Whitaker's brigade of Kimball's division, to which I gave the orders in person, followed Ruger's. Hence that one brigade was the only force we had in line between Hood's bivouac and the turnpike that night. If that fact had been known to the enemy, the result would have been embarrassing, but not very serious. If the enemy had got possession of a point on the pike, the column from Duck River would have taken the country road a short distance to the west of Spring Hill and Thompson's Station, and marched on to Franklin. The situation at Spring Hill in the night was not by any means a desperate one. Veteran troops are not so easily cut off in an open country.

The annotation upon the copy filed in the War Department of the order actually given to the troops on November 29 explains how that mistake occurred. In brief, the draft of an order prepared in writing for another purpose, but not issued, was by some unexplained blunder substituted for the oral orders actually dictated to a staff officer. It was an example of how the improvised staff of a volunteer army, like the "non-military agencies of government," may interfere with military operations.

The serious danger at Spring Hill ended at dark. The gallant action of Stanley and his one division at that place in the afternoon of November 29 cannot be over-estimated or too highly praised. If the enemy had gained a position there in the afternoon which we could not have passed round in the night, the situation would then have become very serious. But, as I had calculated, the enemy did not have time to do that before dark, against Stanley's stubborn resistance.

The following, from the official records, has been quoted as an order from General Thomas to me, though I never received it, the enemy's cavalry having got possession of the road between Franklin and Spring Hill:

NASHVILLE, November 29, 1864, 3:30 A. M.

MAJOR-GENERAL SCHOFIELD, near Columbia:

Your despatches of 6 P. M. and 9 P. M. yesterday are received. I have directed General Hammond to halt his command at Spring Hill and report to you for orders, if he cannot communicate with General Wilson, and also instructing him to keep you well advised of the enemy's movements. I desire you to fall back from Columbia and take up your position at Franklin, leaving a sufficient force at Spring Hill to contest the enemy's progress until you are securely posted at Franklin. The troops at the fords below Williamsport, etc., will be withdrawn and take up a position behind Franklin. General A. J. Smith's command has not yet reached Nashville; as soon as he arrives I will make immediate disposition of his troops and notify you of the same. Please send me a report as to how matters stand upon your receipt of this.

GEO. H. THOMAS,
Major-General U. S. Vols., Commanding.[1]

This despatch does not appear upon any of the records as having been received by me. If it was telegraphed in cipher to Franklin, and there deciphered and sent by courier, the same time being occupied as with other such despatches, this should have reached me not long after noon. But the courier was probably driven back or captured by the enemy's cavalry, who had possession of the direct road, near Spring Hill, about noon.

If any "orders" had been necessary in such a case, they had been rendered unnecessary by Hood's movement to cross Duck River, of which I had already learned at 2 A. M. the same day (November 29). The only question in my mind that General Thomas could solve — namely, to *what place* I must retire — was settled by his despatch of 10:30 P. M., November 28, above quoted, received by me about 8 A. M. of the 29th. But there still remained the question *when* I must do it; and that I must solve myself, for General Thomas was much too far away, and communication was much too slow and uncertain, for him to give me any help on that subject.

I had received information of Hood's movement at 2 A. M., *six hours earlier*, and I had had ample time to get out of his way before morning. After 8 A. M. it would, of course, not have been so easy. Yet a retreat to Franklin that day (November 29), commencing at eight or nine in the morning, and across the Harpeth that night, would not have been at all difficult or dangerous. There would have been some fighting with Hood's cavalry, but little or none with his infantry. Hood would

1 War Records, Vol. XLV, part i, p. 1137.

have had to lay a pontoon bridge at Columbia, after my rear-guard had withdrawn, before his advance from that point could begin; and, as events proved, he could not reach Spring Hill by his mud road from Huey's Mill until late in the afternoon. I had time to pass Spring Hill with my entire army before Hood's infantry advance-guard could reach that place. Hence I had ample time to consider the mathematical and physical questions involved before deciding finally that I would not let Hood drive me back from Duck River that day. But I did not at any time contemplate a retreat that day farther back than Spring Hill, as is shown by my direction to Ruger to have his regiment from Ducktown join him there that night.

I am entirely willing to leave to intelligent military criticism any question in respect to the accuracy of my calculations, also the question whether I was justifiable, under the conditions then existing or understood to exist respecting Thomas's preparations in the rear to fight a decisive battle, in taking the risks, which are always more or less unavoidable, of failure in the execution of plans based upon so close an estimate of what could be done by my adversary as well as by myself. I content myself with the simple remark that, in my opinion, if my own orders had been carried out as I gave them, and my reasonable suggestion to my superior in the rear to bridge the Harpeth at Franklin had been promptly acted on, there would have been far less risk of failure than must frequently be incurred in war.

If I had had satisfactory assurance of the timely arrival of sufficient reinforcements on the line of Duck River, I would have been justified in dividing my infantry into several detachments to support the cavalry in opposing the crossing of Duck River at the numerous places above Columbia. But, sooner or later, Hood could have forced a crossing at some one of those places, and thus have interposed a compact body of troops, larger than my entire army, between my detachments. If that had occurred before my reinforcements arrived, I would have been caught in the worst possible condition. Hence, in the absence of certain information in respect to when reinforcements would arrive, and their aggregate strength, a division of my force was inadmissible. An inferior force should generally be kept in one compact body, while a superior force may often be divided to great advantage.

I now direct attention to the correspondence between General Thomas and myself, on November 30, before the battle of Franklin, showing that he was not ready for battle at Nashville, and his desire that I should, if possible, hold Hood back three days longer; and showing that my estimate of the importance of time when I was at Columbia was by no means exaggerated; also showing General Thomas's views and mine of the military situation before the battle, and the action then determined on and ordered and partially executed by the movement of trains toward Nashville before the battle opened. The results of the battle were not such, even if they had been fully known at the time, as to have rendered admissible any change in those orders.

NASHVILLE, [November] 30, [1864,] 4 A. M.

CAPTAIN W. J. TWINING, Franklin:

Your despatch of 1 A. M. to-day is received. Please inform General Schofield that Major-General Smith's troops have just arrived at the levee and are still on boats, and that it is impossible for them to reach Franklin to-day. He must make strong efforts to cover his wagon-train, protecting it against the enemy, as well as to reach Franklin with his command and get into position there. I will despatch him further in a few hours.

GEO. H. THOMAS.

The next despatch from General Thomas was at 10:25 A. M. By that time he had received two more despatches

from me, as follows, I having arrived at Franklin between
4 and 5 A. M.:

FRANKLIN, November 30, 1864, 5 A. M.

Have just seen your despatch to Captain Twining of 4 A. M.
If Smith is not needed for the immediate defense of Nashville, I
think he had better march for Franklin at once. He could at
least cover my wagon-train if I have to fall back from here.

FRANKLIN, November 30, 1864, 5:30 A. M.

I hope to get my troops and material safely across the Harpeth this morning. We have suffered no material loss so far.
I shall try and get Wilson on my flank this morning. Forrest
was all around us yesterday, but we brushed him away in the
evening and came through. Hood attacked in the front and
flank, but did not hurt us.

This last despatch was written before daylight, on my
arrival at Franklin, before I learned that there were no
bridges across the river. If pontoons had been laid or
the wagon and railroad bridges improved on the 29th, as
was done by me after my arrival, all could have crossed
by noon of the 30th.

General Thomas's reply of 10:25 A. M. was as follows:

Your despatches of 5:30 and 5:50, and Wilson's despatches,
forwarded to you, have been received. It will take Smith quite
all day to disembark; but if I find there is no immediate necessity to retain him here, will send him to Franklin or Brentwood,
according to circumstances. If you can prevent Hood from
turning your position at Franklin, it should be held; but I do
not wish you to risk too much. I send you a map of the en-
virons of Franklin.

Again I telegraphed at 9:50 A. M.:

My trains are coming in all right, and half of the troops are
here and the other half about five miles out, coming on in good
order, with light skirmishing. I will have all across the river

this evening. Wilson is here, and has his cavalry on my flank. I do not know where Forrest is. He may have gone east, but, no doubt, will strike our flank and rear again soon. Wilson is entirely unable to cope with him. Of course I cannot prevent Hood from crossing the Harpeth whenever he may attempt it. Do you desire me to hold on here until compelled to fall back ?

And at 11 A. M. I telegraphed: "Troops and trains in all right."

At noon I answered as follows General Thomas's last despatch :

Your despatch of 10:25 A. M. is received. I am satisfied that I have heretofore run too much risk in trying to hold Hood in check while so far inferior to him in both infantry and cavalry. The slightest mistake on my part, or failure of a subordinate, during the last three days might have proved disastrous. I don't want to get into so tight a place again; yet I will cheerfully act in accordance with your views of expediency, if you think it important to hold Hood back as long as possible. When you get all your troops together, and the cavalry in effective condition, we can easily whip Hood, and, I believe, make the campaign a decisive one. Before that, the most we can do is to husband our strength and increase it as much as possible. I fear the troops which were stationed on the river below Columbia will be lost. I will get my trains out of the way as soon as possible, and watch Hood carefully. Possibly I may be able to hold him here, but do not expect to be able to do so long.

This despatch shows not only my opinion at that time of the kind of "place" I had been in, but my belief that the character of that situation had been due largely to Thomas's action in leaving me without the expected reinforcements, and in not providing the means of crossing the Harpeth River.

The following seems to show that General Thomas did not even then see the importance of prompt concentration of all his available force in front of the enemy, but expected me, with two corps, to fight the entire hostile force until he could complete his concentration at Nashville. Even before the battle of Franklin he seems to have thought he could take his time to concentrate, reorganize his cavalry, and then "try Hood again."

NASHVILLE, November 30, 1864.

MAJOR-GENERAL SCHOFIELD, Franklin :

General Smith reported to me this morning that one division of his troops is still behind; we must therefore try to hold Hood where he now is until those troops can get up, and the steamers return. After that we will concentrate here, reorganize our cavalry, and try Hood again. Do you think you can hold Hood at Franklin for three days longer? Answer, giving your views; and I should like to know what Wilson thinks he can do to aid you in holding Hood.

GEO. H. THOMAS,
Major-General U. S. Vols., Commanding.

Thereupon, in the following telegram, dated 3 P. M., I proposed Brentwood as a point where A. J. Smith's and all the other troops could surely unite with mine :

I have just received your despatch asking whether I can hold Hood here three days. I do not believe I can. I can doubtless hold him one day, but will hazard something in doing that. He now has a large force, probably two corps, in my front, and seems preparing to cross the river above and below. I think he can effect a crossing to-morrow in spite of all my efforts, and probably to-night, if he attempts it. A worse position than this for an inferior force could hardly be found. I will refer your question to General Wilson this evening. I think he can do very little. I have no doubt Forrest will be in my rear to-morrow, or doing some greater mischief. It appears to me that I ought to take position at Brentwood at once. If A. J. Smith's division and the Murfreesboro' garrison join me there, I ought to be able to hold Hood in check for some time. I have just learned that the enemy's cavalry is already crossing three miles above. I will have lively times with my trains again.

This despatch gives a very accurate estimate of the true situation at that time, except perhaps that I did not then fully appreciate how much our cavalry had gained in effective strength by the reinforcements that had joined the corps in the field during the retreat. I judged by the experience of the previous day (November 29). But the result was very different in the afternoon of the 30th, when our cavalry repulsed and drove back that of the enemy; at the same time the infantry assault was repulsed at Franklin. There was no apprehension of the result of an attack in front at Franklin, but of a move of Hood to cross the river above and strike for Nashville before I could effect a junction with the troops then at that place.

The following despatches must have been sent either during the progress of the battle, or very soon afterward:

Please send A. J. Smith's division to Brentwood early to-morrow morning. Also please send to Brentwood to-morrow morning 1,000,000 rounds infantry ammunition, 2000 rounds 3-inch, and 1000 rounds light twelve artillery.

In reply to my advice, the following order to fall back to Nashville was sent by Thomas *before* the battle, but was received by me *after* the heavy fighting had ceased. Communication was interrupted for a short time during the transfer of the telegraph station from the town of Franklin to a place on the north side of the Harpeth, rendered necessary by the battle.

NASHVILLE, November 30, 1864.

Your despatch of 3 P. M. is received. Send back your trains to this place at once, and hold your troops in readiness to march to Brentwood, and thence to this place, as soon as your trains are fairly on the way, so disposing your force as to cover the wagon-train. Have all railroad trains sent back immediately. Notify General Wilson of my instructions. He will govern himself accordingly. Relieve all garrisons in blockhouses and send back by railroad trains last over the road. Acknowledge receipt.

GEO. H. THOMAS, Major-General.

The following is my first report to General Thomas, sent immediately after the battle:

The enemy made a heavy and persistent attack with about two corps, commencing at 4 P. M. and lasting until after dark. He was repulsed at all points with very heavy loss — probably five or six thousand men. Our losses probably not more than one fourth that number.[1] We have captured about one thousand men, including one brigadier-general. Your despatch of this P. M. is received. I had already given the orders you direct, and am now executing them.

Before the battle, and in anticipation of the order from General Thomas, the trains had been sent back and the preparations made for the army to retire to Brentwood, the troops to commence withdrawing from the line on the south side of the river immediately after dark. In consequence of the battle, the movement of the troops was suspended until midnight. General Thomas promptly replied to my first report in these words:

Your telegram is just received. It is glorious news, and I congratulate you and the brave men of your command; but you must look out that the enemy does not still persist. The courier you sent to General Cooper, at Widow Dean's, could not reach there, and reports that he was chased by rebel cavalry on the whole route, and finally came into this place. Major-General Steedman, with five thousand men, should be here in the morning. When he arrives I will start General A. J. Smith's command and General Steedman's troops to your assistance at Brentwood.

[1] At that time I did not know of our loss in prisoners, having thought nearly all of Wagner's two brigades had come in with those I had seen running to the rear.

15

CHAPTER XII

EARLY the next morning (December 1), after receiving
at Brentwood oral orders from General Thomas to
continue the retreat to Nashville, I lay on the ground until
the main body of the troops had passed and I had learned
from the cavalry and from the infantry rear-guard that
nothing could occur in the rear which would require my
attention. I then rode forward and reported to General
Thomas, whom I found waiting for me at the place he
had selected for the Twenty-third Corps in the defensive
line about Nashville. He greeted me in his usual cordial
but undemonstrative way, congratulated me, and said I
had done " well." I have often thought that I may not
have shown due appreciation of his kindness at that moment, for I did not then feel very grateful to him; but
he gave no indication that he thought me unapprecia-
tive of his approbation. On the contrary, he said in the
kindest manner that I appeared " tired." To which I
replied, " Yes, I am very tired." That was about all the
conversation we had that day.

As soon as I saw that my troops were moving into the

position he had indicated to the division commanders before my arrival, I rode to the hotel in Nashville, went to bed, and slept from about noon of the 1st, without awaking to full consciousness, until about sunset the next day. I only hope my weary soldiers enjoyed their rest as much as I did mine, for they must have needed it even more. When I awoke after that thoroughly refreshing sleep the annoyance I had felt on account of the embarrassments experienced during the retreat was replaced by reflections of a much more satisfactory character. From that time forward my relations with General Thomas were of the same cordial character as they always had been; and I was much gratified by the flattering indorsement he placed on my official report, of which I then knew the substance, if not the exact words.

The Fourth Army Corps and the cavalry corps of the Military Division of the Mississippi having been under my command during only the few days occupied in the operations between Pulaski and Nashville (November 14 to December 1), no reports of the operations of those two corps were ever made to me after the close of that brief period. Hence it was not possible for me to give any full account of the distinguished services of those two corps. The cavalry were never seen by me. They were far in front or on the flank, doing all the "seeing" for me, giving me information of vital importance in respect to the enemy's movements. How important that information was then regarded may be learned by a perusal of the despatches to and from General Thomas during those days of anxious uncertainty as to the enemy's plans. I believe no cavalry ever performed that important service more efficiently. At no time in that short campaign did I suffer any inconvenience from lack of information that cavalry could possibly give. If it is true that the operations of our cavalry were to some extent influenced by apprehension of a cavalry raid on Nashville or other vital

point in our rear, that was only what General Thomas
had been apprehending all the time, and to meet which
he had assembled eight thousand troops in Nashville,
perhaps not informing the commander of his own cavalry of that fact quite as early as he might have done.[1]

In fact, the redoubtable Forrest had become famous,
and his troopers were esteemed a very large factor in the
problem then undergoing solution—greater in some respects, as I have pointed out, than the events justified. In
my report of the battle of Franklin I gave all the information in my possession of the gallant action of our cavalry in driving that of the enemy back across the Harpeth
at the very time when his infantry assault was decisively
repulsed.

I have always regarded it as a very remarkable, and to
me a very fortunate, circumstance that the movements
of my infantry columns were at no time seriously interfered with by the enemy's more numerous cavalry — not
even at Spring Hill, where Stanley was attacked by cavalry as well as infantry. Hence I have had no inclination
to make any investigation respecting the details of the
action of troops, only temporarily under my command,
whose gallant conduct and untiring vigilance contributed
all that was needed to the complete success of the military
operations intrusted to my immediate direction by our
common superior, the department commander. I have
now, as always heretofore, only words of highest praise
for the services of the cavalry corps under my command.

The Fourth Corps was under my own eye nearly all the
time; and sometimes, in emergencies, I even gave orders
directly to the subordinate commanders, without the formality of sending them through the corps commander.
Hence I have spoken of that corps with the same freedom
as of my own Twenty-third; and I hope I have not failed

[1] See Thomas's despatch of 8 P. M., November 29, to Colonel H. C. Wharton,
Wilson's staff officer: War Records, Vol. XLV, part i, p. 1146.

to give, so far as the very restricted scope of my account would permit, full justice to that noble corps of veteran soldiers, as well as to its officers. As I have had special occasion to say of the action of Opdycke's brigade and of the 12th and 16th Kentucky of the Twenty-third Corps at Franklin, the conduct of those troops was beyond all praise.

I believe little disputes always arise out of the honorable rivalry which exists between bodies of troops acting together in a great battle. Franklin was no exception to that general rule. For the purpose of "pouring oil on the troubled waters" after Franklin, I said that in my opinion there was glory enough won in that battle to satisfy the reasonable ambition of everybody who was on the field, and of some who were not there, but who were at first given "the lion's share"; but if the disputants were not satisfied with that, they might take whatever share of credit was supposed to be due to me, and divide it among themselves. I was then, as I am now, perfectly satisfied with the sense of triumph which filled my soul when I saw my heroic comrades hurl back the hosts of rebellion with slaughter which to some might seem dreadful, but which I rejoiced in as being necessary to end that fratricidal war. It is not worth while to conceal the fact that most earnest patriotism sometimes arouses in the soldier's breast what might seem to be a fiendish desire to witness the slaughter of his country's enemies. Only a soldier of fortune or a hireling can be a stranger to such feelings. Yet I aver that I had not the slightest feeling of personal enmity toward my old friend and classmate General Hood, or his comrades. It was the "accursed politicians" who had led them into such a fratricidal strife who were the objects of our maledictions. But even that feeling has been softened by time, and by reflection upon the deeper and more remote causes of the war, and that the glorious fruits of final victory have amply repaid, and will continue to repay in all time, for all those immense sacrifices and sufferings.

Hood undoubtedly made a mistake in his plan of operations after he crossed Duck River above Columbia on the night of November 28–9. His march on Spring Hill would have been the best *if it had succeeded.* But he failed to estimate accurately what he could accomplish in a short winter day over a very bad road. In a long day of summer, with that road in the usual summer condition, he might have reached Spring Hill early in the afternoon, with force enough to accomplish his purpose before night, if he had found a single division, or even two divisions, there. But he failed simply because he tried to do what was not possible.

When Hood crossed the river he was not more than five miles (his own journal says three) from the left flank of my position on the north bank. The intervening space was open fields, not much, if any, more difficult for the march of infantry than the dirt road he actually used. If he had moved directly upon my flank, he could have brought on a general engagement about noon, with a force at least equal to mine. In anticipation of such a movement, I sent a brigade toward Huey's Mill to watch Hood's movements, and formed line of battle facing in that direction and covering the turnpike to Spring Hill, for which purpose I detained one of the two divisions of Stanley's corps which, at first, had been ordered to Spring Hill. I was willing to fight Hood in that position, and expected to do so. But I felt relieved when I found he had undertaken the much more difficult task of marching to Spring Hill, where I believed sufficient preparations had been made to oppose him until I could reach that place by a broad macadamized road over which I could march rapidly by day or by night.

I now believe my judgment at that time was correct: that what I had most to apprehend was not an attempt to get in my rear at Spring Hill, but one to dislodge me from my position on Duck River by defeating me in open battle. But I believed I could fight Hood, even where I was, from noon until dark, and then retreat to Spring Hill or Franklin in the night. At least I was willing to try it rather than disappoint the expectation of General Thomas that I would hold Hood in check until he could concentrate his reinforcements. It seems to me clear that Hood's best chance at Duck River was to force a general engagement as early in the day as possible, so as to occupy the attention of all my infantry while his superior cavalry was sent to occupy some point in my rear, and try to cut off my retreat in the night. Perhaps Hood did not appreciate the very great advantage a retreating army has in the exclusive use of the best roads at night, especially when the nights are long and the days correspondingly short — an advantage which cannot be overcome by any superiority of numbers in the pursuing force, except by a rapid circuitous march of a detachment.

As illustrating my accurate knowledge of Hood's character before we ever met in battle, the following incident seems worthy of mention. When Sherman's army, after crossing the Chattahoochee River, was advancing on Atlanta,—my troops being in the center,—General Sherman was on the main road, a little in rear of me. My advance-guard sent back to me an Atlanta paper containing an account of the visit of President Davis, and the order relieving General Johnston and assigning General Hood to the command of the army. General Sherman erroneously says one of General Thomas's staff officers brought him that paper. General Thomas was then off to the right, on another road. I stopped until Sherman came up, and handed him the paper. After reading it he said, in nearly, if not exactly, the following words: " Schofield, do you know Hood? What sort of a fellow is he?" I answered: "Yes, I know him well, and I will tell you the sort of man he is. He 'll hit you like h—l, now, before you know it." Soon afterward, as well described by Sherman, the sound of battle to our right gave indication of the heavy attack Hood's troops made upon Thomas's advancing columns that day, which failed of serious results, as I believe all now admit, mainly if not entirely because Thomas himself was near the head of the column which received the first blow. Soon after, a still more heavy attack was made on the Army of the Tennessee, our extreme left, which resulted in one of the severest and most closely contested battles of the war, and in which the knightly McPherson was killed.

Under the system enforced by the War Department in 1864–5, the commanders of troops in the field were compelled to communicate with each other either in plain language which the enemy could read if a despatch fell into his hands, or else in a cipher which neither of the commanders nor any of their staff officers could decipher. They were made absolutely dependent upon the cipher-operators of the telegraph corps. Of course all this cipher correspondence between commanding generals was promptly transmitted to the War Department, so that the Secretary could know what was going on as well as anybody. Whatever may have been the object of this, perhaps not difficult to conjecture, its effect was to make rapid correspondence in cipher impossible when rapidity was most important and secrecy most necessary. In previous years I and one at least of my staff officers were always familiar with the cipher code, so that we could together, as a rule, quickly unravel a knotty telegram. Indeed, I once had to decipher a despatch to which I had no key, except that I knew from internal evidence that it must be under the War Department code, though written in a different key. It was a despatch from Grant, who was then besieging Vicksburg. It had been sent to

Memphis by steamer, and thence by telegraph to St. Louis, the place from which Grant's army drew its supplies. A cipher despatch sent under the circumstances from Grant to me, who was not at that time under his command, must necessarily be of great importance. My staff officer at once informed me that it was in some key different from that we had in use. So I took the thing in hand myself, and went to work by the simplest possible process, but one sure to lead to the correct result in time—that is, to make all possible arrangements of the words until one was found that would convey a rational meaning. Commencing about 3 P. M., I reached the desired result at three in the morning. Early that day a steamer was on the way down the river with the supplies Grant wanted. I never told the general how he came to get his supplies so promptly, but I imagined I knew why he had telegraphed to me rather than to the quartermaster whose duty it was to furnish supplies for his army—and a most capable and efficient quartermaster he was. I had only a short time before voluntarily sent General Grant 5000 men, and I inferred that there was some connection between the incidents.

The immense change in the whole military situation which was produced in a few minutes at Franklin (for the contest there was in fact decided in that time, by the recovery of the breach in the line), and that by a battle which had not been contemplated by either General Thomas or myself (that is, on the south side of the Harpeth River, with that stream in the rear of the army), nor yet by General Hood until he saw the apparent opportunity to destroy his adversary; and the fact that that dangerous situation had been produced and the battle rendered necessary by slight accidents or mistakes which might easily have been foreseen or avoided, cannot, it seems to me, but produce in every thoughtful mind some reflection upon the influence exercised by what is called "accident" or "chance" in war. The "fortune of war" was, upon the whole, always in my favor, in spite of adverse accidents; yet I have always acted upon the principle that the highest duty of a commander is to anticipate and provide for every possible contingency of war, so as to eliminate what is called chance.

Both Johnston and Hood refer in their narratives to the earnest desire of their commander-in-chief, President Davis, that the army they in succession commanded should undertake an aggressive campaign. Johnston demonstrated that, under the circumstances existing while he was in command, such an undertaking could not possibly have been successful. Hood tried it under far more favorable circumstances, and yet he failed, as had every former like attempt of the Confederate armies. The result in every case was costly failure, and in the last overwhelming defeat. How much greater would have been the military strength of the South if those losses had been avoided, and how much greater would have been her moral strength if she had maintained from the start a firm, consistent, and humane defensive policy! How long would the conservative people of the North have sustained the "invasion" of States where the people were fighting only to "defend their homes and families"? Did not the South throw away a great moral advantage when it waged aggressive war upon the North? No doubt it was necessary at first, from the secession point of view, to "fire the Southern heart" by attacking Fort Sumter. And, also from that point of view, that attack was fully justifiable because that fort was in "Confederate" territory. The invasions of Maryland and Pennsylvania were far different, and much more so were the relentless guerrilla war waged in the border States, attended with horrible massacres like that of Lawrence, Kansas, which, though no one charges them to the government or generals of the South, were unavoidable incidents of that species of warfare; and the inhuman cruelties incidentally suffered by Union prisoners.

It is true that the slavery question was a very powerful factor in our Civil War, and became more and more so as the war progressed. But opinion on that question at the North was very far from unanimous at the first, and it is a fair and important question how far the growth of sentiment in the free States in favor of emancipation was due to the slaveholders' method of carrying on war.

My desire here is to refer to these questions solely from the military point of view, and for the consideration of military students. The conditions upon which depends success or failure in war are so many,— some of them being more or less obscure,— that careful study of all such conditions is demanded of those who aspire to become military leaders.

CHAPTER XIII

GRANT ORDERS THOMAS TO ATTACK HOOD OR RELINQUISH THE
COMMAND — THOMAS'S CORPS COMMANDERS SUPPORT HIM
IN DELAY — GRANT'S INTENTIONS IN SENDING LOGAN TO
RELIEVE THOMAS — CHANGE OF PLAN BEFORE THE BATTLE
OF NASHVILLE — THE FIGHTING OF DECEMBER 15 — EX-
PECTATION THAT HOOD WOULD RETREAT — DELAY IN RE-
NEWING THE ATTACK ON THE 16TH — HOPELESSNESS OF
HOOD'S POSITION — LETTERS TO GRANT AND SHERMAN —
TRANSFERRED TO THE EAST — FINANCIAL BURDEN OF THE
WAR — THOMAS'S ATTITUDE TOWARD THE WAR.

THE perilous character of the situation in Tennessee, in which it was left by Sherman's premature start for the sea and Thomas's tardy concentration of troops, wholly disappeared with the repulse of Hood at Franklin. There was no further obstacle to the concentration of Thomas's forces at Nashville, the organization and equipment of his army, and the necessary preparations to assume the offensive. Hood's army was too much shattered and crippled to make any serious movement for some days, during which it was easy for Thomas to prepare for battle all his troops except the cavalry, of which latter, however, it required a longer time to complete the remount. Indeed, Thomas could have given battle the second or third day after Franklin with more than a fair prospect of success.

Considering the feeling of nervous anxiety which prevailed in Washington and throughout the country at the time, possibly he ought to have assumed the offensive on the 2d or 3d of December. But that state of anxiety was at first unknown at Nashville, even to General Thomas, and was never fully appreciated or understood. No one at Nashville, so far as I am aware, shared that feeling. We knew, or thought we knew, that Hood could do nothing, unless it were to retreat, before we would be prepared to meet him, and that every day's delay strengthened us far more than it possibly could him. His operations, which were closely watched every day, indicated no intention to retreat; hence all at Nashville awaited with confidence the period of complete preparation which was to give us decisive victory.

The anxiety felt elsewhere, especially by General Grant, was probably due to some doubt of the wisdom of Sherman's plan of going off with his main army before disposing of Hood, contrary to Grant's first advice; to the discovery of Sherman's error in supposing he had left Thomas in complete condition to cope with Hood; to some misapprehension as to the degree in which the situation in Tennessee had been changed by the battle of Franklin; as well as to lack of confidence in General Thomas on account of his well-known deliberation of thought and action.

Little was known of this state of anxiety by me, or, I believe, by the corps commanders, until December 9, when General Thomas, calling us together at his headquarters, informed us that he was ordered to attack Hood at once or surrender his command (not saying to whom), and asked our advice as to what he ought to do. One of the officers present asked General Thomas to show us the order, which he declined to do. This confirmed the belief which I had at first formed that the successor named by General Grant could be no other than myself—a belief formed from the fact that I was, next to General Thomas, the highest officer in rank on the ground where immediate action was demanded, and from my knowledge of

General Grant's confidence, which belief has since been fully justified by the record. This, as I conceived, imposed upon me the duty of responding at once to General Thomas's request for advice, without waiting for the junior members of the council, according to the usual military custom. Hence I immediately replied: "General Thomas, I will sustain you in your determination not to fight until you are fully ready." All the other commanders then promptly expressed their concurrence.

I do not know whether or not my declaration of purpose to sustain General Thomas was made known to General Grant, or to any one in Washington, either then or afterward. I have never made any inquiry on that subject. Of course such information must have been conveyed confidentially and indirectly, if at all, and hence would probably not appear in the official records, though despatches and letters marked "confidential" are sometimes published as official. I have only conjectured that some knowledge of my opinion and decision may, perhaps, have influenced General Grant's final determination to go to Nashville himself. If some officer must go there to fight a battle, Grant could get there about as soon as any other he could well select. The records now published seem to verify the belief then (December 9, 1864) existing in my mind, that I had only to withhold my support from General Thomas in his determination to delay, and the chief command would have fallen to my fortune, where I believed brilliant victory was as nearly certain as anything in war can be. But I never had the remotest idea of superseding General Thomas. As I explained to General Sherman, I volunteered to go back to Tennessee, not to supersede Thomas, but to help him. I knew him and his subordinates well, as I did also the antagonist, my West Point classmate, whom they would have to meet. I appreciated Thomas's high qualities, his distinguished services, and, above all, the profound affection and confidence of his troops—an element of strength in a commander far greater than is generally understood, even by military men, some of whom appear to be altogether ignorant of its value as a factor in war. A doubt of our complete success under his leadership, after our troops were united, never entered my mind, much less a desire to diminish or dim the laurels he might win.

General Grant's great anxiety on account of the situation at Nashville was manifested for several days by urgent despatches to General Thomas to attack at once without waiting for further preparations; then by an order to Thomas to turn over the chief command to me, Thomas to become subordinate, which order was suspended; and finally by starting for Nashville himself to direct operations in person. In the meantime he ordered General John A. Logan to go to Nashville to relieve Thomas in command of the Army of the Cumberland, without thought, as he has said, of the question whether Logan or myself should command the combined armies of the Cumberland and of the Ohio. Grant had reached Washington from City Point, and Logan had gone as far as Louisville, when the report of Thomas's victory of December 15 made it unnecessary for either of them to proceed farther. The following letters from Grant to Logan are interesting as explaining the reasons and motives of his action in sending Logan to Nashville, as well as his estimate of the services I had rendered in the preceding operations:

NEW YORK, February 14, 1884.

HON. JOHN A. LOGAN, U. S. Senate, Washington, D. C.

DEAR SIR: In reply to your letter of the 11th, I have to say that my response must be from memory entirely, having no data at hand to refer to; but in regard to the order for you to go to Louisville and Nashville for the purpose of relieving General Thomas, I never thought of the question of who should command the combined armies of the Cumberland and the Ohio. I was simply dissatisfied with the slowness of General Thomas moving, and sent you out with orders to relieve him. No doubt if the order had been carried out, the question would immediately have arisen as to who was entitled to the combined command, provided General Schofield was senior in rank to you, which I do not know that he was. I know that his confirmation as a major-general took place long after yours, but I do not know the date of his commission. The question, in that case, of the command of the whole would have been settled in a very few hours by the use of the telegraph between Nashville and Washington. I was in Washington when you arrived at Louisville and telegraphed me that General Thomas had moved, and, as I remember the telegram, expressing gratification that he had done so. I was then on my way to Nashville myself, and remained over a day in Washington, hoping that Thomas might still move. Of course I was gratified when I learned that he had moved, because it was a very delicate and unpleasant matter to remove a man of General Thomas's character and standing before the country; but still I had urged him so long to move that I had come to think it a duty. Of course in sending you to relieve General Thomas, I meant no reflection whatever upon General Schofield, who was commanding the Army of the Ohio, because I thought that he had done very excellent service in punishing the entire force under Hood a few days before, some twenty-five miles south of Nashville. Very truly yours,

U. S. GRANT

(*per* FRANK F. WOOD).

NEW YORK, February 23, 1884.

GEN. JOHN A. LOGAN, U. S. Senate, Washington, D. C.

DEAR GENERAL: Since I have been confined to my room I have conducted all my correspondence through a secretary, who is a stenographer, and he takes my dictation to the office and writes the letters out there as dictated, and by my direction signs my name. I intended that the letter which I wrote to you should be brought back to me for my own signature, and I sign this myself to show my entire responsibility for the one which you have just received, and which I hope was satisfactory to you.

Very truly yours,

U. S. GRANT.

The passion and prejudice begotten in the minds of Thomas's soldiers and their friends by injustice, real or fancied, done or proposed to be done to him by his superiors in rank, have rendered impossible any calm discussion of questions touching his military career. There is not yet, and probably will not be in our lifetime, a proper audience for such discussion. But posterity will award justice to all if their deeds have been such as to save their names from oblivion.

Time works legitimate " revenge," and makes all things even. When I was a boy at West Point I was court-martialed for tolerating some youthful "deviltry" of my classmates, in which I took no part myself, and was sentenced to be dismissed. Thomas, then already a veteran soldier, was a member of the court, and he and one other were the only ones of the' thirteen members who declined to recommend that the sentence be remitted. This I learned in 1868, when I was Secretary of War. Only twelve years later I was able to repay this then unknown stern denial of clemency to a youth by saving the veteran soldier's army from disaster, and himself from the humiliation of dismissal from command on the eve of victory. Five years later still, I had the satisfaction, by intercession with the President, of saving the same veteran general from assignment to an inferior command, and of giving him the military division to which my assignment had been ordered. When death had finally relieved him from duty, and not till then, did I consent to be his successor. In 1879 I had the satisfaction, after many months of patient investigation, of rendering justice to the other of those two unrelenting soldiers who,

16

of all the thirteen, could not find it in their hearts to recommend clemency to an erring youth: I was president of the board which reversed the judgment of the court-martial in the case of Fitz-John Porter.

I believe it must now be fully known to all who are qualified to judge and have had by personal association or by study of history full opportunities to learn the truth, that General Thomas did not possess in a high degree the activity of mind necessary to foresee and provide for all the exigencies of military operations, nor the mathematical talent required to estimate "the relations of time, space, motion, and force" involved in great problems of war. His well-known high qualities in other respects obscured these imperfections from the great majority of those who surrounded him during the war, and rendered the few educated soldiers who were able to understand his true merits the more anxious to aid him and save him from personal defeat. And no one, I am sure, of his comrades in arms desires to detract from the great fame which is justly his due; for, according to the best judgment of mankind, moral qualities, more than intellectual, are the foundation of a great and enduring fame. It was "Old Pap" Thomas, not General Thomas, who was beloved by the Army of the Cumberland; and it is the honest, conscientious patriot, the firm, unflinching old soldier, not the general, whose name will be most respected in history.

Of the general details of the battle of Nashville I do not propose to speak, but simply to notice a few of its most important points. The plan of battle, as published, placed my command — the Twenty-third Corps — in the left center of our line, where only a feint was to be made. The Fourth Corps was to carry a salient advanced line, while the main attack was to be made on the enemy's extreme left by A. J. Smith's corps and the cavalry. After the order was prepared I went to General Thomas with a map of the position showing the exact length of the several parts of the enemy's line, and explained to him that the force he had assigned to our left wing was at least 10,000 men more than could be used to any advantage unless for a real attack; and that, on the other hand, Smith's force was not large enough for the real attack, considering the extent of the ground occupied by the enemy on that flank. Hence I suggested that my corps should support Smith instead of remaining on the left of Wood. To this suggestion General Thomas readily acceded, and orally authorized me to carry it into effect, but made no change in his written order. The result of this change of plan was that the close of the first day's engagement found the Twenty-third Corps on the extreme right of our infantry line, in the most advanced position captured from the enemy. Yet General Thomas, in his official report, made no mention of this change of plan, but said "the original plan of battle, with but few alterations, [was] strictly adhered to."[1] The "alterations" were certainly "few." A change from 10,000 to 20,000 infantry in the main attacking force may not properly be described as *many* "alterations," but it looks like one very *large* one — sufficient, one would suppose, to determine the difference between failure and success.

The plan of battle issued December 14 had been matured and made known to the principal subordinate commanders several days before, when General Thomas intended to attack, but was prevented by the storm Hence there had been ample time for critical consideration and discussion of the details of that plan, the result of which was the modification made at the conference in the afternoon or evening of December 14, which modification was not embodied in the written order, but was orally directed to be carried out. If General Thomas had caused that clerical work to be done in the evening of December

[1] War Records, Vol. XLV, part i, p. 39.

14, his published orders and his battle of December 15 would have been in complete harmony. There would not, so far as I know, have been even a "few alterations." In this connection, the difference between the "Special Field Order No. 342," of December 14, as recorded in General Thomas's order-book, and the copy embodied in his official report, as explained in a foot-note in the War Records, is not unimportant.[1] In the order-book he says: "Major-General Schofield *will mass* the remainder of his force in front of the works and coöperate with General Wood, protecting the latter's left flank against an attack by the enemy"; but in his report the words "*will move with*" are substituted for "will mass." The latter, in military parlance, meant placing my corps in reserve, with a view to "coöperate with General Wood," etc., whenever such coöperation might be necessary; while the words used in Thomas's final report meant active coöperation with General Wood from the beginning of the engagement. In the body of his report General Thomas spoke of the position of the Twenty-third Corps as "in reserve," from which position it was ordered to the right to join A. J. Smith's troops in the attack. Hence it would seem that a position "in reserve" was what General Thomas had in mind both when he prepared his order of battle and when he wrote his report, and that the change to the words "will move with" was simply a clerical error.

After darkness had ended the first day's battle (December 15), I received an order in writing from General Thomas, which was in substance to *pursue the retreating enemy* early the next morning, my corps to take the advance on the Granny White pike, and was informed that the cavalry had been or would be ordered to start at the same time by a road to the right, and cross the Harpeth below Franklin. These orders seemed to be so utterly inapplicable to the actual situation that I

[1] See Vol. XLV, part i, p. 37.

rode to the rear to where General Thomas's headquarters were supposed to be, and there found that he had gone back to his house in Nashville, to which place I followed him. He appeared surprised at my suggestion that we would find Hood in line of battle ready to receive us in the morning, or even ready to strike our exposed right flank before we could renew the attack, instead of in full retreat, as he had assumed. I told him I knew Hood much better than he did, and I was sure he would not retreat. Finally, after considerable discussion I obtained a modification of the order so far as to direct the cavalry to remain where it was until Hood's action should be known, and an order for some of A. J. Smith's troops to support the right if necessary. But no orders whatever were given, to my knowledge, looking to a battle the next day — at least none for my troops or the cavalry.

The next morning revealed the enemy in his new position, his left remaining where it was the night before, in my immediate front, but the rest of his line far back from the ground on which the other portions of Thomas's army had passed the night. Some time was of course required for the other corps to come up and get in contact with the enemy, and the whole forenoon was passed by me in impatient anxiety and fruitless efforts to get from General Thomas some orders or authority that would enable us all to act together—that is, the cavalry and the two infantry corps on the right. At length the cavalry, without orders from General Thomas, had worked well round on the enemy's left so as to threaten his rear; I had ordered Cox, commanding my right division, to advance his right in conjunction with the movement of the cavalry, and at the proper time to attack the left of the enemy's intrenchments covering the Granny White pike, and that movement had commenced; while, having been informed by General Darius

N. Couch, commanding my left division, that one of Smith's divisions was about to assault, I had ordered Couch to support that division, which movement had also commenced. Then General Thomas arrived near our right, where I stood watching these movements. This, about four o'clock P. M., was the first time I had seen or heard from General Thomas during that day. He gave no order, nor was there time to give any. The troops were already in motion, and we had hardly exchanged the usual salutations when shouts to our left announced that McArthur's division of Smith's corps had already carried the enemy's work in its front, and our whole line advanced and swept all before it.

In my judgment, General Thomas gave a little less than full credit to McArthur's division, and considerably more than full justice to the other troops, in his description of that assault, which was distinctly seen by him and by me.

The resistance along the whole left and center of Hood's line cannot be said to have been strong or obstinate. Our total losses were comparatively insignificant; and whatever may have been the appearance to the troops under fire, to a cool observer out of the smoke the enemy's fire seemed no more than that of an ordinary skirmish. But with the exception of the comparatively feeble resistance of the enemy, that splendid assault of McArthur's division, as I saw it, was very accurately described by its gallant commander in his official report, and also in that of General A. J. Smith.

The fact is that Hood's left wing had been much weakened to strengthen his right, which had been heavily pressed a short time before, as fully described by General Thomas, and his army was already substantially beaten. Its spirit seemed to be gone. What little fight was left in it after November 30 had been greatly diminished on December 15. Hood, almost alone of that army, was not whipped until the 16th. He, the responsible leader of a desperate cause, could not yield as long as there was a ray of hope. Under any ordinary circumstances a commander even of the most moderate capacity must have admitted his campaign a failure the morning after Franklin. It would be absurd to compare the fighting of Hood's troops at Nashville, especially on the second day, with the magnificent assaults at Atlanta and Franklin. My own appreciation of the result was expressed in the following despatch:

HEADQUARTERS, ARMY OF THE OHIO,
December 16, 1864, 7:45 P. M.

MAJOR-GENERAL GEORGE H. THOMAS,
Commanding Department of the Cumberland.

GENERAL: I have the honor to report four pieces of artillery and a considerable number of prisoners captured by General Cox's division this afternoon. General Cox also reported four other pieces and caissons captured in the valley between the hill carried by General McArthur and that taken by General Cox. I learned, however, upon inquiry, that General McArthur's troops claimed, and I have no doubt justly, the honor of capturing the last four. My provost-marshal reports seventy-four prisoners captured this P. M. I have conversed with some of the officers captured, and am satisfied Hood's army is more thoroughly beaten than any troops I have ever seen.

I congratulate you most heartily upon the result of the two days' operations. My messenger will wait for any orders you may have to send me. Very respectfully, your obedient servant,

J. M. SCHOFIELD, Major-General.

It now appears to be fully established by the records that Hood's infantry force in the battle of Nashville was very far inferior to that of Thomas, and he had sent a large part of his cavalry, with some infantry, away to Murfreesboro'. This disparity must have been perfectly well known to Hood, though not to Thomas. Hence it would seem that Hood must have known that it was utterly impossible for his army to resist the assaults which he must expect on December 16. Since all this has become known, it is impossible not to see now that the comparatively feeble resistance offered by the Confederate troops at Nashville was due not so much, perhaps, to any lack of valor on the part of those troops, as to their comparatively small numbers. I recall distinctly the conversation I had with a Confederate field-officer a few minutes after he was captured that day, and which I reported to General Thomas that evening. In answer to my question as to when the Confederate troops recognized the fact that they were beaten, he answered, "Not till you routed us just now." I did not believe him then, for I thought they must have recognized their defeat at Franklin, or at least on the 15th, at Nashville. But now I think he probably told me the exact truth. I doubt if any soldiers in the world ever needed so much cumulative evidence to convince them that they were beaten. "Brave boys were they!" If they had been fighting in a cause that commanded the sympathy and support of the public conscience of the world, they could never have been beaten; it is not necessary to search for any other cause of the failure of the Confederate States.

The most notable feature, on our side, of the battle of December 16 was the wasting of nearly the entire day, so that operations ended with the successful assault at dark. What was left of Hood's army had time to retreat across the Harpeth during the night and destroy the bridges before the pursuit could be commenced.

But the results of the two days' operations at Nashville were too gratifying to admit of contemporaneous criticism. The battle has been generally accepted as a perfect exemplification of the art of war. It is certainly a good subject for the study of military students, and it is partly for their benefit that I have pointed out some of its prominent defects as I understand them. Its com-

mendable features are sufficiently evident; but in studying the actions that have resulted in victory, we are apt
to overlook the errors without which the victory might
have been far more complete, or even to mistake those
errors for real causes of success.

The pursuit from Nashville was necessarily an imperfect one from the start, simply because the successful
assault having been made at the close of day, the broken
enemy had time to get across the Harpeth and destroy
the bridges before morning. The singular blunder by
which General Thomas's pontoon-train was sent toward
Murfreesboro' instead of Franklin added somewhat to
the delay, but probably did not essentially change the
result.

The state of all the roads except the one turnpike, the
soft condition of the fields everywhere, the bad weather,—
rain, sleet, and ice,—made the movements of troops which
were necessary to an effective pursuit extremely difficult,
and often impossible. The energy and determination of
General Thomas and of all who could take any active
part in that pursuit were probably never surpassed in
military history, but the difficulties to be overcome were
often insurmountable. Under the conditions at that
season of the year and in that state of weather, the only
possible chance of reaping fruits commensurate with the
brilliant victory at Nashville and with the great preparations which had been made for pursuit was to make the
final assault at Nashville early enough in the day to
leave time before dark to prevent the enemy from crossing the Harpeth and destroying the bridges.

If Hood had retreated in the night of December 15, as
Thomas presumed he would, the result would doubtless
have been even less serious to the enemy; for he would
not have suffered at Nashville the great losses and de-
moralization which occurred to him on the 16th, and
would have been in better condition to make an effec-

tive retreat, and even better able to cross the Harpeth in the night and destroy the bridges. But this would have been difficult, if not impossible, to prevent on the 15th, on account of the great extent and nature of the movements necessarily required to open the battle on that day. I now recall very distinctly the desire manifested by General Thomas that those initial operations might, if possible, be expedited. As we sat together on horseback just in rear of Wood's right and of Smith's left, on ground overlooking nearly the entire field, the general would frequently reach for my glasses, which he had occasionally used before and said were the only field-glasses he had ever found of much use to him, and try to peer through the misty atmosphere far over the woods and fields where his infantry and cavalry were advancing against the enemy's left. After thus looking long and earnestly, he would return the glasses to me, with what seemed to be a sign of irritation or impatience, for he uttered very few words in that long time, until late in the afternoon, when, after using my field-glasses for the last time, he said to me, with the energy which battle alone could arouse in his strong nature: "Smith has not reached far enough to the right. Put in your troops!"

Occasionally, when a shell struck and exploded near where we were, causing his horse to make a slight start, and only a slight one,— for the nature of the horse was much the same as that of the rider,— the only change visible in the face or form of that stout-hearted soldier was a slight motion of the bridle-hand to check the horse. My own beautiful gray charger, "Frank Blair," though naturally more nervous than the other, had become by that time hardly less fearless. But I doubt if my great senior ever noticed that day what effect the explosion of a shell produced on either the gray horse or his rider. He had on his shoulders the responsibilities of a great battle, while I then had better than ever before opportunity to study the character of my chief.

A wiser commander than Hood might very probably have saved his army from that terrible and useless sacrifice of December 16. But that last and bravest champion of a desperate cause in the west appears to have decided to remain and invite the total destruction of his army. The position which the Confederates occupied in the morning of the 16th was so close to that of more than half of the Union troops that Hood's left could easily have been crushed by an infantry assault and his rear reached by Thomas's cavalry before noon, and nothing less than a miracle could have prevented the capture of Hood's army.

It is worthy of note as instructive comparisons that on November 30 Hood advanced from Spring Hill to Franklin and made his famous assault in just about the same length of time that it took our troops to advance from the first to the second position at Nashville and make the assault of December 16; and that the Fourth and Twenty-third corps on November 29 and 30 fought two battles — Spring Hill and Franklin — and marched forty miles, from Duck River to Nashville, in thirty-six hours. Time is an element in military problems the value of which cannot be too highly estimated, yet how seldom has it been duly appreciated!

The remnant of Hood's army having made its escape across the Tennessee River, the pursuit terminated, and General Thomas issued his remarkable General Orders, No. 169, announcing that "the rear-guard of the flying and dispirited enemy was driven across the Tennessee River. . . ."[1]

Orders were then issued by General Thomas distributing his army along the Tennessee River in winter quarters, and he commenced planning a campaign for the

[1] War Records, Vol. XLV, part i, p. 50.

ensuing spring, the general features of which he telegraphed me, asking my opinion. His proposition seemed to show so different an appreciation from my own of the actual state of the war and of the demands of the country upon its army at that momentous crisis, and views so different from mine in respect to the strategic principles that should govern future operations, that I wrote to General Grant and General Sherman, giving them briefly my views upon the subject, and requesting an order to join them on the Atlantic coast, to aid in terminating the rebellion. My letter to General Grant was promptly followed by a telegram to General Thomas directing him to send me east with the Twenty-third Corps, which enabled me to participate in the closing campaign of the war.

The following are the letters, above referred to, to Grant and Sherman, whose appreciation of the views therein expressed is sufficiently shown by the published history of subsequent operations, and the orders sent to Thomas by General Grant and the War Department during that time:

(Unofficial.)

COLUMBIA, TENN., December 27, 1864.

LIEUTENANT-GENERAL U. S. GRANT, Commanding U. S. Armies, City Point, Va.

GENERAL: My corps was sent back to Tennessee by General Sherman, instead of remaining with him on his march through Georgia, according to his original design, for two reasons, viz.: first, because General Thomas was not regarded strong enough after it became evident that Hood designed to invade Tennessee; and, second, in order that I might fill up my corps from the new troops then arriving in Tennessee. These reasons now no longer exist. By uniting my troops with Stanley's, we were able to hold Hood in check at Columbia and Franklin until General Thomas could concentrate at Nashville, and also to give Hood his death-blow at Franklin. Subsequent operations have shown how little fight was then left in his army, and have taken that little out of it. He now has not more than fifteen thousand infantry, about ten thousand of whom only are armed, and they greatly demoralized. With time to reorganize and recruit, he could not probably raise his force to more than half the strength he had at Franklin.

General Thomas has assigned several new regiments to my command, and I hope soon to make them effective by distributing them in old brigades. I will have from fifteen to eighteen thousand effective men, two thirds of whom are the veterans of the campaigns of East Tennessee and Georgia : a small force, it is true, yet one which would at least be an appreciable addition to your army in Virginia or elsewhere where decisive work is to be done.

It may not be practicable now for me to join General Sherman, but it would not be difficult to transfer my command to Virginia.

I am aware that General Thomas contemplates a "spring campaign" into Alabama or Mississippi, with the Tennessee River as a base, and believe he considers my command a necessary part of the operating force. Without reference to the latter point, permit me to express the opinion that such a campaign would not be an economical or advantageous use of so many troops.

If aggressive operations are to be continued in the Gulf States, it appears to me it would be much better to take Mobile and operate from that point, thus striking vital points, if there are any such, of rebel territory by much shorter lines.

But it appears to me that Lee's army is virtually all that is left of the rebellion. If we can concentrate force enough to destroy that, we will destroy with it the rebel government, and the occupation of the whole South will then be but a matter of a few weeks' time.

Excuse, General, the liberty I have taken in expressing my views thus freely and unsolicited. I have no other motive than a desire for the nation's good, and a personal wish to serve where my little command can do the most.

The change I suggest would of course deprive me of my department command, but this would be a small loss to me or to the service. The present arrangement is an unsatisfactory one at best. Nominally I command both a department and an army in the field; but in fact I do neither. I am, General, very respectfully, your obedient servant,

J. M. Schofield, Major-General.

(Unofficial.)

Columbia, Tenn., December 28, 1864.

My dear General: Accept my hearty congratulations on the happy termination of your "pleasure excursion" through Georgia. You must have had a merry Christmas surely.

As was predicted, you have had the fun, and we the hard work. But altogether your plan has been a brilliant success. Hood did n't follow *you*, . . . but he did *me*. I held him at Columbia several days, and hurt him considerably. Finally he got across the Duck River above, and made for Franklin via Spring Hill. I headed him off at Spring Hill with a division, and concentrated at Franklin. There he made the heaviest assaults I have ever seen, but was fairly repulsed and terribly punished. In fact we pretty much knocked all the fight out of him on that occasion, and he has shown very little since. Now I reckon he has n't any left.

I barely succeeded in delaying Hood until Thomas could get A. J. Smith and Steedman to Nashville, when he became abundantly strong, and after getting Wilson's cavalry together moved out and gave Hood a most thorough beating with all ease. The fact is, Hood's army showed scarcely any fight at all. I have never seen anybody except Jeff Thompson so easily beaten.

Stoneman has cleaned out Breckinridge and destroyed the salt-works and everything else in southwest Virginia; so all together matters are in pretty good shape in this part of the military division.

Thomas has given me nine new regiments, and promises three more. These will make a pretty good division for new troops.

All this being true, I take it the objects for which I was left in this part of the country have been accomplished, and I would like very much to be with you again, to take part in the future operations of the Grand Army. Cannot this be brought about?

Of course I can only conjecture what your operations will now be, and can hardly judge of the practicability of my joining you, but I hope I may be able to do so. I have written to General Grant on this subject, and suggested that if I cannot reach you, I might with propriety be sent to Virginia. I feel certain that I am no longer needed here, for without me Thomas is much stronger than Hood.

I have not talked with General Thomas on the subject, but intend to do so as soon as I can see him.[1] No doubt he will be opposed to any reduction of his force, but I go for concentrating against Lee. If we can whip him now, the rebellion will be virtually ended.

My corps is small, it is true, but it is "powerful willing," and can help some anyhow.

Please present my kindest remembrances to my old comrades, and favor me with an early reply. Yours very truly,

J. M. SCHOFIELD, Major-General.

MAJOR-GENERAL SHERMAN, Com'd'g, etc., Savannah, Ga.

On my passage through Washington in January, 1865, Mr. Stanton, the Secretary of War, confirmed the view I had taken of the situation, and gave reasons for it before unknown to me, by telling me it was regarded by the administration as an absolute financial necessity that the war be ended in the campaign then about to begin. It is, perhaps, not strange that General Thomas had not thought of this; but it does seem remarkable that he should have proposed to let a broken and dispirited enemy have several months in which to recuperate before annoying him any further.

The expectation and instructions of General Grant and General Sherman were that General Thomas should, as soon as he was ready to take the offensive, pursue Hood into the Gulf States. General Thomas appears to have forgotten that part of his instructions. As soon as he had driven Hood across the river, he proposed to go into winter quarters, and "hold the line of the Tennessee" till some time the next spring. If General Sherman

---

[1] I did not see General Thomas after this letter was written.

had confided to General Thomas, as he did to General Grant, his ulterior purpose to march from Savannah toward Richmond, for which reason he wanted Hood kept out of his way, Thomas would have perceived the necessity of pressing the pursuit of Hood into the Gulf States. But if Thomas supposed, as he might naturally have done, that Sherman had only shifted his base with a view to further operations in Georgia and the Gulf States, under the plan of the last autumn, with which Thomas was perfectly familiar, he may well have seen no necessity for his pressing the pursuit beyond the Tennessee River in midwinter.

Some of our military operations in the Civil War remind me of the spirit of "fair play" shown by our old doctors in the West in the days of malarial fever. When the poison had fully developed its power, and threatened the destruction of its victim, the good doctor would come in and attack the enemy with heroic doses of quinine. In a few days medical science would prevail. Then the fair-minded physician would retire, and give the worsted malaria a chance to recuperate and "come to time" for another attack; and so on indefinitely until either the man or the malaria — often the man — finally got "knocked out." It was not until after much study and some practice of the art of war that I conceived for myself the idea of giving the enemy of my youth, which still clung to me, no chance to recover after I once got him down. He has never got the better of me since.

Had Thomas's plan been carried out, he would have been ready, with a fine army splendidly equipped and supplied, to start from the Tennessee River to invade the Gulf States, as had been done the year before, just about the time the plans actually adopted resulted in the surrender of all the Confederate armies. In Thomas's mind war seems to have become the normal condition of the country. He had apparently as yet no thought of its termination. The campaign from the Tennessee River as a base had then become, like the "autumn manœuvers" of a European army, a regular operation to be commenced at the proper time every year. In his general order of December 29, he said the enemy, "unless he is mad, must forever relinquish all hope of bringing Tennessee again within the lines of the accursed rebellion"; but the possible termination of that rebellion appeared to be a contingency too remote to be taken into account in planning future military operations.

CHAPTER XIV

HOOD'S MOTIVE IN ATTEMPTING THE IMPOSSIBLE AT NASH-
VILLE — DIVERSITY OF OPINIONS CONCERNING THAT
BATTLE — NO ORDERS ON RECORD FOR THE BATTLE OF
DECEMBER 16 — THAT BATTLE DUE TO THE SPONTANEOUS
ACTION OF SUBORDINATE COMMANDERS — STATEMENTS
IN THE REPORTS OF THE CORPS COMMANDERS — EXPLA-
NATION OF THE ABSENCE OF ORDERS — THE PHRASEOL-
OGY OF GENERAL THOMAS'S REPORT.

THE official records, Hood's statement, and Sherman's estimate, made at the time, agree pretty closely in placing Hood's infantry force at about 30,000 men when he crossed the Tennessee and began his advance toward Nashville. He lost a considerable number at Spring Hill on November 29, and over 6000, besides thirteen general officers, at Franklin on November 30. Therefore 24,000 must be a liberal estimate of his infantry strength after the battle of Franklin. The infantry strength of the Fourth and Twenty-third corps did not exceed 22,000 present for duty equipped, of which one brigade (Cooper's) of the Twenty-third was sent by General Thomas to guard the fords of Duck River below Columbia, and did not rejoin the corps until after the battle of Franklin. Hence Hood's infantry force at Columbia and Franklin was nearly one half greater than mine. The disparity in cavalry was still greater at first, but was reduced very considerably by the arrival of cavalry sent from Nashville by General Thomas, especially Hammond's brigade, which arrived in the field on the 29th, too late to assist in holding the line of Duck River.

It follows that Hood had an opportunity to conduct operations against an adversary of, at the most, only two thirds his own strength in infantry and in cavalry — an opportunity such as had never before been presented to any Confederate general. That he thought his chance a very brilliant one is not remarkable. If he could cut off my retreat or force me to a pitched battle, he had full reason to hope for the most decisive results. This fact should be given full weight in connection with the question why Hood did not avoid intrenched positions and make a raid into Kentucky, which he could easily have done at that time, because Thomas was not yet ready to meet him in the open field. The moral effect of such a raid would, of course, have been very great; but it must have proved disastrous in the end, for the reason that Thomas would in a short time have had in Hood's rear a far superior force to cut off his retreat and force him to a decisive battle; whereas if Hood could defeat and seriously cripple, if not destroy, the only organized army in the field then opposed to him, he could afterward attend to Thomas's scattered detachments in succession, or invade Kentucky, as he might think expedient. As Hood was operating in the country of his own friends, he did not lack full and accurate information of the strength and movements of his adversary. Indeed, we were also fully informed in due time of all of Hood's movements, but overestimated his strength because we did not have friends residing in his camps.

But the defeat of Hood at Franklin, and Thomas's concentration of troops at Nashville, completely reversed the situation. When Hood recovered from the blow received at Franklin sufficiently to make any further move, he found himself confronted no longer by an inferior force, but by one of more than twice his own strength in infantry, and not far, if at all, inferior to him in cavalry. The artillery in the field is not specially considered in any of these estimates, because it was ample in quantity and efficient in quality on both sides, and need not be compared. This formidable army was now in Hood's immediate front at Nashville, while the important strategic points of Murfreesboro' and Chattanooga were strongly garrisoned and fortified, and the railroads strongly guarded. It had become too late for Hood even to attempt a raid into Kentucky. Thomas would have been close upon his rear with an army at least twice as strong, with all the important points in Tennessee still securely held. But successful operations against Nashville were far less possible to Hood than an invasion of Kentucky. While no commander could possibly think of destroying his own army by assaulting a fortified place in which the garrison was more than double his own strength, or indulge the hope of any valuable results from a less than half investment of such a place, so bold a commander as Hood might possibly attempt a raid into Kentucky, as the only thing he could possibly do except retreat across the Tennessee River, and thus abandon his cause as lost. It was this view of the situation by General Grant and the authorities in Washington that caused such intense anxiety on account of the delay of General Thomas in attacking Hood at Nashville. It was perfectly evident that Thomas could beat Hood whenever he chose to attack him, and that Hood must be fully aware of that fact. Hence it was naturally apprehended that Hood would either make a raid into Kentucky or else retreat across the Tennessee River without suffering any further damage. To those who were watching Hood closely at Nashville, and especially to those who understood his character, there seemed no ground for either apprehension. All his operations indicated a serious attempt to besiege Nashville, though it was impossible to imagine what he could hope to accomplish, unless it was to wait in the most convenient place while his adversary, with all the great resources of the country at his back, got ready to crush him.

As stated in his report, Thomas estimated Hood's strength as being at least equal to his own, and with all the deliberation of his nature, he insisted upon making the full preparations which he considered essential to success not only in battle, but in pursuit of a defeated enemy. From his point of view, Thomas was unquestionably right in his action. How he came to make so great an overestimate of the Confederate strength, in view of the means of information in his possession and the estimate General Sherman had given him before he started for Savannah, it is difficult to conjecture. But the fact is now beyond question that Thomas made all those elaborate preparations to attack an enemy of less than half his own strength, under the belief that his adversary was at least equal in strength to himself. That Hood then knew his own exact strength is a matter of course, and that he did not underestimate the strength of his adversary is almost equally certain. During the two weeks in which his army lay in front of Nashville, if not before, he must have ascertained very closely the strength of the Union forces in his front. Hence Hood's "siege" of Nashville for two weeks could not be regarded otherwise than as a stupendous farce, were it not for the desperate bravery with which he thus kept up the appearance of still fighting for a lost cause rather than be the first to admit by his own action that it was indeed lost. It is now well known that the feeling among the Southern people and that of some of the highest officers of the Confederate government made it impossible for any officer of their army to admit in any public way the failure of the Confederacy until after the enforced surrender of Lee's army in Virginia. Indeed, it required much moral courage on the part of General

Johnston voluntarily to enter into a capitulation even after the capture of Lee.

This is unquestionably the explanation of Hood's desperate act in waiting in front of Nashville and inviting the destruction or capture of his army. The crushing blow he there received was like a death-blow delivered by a giant full of strength and vigor upon a gladiator already beaten and reduced in strength nearly to exhaustion. Sherman was not very far wrong when he said that "the battle of Nashville was fought at Franklin." The gladiator had been reduced to less than one third of his former strength by a long series of combats with a more powerful antagonist all the past summer, and finally by his unexpected repulse at Franklin. It required only one or two more blows from the powerful enemy at Nashville to complete his destruction. Any estimate of the battle of Nashville which fails to take into account the foregoing facts must be essentially erroneous, and it is not doing any honor to the great soldier who fought that battle to compare it with his previous achievements when he heroically met and defeated superior numbers of fresh and vigorous troops.

A wide diversity of opinion has always existed among military men in respect to the battle of Nashville, ranging all the way from the view taken in historical accounts heretofore published to the opinion expressed by General Sherman, in language intended of course to be hyperbolical, namely, that "the battle of Nashville was fought at Franklin." The truth is to be found somewhere between these two extremes. But the exact truth respecting that battle can perhaps hardly yet be told. I will, however, state such facts of my own knowledge and experience, and make such references to data to be found in the voluminous records, as it seems to me may assist the future historian, together with such comments as I deem appropriate upon the information now available. As will be explained hereafter, some important documents which originally formed part of the records have disappeared therefrom. Their influence upon historical opinion, if ever recovered, may now only be suggested.

It must be observed as a very notable fact that the official records, replete with orders and instructions issued every day, and almost every hour, contain no record whatever of any written order or instructions from General Thomas, given after the close of operations on December 15, for the operations which actually took place the next day. The only indications in the records, so far as I have been able to discover, that any orders were given by General Thomas, either orally or in writing, on the night of December 15, are the following "orders of the day" for the Fourth Army Corps, issued by General Wood after a personal interview with General Thomas that night; the order in writing from General Thomas to General Wilson, December 15; and the despatch from General Wilson to myself, dated December 16, 10:10 A. M. They are as follow:

HEADQUARTERS FOURTH ARMY CORPS,
NEAR NASHVILLE, TENN., December 15, 1864, 11:20 P. M.

Orders of the day for the Fourth Army Corps for to-morrow, December 16, 1864:

If the enemy is in their front at daylight to-morrow morning, division commanders will advance at that time, attack, and carry whatever may be before them. If the enemy retreats to-night, we will follow them. General Elliott, commanding Second Division, will cross to the east of the Franklin pike, then move southward parallel to it. He will deploy two regiments, connect with skirmishers, and the rest of his division will move by flank. General Kimball will follow, then General Beatty. The batteries attached to each division to-day will accompany them to-morrow. Ten ambulances and five ammunition-wagons will follow each division.

By order of Brigadier-General Wood:

J. S. FULLERTON,
Lieutenant-Colonel and Assistant Adjutant-General.

HEADQUARTERS, DEPARTMENT OF THE CUMBERLAND,
NASHVILLE, TENN., December 15, 1864.

MAJOR-GENERAL J. H. WILSON, Commanding Cavalry Corps, Military Division of the Mississippi.

GENERAL: I am directed by the major general commanding to say to you that you will remain in your present position until it is satisfactorily known whether the enemy will fight or retreat. In case he retreats, you will move your command on the Hillsborough pike across the Harpeth, and then take the most direct road or roads to the Franklin pike, and endeavor to capture or destroy the enemy's trains in their rear.

I have the honor to be, General, very respectfully your obedient servant,

ROBT. H. RAMSEY, Assistant Adjutant-General.

Both of these orders indicate a not unnatural state of doubt as to whether the enemy would "fight or retreat." The former directs what is to be done by the Fourth Corps in either case, while the latter directs what shall be done in case the enemy retreats, but says nothing about what shall be done if he does not retreat.

HDQRS. CAVALRY CORPS, MIL. DIV. OF THE MISSISSIPPI,
IN THE FIELD, December 16, 1864, 10:10 A. M.

MAJOR-GENERAL SCHOFIELD, Commanding Twenty-third Army Corps.

GENERAL: The regiment sent to the Granny White pike reports it strongly picketed toward us, with troops moving to our left. This is probably Chalmers's division. I have heard nothing from Johnson this morning; but, from what General Croxton reports, there is no doubt that Chalmers crossed the Hardin pike, moving toward Brentwood. The country on the left of the Hillsboro' pike, toward the enemy's left, is too difficult for cavalry operations. It seems to me if I was on the other flank of the army I might do more to annoy the enemy, unless it is intended that I shall push out as directed last night.

Very respectfully,

J. H. WILSON, Brevet Major-General.

(Indorsement.)

Respectfully forwarded to Major-General Thomas.

J. M. SCHOFIELD, Major-General.

This last, while showing that General Wilson had not received at 10:10 A. M. on the 16th any orders from General Thomas later than that above quoted, appears to indicate that he had received some previous order, referred to in the words " unless it is intended that I shall push out as directed last night"; for the order above quoted from the records did not indicate any intention that he should "push out" unless the enemy was in retreat.

An order in writing, as heretofore stated, was received by me very soon after dark on the 15th. It has disappeared from the official records, both those of General Thomas and mine. If any other orders were issued by General Thomas, I have no personal knowledge of the fact.

In my judgment, whatever orders were issued by General Thomas on the night of December 15 or in the morning of the 16th are essential to truthful history; and I am sure they must have been more creditable to General Thomas, though they may have been based upon erroneous foresight of the enemy's action, which is necessarily very common in war, than the absence from the records of any orders from him to govern the operations of the army the next day, and the fact, which appears from the records, that some of the troops at least did not receive any orders from General Thomas, at any time, upon which they could act on December 16.

It seems at least strange that this absence of orders given in the night of the 15th or morning of the 16th should have passed without comment, especially in view of the very full orders issued on the 14th and in the night of the 16th.

It will also be observed that General Thomas, in his official report of the battle of Nashville, dated January 20, 1865, makes no mention of any orders issued in the night of December 15 or morning of the 16th. He simply says in that regard: "The whole command bivouacked in line of battle during the night on the ground occupied at dark, whilst preparations were made to renew the battle at an early hour on the morrow"; but does not say what those preparations were. Then, after describing what had been done in the forenoon of the 16th, he says: "As soon as the above dispositions were completed, and having visited the different commands, I gave directions that the movement against the enemy's left flank should be continued"; but no sub-report mentions the receipt of any such directions. The report then proceeds to give a graphic and, I believe, nearly accurate though brief description of what followed.

It may also be observed that in my official report of the battle of Nashville, dated December 31, 1864, the following appears: "In the night of the 15th I waited upon the major-general commanding at his headquarters, and received his orders for the pursuit of the enemy on the following day." This report was, of course, before General Thomas when he wrote his own, and had necessarily been read by him and doubtless by some of his staff officers; yet no reference was made in his report to the subject referred to in the words above quoted from mine. These facts from the records may perhaps be accepted as sufficient indication of the general purport of whatever orders were issued in the night of the 15th, after the close of that day's operations, and sufficient evidence that no orders of a general character were given by General Thomas, either oral or written, on the 16th until after he had "visited the different commands."

The report of General Steedman, dated January 27, 1865, says: "December 16, at 6 A. M., in obedience to the orders of Major-General Thomas, my command moved on the enemy's works." It is not stated whether these orders were oral or written. No copy of them appears in the records, nor any mention of a personal interview with General Thomas or any of his staff. (Steedman was the man who published a falsehood about an alleged telegram from me to Grant about Thomas. See page 296.)

General T. J. Wood's report, dated January 5, 1865, after describing the operations of the morning of December 16, says: "After the dispositions above recounted had been made, the commanding general joined me near our most advanced position on the Franklin pike, examined the positions of the troops, approved the same, and ordered that the enemy should be vigorously pressed and unceasingly harassed by our fire. He further directed that I should be constantly on the alert for any opening for a more decisive effort, but for the time to bide events. The general plan of the battle for the preceding day — namely, to outflank and turn his left — was still to be acted on. Before leaving me, the commanding general desired me to confer with Major-General Steedman, whose command had moved out that morning from Nashville by the Nolensville pike, and arrange a military connection between his right and my left." This appears from General Wood's report to have occurred a short time before noon, and seems to have been the first information given to any of the corps commanders of the general plan of operations for December 16. General Wood's report does not suggest that even he, who had visited the commanding general the night before, had been given any information about any such general plan; and that statement of Wood's, "the general plan of the battle for the preceding day — namely, to outflank and turn his left — was still to be acted on," was written many days after the battle, and then did not say that General Thomas had at any time so ordered.

In the report of General A. J. Smith, dated January 10, 1865, occurs the following: "About 3 P. M. (December 16) General McArthur sent word that he could carry the hill on his right by assault. Major-General Thomas being present, the matter was referred to him, and I was requested to delay the movement until he could hear from General Schofield, to whom he had sent. . . . General McArthur, not receiving any reply, and fearing that if the attack should be longer delayed the enemy would use the night to strengthen his works, directed the first brigade (Colonel W. L. McMillen, 95th Ohio Infantry, commanding) to storm the hill on which was the left of the enemy's line," etc. This statement, which appears to be nowhere dissented from, seems to show very nearly the hour of the day — not very long after 3 P. M. — when was initiated by General McArthur the general attack which resulted in the brilliant and final success of the day; that this initial movement was not made in pursuance of any orders or directions from General Thomas, but, on the contrary, during a period in which General Thomas had requested General Smith to "delay the movement."

General Wilson's report, dated December 21, says: "About 4:30 P. M. the enemy, pressed in front, flank, and rear, broke in disorder. Croxton's brigade, which had been held in reserve on the Hillsboro' pike, as soon as the success of these dispositions had become apparent was ordered to march rapidly across the country to the Granny White pike, and beyond the right flank of Hammond's brigade; but owing to the lateness of the hour and heaviness of the road over which he was compelled to move, he secured but few prisoners." This report also seems to be silent in respect to any order from General Thomas.

There was another good reason why the cavalry secured but few prisoners at that time: there were very few left to secure behind *that part* of the line, the infantry having captured nearly all of them.

My own official report, dated December 31, gave the following account of the operations of December 16, to the accuracy of which no exception was taken by General Thomas. The only order therein mentioned as coming from General Thomas was that received in the night of the 15th, "for the pursuit of the enemy on the following day."

In the night of the 15th I waited upon the major-general commanding at his headquarters, and received his orders for the pursuit of the enemy on the following day. Our operations during the 15th had swung the right and right center forward so that the general direction of the line was nearly perpendicular to that before the attack; only the right was in contact with the enemy, and was therefore much exposed. Apprehensive that the enemy, instead of retreating during the night, would mass and attack our right in the morning, I requested that a division of infantry be sent to reinforce the right, which was ordered accordingly from Major-General Smith's command. In response to this order, General Smith sent five regiments and a battery (about 1600 men), which were put in reserve near the right. In the morning it was found that the enemy still held his position in our front, of which the hill in front of General Couch was the key, and had thrown up considerable breastworks during the night. He had also increased the force on his left during the night, and continued to mass troops there during the early part of the day. During the morning, therefore, our operations were limited to preparations for defense and coöperation with the cavalry, which was operating to strike the Granny White pike in rear of the enemy. About noon, the troops on my left (Generals Smith and Wood) having advanced and come in contact with the enemy in his new position, the enemy again withdrew from his left a considerable force to strengthen his right and center, when I ordered General Cox to advance in conjunction with the cavalry, and endeavor to carry a high wooded hill beyond the flank of the enemy's intrenched line, and overlooking the Granny White pike. The hill was occupied by the enemy in considerable force, but was not intrenched. My order was not executed with the promptness or energy which I had expected, yet probably with as much as I had reason to expect, considering the attenuated character of General Cox's line and the great distance and rough ground over which the attacking force had to move. The hill was, however, carried by General Wilson's cavalry (dismounted), whose gallantry and energy on that and other occasions which came under my observation cannot be too greatly praised. Almost simultaneously with this attack on the extreme right, the salient hill in front of General Couch was attacked and carried by General Smith's troops, supported by a brigade of General Couch's division; and the fortified hill in front of General Cox, which constituted the extreme flank of the enemy's intrenched line, was attacked and carried by Colonel Doolittle's brigade of General Cox's division, the latter capturing eight pieces of artillery and 200 to 300 prisoners. These several successes, gained almost simultaneously, resulted in a complete rout of the enemy. The cavalry had cut off his line of retreat by the Granny White pike, and such of his troops as were not captured on the line could only escape by climbing the Brentwood Hills. It is believed all of the artillery along the left and center of the enemy's line fell into our hands. Our troops continued the pursuit across the valley and into the Brentwood Hills, when darkness compelled them to desist, and they bivouacked for the night.

In the histories of the battle of Nashville heretofore published, it appears to have been assumed that the plan of battle issued to the troops before the movement of December 15 was equally applicable to the operations of the 16th, was so understood by the subordinate commanders, and was the authoritative guide for their action during the entire day of the 16th. Hence it has seemed to me necessary to direct attention to the above extracts from the official records, as well as to give my own personal recollections, for the benefit of future historians.

Unquestionably the *general plan* of battle embraced in the orders of December 14 for the attack on the 15th was well applicable to the situation which actually existed in the morning of the 16th. It was requisite only to direct in what manner the several corps of the army should act in *concert* in the *changed situation* of both armies, as had so clearly been done for the 15th, in the *situation then existing.* But the detailed orders requisite for such joint action given in the plan for the battle of the 15th were *absolutely inapplicable* in most essential particulars to the situation of the 16th, or to the battle actually fought on that day. In view of the fact that much time had very wisely been spent by General Thomas in remounting his cavalry and in making all other preparations necessary to insure not only the defeat, but the destruction or capture of the enemy, and of the further fact that the operations of the 15th had so damaged the enemy that his retreat that night was thought at least probable, if not certain, it hardly seems possible that General Thomas could have been willing to postpone a renewal of the attack until he could have time to visit "the several commands" in person, and see for himself what the situation actually was the next day, as if the operations he had to determine on and order were the original plans of a battle yet to be opened, instead of the final blow to be struck against an enemy already substantially beaten and quite probably already in full retreat.

The only possible explanation of this very remarkable absence of timely orders from General Thomas for the battle of December 16, and of the long delay on that day, seems to be found in his well-known constitutional habit, sometimes spoken of by his brother officers who had long been familiarly acquainted with him. Unless the opinions of those familiar acquaintances and friends were substantially erroneous, General Thomas's habit of great deliberation did not permit him to formulate in the night of December 15 the comparatively simple orders requisite for the several corps to *resume,* in the morning of the 16th, the movement "against the enemy's left flank," which he says he "directed" to be "continued" some time in *the afternoon* of that day — so late, however, that some of the troops at least, becoming impatient at the long delay, did not wait even for the orders they had asked for, but initiated on their own responsibility the action which resulted in victory before any directions whatever from General Thomas had reached them. Or else, if General Thomas had clearly in his mind the appropriate action of his several corps suggested by the condition of the enemy *as he himself had seen it* just before dark, or as it might be modified during the night, he must, it would seem, have felt so sure of Hood's retreat in the night that he did not think it worth his while to give any orders except for pursuit. However this may be, it seems to be clearly established by the records that the movements which prepared the way for the final assault, and that assault itself, were both made under the orders of subordinates, and not in obedience to any orders or directions from General Thomas, nor in accordance with any general plan which he had informed them was to be the guide for their action that day.

The battle of the 15th was fought in very close conformity to the plan prepared, some time before the 14th, doubtless by General Thomas himself, though spoken of by General Wood, in his confidential letter of the 14th to Thomas, as " our plan," and modified at the conference which was called that day upon the suggestion of Wood in that confidential letter, and, as he said, " at the instance of Schofield and Smith." [1] But the battle of the 16th appears to have been emphatically a battle of the troops themselves, acting under the independent orders of their own subordinate commanders, with such coöperation and support as they had arranged among themselves, in the absence of any orders or instructions from their common superior.

It seems proper for me to say that I have never claimed for myself any part of the credit due to subor-

1 War Records, Vol. XLV, part ii, p. 184.

dinates that day (December 16). Having failed in the night of December 15 to obtain any appropriate orders for my action, or for the conjoint action of the corps on my right and left, and also to obtain any such orders on the 16th, the only orders I gave were those to support the movements on my right and left initiated by the subordinate commanders there. For this action General Thomas, in his report, gave the full credit due to my troops, and, inferentially at least, more than was due to me. I must also add, in order that there may be no misunderstanding on the subject, that General Thomas also gave full credit to me and to the Twenty-third Corps for the part we took in the battle of December 15.

The only special credit to which I have thought myself entitled in respect to Nashville was for two incidental services which General Thomas did not seem to think worthy even of mention. They were, in fact, only such services as any efficient staff officer possessed of unusual knowledge of the character and habits of the opposing commander could have rendered to General Thomas as well as I could. The two services referred to were the suggestion relative to the change in the details of the plan of battle for December 15, by which the infantry attacking force on our right was increased from about ten thousand to nearly twenty thousand men; and the information I gave to General Thomas, in the night of the 15th, that Hood would not retreat without another fight, about which I had not the slightest doubt, and which seemed to me more important than the information I had given about the relative lengths of the several parts of the enemy's line of defense and of his (General Thomas's) line of attack, as proposed in his written orders. But these little services, not worthy of mention in terms of special praise, seemed to me worthy of record, especially the latter, since I had made a long ride in a dark night, after having already been in the

18

saddle from daylight till dark, to carry that information to the commanding general in person, and try to convince him of its correctness. A single word signifies sometimes much more than is imagined by him who uses it. If General Thomas had said *resumed* instead of " continued," his statement of what he said he " directed " would have corresponded very nearly with what was actually done after those directions were given on December 16. But the continuation, at 3 or 4 p. m. of one day, of action which had been suspended at nightfall the preceding day, hardly accords with the rule of accuracy which is demanded in maturely considered military reports. Indeed, when a military movement is suspended at nightfall on account of darkness, it is properly spoken of as *resumed*, not " continued," even at daylight. The word " continued " was used to express what was directed to be done at three or four o'clock in the afternoon—" the movement against the enemy's left flank," which was not any movement that had been going on that day and which could therefore be continued, but the movement which, in fact, had ended the day before in a very important success which had materially altered the military situation under which the orders for the previous day had been given. Hence this use of the word " continued " furnishes food for thought. To have *resumed*, some time in the afternoon, those operations of the preceding day would have been to state that they had been suspended, not only during the night on account of darkness, but during the greater part of the next day for no apparent reason. That would have been manifestly inconsistent with the theory that the operations of the second day were only a continuation of those of the first, all in accordance with the plan of battle published two days before, upon which theory the reports of General Thomas and of some of the subcommanders appear to have been based. The logical conclusion of this reflection, in view of all the facts now established by the records, seems to be that the plan of battle for December 16 was matured and published to the army, as well as to the world at large, some time after the event.

It may be worthy of note that none of the officers whose reports reveal their ignorance of that plan belonged to the Army of the Cumberland, with which General Thomas had so long been identified.

CHAPTER XV

GENERAL THOMAS'S INDORSEMENT ON THE REPORT OF THE
BATTLE OF FRANKLIN — COURTESIES TO HIM IN WASH-
INGTON — PECULIARITIES OF THE OFFICIAL RECORDS IN
REGARD TO FRANKLIN AND NASHVILLE — DOCUMENTS
WHICH HAVE DISAPPEARED FROM THE RECORDS — IN-
CONSISTENCIES IN GENERAL THOMAS'S REPORT — FALSE
REPRESENTATIONS MADE TO HIM — THEIR FALSITY CON-
FIRMED BY GENERAL GRANT.

AFTER I parted from General Thomas in Tennessee,
having at our last meeting there congratulated him
upon his well-deserved promotion to the highest permanent grade, that of major-general in the regular army, I
had no further official intercourse with him, and, so far as
I can recollect, did not see him until after June 1, 1868,
when I entered the War Department. During the intervening time—more than three years—my attention had
been absorbed by important duties, including a mission
to France in defense of the then violated "Monroe doctrine," and command in Virginia during a part of the
period of "reconstruction." I had not even seen the official reports of the campaign in Tennessee, they having
been made public while I was in Europe.

Some time in 1868–9 a staff officer in the War Department brought to my notice the indorsement made by
General Thomas on my report of the battle of Franklin,
and of the preceding operations from the time when, by
his order, I assumed command of the army in the field,
as follows:

HEADQUARTERS, DEPARTMENT OF THE CUMBERLAND,
NASHVILLE, TENN., December 7, 1864.

Respectfully forwarded to the adjutant-general of the army, cordially recommending the gallantry and skill of Major-General Schofield to the commendation of the War Department.

GEO. H. THOMAS,
Major-General U. S. Volunteers, Commanding.

Of course I was much gratified by this high commendation, of which I had never before seen the text, though I had known the substance. I was also shown the telegram from General Thomas to Secretary Stanton recommending that I and Stanley be brevetted one grade in the regular service for our conduct at Franklin. As I received, a short time after that recommendation was made, the appointment of brigadier-general in the regular service, I supposed that General Thomas had based his recommendation for brevet upon his knowledge or belief that I had been, or soon would be, appointed brigadier-general. Hence I had the great satisfaction of believing that I owed my brevet of major-general in the regular army, at least in part, to General Thomas's recommendation.

I cannot now recollect whether or not I saw at that time General Thomas's report of the operations in Tennessee. If I did, there was nothing in it to attract my special attention, as I was too much occupied with the important affairs of the time to think or care very much about anything that was already three years old.

My relations with General Thomas during that time— the winter and spring of 1868-9, when he was, by my selection, president of a very important military court, with General Hancock and General Terry as the other members, and General Holt as the judge-advocate— were very cordial, at least on my part. He was my guest at a large dinner given to the members of the President's cabinet and the Diplomatic Corps, to which the only other gentlemen invited were Generals Thomas and Hancock, as a special mark of distinction to two of my brother officers of the army. When General Grant was inaugurated President I went with General Sherman in person to ask the President to give General Thomas command of the Division of the Pacific, which I had before proposed for him, but which the President had designated for me, under the impression that General Thomas did not want it.

A few days after that we went to our respective commands—General Thomas to San Francisco, and I to Fort Leavenworth. From that time we had no official or personal relations or correspondence during the short remainder of his life.

In respect to what was made public during that brief period, I long since refused to believe that the superior officer whom I had always so highly respected could possibly have been capable, in his own mind and heart, of doing me the grievous wrong which I at one time believed he had done. I now add, as the result of calm and dispassionate judgment, that any criticism at that time, even under great provocation, that could seem unkind, not to say unjust, to that noble, patriotic, and brave soldier, from any source, not excluding myself, was wholly unjustifiable and worthy only of condemnation. His great services had entitled him to the kindest possible consideration of any imperfections, either real or supposed, in his military operations.

Now, in this winter of 1896-7, I have made a careful examination, for the first time since the events, of all the published records of the campaign of 1864 in Tennessee, for the purpose of doing exact justice to the principal actors in that campaign, so far as it is possible for me to do so. In this examination I have discovered some things that have surprised me, but they have not altered my deliberate judgment of the character of the great soldier under whom I had the honor to serve in that campaign. I refer to them only for the consideration of others.

(1) In the report of General Thomas dated January 20, 1865, covering the entire period of the campaign, including both the battles of Franklin and Nashville, in his commendation of subordinates he made no distinction between the corps commanders who had served immediately under him and only in the battle of Nashville, and the army commander who, besides the like service at Nashville, had commanded the army in the field, in the absence therefrom of General Thomas, up to and including the battle of Franklin, where signal victory had prepared the way for the less difficult but brilliant success of General Thomas at Nashville.

(2) In the first letter from General Thomas recommending promotions for services in the campaign, containing the names of a large number of officers, no mention was made of my name or that of General Stanley, who had been conspicuous for gallantry at Spring Hill and at Franklin, where he was wounded.

(3) In a telegram from the Secretary of War calling for recommendations for promotion, General Thomas had been informed that while there was no vacancy in the grade of major-general (the last having, in fact, been given to General Thomas himself), there were then two vacancies in that of brigadier-general; and it was after the receipt of that information, and in view of all it might be understood to imply, that General Thomas sent his telegram to the Secretary of War recommending that Stanley and I be brevetted one grade in the regular service, not, as he had said in his indorsement on my report of the battle of Franklin, for "skill," but for "good conduct." As General Thomas well knew, I was then only a captain in the regular army. Hence he recommended me for the brevet of major — that is, of commander of

a single battalion of four companies — for my services in command of an army of thirty thousand men, including artillery and cavalry.

(4) The telegram from General Thomas to Secretary Stanton recommending those brevets for Stanley and me was dated December 31, 1864, 5 p. m., while my general report including that of the battle of Nashville bears the same date without hour, but may have been, and probably was, received by General Thomas before he sent his telegram recommending my promotion.

(5) Neither the report of General Thomas nor of any of his corps commanders made any mention of orders for "pursuit" in the morning of December 16, and General Thomas himself in his report took no notice whatever of the glaring discrepancy between my report and some of the others, nor of any facts demonstrated or suggested by the correspondence which was made a part of my report, nor made any mention of the change in his plan of battle for December 15, which was made the day before.

(6) In the publication of my report in the War Records there is a foot-note which says that the orders and correspondence referred to are not found with the report filed in the War Department—a fact similar to that which I had found in respect to my own retained copies of orders and correspondence, which I understood had been carefully locked up in a strong leather trunk ever since I left Washington in March, 1869, but which had nevertheless mysteriously disappeared.

In that report of mine was a reference to the modification made in General Thomas's published plan of battle for December 15, though no intimation that it was made at my suggestion; also the statement that I had, after the close of the battle of December 15, "waited upon the commanding general and received his orders for the pursuit," but no mention of the previous written orders to the same effect, which had become obsolete by operation of the subsequent orders received in person. There were attached to my report, and made a part thereof, copies of all the orders and correspondence in my possession relating to the battles of Franklin and Nashville, and to the preceding operations of that campaign, including those about the false position of the troops at Pulaski, those about concentration of the troops in Thomas's department, that about the need of a pontoon bridge at Franklin, that about punishing the telegraph-operator by whose desertion I was deprived of communication with General Thomas during the most critical part of the campaign, and, probably, the order in writing which I had received from General Thomas after the battle of December 15. But of course there were no copies of orders or despatches which I had *not* received; and the desertion of my telegraph-operator and the operations of Forrest's cavalry in my rear had made it probable that there must have been some such despatches sent but not received. There were no annotations or other suggestions as to their significance attached to any of those copies at that time. They were simply included, without comment, as an essential part of the report. The explanations found in this volume were made many years afterward.

In respect to that appendix to my report, I am now compelled to call attention to the fact that it was an absolute necessity. I could not possibly have made a truthful and rational report which would have stood the test of just criticism without reference to the documents in that appendix; and it was far more respectful to General Thomas simply to attach the documents, leaving him to make any explanations he might think necessary, than to call attention myself to the necessity for any such explanations. It would have been impossible to give any rational explanation of the false position occupied by the troops at Pulaski up to the very last moment of safety except by reference to Thomas's orders to Stanley and me, and the subsequent correspondence on that subject. Stanley, with the blunt frankness justified by comradeship, had pointed it out to me the moment we met at Pulaski, while I was governed by the utmost delicacy in discussing the question with General Thomas, so as to avoid suggesting to him that he had made a mistake. Yet so evident was the mistake that I stopped the advance of the Twenty-third Corps some miles north of Pulaski, and no part of that corps actually went to that place. Cox was sent back to a point where he could interpose between Hood and Columbia, and Ruger was stopped at Columbia.

The great tenacity with which I held on at Columbia and on the north bank of Duck River could not have been justified except by reference to the despatches showing Thomas's wishes and his assurance of reinforcements at those points. If I had been free to do so, nothing could have been plainer than my duty to have fallen back behind the Harpeth when I found that Thomas could not or would not reinforce me on the line of Duck River, and before Hood could endanger my retreat. Hence I was compelled to include in the history of that retreat the entire record of facts relating to it.

Again, necessity was the only possible excuse for fighting the battle of Franklin on the south side of the Harpeth, where defeat would have been disastrous; and that necessity had arisen absolutely and solely from the want of a bridge across that river, which I had suggested that General Thomas place there. It was not possible for me, without utter disregard for the truth of history as well as for my own military reputation, to attempt to conceal those facts.

It must seem remarkable that in my report, dated December 7, of operations from November 14 to December

1, 1864, including the battle of Franklin, on which General Thomas placed his indorsement commending my "skill," no mention whatever was made of any orders or instructions from General Thomas. The simple fact was that I could not have quoted the orders and instructions General Thomas had given me for my guidance during those operations without implied criticism of General Thomas; hence it was then thought best to omit any reference to any such orders or instructions, and to limit the report to a simple recital of the facts, thus making the report strictly truthful so far as concerned my own action and that of the troops under my command, without any reference whatever to my superior at Nashville, under whose orders I was supposed to be acting; and that report of December 7 appeared to be entirely satisfactory to General Thomas in that respect as well as in all others. But when the time came to make my final report of the entire campaign, which must go upon the public records as my full and exact contribution to the history of military operations in which I had taken an important part, truth and justice to all required me to make the record complete so far as lay in my power; and if there was anything in the record, as submitted by me to General Thomas, to which he took exception, it was as plainly his duty to truth and justice to place those exceptions also on the public records. So far from suggesting in my final report any possible criticism of General Thomas, I put the best possible construction upon all the despatches I had received from him, by accepting them together as showing me that his object was "to hold the enemy in check" until he (Thomas) could concentrate his reinforcements, and not to fight Hood at Pulaski, as he (Thomas) had at first ordered. I simply submitted to him the plain record, with the best possible construction I could put upon it, and that only so far as it was necessary for me to construe it to give the general basis of my action. If any official duty remained to be done in that regard, that duty devolved on General Thomas, not on me.

In my final report, dated December 31, 1864, I said, as above indicated, that my instructions from the major-general commanding were embraced in a telegram to General Stanley (dated November 8), in which General Thomas said, " Should the enemy overpower them [the cavalry] and march on Pulaski, you must hold that place," " a copy of which was furnished with the order to assume command at Pulaski, and subsequent despatches, explaining that the object was to hold the enemy in check, should he advance, long enough to enable General A. J. Smith's corps, then expected from Missouri, to reach Nashville, other troops in the Department of the Cumberland to be concentrated, and General Wilson's cavalry to be re. mounted and fitted for the field. The reinforcements thus expected were about equal to the force we then had in the field, and would make our entire force, when concentrated, equal, or somewhat superior, to that of the enemy. To effect this concentration was therefore of vital importance, a consideration to which all others were secondary. This required that the enemy's advance should be delayed as much as possible, and at the same time a decisive battle avoided, unless it could be fought on favorable terms."

I refrained from quoting either of the despatches from General Thomas, — that dated November 8 to Stanley, or that dated 19, repeating in substance that of the 8th, — or my reply of November 20 pointing out the reasons why the position at Pulaski was a false one to occupy under the circumstances; and I still think, as I then thought, that that was done as delicately as possible so as to avoid suggesting to General Thomas that I thought his order a blunder. His reply of the same date shows that he so appreciated it. This despatch last referred to from General Thomas, and all the other correspondence after I reached Pulaski, fully justified me in the statement made in my report, above mentioned, as to whence I derived my information of his plans.

But in the report of General Thomas dated January 20, 1865, appears the following: "Directions were then sent to General Schofield to leave a sufficiently strong force for the defense of that point, and with the balance of his command proceed to carry out the instructions already given him, viz., to join the Fourth Corps at Pulaski, and assume command of all the troops in the vicinity, watch the movements of Hood, and retard his advance into Tennessee as much as possible, without risking a general engagement, until Maj.-Gen. A. J. Smith's command could arrive from Missouri, and Maj.-Gen. J. H. Wilson could have time to remount the cavalry regiments dismounted to furnish horses for Kilpatrick's division, which was to accompany General Sherman in his march through Georgia. . . . My plans and wishes were fully explained to General Schofield, and, as subsequent events will show, properly appreciated and executed by him."

Thus, General Thomas, being fully satisfied with the operations of the troops while under my immediate command in the field, asserted that those operations were based upon his "plans and wishes," which had been "fully explained" to me *before I went to Pulaski*, and "properly appreciated," instead of upon what I had gathered from General Thomas's orders to Stanley and subsequent orders to me about fighting Hood at Pulaski, absolutely contradictory to that stated in his report, "without risking a general engagement," and his assent to my *radically different* suggestions made *after I assumed command at Pulaski*, as stated in my report. It is not incumbent upon me to try to reconcile this statement in General Thomas's report with the correspondence, above referred to, found in the official records; and I see no reason for desiring any further corroboration of the strict accuracy of the contrary statement made by me in my report. I am entirely willing to leave any discussion of that subject to others.

In view of the fact that I was not one of General Thomas's corps commanders, but an army commander, holding the same grade of command, by special assignment of the President under the law, as General Thomas himself, he might without military impropriety have left to me in his report, as he had before done in fact, whether intentionally or not, the entire responsibility of the operations of the army under my immediate command from Pulaski to Nashville. The record fully shows that, from the necessities of the case, I was compelled to act, and did act, upon my own judgment from the beginning to the end, not only without any timely orders, but generally without timely or accurate information from General Thomas; and that he approved, from time to time and finally, all that I had done. The question as to why he afterward claimed that all had been done in pursuance of his plans and wishes, fully explained to me *in advance*, I must leave to others. He was certainly under no official obligation to take upon himself any such responsibility. It may be true, as General Sherman said and General Thomas admitted, that it was his duty to take command in the field himself. But it was not his duty, being in the rear, to hamper the actual army commander in the field with embarrassing orders or instructions, nor to take upon himself the responsibility of failure or success. If I had failed in those hazardous operations, nobody could have held General Thomas responsible, unless for neglect of duty in not commanding himself in person, or in not sending me possible reinforcements. No obedience to any erroneous orders or instructions of his, sent from a distance whence the actual situation could not be seen as clearly as at the front, could have justified me in case of failure. The actual commander of an army in the field must act upon his own judgment and responsibility, though with due deference to the plans and wishes of his superior, so far as they are made known to him, having in view the general object of a campaign. This sound military principle appears to have been fully recognized by General Thomas when he made his report. He only claimed that his "plans and wishes were fully explained" and "properly appreciated and executed," not that he had given any specific orders or instructions. Why, then, did he assert, in contradiction of my statement previously made to him, and in contradiction of the official record I had submitted to him with that statement in my report, that those "plans and wishes" of his had been "fully explained" to me *before* instead of *after* I went to Pulaski? What possible difference could it have made to General Thomas, personally or officially, whether the record showed that his plans and wishes were made known to me before or after I assumed command, provided they were received by me in due time for my action? What possible motive could General Thomas have had in putting on the public records what was in substance a flat contradiction of an official statement I had made to him with full documentary evidence to support it, and that in the absence of any possible ground for his own contradictory statement, except his own recollection of some conversation we may have had more than two months before, in which he might have explained to me his "plans and wishes"? I cannot believe that General Thomas ever consciously did any such thing. That feature of the report must have had some other author besides George H. Thomas. It is true that the orders telegraphed to me by General Thomas, November 19, "to fight him [Hood] at Pulaski, if he advances against that place," were inconsistent with the statement in his report that he had fully explained to me his plans and wishes as specified in that report, and in plain disregard of the general principle recognized in his report, as well as likely to lead to disastrous results if obeyed. But those orders were on the records, and could not be expunged, even if such a man as General Thomas could possibly have wished to expunge anything from his official record. Hence, I repeat, that feature of the report signed by General Thomas could not have been his.

In this connection it is to be observed that General Thomas had not, at the time I went back to report to him in Tennessee, any anxiety about his inability to cope with Hood after the arrival of the Twenty-third Corps. He had assured General Sherman of his entire confidence.[1] He had ordered me to march, as Stanley had done, from Tullahoma to Pulaski; but the action of Forrest at Johnsonville about that time caused General Thomas to change his orders and hurry me by rail to Nashville, and thence to Johnsonville, with the advance of my troops, he wishing to see me in person as I passed through Nashville.[2] It would not be an unreasonable presumption that the burden of conversation in that brief interview was in respect to the alarming condition at Johnsonville at that time, rather than in respect to some future defensive operations against Hood, then hardly anticipated. Indeed, the entire correspondence

[1] See Thomas to Sherman, November 12, 1864, 8:30 A.M.: "Your despatch of 12 last night received. I have no fear that Beauregard can do us any harm now; and if he attempts to follow you, I will follow him as far as possible. If he does not follow you, I will then thoroughly organize my troops, and I believe I shall have men enough to ruin him unless he gets out of the way very rapidly. The country through middle Alabama, I learn, is teeming with supplies this year, which will be greatly to our advantage.

"I have no additional news to report from the direction of Florence. I am now convinced that the greater part of Beauregard's army is near Florence and Tuscumbia, and that you will at least have a clear road before you for several days, and that your success will fully equal your expectations."

[2] War Records, Vol. XXXIX, part iii, p. 624.

of that period, including that which occurred between General Thomas and General Sherman, about which it is important to note that I knew nothing at that time, shows that General Thomas then expected to concentrate his troops at Columbia or Pulaski, or both, in a very short time, take command in the field in person, and begin aggressive operations against Hood. It seems extremely probable that General Thomas had given very little thought at that time to the subject of defensive action, except as against what that troublesome cavalryman Forrest might do. It seems far more probable from the record that General Thomas's "plans and wishes" in respect to defensive action against Hood's advance into Tennessee, which I had so "properly appreciated and executed," were, like the plans of the battle of December 16 at Nashville, matured after the event, or at least after Hood's advance into Tennessee had actually begun, and after I had, in my telegram to General Thomas of November 20, pointed out to him the dangers of his previous plan, telegraphed to me the day before.

I do not think much importance is generally to be attached to what any man may or may not recall to memory after the lapse of many years, although the recollection of a recent event, repeated in the memory, for good and sufficient reasons, very frequently during a long time, may continue to be very accurate. However this may be, perfect candor compels me to say here that I have never been able to recall any conversation with General Thomas at any time in respect to his plans or wishes in the event of Hood's advance from the Tennessee before Thomas was ready to assume the offensive. I now believe, as I always have done, that the only information I ever received from General Thomas on that subject was that contained in the telegraphic correspondence quoted in this volume. There is now no doubt in my mind, and, so far as I can recall, never has been any, that when I

19

met General Thomas at Nashville, on my way to Johnsonville, he expected A. J. Smith to arrive from Missouri very soon, when he intended to concentrate all his available troops at Columbia and Pulaski, take command in person, and move against Hood; and that he considered his orders of November 8 to Stanley, to fight Hood at Pulaski or Columbia, as Hood might elect, until he (Thomas) could get there with reinforcements, all the orders that could be necessary, even if Hood did get a little the start of him. The records seem to show, still further, that even after Hood's plans of aggression had developed so long in advance of Thomas's preparations to meet him, Thomas did not then see the great danger that might result from obedience to his orders of November 8 to Stanley, and even went so far as to repeat those orders to me on the 19th; but that he promptly corrected that mistake when I pointed it out to him, and then authorized me to act upon my own judgment.

Now, at this late day, when I am so much older than General Thomas was at the time of these events, I feel at liberty to discuss them without reserve. I am not criticizing the acts of my official superior. In my mature judgment, General Thomas was not justifiable, in 1864–1865, in claiming the credit for what had been done by his inferior in rank in actual command of the army in the field while General Thomas himself was absent.

So, in respect to the battle of Nashville, it would have been utterly impossible to have given any rational explanation of the action of my troops on December 15 under the published orders for that battle. Hence I alluded, as lightly as possible, to the modification in those orders which accounted for what I had done, but gave no hint of the fact that I had suggested that modification. I cannot now recollect whether I had any expectation at that time in respect to what General Thomas would say on that subject in his report; but, in my opinion, his well-known character would have fully justified the expectation that he would say in substance that the foregoing plan of battle, which had been previously prepared, was so far modified, upon the suggestion of General Schofield and with the concurrence of other commanders, as to order the Twenty-third Corps to a position in rear of our right, from which it could reinforce the main attack on the enemy's left, instead of to the reserve position on the left of the Fourth Corps. It does not seem to me that a veteran general could have suffered in his own estimation or in that of the world by such an act of justice or generosity to a young subordinate. But the plain, unavoidable truth is that General Thomas said in his report, besides his statement about the "few alterations": "Finding General Smith had not taken as much distance to the right as I expected he would have done, I directed General Schofield to move his command (the Twenty-third Corps) from the position in reserve to which it had been assigned over to the right of General Smith . . ."—leaving it necessarily to be inferred that "the position in reserve" referred to was that to which it had been assigned in the published orders, and that the Twenty-third Corps moved "over" from that position "to the right of General Smith" after General Thomas gave directions to that effect in the afternoon of December 15. Whereas, in fact, that corps had moved over to the right at daylight in the morning, so as to be ready for the action which General Thomas finally ordered; otherwise it could not possibly have moved over to Smith's right before dark. In fact, one of the divisions (Couch's) of the Twenty-third Corps advanced with Smith's corps, "keeping within supporting distance," as stated in my report, so that Couch was able to take a very important part in the attack that day; while Cox, though much nearer than General Thomas indicated, could not reach the right till near the close of the day's operations, though in time to take part in the final engagement in repelling the enemy's attempt to regain lost ground. When it is remembered that General Thomas was at the rear of our right, where all this could be distinctly seen, no comment seems to be necessary on this feature of his report.

In respect to the statement in my report that I had in the night of December 15 " waited upon the commanding general and received his orders for the pursuit," that was simply a fact without which there was possible no rational explanation of what occurred, or did not occur, the next day. I must have taken it for granted that General Thomas would make some frank and candid explanation of all those matters in his own report, and I could not have imagined that I might incur his displeasure by telling the simple truth. My opinion of his character forbade the possibility of any supposition that he would desire to conceal anything, even if concealment were possible, of facts to which there were so many witnesses. Hence my astonishment at the discovery of so much that I cannot even attempt to explain.

It was publicly stated, soon after the death of General Thomas, that his mortal stroke occurred when he was trying to write something in regard to the use made of the Twenty-third Corps in the battle of Nashville. If he then saw, as it would seem he must have done, the wrong into which he had been betrayed, his sudden death is fully accounted for to the minds of all who knew his true and honest and sensitive nature. He had been betrayed by some malign influence into an outrage upon his own great reputation which it was not possible to explain away, while the slight wrong he had done to me, even if he had intended it, had already proved utterly harmless. His own great record could not possibly suffer from any discussion of the facts, unless those facts themselves proved damaging to him; and he had been too much accustomed to such discussions to be disturbed thereby. There seems no possible explanation of the great shock General Thomas received but the discovery that he had apparently done an irreparable injury to himself. But I do not believe General Thomas himself was the author of those acts which were so foreign to his nature.

At Nashville, in December, 1864, and afterward, General Thomas appears to have been made the victim of a conspiracy to poison his mind by false accusations against his senior subordinate. A press report of a conversation said to have taken place in San Francisco in the year 1869, between General Thomas and General Halleck, gave some indication of the effect which had been produced on the mind of General Thomas. From that time forward there appeared frequent indications of the secret operations of that conspiracy; but no public evidence of its character or authors came to my knowledge until 1881, when there appeared in the " New-York Times " of June 22 an article, copied from the Toledo " Northern Ohio Democrat," which disclosed the character of the false accusations which had been made to General Thomas at Nashville, and the name of their principal, if not sole, author. That publication gave me for the first time the means of refuting a vile slander which had been doing its deadly work in secret for nearly seventeen years. The following correspondence with General Grant shows the character of that slander, and its complete refutation:

LONDON, ENGLAND, July 12, 1881.
GENERAL U. S. GRANT, New York, U. S. A.
MY DEAR GENERAL : For a long time I have been made aware of the fact that a base falsehood was secretly circulated throughout the country, to the effect that while General Thomas's army was at Nashville in December, 1864, I endeavored in some way to influence you or somebody in Washington to remove him from the command and to place me in his stead. I have not heretofore been able to defend myself against this slander because of

its secrecy. But now, for the first time within my knowledge, this falsehood has made its appearance in public print, in the form of an article in the Toledo "Northern Ohio Democrat," copied into the "New-York Times" of June 22, of which I send you a slip.

You, my dear General, are probably the only man now living who is able to make an authoritative statement of the facts in respect to this matter, such as must be accepted without question.

I hope, therefore, it is not asking too much to request you to give me, in a form which I may use publicly, a full and explicit statement of the facts in respect to this accusation.

Perhaps you may also be able to recall the substance of a conversation between you and me, on the subject of the delay of Thomas to attack Hood at Nashville, which occurred on the naval steamer on our way from Hampton Roads to Cape Fear River, when we went down to see Admiral Porter and General Terry while my troops were delayed by the ice in the Potomac.

In that conversation I tried to justify Thomas's delay during the storm at Nashville, and, I thought, perhaps succeeded in modifying to some extent your opinion on the subject. If you are able to recollect the substance of that conversation, a statement of it would be an effective answer to the malicious charges that I was not faithful to Thomas as my commanding officer.

Not knowing where you may be when this letter reaches the United States, I send it to Colonel Wherry, to be sent you by mail or handed you by one of my aides, as may be most convenient. Please do me the great favor to send to Wherry, or the other officer who may call upon you, an answer which he may use in public refutation of the malicious charge which has been made against me.

He can then send it to me. The vipers are taking advantage of my absence to publish falsehoods and give them a long start of the truth which must be sent in pursuit. I am, dear General, as ever, sincerely yours,

J. M. SCHOFIELD.

NEW YORK, August 1, 1881.

GENERAL J. M. SCHOFIELD.

DEAR GENERAL: Your letter of the 12th of July has just been handed me by Colonel Wherry of your staff. I have read it carefully, together with the article from the Toledo "Democrat." The elapse of time since the event spoken of in that article is so great that I feel some hesitation in answering your letter and the article from the "Democrat" as I might do if I had access to the archives at Washington; but, writing from memory, I think I can say with great positiveness there was never any despatch from you to me, or from you to any one in Washington, disparaging General Thomas's movements at Nashville. On the contrary, my recollection is that when I met you on your way to Wilmington, N. C., subsequent to the battle of Nashville, you explained the situation at Nashville prior to General Thomas's movement against Hood, with a view of removing the feeling that I had that Thomas had been slow. I was very impatient at that time with what I thought was tard. ˙˙s on the part of General Thomas, and was very much afraid that while he was lying there at Nashville and not moving his army, Hood might cross the Tennessee River either above or below the city of Nashville, and get between him and the Ohio River, and make a retrograde movement of our army at Nashville a necessity, and very much embarrass and delay future operations of the armies. Laboring under this feeling and impression, I was telegraphing General Thomas daily, and almost hourly, urging him to move out and attack Hood, and finally became so impatient that I contemplated his removal and the substitution of another officer in his place; but this feeling on my part was not added to by any despatches from any person from the scene of action, except those from General Thomas himself. I have certainly no recollection of receiving any despatches from Nashville, during the time spoken of in the article in the "Democrat," from any person but General Thomas himself. I feel very sure that if any despatches had been received from you, I should now recollect it; and I am free to say that it would have created a prejudice to your disadvantage if I had received such despatches. This much you are at liberty to use in any way you may deem proper. The other reflections which the author of the article alluded to [made] against you I of course am not called upon to say anything in regard to. The fact is, your subsequent promotions are proof positive that I entertained none of the views set forth to your disadvantage in this article. Very truly yours,

U. S. GRANT.

The article above referred to asserted that "General Thomas knew three days before the battle of Nashville that Schofield was playing the part of Judas by telegraphing to General Grant, at Washington, disparaging suggestions about the action of Thomas," and pretended to quote the language of one of those despatches, as follows: "It is the opinion of all of our officers with whom I have conversed that General Thomas is too tardy in moving against the enemy . . ." It also stated that "it was known to a number of our officers that . . . Schofield was intriguing with Grant to get Thomas relieved, in order that he might succeed to the command of our army as the general next in rank to Thomas, . . . and he was watched and exposed to Thomas."

This boastful avowal by James B. Steedman of his own crime in making reports which were false and slanderous to his commanding general must doubtless be accepted as conclusive proof of his own guilt. But a statement by such a witness cannot be regarded as proof that any other officer was guilty of the same crime. So far as I know, no other has ever made any avowal, public or private, of his own guilt, or of that of any one else. Nor has any other, so far as I know, denied the truth of my statements, repeated in this volume, of what occurred in the council held at Nashville on December 9, 1864.

It does not seem probable that one such man as James B. Steedman could have exerted such a powerful and baneful influence over General George H. Thomas as that which now appears to have governed his action. There must, it would seem, have been some others, as Steedman asserted. If so, it is time for them, if living, to come to the front and claim their share in the work of falsifying history, of poisoning the mind and heart of their great and noble commander, causing his untimely death, and endangering his great reputation as a man of honor, truth, and justice.

The complete refutation by General Grant of the falsehood ended the hostility which had been shown toward me during all that time, and gradually led to a general recognition of the truth, which had always been known and maintained by the most ardent friends of General Thomas, like the late General J. S. Fullerton and General H. V. Boynton, and the staff officers and the relatives of the general himself. Finally, when it was proposed in Congress to recognize my past services by promotion to the grade of lieutenant-general on the eve of my retirement from active service, not a voice in opposition was heard from the old Army of the Cumberland; and when we met, for the first time in many years, by their cordial invitation, on the historic fields of Chickamauga and Chattanooga, to dedicate those grounds as sacred to the memory of the Army of the Cumberland and its great commander, we met again as brother soldiers, without any trace of the bitterness which malicious slander had for so many years sunk deep into our hearts.

For my part, I had for many years before refused to believe that my old commander, whom I had so faithfully served and so highly respected, could possibly have done me in his own mind and heart the grievous wrong which he appeared to have done. Not long after his death, and many years before the public refutation of the slander which he was said to have accepted and believed, I put on record my deliberate opinion that of General Thomas's character as a man and a soldier his warmest eulogists had not spoken too highly. And now, no matter what injustice General Thomas may have done me under the malign influence which surrounded him, I refuse to alter that deliberate judgment. He is to me in memory the same noble old soldier and commander that he was when he intrusted to me the command of his army in Tennessee, from Pulaski through Columbia, Spring Hill, and Franklin to Nashville, and commended all I had done in that command.

Truthful military history cannot be written without some criticism. "He who never made a mistake never made war." I am keenly sensible of the delicacy of my personal relation to the history of General Thomas, as well as of my obligation to contribute my share to that history, which no other man could ever do if I neglected it. I have written it with the greatest possible care. If I have fallen into error in anything, there are men still living who can correct my mistakes. It will be more just to the memory of General Thomas to publish it now than to wait until all who could correct any errors of mine are silent in death. Thus far none of the several friends of General Thomas to whom I have applied have been able to give me any explanation of the record referred to which modifies that which I have stated. If any one can suggest a more satisfactory explanation, he will earn my gratitude.

CHAPTER XVI

SHERMAN'S "MARCH TO THE SEA" — THE MILITARY THEORY
ON WHICH IT WAS BASED — DID IT INVOLVE WAR
OR STATESMANSHIP? — THE CORRESPONDENCE BETWEEN
GRANT AND SHERMAN, AND SHERMAN AND THOMAS —
THE EFFECT OF JEFFERSON DAVIS'S SPEECH ON SHER-
MAN — RAWLINS'S REPORTED OPPOSITION TO THE MARCH,
AND GRANT'S FINAL JUDGMENT ON IT.

DURING the Atlanta campaign the principal commanders of the army assumed, as a matter of
course, that Atlanta would be ours in due time, and hence
there was much discussion of the question, What next? It
was evident the army could not go much farther and rely
upon its present line of supply, although General Thomas
said, immediately after the capture of Atlanta, that he
had "a plan for the capture of Macon" which he would
like to execute. What the plan was he did not divulge,
General Sherman turning the conversation in another
direction. At that time it was presumed Hood would
oppose whatever move was attempted, and hence a new
base, to be provided in advance, if practicable, by the
capture of some place on the gulf or on the Atlantic,
was evidently essential to further operations in Georgia.
This new base being provided, Sherman could move out
from Atlanta with twenty or thirty days' supplies in
wagons, and swing round Hood so as to place his rear
toward the new base and open communication therewith.
Evidently the march to the sea, as it was actually made,

was impossible, and was not thought of until Hood moved from Sherman's front and cleared the way. In the popular judgment formed immediately after important events, success or failure is the only criterion of wisdom; but the historian must go deeper, and consider the merits of a general plan in view of the greater or less probability of failure of any one of its parts. What would have been the just judgment of mankind upon Sherman's march to the sea if Thomas had failed, as Sherman with a much larger force had done, to destroy or seriously cripple Hood's army? Or what, if Hood had succeeded in his projected invasion of Kentucky — an event much less improbable than many that have actually occurred in war? If Hood had succeeded in overwhelming the smaller force that opposed him at Columbia, Spring Hill, and Franklin, as he came near doing, Nashville would have fallen an easy prey, for it was not defensible by the force Thomas then had there. Thomas's cavalry was not yet remounted, and Forrest, with his troopers, would have had nearly a clear field of Kentucky while Hood marched to the Ohio. What offset to this would have been the capture of Savannah as a "Christmas gift" to the nation?

The situation at that time was certainly a perplexing one to Sherman. He could not permit Hood to put him, with his superior force, on the defensive, nor even to appear to do so for a moment; and it was not easy for him to consent that his enemy should entirely nullify all his elaborately considered plans for future operations in Georgia. What operations Sherman decided on in that unprecedented case is well known.

When Sherman cut loose and started for Savannah on November 12, he had not, as events proved, sufficient reason for assuming "Thomas's strength and ability to meet Hood in the open field," or even to hold Nashville against him, much less to hold "the line of the Tennessee

River firmly," which was the condition upon which Grant at first consented that Sherman might make "the trip to the sea-coast."[1]

Thomas's concurrence in Sherman's opinion, as shown in his despatch of November 12, simply shows that they were both in the same error; for A. J. Smith's troops did not begin to arrive at Nashville until the day of the battle of Franklin (November 30), and they were a very important part of the force relied upon in Sherman's plan. The whole fate of the Tennessee campaign was decided by the delay of Hood at Columbia and Spring Hill and his defeat in the desperate battle of Franklin, and this by two of Sherman's six corps, without the aid of any of the reinforcements upon which he counted so largely, and about which he says so much. It is not too much to say that the hazards of that retreat from Pulaski and of the defense at Franklin were far greater than any portion of Sherman's army had ever before encountered, and far greater than any army ever ought to meet except in case of necessity — hazards which, at that stage of the war, with our vastly superior armies in the field, it would have been inexcusable voluntarily to incur. If it is asked why such hazard was taken, the answer has heretofore been given. By it alone could the time be gained which was necessary for Thomas's reinforcements to reach Nashville. The time gained was barely sufficient; one day less might have been fatal.

The question that at once arises is, Why have taken even a chance of error in a matter of so vital moment — an error that might have led to disastrous consequences? Hood was already on the Tennessee River, preparing to cross and begin his march to Nashville. Thomas had ready to meet him only about two thirds Hood's strength in infantry, and less than half in effective cavalry. A few days' delay on Sherman's part in commencing his

[1] War Records, Vol. XXXIX, part iii, p. 202.

march would have disclosed to him the impossibility of Smith's arrival in time, and have enabled him to send another corps from his superabundant force to assist Thomas. Such delay of only a few days could not have been of serious consequence in respect to Sherman's plans. The near approach of winter was the only reason why an early start was important; and that was not considered any very serious obstacle to the operations of Hood or Thomas in a more unfavorable country for winter operations.

The railroad was in running order to Atlanta, and the enemy's cavalry were then known to be far from it. Sherman could have kept his army supplied, and ready to start any day he pleased. Why not have waited to see whether Thomas could get together troops enough to cope with Hood, and then, when sufficient preparation had been assured to fight the enemy, and only then, start off on a march where there was no considerable enemy to fight?

In the estimate of time, Sherman had no right to disregard even Thomas's well-known "slowness of thought and action," but was bound to take that into account.

I have never yet been able to see the wisdom of taking any hazard of defeat in Tennessee when we had ample force at command to secure victory there, with enough remaining to march wherever its commander pleased through the South, except where Hood's or Lee's army might be. By this I mean to say that three, or even two, of Sherman's corps could have gone to Savannah, or anywhere else, just as well as four, and thus have left Thomas force enough to make the defeat of Hood sure beyond contingency; or that Sherman should have delayed his march to the sea until Thomas had concentrated troops enough to defeat Hood.

The question which now presents itself for critical consideration is, Upon what military theory was Sherman's " march to the sea " based ?

Sherman himself explains it as a change of base, and he estimates its value in comparison with that of his subsequent operations in the ratio of one to ten. But why those subsequent operations, or a change of base with a view to any such ulterior purpose ? Grant had not at that time even suggested the need of Sherman's aid against Lee, and events proved that no such need existed. When Sherman started for Savannah from Atlanta, the Confederate force in the Gulf States was quite equal to Lee's army in Virginia, while Grant's army was larger than Sherman's. Could Sherman have contemplated at that time such a thing as going to Grant's assistance, where he was not needed, and leaving Hood's army behind him ?

A change of base to Savannah or Mobile had been contemplated as a probable necessity of future operations in Georgia or in the Gulf States, upon the capture of Atlanta ; but that of course upon the supposition that there would still be a formidable army of the Confederacy in those States against which operations were to be conducted. When that Confederate army, under Hood, marched toward the west, with the evident intention to carry the war into Tennessee and Kentucky, why a change of base by Sherman in the opposite direction, to Savannah ?

Sherman appears to have supposed at first that Hood would follow him when he started on his march through Georgia, as Hood had supposed that Sherman would follow him into Tennessee. Was there any more reason for the one supposition than the other ? Ought not Sherman as well as Hood to have known his antagonist better than such a supposition would imply ? Was it not extremely unreasonable to suppose that Hood, after he had marched hundreds of miïes west from Atlanta and reached the base of his projected operations in Tennessee, would turn back and follow Sherman at such a distance in his rear? It is perfectly evident that such a stern-chase by Hood was contemplated only as a bare possibility, not by any means as a probable result of Sherman's march. It could have had no influence in forming Sherman's final determination to make that march. In fact, the march does not appear to have been finally decided on—certainly it was not commenced—until Hood had gone so far in the opposite direction as to make his pursuit of Sherman out of the question, and had fully disclosed his plan to invade Tennessee. It was surely, therefore, an extraordinary spectacle to see the main Union army marching where there was no considerable hostile force to meet it, leaving a comparatively small detachment to cope with the formidable enemy!

Of course Sherman could not fall back into Tennessee, and thus let Hood put him on the defensive, even for a short time. He could afford only to send back a detachment large enough to enable Thomas, with the other forces he could assemble, to hold Nashville and prevent Hood from crossing the Cumberland. This is virtually but little more than what Sherman did in that regard.

There then remained to Sherman practically only one line of action at all consistent with the dictates of established principles in the conduct of a military campaign: that was to strike with his superior remaining force for Hood's rear, south of the Tennessee River. Such a movement could have been commenced immediately upon Hood's march in that direction. Supplies would have been drawn, first from Chattanooga and afterward from Stevenson, and then from Decatur, Sherman's line of supply being thus very much shortened. A small detachment at Atlanta could have destroyed the works of military value in that place, and the railroad thence back to Chattanooga, being completely covered in this work by

Sherman's army, without delaying its march a single day. Sherman could thus have easily struck Hood south of the Tennessee before the latter could have made his preparations for crossing that river. Indeed, with Sherman marching in that direction, even so bold a man as Hood could hardly have been so reckless as to have crossed the Tennessee; and if he had, his destruction must have been sure. Hence the least result would have been simply to transfer the theater of operations from Georgia to Alabama, or perhaps to Mississippi, and greatly to shorten Sherman's line of supply. And what possible difference could it make in which part of the revolted States the theater of war might be, so long as the Confederate army, to destroy which was the only important object of a campaign, was there? To avoid a transfer of the battlefield from Georgia to Alabama or Mississippi, was it wise to run the risk of transferring it to Kentucky or Ohio? Perhaps no movement which could have been contemplated by the Confederate authorities would have been more greatly to Sherman's advantage over Hood than the one they adopted.

I cannot better show my own exact impression at the time respecting the operations of Sherman and Hood in 1864, than by an illustration that will be at once appreciated on every farm in America. When two fighting-cocks meet for the first time, battle is joined without delay, and is prosecuted with all possible vigor and skill. If the result is decisive the victor's triumph is loudly proclaimed, while the defeated combatant, with lowered crest, seeks safety in flight. If, on the contrary, the result is a drawn battle, the two antagonists, as if by common consent, slowly separate, carrying their heads high, and sharply watching each other. When distance has assured the close of that contest, they severally go to feeding, as if nothing unusual had happened, or else march off to seek some less formidable foe. Neither

20

utters a note of defiance until he is well beyond the other's reach.

The correspondence between Grant and Sherman, especially the letters from Grant of September 12, and from Sherman of September 20, both carried by Grant's staff officer, Colonel Horace Porter, show a complete understanding of the situation at that time, and perfect accord in respect to the operations appropriate to that situation.[1] Savannah was to be captured, if practicable, by military and naval forces from the east, and Sherman was so to manœuver in respect to Hood's army as to swing round the latter and thus place himself in position to open communication with Savannah as his new base. This was the simple, logical plan dictated by the situation, which had for a long time been considered and worked out after weighing all the advantages and disadvantages of other possible plans.

But very soon after Sherman despatched his letter of September 20 by Colonel Porter, Hood commenced his movement to Sherman's rear, and then far to the west, which was designed to and did radically change the military situation in view of which the carefully matured plan described in Sherman's letter of September 20 had been formed. Sherman, as clearly appears from his despatches later than September 20, considered long and apparently with great doubt what change ought to be made in his own plans in consequence of the altered situation due to the unexpected movements of his enterprising adversary. That some very important change in Sherman's plans was imperative was a matter of course. A general cannot well make his own plans entirely upon his own theory as to what his enemy will or ought to do, but must be governed in some measure by what the other actually does. General Sherman evidently perceived quite clearly what established rules of action re-

1 War Records, Vol. XXXIX, part ii, pp. 364, 411.

quired to be done, and General Grant even more clearly, as was shown in his despatches of October 11, 1864, and others.

It seems hardly possible to speak seriously of many of the reasons given by Sherman for finally deciding to leave his old adversary to the care of Thomas's inferior force. He said, for instance, in his despatch to Grant of November 2: "If I could hope to overhaul Hood, I would turn against him with my whole force. . . . No single army can catch him." [1] Sherman had been "catching" Hood with a single army all summer, and without the slightest difficulty. What reason had he to conclude that it would be impossible to do so later? As my experience proved, it was as easy to "catch" him in November, though with a smaller force, as it had been in July and August with a much larger force, and Thomas had the same experience in December. As Sherman knew from his own experience, as well as I, whether the pursuing force was larger or smaller, Hood was about the easiest man in the world to "catch," even by a "single" army. But Sherman had under his command at that time, in Georgia and Tennessee, as he said with great emphasis and confidence, two armies, each larger than Hood's, even assuming the largest estimate then made of the strength of Hood's army. It appears that Sherman gave Hood credit at that time for only thirty thousand infantry, besides cavalry.[2] If that was his estimate, then he had at least three or four armies (including the reinforcements he counted on for Thomas in Tennessee), each equal in strength to Hood's. Is it possible Sherman thought he could not catch Hood with three or four armies? But another despatch from Sherman, dated November 2, seems to show that his estimate of Hood's army was more than 50,000, instead of 30,000; for in that despatch he said in substance that unless he drew Slocum's corps back from Atlanta, and

---

[1] War Records, Vol. XXXIX, part iii, p. 594. [2] ibid., p. 576.

abandoned that place, his army would be inferior to Hood's.[1] Now Slocum's corps numbered 10,000 men, and Sherman marched to the sea with 60,000 after stripping down to the best possible fighting condition. Hence Sherman, after sending back the Fourth and Twenty-third corps to Thomas, and leaving out Slocum's corps, had 50,000 men, and therefore according to this reckoning Hood had *more* than 50,000. Forty thousand would have been a reasonable estimate for Sherman to have made of Hood's strength, with his more accurate knowledge than any of his subordinate commanders could have. But, somehow, the estimate of Hood's force at that time accepted by Thomas and his subordinates in Tennessee was 45,000, besides cavalry, which was understood to be 10,000, or even 12,000 including Forrest's separate command. But even this was less than half of Sherman's two armies.

Sherman made no attempt to "catch" Hood during his raid in Sherman's rear in September, 1864, nor to interfere with his movement to the west. In his "Memoirs,"[2] Sherman says: "At first I thought of interposing my whole army in the Chattooga Valley, so as to prevent Hood's escape south. . . . He would be likely to retreat eastward by Spring Place, which I did not want him to do." Even thus early in the game Sherman saw the opportunity Hood was probably going to give him to make his projected change of base to Savannah, and hence he took care not to prevent Hood from completing his "coöperative" movement.

Sherman determined to destroy Atlanta and his railroad back to Chattanooga, abandon entirely his former base of operations and line of supply, and assume a new base of future operations on the Atlantic or the gulf. In other words, Sherman decided that he could not attempt to hold any part of the territory he had conquered in the

[1] *Ibid.*, p. 594.　　　　[2] Vol. II, p. 154.

Atlanta campaign; that conquest was valuable only in the opportunity it gave him to destroy everything of military importance in that territory — that is, Atlanta and the railroads. The question then arises, What possible difference could it make in which direction he moved after having decided not to hold any part of that territory, but to destroy it? Why would a move toward the west any more than a move toward the east have the appearance of losing all that had been gained, after he had destroyed it? The simple fact is, the Confederate commander had abandoned Georgia to its fate in the vain hope of putting Sherman on the defensive, not realizing, apparently, that Sherman had ample force for defensive purposes, besides an army superior to Hood's for aggressive operations. The Southern army was thus placed where Sherman could operate against it by a much shorter line, and hence with a much larger force, if that was what he wished to do. He could at the same time, if he thought it necessary or desirable, inflict upon Georgia the destruction which the Confederate commander wanted to prevent, but had in fact invited by abandoning that State, and that without materially impairing the strength of his (Sherman's) main army operating against the main force of the enemy. As suggested by Grant, a cavalry raid through Georgia would have accomplished that destruction as well as a march of 60,000 men. Hence, in the light of all that appears in the records up to the time when Sherman actually started on his march, no valid military reason had been given why Sherman should not have sent a cavalry raid into Georgia, as Grant suggested, to destroy everything there, and thus negative Mr. Davis's promise of protection, while he (Sherman) pursued relentlessly the strictly military plan Grant had prescribed for him to break up Hood's army or capture it, which Sherman had as yet failed to accomplish.

Manifestly some other motive besides the motives stated

in Sherman's telegraphic despatches must have decided him to carry out his plan to make the march to the sea. The boastful assurance and threat of the Confederate commander-in-chief,[1] referred to by Sherman, gave at least some reason for Sherman's defiant response by himself marching through Georgia instead of sending a subordinate; and the partial execution of that threat by Forrest's cavalry, referred to in Sherman's despatch of November 1 to Grant, gave a strong reason for Sherman's eager determination to march at once, without waiting for anything but his own preparations. In his article, "The Grand Strategy of the Last Year of the War,"[2] Sherman reveals one of the reasons for his haste in starting on his march. "How free and glorious I felt," he says, "when the magic telegraph was cut, which prevented the possibility of orders of any kind from the rear coming to delay or hinder us!" A letter written by Sherman to Grant, November 6, on the eve of his start for the sea, also gave reasons, other than military, for his famous march. In Sherman's "Memoirs" no quotation is made from this letter,[3] and it is referred to very briefly without giving any suggestion of its important contents.

General Sherman thus stated his reasons for writing that letter: "I have heretofore telegraphed and written you pretty fully, but I still have some thoughts in my busy brain that should be confided to you as a key to future developments."

Then Sherman explained, with the art of which he was master, clearly, logically, and convincingly, the reasons for the operations of his army from the fall of Atlanta down to the time of his writing, by which he had com-

[1] Mr. Jefferson Davis's speech. See General Sherman's "Memoirs," Vol. II, p. 141.

[2] See the Century War Book,

"Battles and Leaders of the Civil War," Vol. IV, p. 257.

[3] War Records, Vol. XXXIX, part iii, p. 658.

pletely defeated his adversary's designs, closing with the
following language:

> Now, as to the second branch of my proposition, I admit that
> the first object should be the destruction of that army; and if
> Beauregard moves his infantry and artillery up into that pocket
> about Jackson and Paris, I will feel strongly tempted to move
> Thomas directly against him, and myself move rapidly by Deca-
> tur and Purdy to cut off his retreat. . . . These are the reasons
> which have determined my former movements.

General Sherman then continues by explaining the
reasons which induced him not to carry out the movement above suggested.

Now come the reasons for the future movements upon
which Sherman had then fully decided, after having obtained General Grant's consent, and which he was about
to begin. After stating what he had done "in the last
ten days" to prepare for his march, he said:

> Then the question presents itself what shall be done? On the
> supposition always that Thomas can hold the line of the Tennes-
> see, and very shortly be able to assume the offensive as against
> Beauregard, I propose to act in such a manner against the mate-
> rial resources of the South as utterly to negative Davis's boasted
> threat and promises of protection. If we can march a well-ap-
> pointed army right through his territory, it is a demonstration
> to the world, foreign and domestic, that we have a power which
> Davis cannot resist. This may not be war, but rather states-
> manship; nevertheless it is overwhelming to my mind that there
> are thousands of people abroad and in the South who will reason
> thus: If the North can march an army right through the South,
> it is proof positive that the North can prevail in this contest,
> leaving only open the question of its willingness to use that
> power.

It was, perhaps, not *war*, but rather *statesmanship* upon
which Sherman was about to enter — not to defeat and
destroy or capture the Confederate armies, but to demon-

strate in the most positive manner that the "North can prevail in this contest," provided only it is willing to use its power. And by what means was this demonstration to be made? By marching a large army through the South where there was and could be no Confederate army able to oppose it, destroying everything of military value, including food, and continuing this operation until the government and people of the Southern States, and people abroad, should find the demonstration convincing. Again I quote:

Now, Mr. Lincoln's election, which is assured, coupled with the conclusion thus reached, makes a complete, logical whole. Even without a battle, the result, operating upon the minds of sensible men, would produce fruits more than compensating for the expense, trouble, and risk.

The election of Mr. Lincoln meant, of course, continued ascendancy of the "war party" at the North, and that, coupled with the conclusion above reached, made, as Sherman so forcibly stated it, "a complete, logical whole." General Sherman then went on to give in his masterly way the advantages and disadvantages of the several objectives open to him as the goal of his march, reserving to himself finally the choice between three,— Savannah, Mobile, and Pensacola,— trusting to Richmond papers to keep Grant well advised of his movements and of his final choice of the objective; and then, near the close of this letter, in discussing the military aspects of his proposed march, upon which he was about entering, he reverted to the old theory of the line of the Tennessee — "on the supposition always that Thomas can hold the line of the Tennessee, and very shortly be able to assume the offensive as against Beauregard."

It is impossible not to admire the thoroughness with which Sherman had considered all possible or even imaginary difficulties in his way, nor to suppress a smile at the supreme confidence with which he set out, with sixty thousand of the best soldiers in the world, upon a march through a fine healthy country laden with abundance of supplies for men and animals, at a time when only two armies in the South were strong enough to offer him any serious opposition, both of them farther from his line of march than he was from his goal when he started, one besieged by Grant in Petersburg, and the other already commencing an aggressive campaign against Thomas in Tennessee! It is equally impossible to speak seriously of the apprehension of some geographers and logisticians that Hood would interfere in some way with Sherman's march through Georgia. Hood could not have got within two hundred miles of Sherman before the latter had destroyed as much of Georgia as he wished, and then captured Savannah. Of course Sherman was not disturbed by any apprehension that Hood might possibly oppose his march to Savannah. He could have meant by what he said in his despatches on that subject only that Hood would be compelled by "public clamor" to return to Georgia to defend that State against Sherman's *further* operations. Hence his strong insistence that Thomas pursue Hood with energy, and thus keep him out of his (Sherman's) way.

It had never occurred to me, if the fact ever existed, that the rebellion could not be suppressed by crushing or capturing the Confederate armies, or that our vastly superior military strength must necessarily be employed in crushing the Southern people, however much they might deserve crushing, or else that we must give up the contest. Yet while I never saw the necessity for what Sherman called "statesmanship" rather than "war," I would never have hesitated for a moment to say, what I now repeat, if it really was necessary, in order to put down the rebellion and restore the Union, to destroy all the property in the South, in the name of a just and beneficent God, destroy it all! Hence my objection to Sherman's plans was based upon my conviction that such plans were not at that time, and never had been, necessary. Yet such plans are legitimate and often necessary, and no man is wise enough to tell in advance whether they may prove to be necessary or not. The surest way to reach results is the way Sherman adopted. In either a civil or a foreign war, such methods may be very bad policy; but very few men are cool-headed enough in civil war, even if wise enough, to see what good policy dictates, and this is even more true of men at a distance than of those at the front. Men who have been fighting most of the time for three or four years generally become pretty cool, while those in the rear seem to become hotter and hotter as the end approaches, and even for some time after it is reached. They must in some way work off the surplus passion which the soldier has already exhausted in battle. Whatever may be true as to Sherman's methods before Lee surrendered, the destruction inflicted on the South after that time was solely the work of passion, and not of reason. Of this last Sherman was innocent.

Sherman's destruction of military supplies and railroads did undoubtedly render impossible any great prolongation of the war, if that would otherwise have been possible; but it did not materially hasten the actual collapse of the rebellion, which was due to Grant's capture of Lee's army. Besides, if Grant had not captured Lee, Sherman would. Lee could not possibly have escaped them both. Hence Sherman's destruction of property in Georgia, South Carolina, and North Carolina did not hasten the end of the rebellion. If General Sherman was, at the time he planned his march to the sea, informed of the nearly bankrupt condition of the United States treasury, that fact went far toward justifying his action in leaving as small a force as possible with Thomas, and even in starting on his march before Thomas was fully ready to meet Hood. For to make his demonstration early enough and as convincing as possible to the people of the South and all the world, it was important to move at once, and to show that his march was not a mere rapid *raid*, but a deliberate march of a formidable army capable of crushing anything that might get in its way, and that without waiting for anything that might occur in its rear. Such a march of such an army might well have been sufficient to convince everybody that the United States had the military power to crush the rebellion, and even destroy everything in the South, before the world should find out that the resources of the government had been exhausted, and that the United States had not the financial strength necessary to make any further military use of the million of men they then had on the muster- and pay-rolls. To have given the still more convincing proof of the power of the Union, by destroying one of the Confederate armies, would have taken a longer time.

The following despatches fully show Sherman's first plan, assented to by Grant, the essential feature of which was that Thomas should be able to " hold the line of the Tennessee firmly," and the corresponding information and instructions to Thomas:

SHERMAN TO GRANT.

CARTERSVILLE, GA., October 10, 1864, 12 M.

. . . Hood is now crossing the Coosa, twelve miles below Rome, bound west. If he passes over to the Mobile and Ohio road, had I not better execute the plan of my letter sent by Colonel Porter, and leave General Thomas with the troops now in Tennessee to defend the State? He will have an ample force when the reinforcements ordered reach Nashville.

GRANT TO SHERMAN.

CITY POINT, VA., October 11, 1864, 11 A. M.

Your despatch received. Does it not look as if Hood was going to attempt the invasion of middle Tennessee? . . . If he does this, he ought to be met and prevented from getting north of the Tennessee River. If you were to cut loose, I do not believe you would meet Hood's army. . . . Hood would probably strike for Nashville, thinking by going north he could inflict greater damage upon us than we could upon the rebels by going south. If there is any way of getting at Hood's army, I would prefer that, but I must trust to your own judgment. I find I shall not be able to send a force from here to act with you on Savannah. Your movements, therefore, will be independent of mine, at least until the fall of Richmond takes place. I am afraid Thomas, with such lines of road as he has to protect, could not prevent Hood going north. With Wilson turned loose with all your cavalry, you will find the rebels put much more on the defensive than heretofore.

SHERMAN TO GRANT.

October 11, 1864, 10 A. M.

Hood moved his army from Palmetto Station across by Dallas and Cedartown, and is now on the Coosa River, south of Rome. He threw one corps on my road at Acworth, and I was forced to follow. I hold Atlanta with the Twentieth Corps, and have strong detachments along my line. These reduce my active force to a comparatively small army. We cannot remain now on the defensive. With 25,000 men, and the bold cavalry he has, he can constantly break my road. I would infinitely prefer to make a wreck of the road and of the country from Chattanooga to Atlanta, including the latter city, send back all my wounded and worthless, and, with my effective army, move through Georgia, smashing things to the sea. Hood may turn into Tennessee and Kentucky, but I believe he will be forced to follow me. Instead of being on the defensive, I would be on the offensive ; instead of guessing at what he means to do, he would have to guess at my plans. The difference in war is full 25 per cent. I can make Savannah, Charleston, or the mouth of the Chattahoochee. Answer quick, as I know we will not have the telegraph long.[1]

[1] War Records, Vol. XXXIX, part iii, p. 202.

GRANT TO SHERMAN.

October 11, 1864, 11:30 P. M.

Your despatch of to-day received. If you are satisfied the trip to the sea-coast can be made, holding the line of the Tennessee firmly, you may make it, destroying all the railroad south of Dalton or Chattanooga, as you think best.

SHERMAN TO THOMAS.

October 20, 1864.

. . . I want all things bent to the following general plan of action for the next three months. Out of the forces now here and at Atlanta I propose to organize an efficient army of from 60,000 to 65,000 men, with which I propose to destroy Macon, Augusta, and, it may be, Savannah and Charleston, but I will always keep open the alternatives of the mouth of Appalachicola and Mobile. By this I propose to demonstrate the vulnerability of the South, and make its inhabitants feel that war and individual ruin are synonymous terms. To pursue Hood is folly, for he can twist and turn like a fox and wear out any army in pursuit. To continue to occupy long lines of railroads simply exposes our small detachments to be picked up in detail, and forces me to make countermarches to protect lines of communication. I know I am right in this, and shall proceed to its maturity. As to details, I propose to take General Howard and his army, General Schofield and his, and two of your corps, viz., Generals Davis and Slocum. . . . I will send General Stanley, with the Fourth Corps, across by Will's Valley and Caperton's to Stevenson to report to you. . . . I want you to retain command in Tennessee, and before starting I will give you delegated authority over Kentucky, Mississippi, Alabama, etc., whereby there will be unity of action behind me. I will want you to hold Chattanooga and Decatur in force, and on the occasion of my departure, of which you shall have ample notice, to watch Hood close. I think he will follow me, at least with his cavalry, in which event I want you to push south from Decatur and the head of the Tennessee for Columbus, Miss., and Selma, not absolutely to reach these points, but to divert or pursue according to the state of facts. If, however, Hood turns on

you, you must act defensively on the line of the Tennessee. . . .
I do not fear that the Southern army will again make a lodgment on the Mississippi. . . . The only hope of a Southern success is in the remote regions difficult of access. We have now
a good entering wedge, and should drive it home. . . .

SHERMAN TO GRANT.

GAYLESVILLE, ALA., October 22, 1864.

I feel perfectly master of the situation here. I still hold Atlanta and the road, with all bridges and vital points well guarded,
and I have in hand an army before which Hood has retreated
precipitately down the valley of the Coosa. It is hard to divine
his future plans; but by abandoning Georgia, and taking position with his rear to Selma, he threatens the road from Chattanooga to Atlanta, and may move to Tennessee by Decatur. He
cannot cross the Tennessee except at Muscle Shoals, for all other
points are patrolled by our gunboats. I am now perfecting arrangements to put into Tennessee a force able to hold the line
of the Tennessee whilst I break up the railroad in front of Dalton, including the city of Atlanta, and push into Georgia, and
break up all its railroads and depots, capture its horses and
negroes, make desolation everywhere, destroy the factories at
Macon, Milledgeville, and Augusta, and bring up with 60,000
men on the sea-shore about Savannah or Charleston. I think
this far better than defending a long line of railroad. I will
leave General George H. Thomas to command all my division
behind me, and take with me only the best fighting material.

But a few days later Sherman had made a radical
change in his previous plan. He telegraphed Grant, from
Rome, Georgia, November 1, as follows:

As you foresaw, and as Jeff. Davis threatened, the enemy is
now in the full tide of execution of his grand plan to destroy my
communications and defeat this army. His infantry, about 30,-
000, with Wheeler's and Roddey's cavalry, from 7000 to 10,000,
are now in the neighborhood of Tuscumbia and Florence, and,
the water being low, is able to cross at will. Forrest seems to be

scattered from Eastport to Jackson, Paris, and the lower Tennessee; and General Thomas reports the capture by him of a gunboat and five transports. General Thomas has near Athens and Pulaski Stanley's corps, about 15,000 strong, and Schofield's corps, 10,000, en route by rail, and has at least 20,000 to 25,000 men, with new regiments and conscripts arriving all the time; also Rosecrans promises the two divisions of Smith and Mower, belonging to me, but I doubt if they can reach Tennessee in less than ten days. If I were to let go Atlanta and north Georgia and make for Hood, he would, as he did here, retreat to the southwest, leaving his militia, now assembling at Macon and Griffin, to occupy our conquests, and the work of last summer would be lost. I have retained about 50,000 good troops, and have sent back full 25,000; and having instructed General Thomas to hold defensively Nashville, Chattanooga, and Decatur, all strongly fortified and provisioned for a long siege, I will destroy all the railroads of Georgia and do as much substantial damage as is possible, reaching the sea-coast near one of the points hitherto indicated, trusting that General Thomas, with his present troops and the influx of new troops promised, will be able in a very few days to assume the offensive. Hood's cavalry may do a good deal of damage, and I have sent Wilson back with all dismounted cavalry, retaining only about 4500. This is the best I can do, and shall, therefore, when I can get to Atlanta the necessary stores, move as soon as possible.

To that despatch General Grant replied, November 2:

Your despatch of 9 A. M. yesterday is just received. I despatched you the same date, advising that Hood's army, now that it had worked so far north, be looked upon more as the objective. With the force, however, you have left with Thomas, he must be able to take care of Hood and destroy him. I do not really see that you can withdraw from where you are to follow Hood without giving up all we have gained in territory. I say, then, go as you propose.

Thus Grant gave his assent to Sherman's proposition that Nashville, Chattanooga, and Decatur be held defensively, even during a long siege if necessary, instead of the line of the Tennessee, as at first insisted on by Gen-

eral Grant. Yet Grant's assent was given in view of
Sherman's trust that Thomas would be able *in a very few
days* to assume the offensive.

Sherman's despatch to Thomas of the same date (November 1) instructed him as to the policy then determined on, in lieu of that which had contemplated holding
the line of the Tennessee firmly, as follows:

Despatch of last night received. The fact that Forrest is
down about Johnsonville, while Hood, with his infantry, is still
about Florence and Tuscumbia, gives you time for concentration. The supplies about Chattanooga are immense, and I will
soon be independent of them; therefore I would not risk supplies coming in transitu from Nashville to Chattanooga. In like
manner, we have large supplies in Nashville, and if they be well
guarded, and Hood can't get our supplies, he can't stay in Tennessee long. General Schofield will go to you as rapidly as cars
can take him. I have no doubt, after the emergency is past, and
the enemy has done us considerable damage, reinforcements
will pour to you more than can be provided for or taken care of.
In the meantime do your best. I will leave here to-morrow for
Kingston, and keep things moving toward the south; therefore
hold fast all new troops coming to you, excepting such as are
now at Chattanooga, to whom I will give orders.

Yet in his letter to Grant, five days later, Sherman
reverts to the original plan: "On the supposition, always,
that Thomas can hold the line of the Tennessee."

November 7, Sherman telegraphed Grant: ". . . On
that day [November 10] or the following, if affairs should
remain as now in Tennessee, I propose to begin the
movement which I have hitherto fully described . . ."
To which despatch General Grant replied: ". . . I see
no present reason for changing your plan. . . ."

General Grant does not refer to the later despatches in
his general report, July 22, 1865, quoted in his "Memoirs," but uses the following language:

With the troops thus left at his disposal, there was little doubt that General Thomas could hold the line of the Tennessee, or, in the event Hood should force it, would be able to concentrate and beat him in battle. It was therefore readily consented to that Sherman should start for the sea-coast.

General Sherman also omits to make any reference in his "Memoirs" to the despatches respecting a possible long siege of Nashville, Chattanooga, and Decatur; but he says in a despatch of November 2 to Grant, quoted in his "Memoirs":

If I turn back, the whole effect of my campaign will be lost. By my movements I have thrown Beauregard [Hood] well to the west, and Thomas will have ample time and sufficient troops to hold him until the reinforcements from Missouri reach him. We have now ample supplies at Chattanooga and Atlanta, and can stand a month's interruption to our communications. I do not believe the Confederate army can reach our railroad lines except by cavalry raids, and Wilson will have cavalry enough to checkmate them. I am clearly of opinion that the best results will follow my contemplated movement through Georgia.

The following language is found in a despatch dated November 11, midnight, from Sherman to Thomas, which is especially important as giving the last expression of his views of the situation, and of what Thomas would be able to do after Sherman started for the sea:

I can hardly believe that Beauregard would attempt to work against Nashville from Corinth as a base at this stage of the war, but all information seems to point that way. If he does, you will whip him out of his boots; but I rather think you will find commotion in his camp in a day or two. Last night we burned Rome, and in two or more days will burn Atlanta; and he must discover that I am not retreating, but, on the contrary, fighting for the very heart of Georgia. . . . These [some Confederate movements about Rome and Atlanta] also seem to indicate that Beauregard expects me to retreat. . . . To-morrow I begin the movement laid down in my Special Field Orders, No. 115, and shall keep things moving thereafter. . . . By using de-

21

tachments of recruits and dismounted cavalry in your fortifications, you will have Generals Schofield and Stanley and General A. J. Smith, strengthened by eight or ten new regiments and all of Wilson's cavalry. You could safely invite Beauregard across the Tennessee River and prevent his ever returning. I still believe, however, that public clamor will force him to turn and follow me, in which event you should cross at Decatur and move directly toward Selma as far as you can transport supplies. . . . You may act . . . on the certainty that I sally from Atlanta on the 16th instant with about 60,000 well provisioned, but expecting to live chiefly on the country.

The reason for this sudden and radical change of program is made perfectly clear by Sherman's despatch of November 1 and others: "The enemy is now in the full tide of execution of his grand plan to destroy my communications and defeat this army." Sherman's defiant spirit, thus aroused, brooked no delay. He would not wait for anything but his own necessary preparations. Nashville, Chattanooga, and Decatur could stand a long siege, and these alone he regarded as of strategical importance. The enemy would doubtless do " considerable damage," but afterward "reinforcements will pour to you " (Thomas). He convinced himself that Thomas had troops enough; but, "to make things sure," he might "call on the governors of Indiana and Kentucky for some militia "! In the meantime, he (Sherman) would " destroy all the railroads in Georgia and do as much substantial damage as is possible." Thus recklessly challenged by the Confederate chief, Sherman must not only accept that challenge, but do it at once. Perhaps if Jefferson Davis had known William T. Sherman as well as some of us did, he would not have uttered that challenge.

From Grant's "Memoirs"[1] it appears that General Grant not only confirms Sherman's claim in respect to his

[1] Vol. II, pp. 374-6.

independent authorship of the plan, but says he (General Grant) was in favor of that plan from the time it was first submitted to him, and credits his chief of staff, General Rawlins, with having been "very bitterly opposed to it," and with having appealed to the authorities at Washington to stop it.

This recollection of General Grant, after the lapse of so long a time, and when he was suffering almost beyond endurance from a fatal disease, may possibly, it seems to me, not express the views he entertained in October, 1864, quite so fully or accurately as his despatch of October 11, 1864, 11 A. M., to General Sherman, heretofore quoted.

That despatch was a literal prediction of what Hood actually did. It was dictated by clear military foresight, whether of Grant or Rawlins. How far world-wide approval of Sherman's plans after their brilliant success may have obscured the past can only be conjectured. As distinctly stated by Grant himself soon afterward, he clearly saw that somebody ought to be criticized; but, in view of the results, he decided to let it pass.

However all this may be, even my respect for the opinions of the greatest of Union soldiers cannot alter the conclusion I have reached after many years of study and mature consideration. I can only say that the opinion ascribed to General Rawlins, as opposed to General Grant's, was in my judgment the better of the two; and that General Rawlins, though he had not the advantage of an early military education, was a man of great natural ability, and had learned much from more than three years' experience in war, after which the differences in military judgment which had existed at the beginning must have very largely, if not entirely, disappeared. General Rawlins was my immediate successor in the War Department, and would, I doubt not, have made a great reputation there if his life had been prolonged.

I believe Grant's own sound military judgment dictated his first answer to Sherman, dissenting from the proposition to begin the march to the sea before Hood's army was disposed of, or that result assured. His great confidence in the genius of his brilliant subordinate, and in Sherman's judgment that he had given Thomas ample means to take care of Hood, no matter what that bold and reckless adversary might do, dictated Grant's final assent to Sherman's project. Their correspondence shows this so clearly and fully that there would seem to be no need of my making any special reference to it. I do so only because of the statement in General Grant's "Memoirs." Very possibly General Grant may have meant, in his "Memoirs," only that he approved the general project, under the condition that sufficient force would be left "to take care of Hood and destroy him," not caring to say anything about the fulfilment or nonfulfilment of that condition.

From about October 1 till the time Sherman started on his march — six weeks — he seems to have been so intent on the execution of that project, and upon doing it with as large an army as possible, that no question of military principle or of fact could be permitted to stand in his way. He assumed and maintained throughout that the only question was whether he should continue the aggressive, or allow the enemy's movements to put him on the defensive, refusing to consider any other possible plan of aggressive operations, except for a moment in response to advice from Grant, and then brushing it aside as impracticable. — "If I could hope to overhaul Hood," etc. In like manner, he appears to have convinced himself that his arrangements for direct operations against Hood by Thomas in Tennessee were very materially more complete than they were in fact, and he so represented the matter to General Grant. It seems quite certain that Grant was laboring under a serious misapprehension in respect to Thomas's condition to cope with Hood, and no doubt Grant's subsequent impatience in respect to Thomas's action was largely due to this fact. This point deserves close consideration.

Grant's first assent to Sherman's plan was made, October 11, on the condition of "holding the line of the Tennessee firmly." On October 22 Sherman telegraphed: "I am now perfecting arrangements to put into Tennessee a force able to hold the line of the Tennessee."

Even as late as November 1, Grant again suggested to Sherman that Hood ought to be his "objective," now that he "has gone so far north." At an earlier hour the same day, in the despatch above quoted, Sherman telegraphed, "trusting that General Thomas . . . will be able in a very few days to assume the offensive." To this Grant replied November 2: "With the force, however, you have left with Thomas, he must be able to take care of Hood and destroy him." In that despatch of November 1 Sherman had made a statement of the troops Thomas would have, including A. J. Smith's from Missouri, adding, "but I doubt if they can reach Tennessee in less than ten days." Now Smith's troops did not reach Tennessee in less than *thirty* days instead of ten days, and after the crisis of the campaign was passed; and the effective force in Tennessee before Smith's arrival was 13,000 men less than Sherman had stated it. So that the whole brunt of the fight with Hood fell upon the two corps which Sherman had sent back, without any help from the reinforcements upon which Sherman counted so largely. It was, in fact, *six weeks* instead of a "very few days" before Thomas was able "to assume the offensive." It was not even attempted to "hold the line of the Tennessee" either "firmly" or at all.

Having been absent from the army in the field during Hood's raid in Sherman's rear, I knew little personally about those estimates of the strength of the opposing forces. For the same reason, I knew nothing of Sherman's plans or correspondence with Grant which were considered or took place after the fall of Atlanta, though I had been perfectly familiar with the plans discussed previous to that time having in view a change of base to some point on the Atlantic or on the gulf, with a view to further operations in Georgia or the Gulf States, wherever there might be a hostile army to operate against. Yet when I met Sherman at Gaylesburg I was surprised to learn that he was going off to the sea with five sixths of his army, leaving Thomas, with only one of his six corps, and no other veteran troops then ready for field service, to take care of Hood until he could get A. J. Smith from Missouri, incorporate new regiments into the army and make them fit to meet the veteran enemy, remount his cavalry, and concentrate his garrisons and railroad guards in Tennessee! Of course I knew far less than Sherman did about all that, for I had no responsibility and little knowledge about Thomas's department. But I knew enough to feel astonished when Sherman told me what he proposed to do. I plainly told Sherman so, and urged him to send me back with my corps to join Stanley and help Thomas.[1]

Here arise several interesting questions which would be worthy of consideration, although a satisfactory solution of them might not be possible. Under Sherman's assurance as to what he had done for Thomas in Tennessee, Grant appears to have been fully satisfied that Thomas would be able to take care of Hood and destroy him, thus eliminating that Confederate army from the future problem in the Atlantic States. But could Sherman, with his more exact knowledge of what he actually had done, have felt the same confidence? In view of that knowledge and of the results of his own previous operations against Hood, could he have expected any

[1] See my letter to General Sherman, December 28, 1864, p. 254.

such result? Is it not more probable that Sherman simply expected to take advantage of Hood's temporary absence from Georgia to make his own change of base to Savannah? Did Sherman not, in fact, really expect Hood to follow him, even though at so great a distance, and be prepared to resist his future operations from Savannah? Sherman repeatedly said, in his despatches before he started, that he believed Hood would follow him, being compelled to do so by public clamor. What was Sherman's plan when he started for Savannah? Was it simply to effect a change of base, or was it for well-defined ulterior purposes? When did Sherman mature his plan to march to Virginia, and when did that plan first dawn upon Sherman's mind? In this connection, what significance is to be attached to the dates of events in Tennessee, especially the battles of Franklin and Nashville?

By the first mails which reached Sherman after he arrived on the coast, December 14 and 15, containing letters from Grant dated December 3 and 6, full information was received of the battle of Franklin, which had occurred November 30. Thomas's official report of the battle of Nashville was received by Sherman on December 24, but rumors of that victory had reached him earlier. Sherman's first letter to Grant, relative to future operations, written in reply to those from Grant of December 3 and 6, was dated December 16. In that letter was mentioned Sherman's plan in the following words: "Indeed, with my present command I had expected, upon reducing Savannah, instantly to march to Columbia, South Carolina, thence to Raleigh, and thence to report to you." Sherman's second letter to Grant, on the same subject, written in reply to Grant's letter of the 18th, was dated December 24, the day on which he received Thomas's report of the battle of Nashville. In this letter Sherman said: "I am also gratified that you have modified your former orders. . . . I feel no doubt whatever as to our future plans. I have thought them over so long and well that they appear as clear as daylight."

When Sherman first mentioned his future plan he knew that the success of his past plan in Tennessee had been assured. Thomas had succeeded in concentrating his forces at Nashville, and Hood had suffered a serious defeat in attempting to prevent it. At the time of Sherman's second letter, mentioning his very mature consideration of his future plans and perfect confidence in respect to them, he knew that Hood's army had been broken up, and had become a small factor in the future problem. How long, and to what extent, had Sherman anticipated these results in Tennessee, and matured his plans of future operations, which were dependent upon those results? I shall consider these several questions, which involve so intimately the character of my old commander.

CHAPTER XVII

SHERMAN'S PURPOSE IN MARCHING TO THE SEA — HIS EX-
PECTATIONS THAT THE CHANGE OF BASE WOULD BE
"STATESMANSHIP," IF NOT "WAR" — THE THOUSAND-
MILE MARCH OF HOOD'S MEN TO SURRENDER TO SHER-
MAN — THE CREDIT GIVEN BY GRANT TO SHERMAN —
"MASTER OF THE SITUATION" — THE FAME OF SHERMAN'S
GRAND MARCHES — HIS GREAT ABILITY AS A STRATEGIST.

THE actual result in Tennessee was more decisive than
Sherman had any good reason to expect. But he had
good reason to expect, and evidently did, that Thomas
would be able, after he had concentrated his troops, and
after Hood had done considerable damage, to drive the
latter out of Tennessee and pursue him with such force
and energy as fully to occupy his attention and prevent
him from interfering in any manner with Sherman's own
operations. Hence Sherman as well as Grant had reason
to assume that Hood's army would be eliminated from
the military problem in the Atlantic States. Again, the
general military situation as known to General Sherman,
or probably to anybody else, in October and November,
1864, did not indicate that Grant, with the force he then
had in Virginia, would be able to capture or destroy Lee's
army. He might undoubtedly capture Petersburg and
Richmond, but Lee would probably be able to withdraw
his army toward the south, nearer to his sources of supply, and by skilful manœuvers prolong the contest until
the National Government might abandon it. Grant's

letters at that time confirm this view of the military situation.

Some writers have attempted to explain and justify Sherman's action in taking with him so large an army, while leaving with Thomas one so much smaller, on the ground that he might meet in his march to the sea such opposition as possibly to require so large a force to overcome it. But to any one familiar with the facts, and to no one more than to Sherman, his army of 60,000 men was evidently out of all proportion to any possible resistance it could meet in Georgia. But when he should start northward from Savannah the case would become vastly different. At any point in the Carolinas he might possibly meet the whole of Lee's army. That is to say, Sherman's ulterior plan could not be prudently undertaken at all without an army as large as that with which he actually marched to the sea, namely, 60,000 men. Indeed, as the records show, Sherman considered a long time before he decided that he could spare the Twenty-third Corps to go back and help Thomas. If any question can possibly exist as to what was the essential part of Sherman's plan in marching to Savannah, what other possible military reason can be given for that march except to make the subsequent march to Virginia with so large an army? Why change his base to Savannah? What was he to operate against after he got there?

Nothing could have been clearer to any military mind in the fall of 1864, than that if either Lee's or Hood's army could be captured or destroyed, the surrender of the other must necessarily follow very quickly, and the rebellion be ended. No man could have been more earnest than Sherman in his laudable desire to make the capture of his own adversary the beginning of the end. Sherman's well-known character leaves this beyond question. It is not possible that he could have preferred a manifestation of the power of the nation by destroying Southern property rather than by destroying a Southern army.

But there was one objection — absolutely overruling, apparently, in Sherman's mind — to any further attempt by Sherman himself, with the main body of his army then in Georgia, to prosecute the primary military object of his campaign — the destruction or capture of Hood's army. To have done so would have conceded a temporary triumph to the chief of the Confederate armies, who had loudly proclaimed his purpose to drive Sherman out of Georgia, and protect that State from any further invasion. Such a concession, however temporary, was manifestly intolerable to Sherman's mind.[1] Besides, Sherman had formed and announced, with Grant's cordial concurrence, a well-matured plan of future operations. As "master of the situation," he could afford to go on and substantially execute that plan, or at least the primary part of it,— the change of base,— treating almost with contempt the enemy's bold design to thwart him. Although this must, at least for the time being, compel him personally to forego and leave to a subordinate the primary operations of a military campaign,—those directly against the opposing army,—the joint action of Sherman and Grant, each with a powerful army, directly against Lee's army in Virginia, was the surest and probably the shortest possible way to end the war. Hence Sherman's broad view of the entire national military situation, including the moral aspect of it, which was then of very great importance, gave rise to that grand conception of far-reaching strategy which must ever stamp its author as a master of that great art.

Sherman having thus come to the conclusion that he personally must abandon the attempt to "catch Hood," as he called it, his "busy brain" did not fail to perceive every possible alternative plan of operations. The aban-

[1] Sherman's "Memoirs," Vol. II, p. 141.

donment of Georgia by Hood had completely opened up two other alternatives, one of which was before not possible, and the other only partly so. The one was a movement upon Richmond or its communications to join with Grant in the capture of Lee's army, and the other was to destroy the military resources of the Southern Atlantic States. The first was too grand, and perhaps might seem too visionary, to be talked about at first, nor was any mention of it at that time necessary. Besides, events might possibly render the march to Richmond unnecessary or impracticable; or, possibly, Sherman might be compelled for some reason to make his new base at Pensacola or Mobile, though he was determined to make it at Savannah, if possible; and hence it was necessary to have, in reserve as it were, a sufficient logical reason for the preliminary operation, if that finally had to stand alone.

Again, that part of the original plan which contemplated the capture of Savannah in advance could not be carried out. Grant could not spare the troops from the east for that purpose. If that had been done, Sherman could have marched to Augusta, there replenished his supplies by the river from Savannah, and marched thence northward by the upland route instead of through the swamps of South Carolina. But, as it was, Sherman was, as he thought, compelled to go to Savannah first, capture that place himself, and make that the base for his northward march. Hence there was no need to say anything to anybody about what further was to be done until after Savannah was in Sherman's possession, and the time had arrived for him to consult Grant about the future. Yet in Sherman's remarkable letter to Grant, dated November 6, 1864,[1] written after it was too late to have any influence upon Grant's approval of Sherman's march, he disclosed to Grant the ulterior object he had in

[1] War Records, Vol. XXXIX, part iii, p. 658.

view. In discussing the reasons for selecting the route
to Savannah rather than either of the others, he said:
"Incidentally I might destroy the enemy's depots at
Macon and Augusta, and reach the sea-shore at Charleston or Savannah, from either of which points I could reinforce our armies in Virginia."

Of course Grant, no less than Sherman, must have
perceived instantly the full significance of Sherman's
change of base to Savannah the moment that move was
suggested. The question in what manner that concerted
action between Grant and Sherman against Lee should
be arranged could well be considered later, after that
march had been made and a new base established at Savannah. The correspondence between Grant and Sherman previous to Hood's march to the west, including
the letters of September 12 and 20, simply shows that
neither had at that time conceived the possibility of
any movement of Sherman toward Virginia. All their
thoughts had reference to continuing operations in the
south, Sherman's most important object being to get control of the Savannah River; or, as expressed, in his last
words: "If you can whip Lee, and I can march to the
Atlantic, I think Uncle Abe will give us a twenty days'
leave of absence to see the young folks." Their joint action against Lee does not appear to have been suggested
by either until Sherman's letter of November 6, which
was probably received by Grant after Sherman started.

The first thought suggested to Sherman by Hood's
movement "leaving open the road to Macon, as also to
Augusta," as embodied in his despatch to Halleck on
September 25, related simply to the opportunity thus
offered to carry into effect without difficulty the original
plan of a change of base to Savannah. But when Hood's
movement had gone so far, and his designs were so fully
disclosed, as practically to eliminate his army from the
problem in the Atlantic States, Sherman determined to

march as soon as possible, with the ulterior purpose to "reinforce our armies in Virginia." He telegraphed his determination to Grant on November 1, and on November 6 wrote him very fully, giving his reasons, including that to reinforce Grant. Hence Sherman was well able to say at Savannah on December 24: "I feel no doubt whatever as to our future plans. I have thought them over so long and well that they appear as clear as daylight."

It should be observed that Sherman's letter of November 6 to Grant was strictly confidential. "I have still some thoughts . . . that should be confided to you [that is, to Grant and to nobody else] as a key to future developments." Neither Grant nor Sherman appears to have made any use of that "key" for the public benefit. But it now unlocks the store-house of Sherman's mind, and shows to the world more of the real character of the great strategist than any other public document he ever wrote.

Then Grant was ready with his plan, first to seize and hold the Southern railroads by which supplies could reach Lee, and second, for Sherman and the most of his army to come to Virginia by sea, to which Sherman responded with all the loyalty of his most loyal nature, only mentioning incidentally his own plan. Thereupon, when Grant gave him an invitation to speak freely, he replied as above quoted, and explained in detail his plans for the northward march, to "be on the Roanoke, either at Raleigh or Weldon, by the time the spring fairly opens; and if you feel confident that you can whip Lee outside of his intrenchments, I feel equally confident that I can handle him in the open country."

But Sherman's "busy brain" had provided in advance even for the worst possible contingency — that after all his long march, however long it might prove to be, that march might have to "stand alone"— he might not actually take part in the capture of either of the Confederate armies.   Hence, before starting on his march, in his letter of November 6 to Grant he explained that his march would be "statesmanship" anyway, even if it was not "war." Sherman was not a man to be "left out," no matter what might happen.

But Sherman's good fortune was almost equal to his strategy and his skill in marching an army.   Although, as fate would have it, he did not have a chance to assist in the capture of Lee, Thomas had failed to obey his instructions to pursue Hood into the Gulf States, whereby the fragments of that "broken and dispirited" army, as Thomas well called it, were gathered together, under their old, able commander, General Johnston, and appeared in Sherman's front to oppose his northward march, and finally to capitulate to him at "Bennett's House" in North Carolina.   The remnant of that army which Sherman had disdained to pursue into Alabama or Mississippi had traveled a thousand miles to surrender to him!   No story of fiction could be more romantic than that fact of real war history.

It was not necessary for Sherman to produce his letter of November 6, 1864; but I have quoted from it here very largely to show that there was no possible contingency which his far-reaching mind had not foreseen and provided for.

Sherman's plan was so firmly fixed in his own mind, almost from the very start, that he was determined to adhere to it in spite of all possible opposition, even including the adverse opinions and advice of General Grant. Hence, as was his habit in such cases, he invented every imaginable reason, without regard to their logical or illogical character, to convince others of the soundness of his conclusion.   But the logic of the real reasons which convinced his own mind is, when the chaff is all winnowed away, as clear and bright as the golden grain.

In view of the great strategical project which Sherman

had mapped out for himself and which required a formidable army, and of his responsibility for what might be the result of operations against Hood in Tennessee, it was a difficult and delicate question to decide what force he should take with him, and what send back. My own belief always has been, and is now, that in view of his exact knowledge of Thomas's character and habits of thought and action, Sherman ought to have sent back another corps of veteran troops, or else have waited to see that Thomas was actually prepared to cope with Hood, preferably the latter, before going so far away that he could not render him any assistance. Yet, as has heretofore been shown, if Thomas had carried out Sherman's instructions by promptly concentrating his troops, there would have been no risk of serious results in Tennessee.

In connection with Sherman's operations it is essential to bear in mind the distinction between two radically different kinds of strategy, one of which has for its object the conquest of territory or the capture of places by defeating in battle or out-manœuvering the defending armies; while the other has for its object the destruction or capture of those armies, resulting, of course, in the conquest of all of the enemy's territory. The first kind may be all-sufficient, and hence best, in a foreign war having for its object anything less than total conquest; but in the suppression of a rebellion, as in a foreign conquest, the occupation of places or territory ought to be entirely ignored except so far as this contributes to the successful operation of armies against opposing forces. This fundamental principle appears to have been duly appreciated by the leading Union commanders near the close of the Civil War, though not so fully in its earlier stages. Military critics are apt to fall into error by not understanding the principle itself, or by overlooking the change of policy above referred to.

It is necessary not to confound the "march to the

sea" as actually conceived and executed by Sherman as a preliminary to the march northward for the capture of Lee's army, with the previous far-reaching strategic plans of Grant, of which Sherman and other chief commanders were informed in the spring of 1864.

Grant's plans had in view, as their great object, again to cut in two the Confederate territory, as had been done by the opening of the Mississippi River to the gulf. This next line of section might be Chattanooga, Atlanta, and Savannah, or Chattanooga, Atlanta, Montgomery, and Mobile. But with the disappearance of Hood's army from that theater of operations, all reason for that plan of "territorial" strategy had disappeared, and the occasion was then presented, for the first time, for the wholly different strategical plan of Sherman, of which Lee's army was the sole military objective. Grant was perfectly just to himself as well as to Sherman in giving the latter full credit for this last plan; and he modestly refrained from any more than a brief mention of his own plans, which unforeseen events had made it unnecessary fully to execute. But history will do justice to Grant's great strategical designs as well as to his great achievements. I trust it may be my good fortune to contribute something hereafter toward the payment of this debt of gratitude which all Americans owe to the greatest soldier of the Union.

The fact that Savannah was one of the points in both Grant's plans and Sherman's was merely an incident, and a very unimportant one. Indeed, after Hood got out of his way, Sherman might as well, and I think better, have marched direct to Augusta, and thence northward, wholly ignoring Savannah as well as Charleston, except that he would have arrived in Virginia rather early in the season. Savannah was a good place to go to in order to spend the winter, besides destroying Georgia en route.

Of course it is much easier to see what might have been

22

done than to see in advance what can or ought to be done. But it can hardly be believed that Sherman did not think of everything that was possible, as well as many things that were not. At least, so simple a proposition as the following could not have escaped his mind.

Sherman was, as he so confidently said, absolute "master of the situation" before he started for Savannah. Hood and Forrest had utterly failed so to damage his communications that they could not be put in order again in a few days. He was able, if he chose, to remain in perfect security at Atlanta all winter, with two or three corps, while he sent back to Thomas ample force to dispose of Hood. Then, if the result of the operations of a larger force in Tennessee had been as decisive as they actually were with the smaller one Thomas had, Sherman could have recalled to Atlanta all of the troops he had sent to Tennessee, and thus marched toward Virginia with eighty-five or ninety or even one hundred thousand men, instead of sixty thousand. All this could have surely been accomplished by the middle of January, or before the time when Sherman actually began his march from Savannah. From Atlanta to Columbia, South Carolina, crossing the Savannah River at or above Augusta, is an easier march than that from Savannah to Columbia. Or if Sherman had not cared about paying a visit to Columbia en route, he could have taken the much shorter "Piedmont route" to Charlotte, North Carolina, and thence northward by whichever route he pleased. Instead of retaining the dominant attitude of "master," Sherman lost it the moment he started eastward with his main army, leaving an inferior force to cope with his enemy ; and the march through Georgia and the capture of Savannah did not by any means restore that mastery to Sherman. It was not restored until Hood was actually defeated in Tennessee.

I have referred to the possibilities of a direct march

from Atlanta via Columbia or Charlotte, with a much larger army, at exactly the same time, for the purpose of showing that even Sherman's grand strategic plan to assist in the capture of Lee's army did not necessitate or justify his action in marching to Savannah and quitting his own theater of operations before his adversary there had been disposed of. The plan above suggested would have negatived even more positively the boast and promise of the Confederate chief that Sherman should be driven out of Georgia. The fact that Sherman personally, with an army about as large as, or larger than, Hood's, could and did remain quietly at Atlanta while one of his subordinates disposed of Hood and his army, would have been the most emphatic possible defeat of the Confederate plan to force him back by operations in his rear. Only one part of Sherman's earnest desires would have been unrealized — namely, to destroy Georgia. But even that could have been, at least in a great measure, compensated for by the more complete destruction of South Carolina, the cradle of secession and rebellion.

The more carefully Sherman's great operations are examined, the more clearly it will appear that while his plans were magnificent, their execution was not perfect. And this is the legitimate aim of just military criticism, not to build up or pull down the reputations of commanders, but to assist military students in their efforts to perfect themselves in the art and science of war.

Sherman's great marches, especially through the enemy's country and over such obstacles as those found from Savannah to Goldsboro', showed him to be a master of the auxiliary art of logistics no less than of the great science of strategy. Even to those who have had no means of duly appreciating the higher merits of Sherman's general plans, his marches have seemed the wonder of the world. Yet, strangely enough, the march through Georgia, which was in fact the simplest thing possible, has been regarded as the great exploit, while the vastly more difficult and important march through the Carolinas appears to have been taken as a matter of course, perhaps because of the conviction, which had by that time become general, that Sherman could do anything he might undertake.

In respect to Sherman's skill in grand tactics, I have only a few words to say here. The part assigned him in Grant's general plan of operations for all the armies, in 1864, in his "private and confidential" letter of April 4, was as follows: "You I propose to move against Johnston's army to break it up, and to get into the interior of the enemy's country as far as you can, inflicting all the damage you can against their war resources." It is a simple, plain matter of history that Sherman did not accomplish the first and more important part of the task assigned him—"to break it up"—in the four months of almost constant fighting with Johnston's army. In the comments I have made upon the Atlanta campaign, I believe I have shown clearly why Sherman did not accomplish that result by the tactical operations to which he limited himself. The manner in which that army, then under Hood instead of Johnston, was finally broken up, by Sherman's subordinates in Tennessee, shows clearly enough what kind of modification of Sherman's tactical methods was requisite to enable him to reach the same result in Georgia.

Sherman's tactical operations during the entire Atlanta campaign were marked by the highest degree of prudence and caution. Even his one assault upon fortified lines at Kenesaw was no exception; for the worst that could happen in that was what actually did happen, namely, a fruitless loss of a considerable number of men, yet a number quite insignificant in comparison with the total strength of his army. Johnston displayed similar qualities in an equal degree so long as he was in command; and his well-known ability may have suggested to Sherman the wisdom of like prudence in all his own operations. But Hood signalized his accession to the command by the boldest kind of tactics, amounting even to rashness in the commander of a force so inferior to that of his adversary. Yet Sherman continued his own cautious methods to the end. Even his last move, which resulted in the capture of Atlanta,—the only one which had even the general appearance of boldness,—was, in fact, marked by the greatest prudence throughout. The Twentieth Corps occupied a strongly fortified bridge-head at the Chattahoochee River, and the Twenty-third Corps another equally strongly fortified " pivot " around which the grand wheel of the army was made. That moving army was much larger than Hood's entire force, and had all the advantage of the initiative, which completely disconcerted the opposing commander, and caused him to commit a blunder that ought to have proved fatal, namely, that of dividing his inferior force and permitting his superior opponent to occupy a position between the widely separated wings of his own army. Yet Sherman refused to take any advantage of that blunder, and sat still while Hood leisurely reunited his divided forces.

Even if such extreme caution in handling a superior force against such an antagonist as Johnston could be regarded as wise, it surely could not against such an antagonist as Hood, whose character of extreme audacity in the aggressive should have assured his destruction by a more skilful adversary in command of a superior force. But Sherman's own knowledge of his own impulsive nature made him unduly distrustful of his own judgment when under great responsibility in emergencies, and this in spite of his unusual intellectual activity and his great confidence in his deliberately matured judgment. This is the opinion of Sherman's character formed by me after the closest possible observation and study. For this reason Sherman's capacity as a tactician was not by any means equal to his ability as a strategist. He lacked the element of confident boldness or audacity in action which is necessary to gain the greatest results by taking advantage of his adversary's blunders, and by tempting or forcing his adversary into positions of which he might take advantage. Yet Sherman was very far from lacking skill as a tactician. Both he and Johnston might well be likened to masters of the sword so skilful and so equally matched that neither could gain any material advantage over the other. In my opinion, their duel of ten weeks' duration was never surpassed in the history of the world for the masterly skill and caution with which the one pressed the other back step by step, and the other disputed every foot of the ground, neither giving nor attempting to make an opportunity to strike a decisive blow. If the object of that campaign was to capture Atlanta on the one side, and to defend it on the other, the handling of those two splendid armies was simply magnificent. It would be a great pity that an end was put to that duel by the removal of Johnston, and the military world thus deprived of a complete lesson, except for the fact that, whether or not the contest finally resulted in the fall of Atlanta, the rebellion in that part of the South would have been practically as far from an end as it was the first of May! Johnston would have been there in front of Sherman, all the same, and at least one more campaign would have been required before the march to the sea could have been made.

Although Sherman did not himself accomplish the first part of Grant's plan in respect to Johnston's army,— namely, " to break it up,"— the second part, " to get into the interior of the enemy's country, . . . inflicting all the damage you can against their war resources,"[1] was carried out as thoroughly as Grant or anybody else could have

[1] War Records, Vol. XXXII, part iii, p. 245.

wished. It is also true that Sherman claimed the credit for the breaking up of Hood's army in Tennessee, while he was marching to Savannah, as a legitimate and foreseen part of his general plan, like his successful march and capture of Savannah. But he appeared not to see that in such a claim he was condemning himself for not having done with a superior force what Thomas actually did with a smaller one. That result was, in fact, due largely to an accident which, in the ordinary course of military operations, ought not to have happened, and by which Hood was tempted to make at Franklin one of those furious assaults upon troops in position and ready to receive him which are almost always disastrous. It was just the kind of temptation to Hood's army that was necessary "to break it up," and it did so very effectually. The old "Army of Tennessee," which had been so formidable, ceased to be a formidable army on November 30. Its fighting days were nearly over. After that it never did any fighting at all worthy of its old record. And there was hardly a single day while Hood was in command in the Atlanta campaign when a similar result might not have been reached by a similar method, and that without any risk of disaster to the Union army, because the force assaulted by Hood might always have had a more powerful army near at hand to support it if necessary.

In his special field order of January 8, 1865, announcing to all the troops of his military division the results of his great campaign, General Sherman said: "Generals Thomas and Schofield, commanding the departments to our rear, returned to their posts and prepared to decoy General Hood into their meshes." If the purpose that prompted Sherman to send me back to Tennessee was to serve as a "decoy" to Hood, I must say that my part of the sport would have been more enjoyable if it had taken place earlier in the season, when

Sherman was near by with his sixty thousand men to help " bag the game."

It has occurred to me as at least possible that Sherman's recollection of the suggestions I had repeatedly made to him during the Atlanta campaign may have been in his mind when he ordered me back to report to Thomas, and when he wrote his special field order. If so, I must protest my innocence of any intention to play the role of " decoy " at Franklin when one of the great gunners was twenty miles away, and the other several hundred!

Yet, accepting even the most unfavorable view of Sherman's tactical as well as of his strategical operations in connection with the operations of all the other armies under Grant's general plans and direction, there was nothing in them all that could possibly have prevented their complete ultimate success in the capture of Lee's army. If Grant had not captured that army, Sherman would. And the surrender of Lee was necessarily followed by that of all the other Confederate armies. Hence, whatever might have happened if Sherman's great march had not been made, that march with so large an army made the end of the rebellion in the spring of 1865 sure beyond any possible doubt. In view of a public service so original in its conception, so grand in its magnitude, and so brilliant in its execution, any criticism respecting details cannot diminish the fame of the general who planned and executed that grand campaign, nor that of the general-in-chief, the success of whose far-reaching plans had made the brilliant exploit of his subordinate possible. Such criticisms are justifiable only in the interest of exact truth and of exact military science, so that imperfections in the operations of the greatest commanders may not be mistaken by the military student as having been among the causes which led to success.

CHAPTER XVIII

TRANSFER OF THE TWENTY-THIRD CORPS TO NORTH CARO-
LINA — SHERMAN'S PLAN OF MARCHING TO THE REAR OF
LEE — THE SURRENDER OF J. E. JOHNSTON'S ARMY —
AUTHORSHIP OF THE APPROVED TERMS OF SURRENDER
— POLITICAL RECONSTRUCTION — SHERMAN'S GENIUS —
CONTRAST BETWEEN GRANT AND SHERMAN — HALLECK'S
CHARACTERISTICS — HIS ATTEMPT TO SUPPLANT GRANT
— PERSONAL FEELING IN BATTLE — THE SCARS OF WAR.

UPON the termination of the campaign of 1864 in
Tennessee, General Grant ordered me, with the
Twenty-third Corps, to the coast of North Carolina, via
Louisville, Cincinnati, Pittsburg, Washington, and the
sea. Under the direction of the Assistant Secretary of
War, Charles A. Dana, and the personal management of
Colonel Lewis B. Parsons of the quartermaster's department, that movement was made without any necessity for the exercise of direction or control on my part,
in respect to routes or otherwise. I enjoyed very much
being a simple passenger on that comfortable journey,
one of the most remarkable in military history, and exceedingly creditable to the officers of the War Department who directed and conducted it. I did not know at
the time anything about the details of the arrangements
made for transportation, nor who made them; but I
have always thought it an excellent illustration of the
good results to be obtained by a judicious distribution
and division of duty, authority, and responsibility in
military operations on a large scale. This being done

under one common, competent head, to whom all subordinates are alike responsible, the military system becomes as nearly perfect as possible.

While the transports were detained by an ice blockade in the Potomac, I joined General Grant at Fort Monroe, and went with him on the war-steamer *Rhode Island* to Cape Fear River, where we met General Terry and Admiral Porter, discussed the military situation, and decided on the general plan of operations for the capture of the defenses of Cape Fear River and the city of Wilmington, and subsequent operations. On our return to Fort Monroe, I proceeded to Washington, and sailed with the advance of the Twenty-third Corps, arriving at the mouth of Cape Fear River on February 9, 1865, where we joined General Terry, who with two divisions had already captured Fort Fisher. I was then assigned to command the new department of North Carolina. We turned the defenses of Cape Fear River by marching round the swamps, and occupied Wilmington with little loss; then we captured Kinston, after a pretty sharp fight of three days, and occupied Goldsboro' on March 21, within one day of the time indicated by Sherman, from Laurel Hill, N. C., March 8, for our junction at Goldsboro'. General Sherman, who had been delayed by his battle at Bentonville, did not reach Goldsboro' until the 23d, but the sound of his guns on the 20th and 21st informed me that he was near, and I put a bridge across the Neuse River, so as to go to his assistance if necessary. After the junction at Goldsboro', I commanded the "center," one of the three grand divisions of Sherman's army.

For the elucidation of some things in this campaign which have seemed obscure, and some acts of General Sherman which have been severely criticized, it is necessary to know the ruling ideas which actuated him. As Sherman says, in his own estimate of the relative importance of his march through Georgia and that through the Carolinas, the former was only a change of base preparatory to the latter, the great final campaign of the war, which had for its end the defeat and capture of Lee's army. Sherman and his army expected to share the glory of capturing Richmond and Lee's army, which had baffled the Eastern troops for four years. This feeling in the army was very general and very manifest at the time.

After the concentration at Goldsboro', Sherman's plan was to march straight for Lee's rear at Petersburg, and he expected Johnston to keep ahead of him and to unite with Lee for the final struggle at or near Richmond. Grant's idea was quite different: he wanted Sherman to keep between Lee and Johnston and prevent their union, as well as to cut off Lee's retreat if he should escape before Grant was ready to move, the latter alleging that he had ample force to take care of Lee as soon as the necessary preparations were made and the roads would permit him to move. It was this important difference of plan that occasioned Sherman's visit to City Point, where he hoped to gain Grant's acquiescence in his own plans. The result was the movement ordered by Sherman on his return to Goldsboro', which was substantially the same as that which Grant had before proposed. Grant's immediate army proved to be, as he predicted it would, amply sufficient for the capture of the whole of Lee's army. Hence it is difficult to see in what respect Sherman's campaign of the Carolinas was essential to that great result, or proved to be more important than his march through Georgia. Each was a great raid, inflicting immense damage upon the enemy's country and resources, demoralizing to the people at home and the army in Virginia, cutting off supplies necessary to the support of the latter, possibly expediting somewhat the final crisis at Richmond, and certainly making the subjugation more complete of those of the Southern people who were thus made to "feel the weight of war." Considered as to its military results, Sherman's march cannot be regarded as more than I have stated — a grand raid. The defeat and practical destruction of Hood's army in Tennessee was what paved the way to the speedy termination of the war, which the capture of Lee by Grant fully accomplished; and the result ought to have been essentially the same as to time if Sherman's march had never been made. The capitulation of Johnston was but the natural sequence of Lee's surrender; for Johnston's army was not surrounded, and could not have been compelled to surrender. Indeed Sherman could not have prevented that army from marching back into the Gulf States and continuing the war for a time. In military history Sherman's great march must rank only as auxiliary to the far more important operations of Grant and Thomas. Sherman at the time saw clearly enough this view of the case; hence his undeviating bent toward the final object of his march, disregarding all minor ends — to take part in the capture of Lee's army.

During General Sherman's interviews with the President and General Grant at City Point, his mind must have been absorbed with this one idea which was the sole reason of his visit. Terms of surrender and the policy to be pursued toward the conquered South must have been referred to very casually, and nothing approximating instructions on the subject can have been received or asked for by General Sherman. Else how is it possible that the very pointed and emphatic instructions of the President to General Grant, dated March 3, 1865,[1] were not made known to him or the spirit of them conveyed to him in conversation?

The question of the abstract wisdom of the terms of the

[1] War Records, Vol. XLVI, part ii, p. 802.

Sherman-Johnston "memorandum" has little to do with that of Sherman in agreeing to it. Any person at all acquainted with the politics of the dominant party at that time would have known that it was at least unwise to introduce political questions at all. Besides, he had the example of his superior, the general-in-chief, who had just accepted the surrender of the principal Confederate army from the Confederate generalissimo without any political conditions; and the knowledge of President Lincoln's assassination, which must have made the country unwilling to consent to more liberal terms than had before been granted. Yet, however unwise Sherman's action may have been, the uproar it created, and the attacks upon his honor and integrity for which it was made the excuse, were utterly inexcusable. They were probably unexampled as an exhibition of the effect of great and unusual excitement upon the minds of men unaccustomed to such moral and mental strain.

The most charitable view of this matter seems also to be the most just—namely, that the high officers of government were completely unnerved and lost their heads under the terrible strain produced by President Lincoln's assassination, increased somewhat, perhaps, by a natural apprehension of what might come next. The contrast between this state of excitement in Washington and the marked calm that prevailed throughout the army was very instructive, and it was difficult for any soldier to understand at that time the state of mind in Washington. No part of the people could have felt more deeply or with greater indignation the loss the country had suffered, and the infamous crime by which it had been accomplished. Yet not a ripple of excitement could be seen anywhere in the army. The profound calm which pervades the atmosphere surrounding a great, disciplined, self-confident army is one of the most sublime exhibitions of human nature.

That Sherman felt "outraged beyond measure," was natural and indeed inevitable. He had committed an error of judgment arising from political inexperience and a failure to appreciate the difference between Mr. Lincoln's humane purposes toward individual Confederates and his political policy. But the error was of the least possible practical consequence, and there was not the slightest excuse for making it public at the time, in violation of all rules of official courtesy. All that it was necessary or right to do was to tell Sherman to correct his error.

While the effect of these ferocious bulletins received some time later was such as General Sherman fully describes, the first effect of the simple disapproval of the convention, both upon Sherman and Johnston, not referred to by either in their published narratives, may be interesting to the readers of history. General Sherman was manifestly much disappointed and mortified at the rejection of his terms, although he had been prepared somewhat by expressions of opinion from others in the interval, and both he and Johnston at their last meeting seemed sad and dejected.

To understand this, it must be remembered that Johnston's army was not surrounded, and its surrender could not have been compelled. Unless the terms of capitulation could be made such as the troops themselves would be willing to accept, they would, it was apprehended, break up into guerrilla bands of greater or less strength and carry on the war in that way indefinitely. So strongly was I impressed at the time with General Johnston's apprehension, that I was often thereafter haunted in my dreams with the difficulties I was actually encountering in the prosecution of military operations against those remnants of the Confederate armies, in marshy and mountainous countries, through summer heats and winter storms. It was several years after the war that

I became fully satisfied, at night, that it was really over.

At the time of Sherman's first interview with Johnston I hinted that I would like to accompany him; but he desired me to remain in immediate command, as I was next in rank, and we could not tell what might happen. He took some others with him, but I believe had no one present in the room to assist him in his discussion with Johnston and Breckinridge. At his last interview I accompanied him, by his special request. On meeting at Bennett's House, after the usual salutations Generals Sherman and Johnston retired to the conference room, and were there a long time with closed doors. At length I was summoned to their presence, and informed in substance that they were unable to arrange the terms of capitulation to their satisfaction. They seemed discouraged at the failure of the arrangement to which they had attached so much importance, apprehensive that the terms of Grant and Lee, pure and simple, could not be executed, and that if modified at all, they would meet with a second disapproval. I listened to their statements of the difficulties they had encountered, and then stated how I thought they could all be arranged. General Johnston replied, in substance, "I think General Schofield can fix it"; and General Sherman intimated to me to write, pen and paper being on the table where I was sitting, while the two great antagonists were nervously pacing the floor. I at once wrote the "military convention" of April 26, handed it to General Sherman, and he, after reading it, to General Johnston. Having explained that I, as department commander, after General Sherman was gone, could do all that might be necessary to remove the difficulties which seemed to them so serious, the terms as written by me were agreed to, as General Sherman says, "without hesitation," and General Johnston, "without difficulty," and after being copied *without alteration* were signed by the two commanders. Johnston's words, on handing the paper back to Sherman, were: "I believe that is the best we can do." It was in pursuance of this understanding that I made with General Johnston the "supplemental terms," and gave his disbanded men the two hundred and fifty thousand rations, with wagons to haul them, to prevent the troops from robbing their own people, for which, in his "Narrative," he very properly credits General Sherman.

But I also gave to the troops from each State arms enough to arm a guard to preserve order and protect citizens en route, the arms so used to be turned over to United States officers after the troops got home. This was one of the things most bitterly condemned in Sherman's first agreement. Yet not a word was said when I did it! It would be difficult for a soldier to imagine anything more monstrous than the suggestion that he could not trust the officers and men whom he had been fighting four years to go home and turn in their arms after they had voluntarily surrendered and given their parole of honor to do so. Yet there seem to be even in high places some men who have no conception of the sense of honor which exists among brave men.

When that second "convention" was handed to General Grant the same evening, he said that the only change he would have made would have been to write General Sherman's name before General Johnston's. So would I if I had thought about it; but I presume an unconscious feeling of courtesy toward a fallen foe dictated the order in which their names were written.

It seems to me a little singular that neither General Sherman nor General Johnston thought the circumstances above referred to worthy of being preserved in memory, and I am not quite willing that General Breckinridge shall carry off all the honor of assisting the great commanders to make "memoranda" and "military conventions" at "Bennett's House." But Sherman and Johnston were writing their own defense, and it was natural that they should omit matter not pertaining thereto. Besides, I was General Sherman's subordinate, and owed him all the help I could give in every way. He may have regarded my services, and perhaps justly, as little more than clerical, after it was all over, even if he thought of the matter at all.[1]

The Confederate troops were promptly furnished with all needed supplies of food and transportation and sent in comfort to their homes, freed from the necessity of taxing the slender resources of the impoverished people on their routes. The surplus animals and wagons remaining with the army were given to the people of North Carolina in large numbers, and they were encouraged at once to resume their industrial pursuits. In the meantime, all who were in want were furnished with food.

It may not be possible to judge how wise or unwise Sherman's first "memorandum" might have proved if it had been ratified. It is always difficult to tell how things that have not been tried would have worked if they had been. We now know only this much — that the imagination of man could hardly picture worse results than those wrought out by the plan that was finally adopted—namely, to destroy everything that existed in the way of government, and then build from the bottom on the foundation of ignorance and rascality.

The de facto State governments existing at the time of the surrender would have been of infinite service in restoring order and material prosperity, if they had been recognized by the military authority of the United States

---

[1] For the military convention of April 26, 1865, signed by Sherman and Johnston, and the supplemental terms, signed by Johnston and Schofield, see War Records, Vol. XLVII, part iii, pp. 313, 482.

and kept under military control similar to that exercised
by the district commanders under the "reconstruction
acts." And such recognition would in no manner have
interfered with any action Congress might have thought
it wise to take looking to the organization of permanent
governments and the admission of senators and representatives in Congress. After two years of "reconstruction" under President Johnson's "policy," the Southern
State governments were no better than those he had
destroyed. Then Congress took the matter in hand, and
after years of labor brought forth State governments far
worse than either of those that had been torn down.

Party ambition on the one hand, and timidity on the
other, were the parents of these great follies. The presidential succession was the mainspring of the first movement and of the opposition thereto, while that and party
majority in Congress were the motives of the later "reconstruction." Both ingloriously failed, as they deserved
to do. How much stronger the Republican party would
have been if it had relied upon the loyal States which
had sustained it through the war, instead of timidly dis-
trusting them and trying to bolster itself up by the aid
of the negro and "carpet-bag" governments in the South!

Political reconstruction ought not to have been thought
of at the close of the war. What was then needed was
local civil government under such military control as
might be necessary, restoration of order, industry, and
material prosperity, leading to a gradual reorganization
of the society which had been completely broken up by
the war. After this had been done, and Congress had
decided upon the conditions of full restoration, it would
have been time enough to inaugurate political reconstruction. This was clear enough at the time to those
who had studied the subject and knew by personal observation the real condition and feeling of the Southern
people. But the leading politicians of either party do

not appear to have had the wisdom and moral courage to advocate such a policy. Both were impatient to see their party represented on the floors of Congress by members from the South. It was something of the kind above suggested which was aimed at by Generals Sherman and Johnston, and which was deemed wise by the leading generals both North and South. There were several conditions in the memorandum that were clearly inadmissible, though easy of correction without changing the essential features of the document. This was to be expected from a hasty effort to solve a great political problem by a man without political education or experience. Sherman's failure was not unlike that of great politicians who undertake to command armies. Their general ideas may be very good, but they have no knowledge of details, and hence make mistakes resulting in failure.

As now seen, projected upon the dark background of the political history of the Southern States during the twelve years from 1865 to 1877, and compared with the plans of political doctrinaires in 1865, under the light of experience and reason, the Sherman-Johnston memorandum and Sherman's letters of that period seem self-luminous with political wisdom. Sherman needed only the aid of competent military advisers in whom he had confidence to have made him one of the greatest generals of any age, and he would have needed only the aid of competent political advisers to have made him a great statesman. But he looked almost with contempt upon a "staff," and would doubtless have thought little better of a "cabinet."

The efforts of political leaders to establish an absolutely impossible popular government in the South seem to show the necessity of general political education, no less than the military blunders of the war show the necessity of general military education. If our schools would drop from their course of studies some of the comparatively unimportant " ologies," and substitute the qualifications for good citizenship, the change would be greatly for the better.

General Sherman was one of those rare actors in historic events who require no eulogy. All his important acts were so unqualifiedly his own, and so emphatically speak for themselves, that it is only necessary to judge of the quality and merits of those acts. There is no question of division of honors between him and any other respecting any of his important operations. It is not meant by this that he was disdainful of the advice or opinions of others. On the contrary, although naturally impulsive and self-reliant, his acquired habit was to study carefully and consult freely with his subordinate commanders respecting all important movements. Yet discussion resulted almost if not quite invariably in the adoption of his own original plans. As to details, he was wont to leave them very much to his subordinates, and, I think, did not estimate very accurately the possibilities or probabilities of the accomplishment of the details necessary to the success of his general plans. It is certainly not too much to say that his expectations in this regard were very frequently unrealized. But of this it must be observed that the character of the theater of war made the handling of a large army extremely difficult, precision of movements impossible, and any accurate estimate of the time in which projected operations could be accomplished by no means easy. Criticism of General Sherman, or of his subordinates, based upon military experience in other countries or upon the success of his able antagonist General Johnston, to whom Sherman's difficulties were corresponding advantages, is likely to be extremely unjust. In short, Sherman's campaigns stand alone, without a parallel in military history; alike unique in their conception, execution, and final results;

in most respects among the highest examples of the art of war. Plans so general and original in conception and successful in execution point unmistakably to a very high order of military genius.

In the order of nature, comparison with those that follow as well as those that precede is needed to establish the merits of any individual. A commander may be a great captain compared with his military predecessors, and yet some of his operations be regarded as very faulty by more modern commanders.

Some future historian, with the example before him of a later chieftain who, on a similar field and under similar but improved conditions, may have won more brilliant successes, may be able to determine Sherman's rank among the commanders of past, present, and future ages.

Sufficient is not yet known in this country of the credit due any one individual for the success achieved in the recent campaigns in Europe to furnish the means of just comparison between the European and American commanders of this generation. And even between Grant and Sherman there are so few points of resemblance in military character or methods, that they must be judged by contrasts rather than by comparison. Hence it may always be difficult to determine their exact relative merits as military leaders. Upon this point I forbear, for the present, to express any opinion.

In some other respects Grant and Sherman were hardly less in contrast than in their military characteristics. At the close of the Atlanta campaign, in his letter of September 12, 1864, Grant paid to Sherman the following generous and glowing tribute: "In conclusion, it is hardly necessary for me to say that I feel you have accomplished the most gigantic undertaking given to any general in this war, and with a skill and ability that will be acknowledged in history as unsurpassed, if not unequaled. It gives me as much pleasure to record this in your favor as it would in favor of any living man, myself included."

To this Sherman replied, September 20: "In the meantime, know that I admire your dogged perseverance and pluck more than ever."

There has been much learned discussion of the relative merits of McClellan's, Grant's, and other plans for the "capture of Richmond," as if that was the object of the campaign. In fact, though the capture of Richmond at any time during the war would have produced some moral effect injurious to the rebellion and beneficial to the Union in public opinion, it would have been a real injury to the Union cause in a military sense, because it would have given us one more important place to garrison, and have increased the length of our line of supplies, always liable to be broken by the enemy's cavalry.

The worst form of operations in such a war is "territorial" strategy, or that which aims at the capture and occupation of territory as a primary object. The best is that which aims at the destruction or capture of the opposing armies as the first and only important object. Grant at Donelson, Vicksburg, and in Virginia best illustrated this kind of strategy.

Halleck was probably the chief of the "territorial" strategists of our Civil War period. In the winter of 1861–1862 the counties of north Missouri bordering on the Missouri River were infested with guerrillas. Halleck sent Pope, with a force of all arms amounting to a considerable army, to "clear them out." Pope marched in triumph from one end of that tier of counties to the other, and Halleck then informed me with evident satisfaction that north Missouri was cleared of rebels, and that the war was ended in that part of the State! In fact, the guerrillas, "flushed" like a flock of quail by Pope's advance-guard, had taken to the bush until the rear-guard had passed out of sight, and then were found "feeding" again on their old ground.

I felt greatly complimented when Halleck, on his return from Corinth to St. Louis, en route to Washington to take command of the army, gave me a full explanation of his "siege of Corinth," including his application of the standard European tactics of a former generation, with its rule of 10,000 men to the mile in line and regular approaches.

I was many years younger than Halleck, Thomas, Sherman, Grant, and the other chief commanders, and hence had much more to learn than they. Perhaps I was also, on account of comparative youth, more teachable. At any rate, the two lessons from Halleck above referred to, and later experience, caused me to do "a world of thinking"; so that I was amazed beyond expression when, in the winter of 1863–64, just before Grant was made lieutenant-general, Halleck told me that *his* plan for the next campaign was to send west of the Mississippi River force enough to finish the war in all that region of country, and then return and clear up the States east of that river! I said nothing, but could not help thinking that it was, sure enough, time to have another general-in-chief of the army. But accepting his strategic theory of operations in the American Civil War,—territorial conquest,—his plans of campaign were unquestionably sound.

Halleck was, I believe, a man of great ability and of high military education, though with little practical experience in war; yet his peculiar views, and still more singular action, have seemed to me very remarkable. He remained in Washington, practically inert, while one of the great armies of which he was general-in-chief was suffering sore reverses, almost in sight of the Capitol, and the country's cause greatly imperiled for want of a competent commander for that army. How could a soldier resist the impulse to "do or die" at the head of that army? But General Halleck must have known better than any one else at that time the limits of his own capacity. He probably knew that even his great ability and education did not suffice to qualify him for the command of an army in the field. If so, his action afforded a patriotic example which some others would have done well to imitate.

As I have before stated, General Halleck was always kind and just to me, so far as I ever knew, and I was much indebted to him for support when it was needed. Now I find in the records the following letter:

RICHMOND, VA., May 10, 1865, 10:30 A. M.

HON. EDWIN M. STANTON, Secretary of War:

I beg leave to withdraw for the present my recommendation of Schofield as military governor of North Carolina. It is represented to me that he and General Blair were the principal advisers of Sherman in his armistice with the rebel General Johnston. If so, he is not a proper person to command in North Carolina. I therefore suspend my recommendation for further developments.

H. W. HALLECK, Major-General.

The fact was that I had not been present when Sherman's memorandum was agreed upon, had not been consulted about it in any way, and knew nothing of its character until after it had been sent to Washington. All of this Halleck could have learned at once if he had inquired, which he did not. So far as I know, he left on record, without any subsequent explanation or correction, a report which was without the slightest foundation in fact, and which he understood to be very damaging to my reputation. Hence it seems necessary for me to record the fact that there was no foundation for that report. Beyond this I will only say that I think General Halleck, in this slight matter, as in his far more serious conduct toward General Sherman, was inexcusably thoughtless respecting the damage he might do to the reputation of a brother soldier. The least a true man can do is to make suitable public reparation if he has for any reason done publicly a personal injustice. I knew personally at the time the exact truth respecting the action of General Halleck toward General Grant before the battle of Shiloh, especially in ordering Grant to remain in the rear while General C. F. Smith was sent with the advance of the army to Pittsburg Landing, as described by General Grant in his "Memoirs." Halleck hoped Smith might fight a battle and win a victory in Grant's absence, which would naturally be followed by an order putting Smith in command in place of Grant. But Halleck had not anticipated Grant's soldierly action in applying to be relieved, and was not prepared to face that emergency. As soon as Grant's application reached St. Louis, Halleck abandoned that line of action, but he did not abandon his purpose to supersede Grant in some way until some time later. Whatever excuse there may have been at that time for Halleck's opinion of Grant, nothing can be said in favor of the method he adopted to accomplish his purpose to supersede him.

The action of Grant in this case well foreshadowed that which occurred when he was tendered the commission of lieutenant-general and the command of all the armies. Grant would not hold any commission or command without full authority to perform the duties belonging to it. In his "Memoirs" he modestly refrains from relating the most important part of that action, as he told it to me on the war-steamer *Rhode Island* the next January. Before accepting the commission from President Lincoln, as Grant describes, he said in substance that if it meant that he was to exercise actual command of all the armies, without any interference from the War Department, he was willing to accept it, otherwise he could not. To illustrate what he meant, Grant said to me that when he was coming East to accept that commission he determined that he would not be "McClellanized."

The personal observation, experience, and emotions of an individual soldier may perhaps be interesting to the reader. I have never been a lover of war or strife, and have never been disposed to seek a fight or quarrel. But when once engaged in or challenged to battle all the combativeness in human nature is at once aroused. It is then difficult, if not morally impossible, to decline the challenge. At all events, that question is not even thought of at times. One of the most difficult lessons a commander has to learn is when to offer or accept battle, and when to refrain or decline — that is, to be complete master of his own natural combativeness. That courage which is the highest quality of a private or a subordinate officer may become extremely dangerous in a commander, unless dominated by that higher moral courage which is undisturbed by excitement or passion. Grant probably possessed this higher quality in a greater degree than any other commander of our time. Sherman and Thomas also possessed it in a very high degree. In Sherman it was the more remarkable because he was naturally impulsive, and often manifested this trait, especially in minor matters. He acquired the power of absolute self-command in battle. With Thomas this quality appeared to be perfectly natural, as it did with Grant.

Since I had to fight, I sometimes regretted that I could not have a chance with a musket in the ranks (behind a good parapet and "head-log," of course!), for I was a remarkably good shot in my youth. But I never had a chance to fire a shot in battle except once, and that was with my artillery at Fredericktown, Missouri, where not an officer or man in the battery had any idea how to point a field-piece and give it proper elevation according to the distance. I quickly found the proper elevation by the means well known to artillerists, and then directed the battery to go on firing at that elevation, while I was called upon by the commanding officer to devote myself to some men with muskets. I have seen this passion so strong that a major-general commanding an army corps would dismount and act the part of gunner to a field-piece, apparently oblivious to the battle raging all along the line of his corps.

Personal feeling in battle is sometimes remarkable, even to the person himself. In my own experience, the degree of danger was not often entirely unthought of; and in the comparatively few cases where it was, the actual danger was much the greatest ever experienced by me. That such should be the experience of a general in chief command, under the responsibilities of a great battle, is natural enough; but that the same should occur when there is little or no responsibility seems worthy of remark in reference to its apparent cause. In my first battle,—that of Wilson's Creek,—where I was a staff officer under a soldier of great experience, ability, and unsurpassed courage,—General Lyon,—I felt for a long time no sense of responsibility whatever. I had only to convey his orders to the troops. Yet the absorption of my mind in the discharge of this simple duty, and in watching the progress of the battle, was so complete that I absolutely had no thought whatever of self. Even after Lyon had been twice wounded, both of our horses killed, the troops on our left given way in disorder, leaving us standing in the line, only a few feet to the left of Totten's battery, under a murderous fire, it did not occur to me that I also might possibly be hit. I had not even thought for a moment that the commanding general ought not to be in such an exposed position, or that his wounds ought to have surgical treatment! My absolute confidence in my chief left no room in my mind for even such thoughts as those. It was not until wounds had produced discouragement in the bravest soul I ever knew that I was aroused to some sense of my own responsibility as his senior staff officer, and spontaneously said: "No, general; let us try it again." I was so much absorbed in the battle itself at that time, and even after Lyon's death, that it did not occur to me that wounds and death, even of the commanding general himself, were of any consequence except as they might influence the progress and final result of the battle. This is the feeling that must dominate the action of every successful commander. It is remarkable only because of its early development in one not then under any such responsibility.

It may not be a proper subject for criticism at this time, and certainly is not for any that might seem harsh or unkind, yet it is an instructive lesson which ought never to be forgotten, that feeling and passion sometimes more than reason, sound military principles, or wise statesmanship, dictated military as well as political policy during and long after the Civil War.

No doubt all are now ready to admit this in respect to the political measures which wrought so much evil in the South during the so-called reconstruction period. But those who are not familiar with the facts will, I think, be amazed when they see the evidences of this influence in military operations, and perhaps at no time more strikingly than during the last period of the Civil War. It would seem that the official correspondence of that period ought to be a sufficient warning to deter any future generation from bringing the country into a condition where even some of the most distinguished citizens, statesmen, and soldiers seem to be governed more by passion than by reason in the conduct of public affairs. The inevitable horrors of war are bad enough in any case, but they are vastly increased when the passions begotten of civil strife become dominant. While all parts of the United States have reason for pride in the manhood and valor of American soldiers, and in the patriotic devotion of citizens to the cause which they believed to be right, and profound gratitude for the restoration of the Union of the States, the people of this entire country should bow their heads in humiliation when they think of the general low state of civilization which made such a war possible, and much of its conduct the dictate of passion and hate rather than of reason or regard for the public good. Even if it is true, as some soldier-statesmen have said, but which I do not believe, that occasional wars are necessary to the vitality of a nation,—necessary to keep up the fires of patriotism and military ardor upon which the national life depends,—let them be foreign and not civil wars. It is a great mistake, though apparently a common one, to suppose that a country benefits ultimately, in some mysterious way, by civil war, in spite of all its losses during the war. That able scientist General M. C. Meigs demonstrated years ago that this country had, in accordance with a general law, suffered permanent national injury, irreparable in all future time, by its Civil War, and showed very closely the amount of that injury.

It is, no doubt, true that the body politic, like the natural body, may in extreme cases be so diseased either by inheritance or from violation of natural laws, as to require the surgeon's knife to remove the diseased part. But in such a case there is little cause for pride except in the skill of the surgeon, and little cause for rejoicing except in the fact that the operation was successful, that neither the disease nor the surgeon's knife killed the patient.

While the great Von Moltke and others were unquestionably right in their views of the necessity for thorough preparation for war at all times, I believe that indispensable preparation can be made in a way vastly more satisfactory than by actual war. And this can be done with only a trifling expenditure of treasure, and at no cost whatever in blood and sorrow, nor in suspension of peaceful pursuits, nor in burdensome debts, nor in enormous disbursements for pensions. Let the schools of all kinds and all grades teach patriotism, respect for law, obedience to authority, discipline, courage, physical development, and the rudiments of practical military manœuvers; let the national and State military schools be fostered and perfected, and the volunteer citizen soldiery given material aid proportionate to their patriotic military zeal. Let the fortifications of the sea-coasts and the fleets of battle-ships and cruisers on the ocean be commensurate with the vast national interests and honor intrusted to their protection and defense; let the standing army be sufficient to discharge the duties which require long and scientific education and training, and to serve as models and instructors for the millions of young citizens: then will the United States, by being always ready for war, insure to themselves all the blessings of peace, and this at a cost utterly insignificant in comparison with the cost of one great war. It is a source of profound gratification to an old soldier who has long worked toward this great end to know that his country has already, in his short lifetime, come so near this perfect ideal of a peace-loving yet military republic. Only a few more years of progress in the direction already taken, and the usual prolongation of natural life will yet enable me to witness the realization of this one great object of my earthly ambition.

CHAPTER XIX

THE RESTORATION OF CIVIL GOVERNMENT IN THE SOUTHERN
STATES — THE COURSE PURSUED IN NORTH CAROLINA
— AN ORDER FROM GENERAL GRANT IN REGARD TO
COTTON AND PRODUCE — SUGGESTIONS FOR THE REOR-
GANIZATION OF CIVIL GOVERNMENT — A PROVISIONAL
GOVERNOR FOR NORTH CAROLINA.

BEING in command in North Carolina at the close of
the war, I was connected for a short period with
the very earliest consideration of the vital question of
the restoration of civil government in the Southern
States, in which I acted a more important part at a later
period. The moment the surrender of Johnston's army
made it evident that the end was near, the question
arose, and was much discussed among some of the
prominent officers, as to the status of the negroes in
the South. The position was promptly taken by me,
as the responsible commander in North Carolina, that the
question at that time was solely one of fact. The President's proclamation of emancipation was virtually a
military order to the army to free all the slaves in the
insurgent States as rapidly as military operations should
bring them within its control. Whatever the legal effect
of the proclamation upon the status of slaves not within
the reach of the army when it was issued, there could be
no question of its binding obligation, as an order to the
army, to be executed and made practically effective as
rapidly as it came within the power of the army to execute it. Accordingly, the following order was issued by
me to give full practical effect to the proclamation, and

to maintain the freedom of all former slaves, so long as the subject-matter should remain under military control. This order, which was the first public official declaration on the subject, was mentioned by one of the leading journals of New York at the time as having at least the merit of "saving a world of discussion." However this may be, little or no discussion followed, and the freedom of all slaves in the States lately in insurrection at once became an established fact.

(General Orders, No. 32.)

HDQRS. DEPT. OF NORTH CAROLINA, ARMY OF THE OHIO,
RALEIGH, N. C., April 27, 1865.

To remove a doubt which seems to exist in the minds of some of the people of North Carolina, it is hereby declared that by virtue of the proclamation of the President of the United States dated January 1, 1863, all persons in this State heretofore held as slaves are now free, and that it is the duty of the army to maintain the freedom of such persons.

It is recommended to the former owners of the freedmen to employ them as hired servants at reasonable wages; and it is recommended to the freedmen that, when allowed to do so, they remain with their former masters, and labor faithfully so long as they shall be treated kindly and paid reasonable wages, or that they immediately seek employment elsewhere in the kind of work to which they are accustomed. It is not well for them to congregate about towns or military camps. They will not be supported in idleness.

By command of Major-General Schofield:
J. A. CAMPBELL, Assistant Adjutant-General.

On the same day I issued the following:

(General Orders, No. 31.)

HDQRS. DEPT. OF NORTH CAROLINA, ARMY OF THE OHIO,
RALEIGH, N. C., April 27, 1865.

The commanding general has the great satisfaction of announcing to the army and to the people of North Carolina that hostilities within this State have definitively ceased; that for us the war is ended; and it is hoped that peace will soon be restored throughout our country.

It is now the duty of all to cultivate friendly relations with the same zeal which has characterized our conduct of the war, that the blessings of Union, peace, and material prosperity may be speedily restored to the entire country. It is confidently believed and expected that the troops of this army and the people of North Carolina will cordially unite in honest endeavors to accomplish this great end.

All good and peaceable citizens will be protected and treated with kindness, while those who disturb the peace or violate the laws will be punished with the severity of martial law.

The troops will be distributed so as best to secure the interests of the United States government and protect the people until a civil government can be established in harmony with the constitution and laws of the United States.

The most perfect discipline and good conduct are enjoined upon all officers and soldiers, and cordial support upon all good citizens.

All who are peaceably disposed are invited to return to their homes and resume their industrial pursuits. Such as have been deprived of their animals and wagons by the hostile armies will be temporarily supplied, as far as practicable, upon application to the nearest provost-marshal, by loans of the captured property in possession of the quartermaster's department. The needy will also be supplied, for the time being, with subsistence stores from the commissary department. . . .

By command of Major-General Schofield:

J. A. CAMPBELL, Assistant Adjutant-General.

On May 4, I issued a circular to this effect:

Local commanders and provost-marshals will encourage all refugees, white and colored, to return to their homes; and for this purpose will furnish them the necessary railroad passes and subsistence.

Such persons must not be given passes to Raleigh or points on the sea-coast, nor be permitted to congregate about towns or camps, there to live in idleness.

24

On May 5, I wrote to General Sherman:

When General Grant was here, as you doubtless recollect, he said the lines had been extended to embrace this and other States south. The order, it seems, has been modified so as to include only Virginia and Tennessee. I think it would be an act of wisdom to open this State to trade at once. I hope the government will make known its policy as to organization of State governments without delay. Affairs must necessarily be in a very unsettled state until that is done. The people are now in a mood to accept almost anything which promises a definite settlement. What is to be done with the freedmen is the question of all, and it is the all-important question. It requires prompt and wise action to prevent the negro from becoming a huge elephant on our hands.

If I am to govern this State, it is important for me to know it at once. If another is to be sent here, it cannot be done too soon, for he will probably undo the most of what I shall have done. I shall be most glad to hear from you fully when you have time to write. . . .

Two days later I wrote to General Halleck:

I have received your despatch concerning slavery, the treatment of freedmen, etc. I will send you my orders issued some days ago, which agree perfectly with your views on this subject. I have not recognized in any way any of the civil officers of the State — not being willing to act in such matters in the absence of any indication of the policy of the government, and taking it for granted that instructions would be given soon. In this connection, I desire to suggest that the sooner a military governor is appointed for this State, and steps taken to organize a civil government, the better. The people are now in a mood to accept anything in reason, and to do what the government desires. If I am, by virtue of my command, to perform the duties of military governor, I would like to know it.

If another is to be appointed, it ought to be done before I have been compelled to do something which he may think it necessary to undo. I think it would be eminently wise to retain in office justices of the peace, sheriffs, and other inferior officers who may prove to be loyal and worthy; but this should be done by the military governor. I believe the administration need have no anxiety about the question of slavery, or any other important question, in this State. But the proper care of the freedmen should be provided for by State legislation as soon as possible. I shall be thankful for any information or instructions you may be able to give me on these subjects.

A week later more precise rules governing the freedmen were issued:

(General Orders, No. 46.)

HDQRS. DEPT. OF NORTH CAROLINA, ARMY OF THE OHIO,
RALEIGH, N. C., May 15, 1865.

The following rules are published for the government of freedmen in North Carolina until the restoration of civil government in the State:

I. The common laws governing the domestic relations, such as those giving parents authority and control over their children, and guardians control over their wards, are in force. The parent's or guardian's authority and obligations take the place of those of the former master.

II. The former masters are constituted the guardians of minors and of the aged and infirm, in the absence of parents or other relatives capable of supporting them.

III. Young men and women under twenty-one years of age remain under the control of their parents or guardians until they become of age, thus aiding to support their parents and younger brothers and sisters.

IV. The former masters of freedmen may not turn away the young or the infirm, nor refuse to give them food and shelter; nor may the able-bodied men or women go away from their homes, or live in idleness, and leave their parents, children, or young brothers and sisters to be supported by others.

V. Persons of age who are free from any of the obligations referred to above are at liberty to find new homes wherever they can obtain proper employment; but they will not be supported by the government, nor by their former masters, unless they work.

VI. It will be left to the employer and servants to agree upon the wages to be paid; but freedmen are advised that for the present season they ought to expect only moderate wages, and where their employers cannot pay them money, they ought to be contented with a fair share in the crops to be raised. They have gained their personal freedom. By industry and good conduct they may rise to independence and even wealth.

VII. All officers, soldiers, and citizens are requested to give publicity to these rules, and to instruct the freed people as to their new rights and obligations.

VIII. All officers of the army and of the county police companies are authorized and required to correct any violation of the above rules within their jurisdiction.

IX. Each district commander will appoint a superintendent of freedmen,— a commissioned officer,— with such number of assistants — officers and non-commissioned officers — as may be necessary, whose duty it will be to take charge of all the freed people in his district who are without homes or proper employment. The superintendents will send back to their homes all who have left them in violation of the above rules, and will endeavor to find homes and suitable employment for all others. They will provide suitable camps or quarters for such as cannot be otherwise provided for, and attend to their discipline, police, subsistence, etc.

X. The superintendents will hear all complaints of guardians or wards, and report the facts to their district commanders, who are authorized to dissolve the existing relations of guardian and ward in any case which may seem to require it, and to direct the superintendent to otherwise provide for the wards, in accordance with the above rules.

By command of Major-General Schofield:

J. A. CAMPBELL, Assistant Adjutant-General.

On May 29, General Grant, from Washington, ordered me to " give every facility and encouragement to getting to market cotton and other Southern products. Let there be no seizure of private property or searching to look after Confederate cotton. The finances of the country demand that all articles of export should be gotten to market as speedily as possible." I answered at once:

Your despatch concerning cotton and other products is received. I some time ago removed all military restrictions upon trade, and have given every facility for carrying cotton and other products to market. The only obstacles in the way are the restrictions of the Treasury Department. It would be a blessing to the country if the whole system could be abolished. Now only one man in North Carolina is authorized to buy cotton, and he does not pay money for it. It is impossible for people to get their products to market in this way.

The imperative need of the Southern States at the close of the war was temporary military government, and permission, under such full military protection, to reorganize their civil governments. In the following letter to General Grant, dated May 10, I submitted my views concerning the policy that ought to be pursued:

I desire to submit to you my views concerning the policy that ought to be pursued in North Carolina, leaving it to your judgment whether or not to submit them to the President or Secretary of War. I am now led to this mainly by a letter which I received on the 7th from Chief Justice Chase, giving some points of the policy advocated by him, which, if adopted in this State, would in my opinion lead to disastrous results.

The points I refer to are briefly as follows, viz.:

The organization of the State government to be left to the people acting in their original sovereign capacity.

In determining the right of suffrage, the old Constitution, amended in 1835, to be followed in preference to the new one which was in force at the commencement of the rebellion — the object being to give negroes the right to vote.

The first proposition is not, I think, open to serious objection. With proper assistance from the military authorities, it can be successfully carried out.

The second proposition is the one to which I refer as specially objectionable, and this for two reasons.

First. The Constitution of the State as it existed immediately prior to the rebellion is still the State Constitution, and there is no power on earth but the people of the State that can alter it.

The operations of the war have freed the slaves in this and most other States, and, doubtless, slavery will be constitutionally abolished throughout the country. But the United States cannot make a negro, nor even a white man, an elector in any State. That is a power expressly reserved by the Constitution to the several States. We cannot alter or amend the Constitution of North Carolina, as it now exists, without either first altering or else violating the Constitution of the United States.

If we hold that by the rebellion the States have lost their existence as States, and have been reduced to unorganized Territories under the absolute sovereign authority of the United States, then undoubtedly we may declare that all inhabitants, white and black, shall have equal political rights and an equal voice in the organization of a State to be admitted into the Union. But I understand President Johnson repudiates this doctrine; hence it may be left out of the question.

It appears to me beyond question that the Constitution of North Carolina is now valid and binding as the law of the State, and that any measures for the reorganization of the State government must be in accordance with the provisions of that instrument. This, I am convinced, is the unanimous opinion of the leading Union men of the State.

My second reason for objecting to the proposition is the absolute unfitness of the negroes, as a class, for any such responsibility. They can neither read nor write. They have no knowledge whatever of law or government. They do not even know the meaning of the freedom that has been given them, and are much astonished when informed that it does not mean that they are to live in idleness and be fed by the government.

It is true they are docile, obedient, and anxious to learn; but we certainly ought to teach them something before we give them an equal voice with ourselves in government. This view is so fully recognized as correct by all who are familiar, by actual contact, with the negro character and condition, that argument seems superfluous. I have yet to see a single one among the many Union men in North Carolina who would willingly submit for a moment to the immediate elevation of the negro to political equality with the white man.

They are all, or nearly all, content with the abolition of slavery. Many of them are rejoiced that it is done. But to raise the negro, in his present ignorant and degraded condition, to be their political equals would be, in their opinion, to enslave them [the white citizens]. If they did not rebel against it, it would only be because rebellion would be hopeless. A government so organized would in no sense be a popular government.

After careful consideration of all the questions involved, I am fully convinced as to the best policy to be adopted in this State, which I will submit in outline:

A military governor to be appointed, who shall have command of all the troops in the State; or the department commander be authorized to assume, by virtue of his command, the functions of military governor, which naturally devolve upon him.

The military governor to declare the Constitution and laws of the State in force immediately preceding the pretended Act of Secession (so far as the same are not inconsistent with the Constitution and laws of the United States and the war proclamations of the President) to be still in force.

To make provisional appointments of justices of the peace, sheriffs, and such other inferior officers as the State laws empower the governor to appoint, to serve until the organization of a civil government.

To order an enrolment of all electors who may take the President's amnesty oath.

As soon as this enrolment shall be completed, to call an election for delegates to a State convention. The qualifications of voters and candidates to be those prescribed by the State laws, and that they shall take the amnesty oath. All acts of the convention to be submitted to the people, for their ratification or rejection, at the same time with the election of governor and members of the legislature, which would be ordered by the convention.

I would confidently expect a convention, so chosen, to repudiate the doctrine of secession, abolish slavery, and fully restore the State to its practical constitutional relations to the Government of the United States. The people are now ripe for such action. They only ask to know what the government desires them to do, and how they are to do it.

If, however, they should fail to do this, I would regard them as having violated their oaths, would dissolve the convention, and hold the State under military government until the people should come to their senses. I would have a lawful popular government or a military government — the latter being a necessary substitute in the absence of the former.

I am willing to discharge, to the best of my ability, any duty which may properly devolve upon me. Yet if a policy so opposed to my views as that proposed by Mr. Chase is to be adopted, I respectfully suggest that I am not the proper person to carry it out.

If, however, after knowing my views fully, it be desired that I execute the President's wishes, would it not be well for me to have a personal interview with him, in order that I may fully understand his plan and the principles upon which it is founded?

The fundamental principles of my suggestion were:

First. The Constitution and laws as they were before secession, modified to embrace the legitimate results of the war — namely, national integrity and universal freedom.

Second. Intelligent suffrage, to be regulated by the States themselves; and

Third. Military governments, in the absence of popular civil governments, as being the only lawful substitute, under our system, for a government by the people during their temporary inability, from whatever cause, to govern themselves.

But these constitutional methods were rejected. First came the unauthorized system of "provisional" governors, civilians without any shadow of lawful authority for their appointments, and their abortive attempts at "reconstruction."

Next the Fourteenth Amendment, disfranchising nearly all the trusted leaders of the Southern people, and then the "iron-clad oath," universal enfranchisement of the ignorant blacks, and "carpet-bag" governments, with all their offensive consequences. If wise statesmanship instead of party passion had ruled the hour, how easily could those twelve years of misrule in the South, and consequent disappointment and shame among its authors in the North, have been avoided!

A "provisional" governor (William W. Holden) having been appointed for North Carolina, I relinquished command of the department in June, 1865, to enter upon more important service in respect to the then existing military intervention in Mexico by the Emperor of the French.

CHAPTER XX

FRENCH INTERVENTION IN MEXICO — A PLAN TO COMPEL THE
WITHDRAWAL OF THE FRENCH ARMY — GRANT'S LETTER
OF INSTRUCTIONS TO GENERAL SHERIDAN — SECRETARY
SEWARD ADVOCATES MORAL SUASION — A MISSION TO
PARIS WITH THAT END IN VIEW — SPEECHMAKING AT THE
AMERICAN THANKSGIVING DINNER — NAPOLEON'S METHOD
OF RETREATING WITH DIGNITY — A PRESENTATION TO THE
EMPEROR AND EMPRESS.

WHILE the government of the United States was
fully occupied with the contest for the preservation of the Union, Napoleon III, Emperor of the French,
attempted to overthrow the republican government in
Mexico, and establish in its stead an empire under the
Archduke Maximilian of Austria. If the American conflict had resulted in the triumph of secession, so also might
Napoleon have succeeded in reëstablishing monarchical
government on the American continent. But from the
moment when the Union of the States became reassured,
European interference in the political affairs of the
American republic became impossible. Upon this subject there appeared to be no division of sentiment among
the people of the United States. Certainly there was
none among the responsible American statesmen of that
time. It was their unanimous voice that the French intervention in Mexico must be speedily terminated; but
there was naturally some division of opinion respecting
the means by which this should be effected. Some fa-

vored the most prompt and vigorous military action, while others, not unmindful of the long-existing friendship between the people of the United States and France, preferred more peaceful measures.

As the first and necessary step in either line of policy, whether for immediate active military operations or as conclusive evidence of ultimate military purpose in aid of diplomacy, General Sheridan was sent, with an army of about fifty thousand men, to the line of the Rio Grande. But Sheridan's troops were Union volunteers who had been enlisted especially for the Civil War, then terminated; and the necessity was at once recognized of organizing a new army for the express purpose of acting against the French army in Mexico, in case of need. It was proposed that this new army should be enlisted and organized under the republican government of Mexico, the only government recognized by the United States in that country. This course would avoid the necessity of any political action of the government of the United States in the premises. Lieutenant-General U. S. Grant, then commander-in-chief of the armies of the United States, was requested to select an officer to organize and command the proposed army.

In June, 1865, at Raleigh, North Carolina, I received a message from General Grant informing me of my selection, and desiring me, if I was willing to consider the proposition, to come to Washington for consultation on the subject. Upon my arrival in Washington, I consulted freely with General Grant, Señor Romero (the Mexican minister), President Johnson, Secretary of State Seward, and Secretary of War Stanton, all of whom approved the general proposition that I should assume the control and direction of the measures to be adopted for the purpose of causing the French army to evacuate Mexico. Not much was said between me and the President or either of the secretaries at that time about the means to be employed; but it appeared to be understood by all that force would probably be necessary, and for some time no other means were considered. The subject was fully discussed with General Grant and Señor Romero, and I then consented to take charge of the matter, with the understanding that I should have perfect freedom of action and choice of means and of time, so far as circumstances would permit. To enable me to do this, the War Department gave me leave of absence for twelve months, with permission to go beyond the limits of the United States and to take with me any officers of my staff whom I might designate. It was proposed to organize in Mexican territory an army corps under commissions from the government of Mexico, the officers and soldiers to be taken from the Union and Confederate forces, who were reported to be eager to enlist in such an enterprise.

The Mexican authorities proposed to furnish the means by which this army should be paid and the expenses of military operations defrayed, and to that end a loan was to be negotiated in the United States. To facilitate the enlistment and equipment of the proposed army corps, General Grant gave me a manuscript order, dated West Point, July 25, 1865, addressed to General P. H. Sheridan, then commanding the Military Division of the Gulf, with a large force near the Mexican frontier. The following is a copy of General Grant's order:

HEAD QUARTERS ARMIES OF THE UNITED STATES.

WEST POINT, N. Y., July 25, 1865.

MAJ.-GEN. P. H. SHERIDAN, Com'd'g Mil. Div. of the Gulf.

GENERAL: Maj.-General J. M. Schofield goes to the Rio Grande on an inspection tour, carrying with him a leave of absence for one year, with authority to leave the United States. If he avails himself of this leave he will explain to you the object more fully than I could do in the limits of a letter, and much more fully than I could do now, under any circumstances, because much that will have to be learned to fix his determination, whether to go or not, has yet to be found out in Washington whilst I shall be away. This, however, I can say: Gen. Schofield's leave has been given with the concurrence of the President, he having full knowledge of the object. I have both written my views to the President and had conversations with him on the subject. In all that relates to Mexican affairs he agrees in the duty we owe to ourselves to maintain the Monroe doctrine, both as a principle and as a security for our future peace.

On the Rio Grande, or in Texas, convenient to get there, we must have a large amount of surrendered ordnance and ordnance stores, or such articles accumulating from discharging men who leave their stores behind. Without special orders to do so, send none of these articles back, but rather place them convenient to be permitted to go into Mexico if they can be got into the hands of the defenders of the only Government we recognize in that country. I hope Gen. Schofield may go with orders direct to receive these articles; but if he does not, I know it will meet with general approbation to let him have them if contrary orders are not received.

It is a fixed determination on the part of the people of the United States, and I think myself safe in saying on the part of the President also, that an empire shall not be established on this continent by the aid of foreign bayonets. A war on the part of the United States is to be avoided, if possible; but it will be better to go to war now, when but little aid given to the Mexicans will settle the question, than to have in prospect a greater war, sure to come if delayed until the empire is established. We want, then, to aid the Mexicans without giving cause of war between the United States and France. Between the would-be empire of Maximilian and the United States all difficulty can easily be settled by observing the same sort of neutrality that has been observed toward us for the last four years.

This is a little indefinite as a letter of instructions to be governed by. I hope with this you may receive them — instructions — in much more positive terms. With a knowledge of the fact before you, however, that the greatest desire is felt to see the Liberal Government restored in Mexico,— and no doubt exists of the strict justice of our right to demand this, and enforce the demand with the whole strength of the United States,— your own judgment gives you a basis of action that will aid you.

I will recommend in a few days that you be directed to discharge all the men you think can be spared from the Dept. of Texas, where they are, giving transportation to their homes to all who desire to return. You are aware that existing orders permit discharged soldiers to retain their arms and accoutrements at low rates, fixed in orders.

Very respectfully, your obt. svt.,

U. S. GRANT, Lt.-Gen.

In effect this order required General Sheridan to turn over to me all of his volunteer troops who might wish to take part in the Mexican enterprise, with their arms and equipments, and all "surrendered ordnance and ordnance stores," etc., thus making it easy for me to arm and equip at small cost the ex-Confederates and others who would join my standard. Soon after the date of General Grant's order to General Sheridan, and at the request of Secretary Seward, conveyed to me by Mr. Stanton, I met Mr. Seward at Cape May. He then proposed to me to go to France, under authority of the State Department, to see if the French emperor could not be made to understand the necessity of withdrawing his army from Mexico, and thus save us the necessity of expelling it by force. Mr. Seward expressed the belief that if Napoleon could be made to understand that the people of the United States would never, under any circumstances, consent to the existence in Mexico of a government established and sustained by foreign power, he would withdraw his army from that country. If this were done, the friendly relations between the people of France and the United States would not be disturbed, while the expulsion of a French army from Mexico by American volunteers would engender great bitterness of feeling among the French people, even if it did not lead to war between France and the United States.

This proposition from Mr. Seward seemed to put upon me the responsibility of deciding the momentous question of future friendship or enmity between my own country and our ancient ally and friend. I had, on the one hand, full authority from the War Department and the general-in-chief of the army, given with the knowledge and consent of the President of the United States, to organize and equip an army for the purpose of driving the French out of Mexico, and on the other hand a request from the State Department to go to France and try by peaceful means to accomplish the same end.

As the negotiation of the Mexican loan had not made great progress, the funds were not yet available for the support of an army. It was expected that the actual beginning of operations on the Rio Grande would stimulate subscriptions to the loan, yet the lack of ready money was a sufficient cause for some delay in making the proposed "inspection tour" to the Rio Grande; and this fact, added to a natural love of peace rather than of war, and a due sense of the dictates of patriotism as contrasted with mere military ambition, determined the decision of that question. It is reason for profound thankfulness that the peaceful course was adopted.

In a letter dated August 4, 1865, I informed Mr. Seward of my decision, "after mature reflection," "to undertake the mission" which he had proposed. Mr. Seward acknowledged my letter on August 9, and on the 19th I received a telegram from the War Department to "report at the State Department upon your [my] next visit to Washington." This order was promptly obeyed. On August 23 the Secretary of War sent a letter to the Secretary of State, accrediting me as an officer of the army, in which capacity, and unofficially, I was to be understood by the public as visiting Europe. A copy of this letter, inclosed in one from the State Department, was sent to Mr. Bigelow, United States minister at Paris; and similar letters were sent to several other United States ministers in Europe. But time passed until November 4, and thus more than two months elapsed before the Secretary of State was ready for me to start for Europe. Mr. Seward then gave me a confidential letter, dated November 4, 1865, addressed to Mr. Bigelow, and a letter of credit on the Barings, and requested me to proceed on my mission.

In his letter to Mr. Bigelow he said: "General Schofield proceeds to Paris. He is, I believe, fully informed of the feelings and sentiments, not only of this government, but of the American people. I commend him to your confidence," etc. Mr. Seward explained to me several times during this period of delay that correspondence then going on with the French government rendered it advisable that my visit be delayed until he should receive expected answers from that government. The Atlantic cable did not then exist, and hence correspondence across the ocean was necessarily slow. The expected despatch — viz., that from the French Foreign Office to their minister at Washington, dated October 18, 1865, and communicated to Mr. Seward on the 29th of the same month — was no more satisfactory, though in better tone, than those which had preceded. In effect it demanded a recognition by the United States of the government of Maximilian in Mexico as a condition precedent to the recall of the French army. The time had evidently arrived when Napoleon must be informed in language which could not be misunderstood what was the real sentiment of the government and people of the United States on the Mexican question. It was difficult, perhaps impossible, to express that sentiment in official diplomatic language that an emperor could afford to receive from a friendly power. It was therefore desirable that the disagreeable information be conveyed to Napoleon in a way which would command his full credence, and which he yet need not regard as offensive. Mr. Seward's explanation and instructions to me, after several long conversations on this subject, were summed up in the words: "I want you to get your legs under Napoleon's mahogany, and tell him he must get out of Mexico."

In my visit to Paris I was accompanied by two officers of my staff, Brevet Brigadier-General William M. Wherry and Brevet Brigadier-General G. W. Schofield, who had been given leave of absence for the purpose of going with me to Mexico or elsewhere. We sailed from New York, November 15, 1865, on the Cunard steamer *Java*, and stayed a day in Liverpool and several days in London, where I explained to Mr. Adams, United States minister, the purpose of my visit.

Mr. Adams expressed hearty sympathy with the object of my mission, and gave cordial assent to my wish that I might feel at liberty to consult him in regard to it at any time.

Mr. Motley, United States minister at Vienna, whom I had the pleasure of meeting at the residence of Mr. Adams, assured me that the government of Austria was especially desirous of not being regarded by the United States as responsible in any manner for the attempt to establish an empire under the Austrian archduke in Mexico. Mr. Motley thought a visit by me to Vienna while the Mexican question was pending might produce undue excitement. Hence I limited my tour in that direction to Italy.

We proceeded to Paris on the 2d of December. Our arrival had been preceded by vague rumors of an official mission more or less hostile to the interests of France, which caused great excitement among the French people and the American residents in Paris, and serious depression of United States, Mexican, and French securities in the financial markets of Europe. It was also understood that no little anxiety was felt at the French court, then

25

at Compiègne. It was manifestly desirable to allay so far as possible this undue excitement in the public mind. Hence I availed myself of an early opportunity, given by the American Thanksgiving dinner at the Grand Hotel, to intimate in unmistakable terms that my mission, if any, was one entirely friendly to the people of France.

The following is a part of the account of that banquet given by the Paris correspondent of the "New York Herald," under date of December 8, 1865:

The American residents and transient sojourners in Paris celebrated the national Thanksgiving by a grand dinner at the Grand Hotel, which passed off in splendid style. . . . The next toast was the long-looked-for one of the evening, for it was known that it would call up a distinguished guest from whom all were anxious to hear. It was "The Army and Navy of the United States." When the band had ceased playing "Yankee Doodle," Major-General Schofield rose to reply to this toast, and was received with tremendous enthusiasm. The ladies rose and waved their handkerchiefs, and gentlemen shouted until they were hoarse. The general, after bowing his acknowledgments, said: "Fellow-countrymen — I want words to express to you the satisfaction which will be felt in the heart of every soldier and sailor when he learns the manner in which the names of the army and navy have been received by you to-night. I will at this time allude but briefly to one of the great lessons taught by the American war — the grandest lesson of modern times. A great people who have heretofore lived under a government so mild that they were scarcely aware of its existence have found, in time of war, that government to be one of the strongest in the world [cheers], raising and maintaining armies and navies vaster than any ever before known [cheers]. In point of character, in point of physical and moral qualities, in point of discipline and of mobility in large masses, the armies of the United States have never before been equaled [loud cheers]. Yet this, great as it is, is not the greatest wonder of the American war. This vast army, as soon as its work was done, was quietly disbanded, and every man went to his home, as quietly as the Christian goes back from church on Sabbath morning; and each soldier reëntered upon the avocations of peace a better citizen than he was before he became a soldier [renewed applause]. This was the grandest lesson of the war. It shows that the power of a nation to maintain its dignity and integrity does not result from or depend upon its form of government; that the greatest national strength — the power to mass the largest armies in time of war — is entirely consistent with the broadest liberty of the citizen in time of peace [enthusiasm]. Permit me, in conclusion, to propose a toast which I know will be heartily responded to by every true American — 'The old friendship between France and the United States: may it be strengthened and perpetuated!'" General Schofield's toast was drunk with great enthusiasm, and upon his taking his seat the applause which followed his remarks was deafening.

The situation of Napoleon's government at that time was extremely critical. The opposition was powerful and aggressive. The intervention in Mexican affairs was very unpopular in France, and yet the national pride of the people would not permit the Emperor to yield to menace even from the United States, nor allow his army to be driven by force from Mexico without a supreme effort to maintain it there. Napoleon could not have submitted to such humiliation without the loss of his throne. In short, forcible intervention by the American people in the Mexican question, or the public threat of such action, arousing the national pride of France, must have led to a long and bloody war, resulting, doubtless, in final success in America and probably in a revolution in France.

Such a result would have been a just punishment to Napoleon for his conduct toward the United States and Mexico during our Civil War. But why involve the people of France and the people of the United States in this punishment? Why make enemies of our ancient friends? Our sister republic of Mexico must be relieved from foreign domination, at whatever cost; but strife and lasting enmity between the United States and France would be a fearful price to pay for even so great a good as the freedom of Mexico. Manifestly such extreme measures should not be resorted to until all peaceful means had failed. Considerations of this nature determined my course while in Paris. I had sufficient opportunity in two interviews with Prince Napoleon, and in several conversations with officers of high rank on the Emperor's staff, to make known to the Emperor the views and purposes of the government and people of the United States in respect to Mexican affairs. Our conversation was without reserve on either side, and with the understanding that nothing said by me would be withheld from the Emperor.

The principal of these staff-officers was the distinguished Admiral de la Gravière, who had commanded the French squadron in American waters in the early part of our Civil War and in the capture of Vera Cruz. This gallant and honest old sailor had reported to his government the exact truth about the enterprise which Napoleon had undertaken when he ordered the bombardment and capture of the Mexican seaport for the alleged purpose of collecting a French claim — namely, that he was no better able to collect that claim after the city was in his possession than he had been before, and that the conquest of Mexico by the operations of a large army would be necessary before any financial return could be expected. This unwelcome report led to the admiral's recall to France, and he was sent to his home in disgrace. But in due time the Emperor learned that while all others had deceived him, the admiral had told him the truth, whereupon he was called to Paris, restored to the confidence of his chief, and appointed aide-de-camp on the staff of the Emperor. Admiral de la Gravière was a warm friend of America, rejoiced in the triumph of the Union cause, understood and appreciated the sentiments of the people of the United States, among whom he had made many friends, and was a very willing medium of communication to the Emperor of the exact attitude of the American people respecting the Monroe doctrine, which the Emperor of the French had been betrayed into violating through the influence of persons high in his confidence, but governed by sordid motives.

Admiral Reno, Assistant Minister of Marine, was another of the high French officials with whom free conversation was held.

The fidelity with which Prince Napoleon and others reported to the Emperor the character of the unofficial message which I had to deliver rendered it quite unnecessary that it be delivered in person, and quite impossible that the Emperor should be willing to receive it in that way. Hence, though I received several intimations that I would be invited to a private interview, no invitation came, and none was sought. My letters from Paris to Mr. Seward, to General Grant, and to Señor Romero, reported the progress made, and the nature of the situation as it then appeared to me.

On January 22 I was present at a dinner given by Prince Napoleon in the Palais Royal. Every shade of political opinion in Paris was represented among the guests. Political discussion seemed to be entirely unrestrained, with one exception, when a remark which savored of disloyalty to the empire was rebuked by the prince.

In the Emperor's address to the French legislature on January 22, his future policy in respect to Mexico had been hinted at in the words: "[Our expedition] *touche à son terme.*" The declared purpose of speedily terminating the intervention in Mexico having been applauded by all, the prince inquired pointedly of me whether, in my opinion, the Emperor's declaration would be satisfactory to the United States, and received the unreserved reply that it would, as I believed, be accepted as satisfactory.

In my report to Mr. Seward of January 24, I expressed the belief that even his enemies in France would not be disposed to embarrass the Emperor in respect to Mexico, "well satisfied to see him get out of that country by any means, and thus avoid war with the United States"; and I ventured the suggestion that "this course would also seem wise on our part." In my letter of the same date to General Grant I said:

You will get by this mail Napoleon's speech delivered at the opening of the French legislative session. I was present and heard the speech delivered. That part of it relating to Mexico and the United States was received with very general tokens of approbation, while most of the remainder met with a cold reception. I have since heard it discussed very freely by many prominent men of all shades of political opinion, among others the Prince Napoleon. All seem to recognize the falsity of the Emperor's assumptions where he says: "In Mexico the government founded by the will of the people is consolidating itself," etc. Yet his statements are, no doubt, believed by a large majority of the French people, and therefore afford him a very good reason for yielding to the demand, made in common by the people of France and the United States, that his intervention in Mexico shall be brought to an end. This is the logic of his position and his solution of his difficulty, viz.: to assert that he has accomplished the object of his expedition to Mexico, and hence to end it. While we laugh at the absurdity of his premises, we can hardly find fault with his conclusion, and hence it is not worth while to criticize any part of his argument. Rather I think it well to let him make the most of his audacity in the creation of convenient facts. The opinion seems to be universal here that the Emperor is sincere in his declarations of intention as to Mexico; indeed, that he has adopted the policy of making the strongest possible bid for the friendship of the United States. It is certainly easy to derive such an opinion from his speech, and I am strongly inclined to believe it correct. Yet we cannot forget the fact that in his speech of last year he used quite as strong language as to the speedy termination of his Mexican expedition. Hence I shall indulge in some doubt until I see the actual development of his present plans. I have no idea that Napoleon believes that Maximilian can remain long in Mexico after the French troops are withdrawn; but it is very important for him, in order to give some appearance of truth to his assumed grounds of action, that Maximilian be allowed to stay there some time without French aid. And for this reason he wants some assurance of neutrality from the government of the United States. Prince Napoleon and others with whom I have conversed express the decided opinion that Maximilian will come away with Marshal Bazaine, in spite of all the Emperor may say to induce him to try to stand alone. This, I apprehend, will be the difficulty, and may cause much delay, unless the United States kindly lend a helping hand. Would it not be wise for us to abstain for a few months from all interference, direct or indirect, and thus give Napoleon and Maximilian time to carry out their farce? Mexico would thus be rid of the French flag in the least possible time. If the French troops come also, Juarez can easily dispose of Maximilian at any time. If they succeed in getting the French troops to remain as colonists, then the United States can easily find a good reason for disposing of the whole matter, and Napoleon will not dare to interfere. . . . An officer of the Emperor's household left here about ten days ago with despatches for Mexico which, it is understood, contained the Emperor's declaration to Maximilian of his intention to recall his troops. This will give you some idea of the time when the matter may be arranged if all works well.

My views relative to the purposes of the French government appear to have been in accord with those of Mr. Bigelow at the time, as shown in his official despatches afterward published, and adopted by Mr. Seward in his subsequent correspondence with the French minister at Washington. They were soon afterward confirmed by the official announcement which the French minister was authorized to make to the government of the United States. In fact, I was in almost constant conference with Mr. Bigelow during that time, and knew that my views, as communicated to Mr. Seward and General Grant, were in close accord with his, although I could not know anything of Mr. Bigelow's despatches to the State Depart-

ment until they were published. Mr. Bigelow's compre-
hension of the French view of the Mexican question proved
to be perfectly exact. While awaiting further instructions
in reply to my report of January 24, I occupied my time
in visits to the south of France, Italy, Switzerland, and
England.

Among the personal incidents connected with my stay
in Paris which seem worthy of record were the following:

Soon after my arrival in Paris, in company with Mr.
Bigelow I called upon Marshal Randon, Minister of
War, who was the only minister of the French government then in Paris. We were received with cold and
formal politeness. Some days later, the Emperor having
returned to Paris, and having apparently become satisfied
that I was not occupied with any designs hostile to France,
I received a very courteous letter from the Minister of
War, dated December 13, and addressed to Mr. Bigelow;
and Captain Guzman, the officer therein named, reported
to me immediately. Under the guidance of this accomplished officer I saw in the most agreeable manner all the
military establishments about Paris. These courtesies
were acknowledged in a letter dated February 25, 1866,
addressed to Mr. Bigelow.

My presentation to the Emperor and Empress occurred
at one of those brilliant occasions at the Tuileries for
which the second empire was famous. In conversing
with the Emperor, he desired to know something of the
operations of the American armies, and especially their
marvelous methods of supply at great distances from a
base of operations.

It gives me great pleasure to record here, as I did in
my correspondence at the time, the great courtesy, the
kindness, and the charming hospitality shown me by Mr.
Bigelow and his amiable family during my stay in Paris.
Mr. Adams, United States minister at London, was
also exceedingly kind, inviting a very distinguished

company to meet me at dinner, taking me to several charming entertainments, and presenting me to the Prince of Wales, who then received in place of the Queen. General King at Rome, and Mr. Marsh at Florence, also entertained me very courteously during my short stay at those places. The warmth of greeting by Americans everywhere, and the courteous reception by all foreigners whom I met, lent a peculiar charm to the first visit of a Union soldier among those who had watched from a distance the great American conflict.

I now have the satisfaction of knowing, in the light of subsequent events, that whatever my mission to France contributed toward the solution of the momentous question of that day was wisely directed in the interest of peace at home, continued friendship with our former allies, the people of France, and the relief of an American republic from foreign domination; these great blessings were combined in the final result.

Too much cannot be said in praise of the able and patriotic statesmanship displayed by Secretary Seward in his treatment of the French violation of the Monroe doctrine.

Early in May, 1866, I received from Mr. Seward his final reply to my report of January 24, in which he said: "The object for which you were detailed to visit Europe having been sufficiently accomplished, there is considered to be no further occasion for you to remain in that quarter in the service of this department." Whereupon I returned to the United States, and reported at the State Department on the 4th of June.

The condition of the Franco-Mexican question at the time of my return from Europe gave no further occasion for my offices in either of the ways which had been contemplated in behalf of Mexico. Subsequent events in Mexico included the sad fate of Maximilian and the sadder fate of Carlotta.

CHAPTER XXI

RECONSTRUCTION IN VIRGINIA — THE STATE LEGISLATURE
ADVISED TO ADOPT THE FOURTEENTH AMENDMENT —
CONGRESSIONAL RECONSTRUCTION AS A RESULT OF
THE REFUSAL — THE MANNER IN WHICH THE ACTS OF
CONGRESS WERE EXECUTED — NO RESORT TO TRIAL BY
MILITARY COMMISSION — THE OBNOXIOUS CONSTITUTION
FRAMED BY THE STATE CONVENTION — HOW ITS WORST
FEATURE WAS NULLIFIED — APPOINTED SECRETARY OF
WAR.

IN August, 1866, after my return from Europe, I was
assigned to command the Department of the Potomac, which included the State of Virginia, then governed
in part by the Freedmen's Bureau and in part by the
provisional government which had been organized at
Alexandria while the war was still in progress. The
State had yet to obtain from Congress a recognition
of its government, which recognition was understood
to depend upon the ratification by the State legislature of the then pending Fourteenth Amendment to
the Constitution of the United States. This subject
was very fully discussed between me and the leading
members of the legislature. I advised them to accept
the proposed amendment as the only means of saving
the State from the more "radical" reconstruction under
act of Congress, which was then threatened. It was
urged that Virginia would not suffer much from the operation of the Fourteenth Amendment, because of the
general intelligence of her white population and their

superiority in numbers over the negroes — advantages which some of the other Southern States did not enjoy; that if the Virginia legislature would ratify the pending amendment, Congress could not refuse to recognize the existing State government and make it permanent; and that Virginia would thus be restored at once to her full privileges as a State in the Union. I visited Washington, and obtained from leading Republicans in Congress the assurance, so far as it was in their power to give it, that such would be the result. On my return to Richmond, it at first seemed that the amendment would be speedily ratified. But other influences, understood to come from some source in Washington (probably President Johnson), finally prevailed; the amendment was rejected; and Virginia was thus doomed to undergo "congressional reconstruction" in company with her sister States.

The "policy" of President Johnson having resulted in an "irrepressible conflict" between him and Congress, finally culminating in his impeachment, the reconstruction of the States lately in insurrection was undertaken by Congress. First an act dated March 2, 1867, was passed for the military government of the "rebel States," and then another act, dated March 23, 1867, prescribing the conditions of organization of State governments preparatory to restoration to the Union; the last-named act was supplemented by the act dated July 19, 1867. All of these acts were passed over the President's veto. They provided for the assignment of military commanders in the several districts, with nearly absolute powers to govern those States and direct the steps in the process of reconstruction. It fell to my lot to command the First Military District, into which Virginia was converted by the act of Congress.

The terrible oppression of the Southern people embodied in those acts of Congress has hardly been appreciated by even the most enlightened and conservative people of the North. Only those who actually suffered the baneful effects of the unrestrained working of those laws can ever realize their full enormity. The radical Congress was not content to impose upon the Southern States impartial suffrage to whites and blacks alike. They were not content even to disfranchise the leading rebels, according to the terms of the Fourteenth Amendment to the Constitution. Even those would not be sufficient to put the Southern whites under the domination of their former slaves and of adventurers from the North, and thus to secure the radical supremacy in the reconstructed States. Hence another and an enormous stride was taken, with the purpose of putting those States under what became known as "carpet-bag" governments, so offensive as to be nearly intolerable even to their authors. That stride consisted in imposing the so-called "iron-clad oath" upon all officers, of whatever grade or character, in all the former Confederate States. That oath excluded from office not only all who had in any way taken active part in the rebellion, but even the most constant Union men of the South who had remained at home during the war; for not one of them had escaped "giving aid or comfort" in some way to those engaged in the rebellion. Even so conspicuous a loyalist as Judge Rives, afterward United States district judge, declared, after mature deliberation, that he could not take that oath, although his constant fidelity to the Union was known to all in Virginia.

I asked this noted Union man to accept the office of chief justice of the State, but he could not take the prescribed oath. He had permitted his boy, about to join the Confederate army, to take one of his horses rather than see him go afoot. Perhaps the judge was too conscientious. But it was the evil effect of the law to exclude the highly honorable and let the rascals in. Thus the Union could not have the benefit of Judge Rives's eminent services in the vital work of reconstruction, and some " carpet-bagger " had to take his place. And thus, although the acts of Congress permitted a majority of the whites to vote, their choice of officers was restricted to negroes and "carpet-baggers"! To these latter, therefore, was committed the entire work of organizing and administering the Southern State governments, which required the aid of the United States troops to support them, and which fell by their own weight the moment that support was withdrawn.

The manner in which I executed those " reconstruction " acts of Congress in Virginia, so as to save that State from the great evils suffered by sister States, is perhaps an instructive part of the history of that time. The following extracts from my orders and correspondence clearly show the constitutional principles upon which my administration was based. They also give the essential points in the history of Virginia reconstruction up to the time when the Convention had completed its work of framing a constitution. My " General Orders, No. 1," dated Richmond, Va., March 13, 1867, was as follows:

I. In compliance with the order of the President, the undersigned hereby assumes command of the First District, State of Virginia, under the act of Congress of March 2, 1867.

II. All officers under the existing provisional government of the State of Virginia will continue to perform the duties of their respective offices according to law, unless otherwise hereafter ordered in individual cases, until their successors shall be duly elected and qualified in accordance with the above-named act of Congress.

III. It is desirable that the military power conferred by the before-mentioned act be exercised only so far as may be necessary to accomplish the objects for which that power was conferred, and the undersigned appeals to the people of Virginia, and especially to magistrates and other civil officers, to render the necessity for the exercise of this power as slight as possible, by strict obedience to the laws, and by impartial administration of justice to all classes. . . .

On April 20 was issued "General Orders, No. 16":

I. Temporary appointments to fill vacancies which may occur in county or city offices will, in general, be made upon the concurrent recommendations of the County Court or City Council and of the President of the Board of Registration [1] for the county or city.

II. The several County Courts and City Councils are requested to confer with the Presidents of the Boards of Registration concerning such appointments, and to agree upon a suitable person to fill any vacancy that may occur.

III. The President of the Board of Registration will forward to the assistant adjutant-general the recommendation of the court or council, with his own indorsement thereon.

IV. When a County Court is not in session, a recommendation signed by five justices, including the presiding justice, will be received in lieu of the recommendation of the court.

V. County and corporation officers appointed by the commanding general will be required to give the bonds required by law, and will be subject to indictment for malfeasance, misfeasance, or neglect of official duty, the same as if they had been elected by the people.

On May 28 was issued "General Orders, No. 31," in part as follows:

. . . IV. The military commissioners [officers of the army] will make a prompt report to these headquarters of each case of which they may take jurisdiction, and the disposition made of such case. Where parties are held for trial, either in confinement or under bail, such full statement will be made of the facts in each case as will enable the commanding general to decide whether the case shall be tried by a military commission or be brought before a civil court.

---

[1] The presidents of Boards of Registration were army officers detailed by me for that duty.

V. Trial by the civil court will be preferred in all cases where there is satisfactory reason to believe that justice will be done. But until the orders of the commanding general are made known in any case, the paramount jurisdiction assumed by the military commissioner will be exclusive.

VI. All persons, civil officers and others, are required to obey and execute the lawful orders of the military commissioners to the same extent as they are required by law to obey and execute writs issued by civil magistrates. Any person who shall disobey or resist the lawful orders or authority of a military commissioner shall be tried by a military commission, and upon conviction shall be punished by fine and imprisonment according to the nature and degree of the offense. . . .

VIII. This order will not be construed to excuse civil officers, in any degree, from the faithful discharge of their duties. It is intended to aid the civil authorities, and not to supersede them, except in cases of necessity.

No case arose in Virginia in which it was found necessary, in my opinion, to supersede the civil authorities in the administration of justice. Not a single citizen of that State was tried by military commission. Yet some cases arose which well illustrate the fascinations of absolute power to those who desire the benefit of its exercise in their own interests. Some of the most prominent citizens of Virginia, men who had earnestly opposed the general policy of military government then in force, came to me to settle their petty differences summarily. They seemed much disappointed when I declined to adjudicate such cases, and informed them that they must be content with the slow process of trial before their own civil magistrates. Other orders were in part as follows:

RICHMOND, VA., July 26, 1867.

. . . III. The governor and other executive officers, the courts of law, and councils of cities are invited to recommend suitable persons for appointment to such offices as, under the existing laws of Virginia, are usually filled by their appointment or upon their nomination. . . .

RICHMOND, VA., August 8, 1867.

. . . VI. Military commissioners are reminded that they are to be "governed in the discharge of their duties by the laws of Virginia, so far as the same are not in conflict with the laws of the United States, or orders issued from these headquarters," and that they are not to supersede the civil authorities, except in cases of necessity. In such cases the action, or failure to act, of the civil officers should be fully reported, in order that the commanding general may hold them to a proper accountability for any neglect of duty. . . .

Upon the adjournment of the State Convention, I sent the following letter to General Grant:

RICHMOND, VA., April 18, 1868.

DEAR GENERAL: In spite of every effort that could be made to prevent it, the Virginia Convention has adhered to its proscriptive measures, or rather to the most objectionable of them.

After every other means had failed, I even went so far as to visit the Convention and urge the repeal of the test oath. But what I said seemed not to have the slightest influence. I inclose a newspaper report, which is a pretty accurate one, of what I said, and which will show that I have at least done my duty in that regard, if not more.

The same baneful influence that secured the election of a majority of ignorant blacks, and equally ignorant or unprincipled whites, to the Convention, has proved sufficient to hold them firmly to their original purpose. They could only hope to obtain office by disqualifying everybody in the State who is capable of discharging official duties, and all else to them was of comparatively slight importance. Even the question whether their Constitution will be ratified or rejected, they treat with indifference. Congress, they say, will make it all right anyway. . . .

Of course I may be mistaken, but my opinion is that the Constitution must be adopted. This would not be a serious matter if it (the Constitution) were a good one, and good officers could be elected under it. But it seems hardly possible that the Union party can organize upon a satisfactory basis for the election. The negroes and their associates will doubtless insist upon unqualified indorsement of the Constitution by their nominees. This the respectable whites will not give. Hence the late Convention will be reproduced in the legislature, a large majority being either worthless radicals, white and black, or bitter opponents of reconstruction upon the congressional plan. The danger is that we will have on our hands, not only one big elephant in the Constitution, but a host of little ones in the shape of officers-elect who are not fit to be installed — a prospect not very encouraging, at least.

My impression is that the wisest course would be to let the thing fall and die where it is — not submit it to the people at all. We can then go on putting Union men in office and reorganizing the provisional government upon a loyal basis, until the friends of reconstruction get control of the State. Then a convention can be called which will frame a Constitution fit to be ratified by the people of the State and approved by Congress and the country at large.

If Congress would give a little more latitude in the selection of officers, by modifying the test oath, there would be no difficulty in filling all the offices in the State with men who would aid restoration. Without some such change, the work of reorganization cannot be carried very far. The view of the question which I have given above is, of course, the local one; but it seems to me the national one leads to the same conclusion. I can't see how the indorsement of such a Constitution as this one, by the Republican party, can be otherwise than damaging to them in the North. Would it not be wise for Congress to say at once, We reject, once and for all, proscriptive constitutions?

I have written this letter merely to suggest points that occur to me as worthy of very careful consideration. I suppose Congress alone can determine what is to be done.

As explained in my official letter to-day, I feel bound to await the action of Congress before ordering an election. The nominating conventions of the two parties meet in Richmond on the 6th and 7th of May. Perhaps it may be best for Congress to await their action before determining the question. . . .

The newspaper clipping inclosed in the above letter to General Grant was a report of the proceedings of the Convention which appeared in the "Richmond Dispatch"

26

of April 18, 1868. Several other letters to General Grant, near the same time, explained the situation in detail.

As was to be expected, and in spite of any influence which the military commander could properly exert, that proposed Constitution, like those framed in the other States, perpetuated the worst features of the acts of Congress. It disqualified all the respectable whites from any active part in the government, leaving the negroes and " carpet-baggers " full sway. So sweeping was this disqualification that in many parts of the State not a native Virginian, white or black, could be found who could read or write, and who would be eligible for election or appointment to any office. In my great anxiety to save the State from so great an evil, I went to the hall of the Convention and explained the impossibility of organizing a government under such a Constitution, and besought the Convention to strike out the disqualifying clause. I was listened to with cold respect, my advice was disregarded, and promptly after my departure the Constitution was finally adopted, and the Convention adjourned *sine die.*

But the State was, nevertheless, saved from the impending disaster. The act of Congress required that the Constitution be submitted to the people for ratification or rejection ; but Congress had failed to appropriate money to pay the expenses of an election. If an election was to be held, the money must be taken from the treasury of the State, by the order of the district commander, or else Congress must make a special appropriation for that purpose. I declined to sanction the use of the people's money for any such purpose, refused to order an election for ratification or rejection of the obnoxious Constitution, and referred the matter to Congress, with a recommendation that the people be authorized to vote separately on the disqualifying clause — a privilege which the Convention had denied.

The radicals in Congress were so glad, apparently, of this mode of escape from a result so obnoxious to the better sense of the Union people at that time, that not a voice was raised in favor of the "carpet-bag" Constitution or in disapprobation of my action in regard to it. The instrument was permitted to rest quietly in the pigeonhole of the district commander's desk until the next year. Then an act was passed providing for submitting that Constitution to the people of Virginia, with the privilege of voting separately on the disfranchising clause, which clause they, of course, rejected. Thus Virginia was saved from the vile government and spoliation which cursed the other Southern States, and which the same radical Congress and its successors sustained until the decent public sentiment of the North would endure them no longer.

It is, perhaps, not too much to say that if the other district commanders had in like manner refused to make themselves parties to the spoliation of the people placed under their charge, Congress would have shrunk from the direct act of imposing upon them such obnoxious governments, and the country might have been saved the disgrace of the eight years of carpet-bag rule in the South. At least it is certain that a large proportion of the more moderate among the Republican majority in Congress at that time indulged the hope that respectable governments might be organized under the acts of Congress. But they made this difficult, if not impossible, when they gave their assent to the amendment of those acts, prepared by the extremist radicals, depriving the Southern whites of any active part in the organization of their governments. Impartial justice, as expressed in "impartial suffrage," might have led to tolerable results even in those States where the blacks were in the majority. But under a law which gave universal suffrage to the blacks and disfranchised the influential whites, any tolerable result was impossible unless under the administration of a man who had the independence and courage to disarm such a law of its poisonous sting. However this may be, it is certain that Virginia owes her escape from the sad fate of her sister States to the action of her district commander, who has abundant reason for the belief that the good people of that State fully appreciated the fact.

With this service to the people of Virginia, my duty in that State practically terminated. The impeachment trial of President Johnson had reached its crisis. It had become evident to those who were wise enough to discern the "signs of the times" that the Senate would probably not sustain the articles of impeachment by the necessary two-thirds majority. This would leave unsettled the quarrel between the President and Congress over the War Department, and that on the eve of an exciting Presidential election, in which several of the newly reconstructed States were expected to take part. In not one of these States was the new government able to stand alone or to preserve the peace within its borders. A firm and impartial administration of the War Department in the sole interest of peace and order during the coming contest was the one indispensable want of the country. Without that, a revival of civil strife seemed inevitable. Under these circumstances, I was urged to accept the office of Secretary of War, with the assurance that in this way the contest which endangered the peace of the country could be adjusted. I gave my consent, the nomination was promptly sent to the Senate, and that body, in spite of its very large majority in opposition to the President, confirmed the appointment with almost entire unanimity. The impeachment was dismissed, and that dangerous farce, which had come within one or two votes of inflicting lasting disgrace upon the country, happily came to an end.

Upon the inauguration of the newly elected President in March, 1869, I laid down the war portfolio without having incurred censure from either party for any of my official acts, and with the approbation of all for impartial discharge of duty. But, apparently lest such a thing might possibly happen again, Congress made haste to pass a law prohibiting any army officer from thereafter holding any civil office whatever! In 1895 that law was so modified as not to apply to officers on the retired list! It is a singular coincidence that I had just then been retired.

CHAPTER XXII

DIFFERENCES BETWEEN THE COMMANDING GENERAL OF THE
ARMY AND THE WAR DEPARTMENT — GENERAL GRANT'S
SPECIAL POWERS — HIS APPOINTMENT AS SECRETARY OF
WAR *AD INTERIM* — THE IMPEACHMENT OF PRESIDENT
JOHNSON — MEMORANDUM OF INTERVIEWS WITH WILLIAM
M. EVARTS AND GENERAL GRANT IN REGARD TO THE
SECRETARYSHIP OF WAR — FAILURE OF THE IMPEACH-
MENT TRIAL — HARMONY IN THE WAR DEPARTMENT —
A NEW POLICY AT ARMY HEADQUARTERS.

DURING nearly the entire history of the government of the United States the relations between the general-in-chief, or nominal commanding general of the army, and the War Department have been the cause of discord, sometimes descending to bitter personal controversy, and in a few instances leading to very serious results.

The differences between General Scott and the Secretary became so serious that the general removed his headquarters from Washington to New York, and remained away from the capital several years, until the time when civil war was imminent. General Sherman also found it necessary to escape from an intolerable situation by removing to St. Louis, and did not return to Washington until the condition of the War Department led to the impeachment of the Secretary of War. During their long absence from the capital neither of these generals could exercise any appreciable influence over either the administration or the command of the army. It is thought to be worthy of note that during one of those periods of absence of the general-in-chief the military resources of the country were mostly placed within easy reach of those about to engage in an effort to break up the Union, and that during the other period corruption in the War Department led to impeachment. It is no reflection upon the many eminent, patriotic citizens who have held the war portfolio to say that the very few men who have proved unworthy of that great trust would have been much less likely to do serious harm to the public interests if they had been under the watchful eye of a jealous old soldier, like Scott or Sherman, who was not afraid of them.

As hereafter explained, the controversy between General Grant and the Secretary of War was the primary cause which finally led to the impeachment of the President of the United States. The cause of this trouble has seemed to be inherent in the form and character of the government. An essential provision of the Constitution makes the President commander-in-chief of the army and navy. It is manifestly indispensable that the executive head of a government be clothed with this authority. Yet the President is not, as a rule, a man of military education or experience. The exigencies of party politics also seem to require, in general, that the Secretary of War be a party politician, equally lacking with the President in qualifications for military command.

The art of war has in all ages called forth the highest order of genius and character, the great captains of the world having been esteemed as among the greatest men. So, also, and in continually increasing degree in modern times, the military art has called for scientific education of the very highest character, supplemented by practical experience. It cannot be questioned that the military profession requires ability, education, and practical training no less than the legal or any other profession. A

Supreme Court of the United States composed of merchants and bankers would be no more of an anomaly than a body of general and staff officers of like composition. The general policy of our government seems to be based upon a recognition of this self-evident principle. We have a national military academy and other military schools inferior to none in the world, and well-organized staff departments which are thoroughly efficient in war as well as in peace. The laws also provide a due proportion of subordinate general officers for the command of geographical departments in time of peace, or of divisions and brigades in the field in time of war. But no provision is made for an actual military commander of the entire army either in peace or in war. During only one single year since the adoption of the Constitution of the United States has this not been the fact. In pursuance of a special act of Congress and the orders of President Lincoln, General Grant in fact commanded "all the armies of the United States" during the last year of the Civil War; but at no other time has there been an actual military commander of the army or armies whose authority as such was recognized by the War Department.

Why, it may be asked, this strange departure from the recognized rule of organization in all governmental and business affairs? Why provide educated and trained experts for all subordinate positions, and none for the head or chief, vastly the most important of all?

In the first place, it is important to observe that the matter rests absolutely in the hands of the President: Congress has no power in the matter. To create by law a military head for the army would be a violation of the essential provision of the Constitution which makes the President commander-in-chief.

In the case of General Grant, Congress fully recognized this fact, saying: "Under the direction and during the pleasure of the President" he "may" command the armies of the United States. Even this, if intended as conveying authority to the President, was superfluous, and if intended as more than that would have been unconstitutional. In fact, it was only a suggestion, intended to be entirely within the limits of constitutional propriety, of what was the general opinion of the people and of Congress, that after three years of failure the President ought to select a soldier and put him in actual command of all the armies. The President then went far beyond the suggestion of Congress, and even to the extreme limit of military abdication. He not only gave General Grant absolute, independent command, placing at his disposal all the military resources of the country, but he even denied to himself any knowledge whatever of the general's plans. In this patriotic act of extreme self-abnegation President Lincoln undoubtedly acted in exact accord with what he believed to be the expressed popular opinion, and probably in accord with his own judgment and inclination; for no one could have been more painfully aware than he had by that time become of the absolute necessity of having a military man actually in control of all the armies, or more desirous than he of relief from a responsibility to which he and his advisers had proved so unequal. But it must be admitted that in this President Lincoln went beyond the limit fixed by his constitutional obligation as commander-in-chief. He would have more exactly fulfilled that obligation if he had endeavored faithfully to comprehend and adopt as his own all the plans proposed by his chosen and trusted general-in-chief, guarding the latter against all possible interference, theretofore so pernicious, from the War Department or any other source. By such means the President could have actually exercised the chief command imposed upon him by the Constitution, sharing in due measure with his chief military officer the responsibilities imposed by their high offices.

In no other way, it is believed, can the duties imposed upon a constitutional commander-in-chief who is not possessed of military education and experience be fully and conscientiously performed. Indeed, such is the method pursued by great military sovereigns all over the world, except in the few instances where the monarch believes himself, either truly or falsely, superior in military ability to his chief of staff. It is only in this country, where the chief of state has generally no military training, and his war minister the same, that a chief of staff of the army is supposed to be unnecessary. While it is easy to understand the reasons which led to the action of the government in the spring of 1864, it is much less easy to understand why some reasonable approximation to that course, as above suggested, and in accord with the practice of all military nations, has never been adopted as a permanent system in this country. Perhaps it may be like the case of that citizen of Arkansas who did not mend the roof of his house when it was not raining because it did not then need mending. But it would seem the part of wisdom to perfect the military system so far as practicable in time of peace rather than continue a fruitless controversy over the exact location of an undefined and undefinable line supposed to separate the military administration from the command in the army, or the functions of the Secretary of War from those of the commanding general. The experience of many years had shown that the Secretary was sure to get on both sides of that line, no matter where it was drawn. But it is encouraging to note that some experiments made in more recent years, in the direction of the generally recognized sound military system, have not proved by any means unsatisfactory.

This chronic controversy between the military administration and the command once gave rise to one of the most dangerous crises in American history. The facts in respect to the origin of that crisis soon became obscured by other events, and have never been correctly published.

The assassination of President Lincoln occurred a very short time before the end of the Civil War. It appears that his successor in the Presidential office did not withdraw any part of the supreme authority which had been conferred upon General Grant by President Lincoln a year before. Nevertheless, Secretary Stanton, who had very reluctantly yielded to President Lincoln's order, began, soon after the end of hostile operations, to resume the exercise of those functions which had formerly been claimed as belonging to the War Department, and which had been suspended by President Lincoln. Stanton "boldly took command of the armies."[1] By this General Grant was deeply offended, and finally declared that the action of the Secretary of War was intolerable; although he refers to it in his "Memoirs" as "another little spat." The authority which Stanton assumed was the constitutional authority of the commander-in-chief of the army, a large part of which authority had been delegated by the President to General Grant, not to Secretary Stanton. Hence the Secretary's assumption was offensive alike to the general and to the President. General Grant acted with great forbearance, and endeavored to obtain from Secretary Stanton due recognition of his rightful authority as general commanding the army, but with no permanent effect.[2]

General Grant opposed the removal of Mr. Stanton by the exercise of the President's prerogative alone, for the reason, with others, that such action would be in violation of the Tenure-of-Office Act.[3] He also objected at

---

[1] Grant's "Memoirs," Vol. II, p. 105.

[2] Grant's "Memoirs," Vol. II, pp. 104, 105; Sherman's "Memoirs," second edition Vol. II, pp. 446–450.

[3] See General Grant's letter to President Andrew Johnson, August 1, 1867, in McPherson's "History of Reconstruction," p. 307.

first to either removal or suspension, mainly for fear that an objectionable appointment might be made in Stanton's place.[1] But those two objections being removed by Johnson's tender of the appointment to Grant himself, *vice* Stanton suspended instead of removed, General Grant gave his full countenance and support to President Johnson in the *suspension* of Mr. Stanton, with a view on the part of the President to his ultimate removal, either with the concurrence of the Senate or through a judicial decision that the Tenure-of-Office Act was, as Johnson claimed, unconstitutional.[2]

On August 12, 1867, Grant himself accepted the appointment of Secretary of War *ad interim*, and informed Stanton that he had done so. Stanton denied the right of the President to suspend him without the consent of the Senate, but wrote to the President, and to the same effect to General Grant: "But inasmuch as the general commanding the armies of the United States has been appointed *ad interim*, and has notified me that he has accepted the appointment, I have no alternative but to submit, under protest, to superior force."[3]

In 1866, 1867, and 1868 General Grant talked to me freely several times of his differences with Secretary Stanton. His most emphatic declaration on that subject, and of his own intended action in consequence, appears from the records to have been made after Stanton's return to the War Office in January, 1868, when his conduct was even more offensive to Grant than it had been before Stanton's suspension in August, 1867, and when Grant and Sherman were trying to get Stanton out of the War Office.[4] At the time of General Grant's visit

[1] See General Grant's letter to President Andrew Johnson, February 3, 1868, in McPherson's "History of Reconstruction," p. 286.

[2] Sherman's "Memoirs," second edition, Vol. II, p. 241; and McPherson's "History of Reconstruction," pp. 282–293.

[3] McPherson's "History of Reconstruction," pp. 261, 262.

[4] Sherman's "Memoirs," second edition, Vol. II, pp. 422–424.

to Richmond, Va., as one of the Peabody trustees, he said to me that the conduct of Mr. Stanton had become intolerable to him, and, after asking my opinion, declared in emphatic terms his intention to demand either the removal of Stanton or the acceptance of his own resignation. But the bitter personal controversy which immediately followed between Grant and Johnson, the second attempt to remove Stanton in February, 1868, and the consequent impeachment of the President, totally eclipsed the more distant and lesser controversy between Grant and Stanton, and, doubtless, prevented Grant from taking the action in respect to Stanton's removal which he informed me in Richmond he intended to take.[1]

Of the impeachment and trial of President Johnson it is not my province to write. My special knowledge relates only to its first cause, above referred to, and its termination, both intimately connected with the history of the War Department, the necessities of which department, real or supposed, constituted the only vital issue involved in the impeachment trial. The following memorandum, made by me at the time, and now published with the consent of Mr. Evarts, explains the circumstances under which I became Secretary of War in 1868, and the connection of that event with the termination of the impeachment trial:

MEMORANDUM
May, 1868.

In compliance with a written request from Mr. W. M. Evarts, dated Tuesday, April 21, 1868, 2 p. m., I called upon that gentleman in his room at Willard's Hotel, Washington, a few minutes before three o'clock p. m. of the same day.

Mr. Evarts introduced conversation by saying something about the approaching trial of Mr. Jefferson Davis, but quickly said that was not what he wished to see me about. The business

---

[1] The records of the Peabody trustees show that their meeting in Richmond, when General Grant was present, occurred January 21 and 22, 1868.

upon which he wished to see me was of vastly greater importance, involving the safety of the country and the maintenance of the Constitution. Mr. Evarts then asked my consent that the President might at any time before the close of the impeachment trial send my nomination to the Senate as Secretary of War in place of Mr. Stanton. I asked upon what ground, and for what reasons, the proposition was made, which question was then answered in part, and in the evening of the same day more fully, as hereafter related. It having been announced that General Grant was waiting at the door for me, this first interview was cut short with an agreement to renew it about eight o'clock the same evening. Before separating I asked Mr. Evarts whether I was at liberty to mention the subject to any other person. Mr. Evarts replied: " I suppose you mean General Grant." I said: " Yes; my relations with General Grant, and his with the President, are such that I do not wish to act in such a matter without consulting him." Mr. Evarts said he could not give consent that any person should be informed that such a proposition had been made on behalf of the President, and suggested some objections to consulting General Grant on the subject, for the reason of his being a candidate for the Presidency, but finally intimated that it might be well to talk to General Grant about it incidentally, and thus learn his views.

While walking with General Grant after dinner the same day, I said to him, in effect, that I had reason to believe that a proposition like the one referred to above would probably be made to me, and that upon the theory, as I understood, that the President would not be convicted by the Senate, and I asked General Grant's opinion in regard to it. General Grant replied that he had supposed there was no reasonable doubt of the President's removal, but if that was not the case, or if it were, he (General Grant) would be glad to have me as Secretary of War during the remainder of the term; that Mr. Wade would have some difficulty in making up a cabinet for so short a portion of a term.

About eight o'clock P. M. of the same day (April 21) I again called upon Mr. Evarts at the hotel, when a long conversation took place upon the subject referred to in the morning. The substance of what Mr. Evarts said was as follows: He was fully satisfied that the President could not be convicted upon the evidence; if he was removed, it would be done wholly from supposed party necessity; that this was the opinion and feeling of a considerable number of the ablest lawyers and statesmen among the Republican senators; that it was his and their opinion that if the President was removed, it would be not really from anything he had done, but for fear of what he might do; that he (Mr. Evarts) did not believe the President could possibly be convicted in any event, but that senators were at a loss how to remove the apprehensions of the Republican party as to what the President would do in case of acquittal, unless the War Department was placed in a satisfactory condition in advance. He said: "A majority of Republicans in both houses of Congress and throughout the country now regret the commencement of the impeachment proceedings, since they find how slight is the evidence of guilty intent. But now the serious question is, how to get out of the scrape? A judgment of guilty and removal of the President would be ruinous to the party, and cause the political death of every senator who voted for it as soon as the country has time to reflect upon the facts and appreciate the frivolous character of the charges upon which the removal must be based. The precedent of the impeachment and removal of the President for political reasons would be exceedingly dangerous to the government and the Constitution; in short, the emergency is one of great national peril." He added that this was the view of the case entertained by several among the most prominent Republican senators, and that from such senators came the suggestion that my nomination as Secretary of War be sent to the Senate, in order that the Senate might vote upon the President's case in the light of that nomination. Mr. Evarts believed that I was so named because my appointment would be satisfactory to General Grant, and would give the Republican party a sense of security as to the President's future action in reference to the War Department and the military districts of the South; that it was not with anybody a question of friendship or hostility toward the President personally, for he really had no friends. That while the Democrats in the Senate would of course vote for his acquittal, and do their whole duty in the case, just so soon as he was removed they would rejoice that it was done, feeling confident that it would cause the overthrow of the Republican party and the defeat of General Grant. Mr. Evarts was not at liberty to mention names of senators holding these views and originating the proposition of my nomination.

I suggested a number of objections, some personal as to myself, and others of a public character, to giving my assent to the proposed nomination, in reply to which objections many of the above statements by Mr. Evarts were made. I then said I would again talk with General Grant upon the subject, and give a definite reply the next morning. About eleven o'clock the same night (April 21) I informed General Grant at his house that the proposition above named had been (or it would be) made to me; that it originated with Republican senators; and I gave in substance the reasons above stated as what I understood to be the grounds upon which the proposition was made. I did not give any names of senators, nor the channel through which my information or the proposition came. My remarks to General Grant were prefaced by the statement that while I would be glad of General Grant's advice if he felt at liberty to give it, I did not wish to ask General Grant to commit himself in so delicate a matter unless he desired to do so; but that the matter was one of so great importance that I thought it my duty to tell him all about it, and what I believed I ought to do, and leave General Grant to advise or not, as he thought best. I said that although the statement of the views and wishes of senators above referred to came to me indirectly, they came in such a way as not to permit me to doubt their correctness, and I believed it my duty to yield to the request. General Grant at once replied that under those circumstances he did not see how I could do otherwise. General Grant said he did not believe in any compromise of the impeachment question. The President ought to be convicted or acquitted fairly and squarely on the facts proved. That if he was acquitted, as soon as Congress adjourned he would trample the laws under foot and do whatever he pleased; that Congress would have to remain in session all summer to protect the country from the lawless acts of the President; that the only limit to his violation of law had been, and would be, his courage, which had been very slight heretofore, but would be vastly increased by his escape from punishment. General Grant said he would not believe any pledge or promise Mr. Johnson might make in regard to his future conduct. In his opinion, the only safe course, and the most popular one, would be to remove the President. He could understand the grounds of apprehension in the minds of some leading Republicans, but he did not agree with them. He believed the safest and wisest course was the bold and direct one. In this General Grant was very emphatic; he said he would not advise me to enter into any project to compromise the impeachment question, but if the facts were as represented that I could not well do otherwise than to acquiesce in the nomination.

The next morning (April 22), about ten o'clock, I called upon Mr. Evarts at Willard's Hotel, and informed him that I had considered the matter as carefully as I was able to do, and that there was then only one difficulty in my mind. That was as to what would be the policy of the President during the remainder of his term, in the event of his being acquitted. I mentioned some of the President's recent acts, such as the creation of the Military Division of the Atlantic, disregard of military usage in sending orders to army officers out of the regular channels, etc., — acts for which no good reason could be given, and which at least tended to create discord and trouble. Mr. Evarts replied that he could not tell anything about those matters, but presumed that such annoying irregularities would disappear with the removal of their cause, namely, hostility between the President and the Secretary of War. Mr. Evarts said he did not see how I could satisfy myself on that subject without a personal interview with the President, which would not be advisable in the circumstances. I then said I did not expect any pledge from the President, and did not expect to receive any communication from him on the subject, either directly or indirectly; and that I was not willing to converse with the President, nor with any other person except Mr. Evarts, on the subject; but that I wished the President to understand distinctly the conditions upon which I was willing to accept the appointment, and desired Mr. Evarts to inform the President of these conditions. If the nomination was then made, I would take it for granted that the conditions were satisfactory. I then said I had always been treated kindly by the President, and felt kindly toward him; that I had always advised him, whenever any excuse had been given for offering advice, to avoid all causes of irritation with Congress, and try to act in harmony with the legislative department; that I regarded the removal of Mr. Stanton, in the way it was done, as wrong and unwise; that I understood this proposition as coming originally from the Republican side of the Senate, and as being accepted by the President in the interest of peace, and for the purpose of securing harmony between the legislative and executive departments of the government, and

27

a just and faithful administration of the laws, including the reconstruction acts. I added: "And the President knows from General Schofield's acts what he means by this,—if, after these conditions have been fully stated to the President, he sends my name to the Senate, I will deem it my duty to say nothing on the subject of accepting or declining the appointment until the Senate has acted upon it."

Mr. Evarts intimated that the above was satisfactory, and the interview then ended.

I returned to Richmond on Thursday, April 23, being then in command in Virginia, executing the reconstruction acts. On the 24th the President sent to the Senate my nomination as Secretary of War. On the morning of the 26th I received from General Grant a confidential letter, dated April 25, advising me under the circumstances to decline the secretaryship in advance.[1]

To the above letter I sent the following letters in reply :

(Confidential.)

RICHMOND, VA., April 26, 1868.

DEAR GENERAL: I regret exceedingly that your advice came too late. I have already promised not to decline the nomination in advance of any action of the Senate.

Yours very truly,   J. M. SCHOFIELD, Bvt. Maj.-Gen.

GEN'L GRANT, Washington, D. C.

RICHMOND, VA., April 26, 1868.

DEAR GENERAL: I see from the papers that the President has nominated me to the Senate as Secretary of War. You are aware that I do not want that office; yet under existing circumstances, if the Senate should wish me to serve I could not decline. I presume my nomination will not be confirmed, but have no right to act upon such presumption.

Yours very truly,   J. M. SCHOFIELD, Bvt. Maj.-Gen.

GEN'L GRANT, Washington, D. C.

---

[1] From all the circumstances it is fair to assume that General Grant's change of attitude was owing to his opinion as to the effect the nomination would have on the impeachment proceedings.

I have no means of knowing to what extent, if any, the Senate was influenced by this nomination, but anxiety about the ultimate result seemed to be soon allayed. About a month later a vote was taken in the Senate, and the impeachment failed; my nomination was then confirmed, as stated at the time, by a nearly unanimous vote of the Senate.

I entered upon the duties of the office as Secretary of War on the first day of June, and continued to discharge them until a few days after General Grant's inauguration in March. I was greeted very cordially by the President, by all the members of his cabinet, by General Grant, and by a large number of senators who called upon me at the War Department.

The duties devolved upon me were often of a very delicate character, and it required at times no little tact to avoid serious trouble. President Johnson's views were sometimes in direct conflict with those which I felt compelled to maintain under the acts of Congress affecting the States lately in rebellion; but it is due to the memory of President Johnson to say that he did not at any time require me to do anything contrary to my interpretation of the acts of Congress, and that he in general acquiesced without objection in all the measures I deemed necessary to preserve the peace and secure a fair vote of the newly enfranchised citizens of the Southern States in the Presidential election. The cordial assistance of Mr. Evarts as Attorney-General was a great help to me in such matters. When he was present I had little difficulty in respect to the law involved in any question; but when he happened to be absent, and I was compelled to stand alone against all the cabinet, or all who chose to take any interest in the question, it was hard work. But I always carried the day—at least, in act if not in argument. The President never decided against me. He thus fulfilled to the letter the implied promise made when he submitted my nomination to the Senate.

If there ever had been any real ground for the wide-spread apprehension of criminal purpose on the part of President Johnson, certainly all indication of any such purpose disappeared with the failure of his impeachment and the settlement of the long-standing controversy respecting the War Department. The so-called reconstruction laws, which the President so emphatically condemned as being unconstitutional, were carried out without further objection from him; the Presidential election in the Southern States was conducted with perfect good order; a free ballot and a full count were secured under the supervision and protection of the army—a thing supposed to be so dangerous to the liberties of a free people. This and many other examples in the history of this country, from the time when Washington surrendered his commission to the Continental Congress down to the present time, show that a "free people" have nothing to fear from their army, whether regular, volunteer, or militia; the soldiers are, in fact, among the most devoted and loyal citizens of the republic, and thoroughly imbued with the fundamental principle of subordination of the military to the civil power.

With General Grant my relations while in the War Department were of the most satisfactory character. As a candidate for the Presidency, and as President-elect, he naturally desired to be as free as possible from the current duties of his office as general of the army, and he was absent from Washington much of the time, his chief of staff, General Rawlins, remaining there to promulgate orders in his name. Thus it devolved upon me to exercise all the functions of "commander-in-chief of the army"—functions which it is usually attempted to divide among three,—the President, the Secretary of

War, and the general-in-chief,—without any legal definition of the part which belongs to each. Of course "the machine" ran very smoothly in the one case, though there had been much friction in the other. In compliance with the wish of General Grant, I remained in office under him for a few days, for the purpose of inaugurating the system which he hoped would end the long-standing controversy between the War Department and the headquarters of the army. The order which was issued assigning General Sherman to command the entire army, staff as well as line, was prepared by me under General Grant's instructions, and the draft of the order was approved by him as expressing the views he had maintained when he was general-in-chief. As President he very soon yielded to the opposite views, and caused the order to be amended accordingly.

That General Sherman then entertained views of his authority which were too broad, as General Grant had also done, is no doubt true; but it ought not to have been very difficult to correct such errors. It was easier to take away all administrative authority and all command over the general staff of the army, and the latter course was adopted. The ancient controversy was up to 1888 no nearer settlement than it was in 1869, though in General Sheridan's time some progress had been made in the persistent efforts to deprive the general-in-chief of the little authority which had been left to General Sherman. General Sheridan had, with his usual gallantry and confidence, renewed the contest, but had been worsted in his first encounter with the Secretary, and then gave up the struggle.

Upon my assignment to the "command of the army" in 1888, I determined to profit so far as possible by the unsatisfactory experience of Generals Scott, Grant, Sherman, and Sheridan — at least so far as to avoid further attempts to accomplish the impossible, which attempts have usually the result of accomplishing little or nothing. In fact, long study of the subject, at the instance of Generals Grant and Sherman, earnest efforts to champion their views, and knowledge of the causes of their failure, had led me to the conclusion heretofore suggested, namely, that under the government of the United States an actual military commander of the army is not possible, unless in an extreme emergency like that which led to the assignment of Lieutenant-General Grant in 1864; and that the general-in-chief, or nominal commanding general, can at most be only a "chief of staff,"— that or nothing, — whatever may be the mere title under which he may be assigned to duty by the President.

As the first step in the experimental course decided upon, I sent an order in writing to the adjutant-general, directing him never, under any circumstances, to issue an order dictated by me, or in my name, without first laying it before the Secretary of War; and I made it known to all the staff that I disclaimed the right to issue any order to the army without the knowledge of the President or the Secretary. I also forbade the issuing of any order in my name without my knowledge. The first rule was easy, the latter very difficult, to enforce. I found, with no little surprise, that the office of the "commanding general" usually learned for the first time of routine orders issued in his name by seeing them published in the New York papers the next day; and it was quite difficult at first to make it distinctly understood that such a practice could not be tolerated. In fact, it became necessary to call attention to the question of veracity involved in such a use of the general's name. Such was the condition the War Department had reached. The adjutant-general had acquired the habit of issuing nearly all orders to the army without the knowledge of any one of his superiors — the President, the Secretary of War, or the general-in-chief. In fact, the adjutant-general had in practice come very near being "commander-in-chief."

Some time and much patience were required to bring about the necessary change, but ere long the result became very apparent. Perfect harmony was established between the War Department and the headquarters of the army, and this continued, under the administrations of Secretaries Proctor, Elkins, and Lamont, up to the time of my retirement from active service. During all this period,— namely, from 1889 to 1895, under the administrations of Presidents Harrison and Cleveland,— the method I have indicated was exactly followed by the President in all cases of such importance as to demand his personal action, and some such cases occurred under both administrations. The orders issued were actually the President's orders. No matter by whom suggested or by whom formulated, they were in their final form understandingly dictated by the President, and sent to the army in his name by the commanding general, thus leaving no possible ground for question as to the constitutional authority under which they were issued, nor of the regularity of the method, in conformity with army regulations, by which they were communicated to the army.

It is, I think, to be hoped that the system thus begun may be fully developed and become permanent, as being the best practicable solution of a long-standing and dangerous controversy, and as most in accord with the fundamental principles of our constitutional government, under which the President, whether a soldier or a civilian, is in fact as well as in name the commander-in-chief of the army and navy.

CHAPTER XXIII

ASSIGNMENT TO THE DEPARTMENT OF THE MISSOURI — A CORDIAL RECEPTION FROM FORMER OPPONENTS IN ST. LOUIS — ORIGIN OF THE MILITARY SCHOOL AT FORT RILEY — FUNERAL OF GENERAL GEORGE H. THOMAS — DEATH OF GENERAL GEORGE G. MEADE — ASSIGNED TO THE DIVISION OF THE PACIFIC — A VISIT TO HAWAII — MILITARY MEN IN THE EXERCISE OF POLITICAL POWER — TROUBLE WITH THE MODOC INDIANS — THE CANBY MASSACRE.

WHEN I went into the War Office in 1868, the cordial greeting extended from all quarters was exceedingly gratifying to me, and, I thought, highly honorable to those gentlemen, especially in the Senate, who had so long opposed me, only one of whom, I believe, failed to call at the office and express a kindly welcome; and that one was so great a man, in his own estimation, I flattered myself that was the only reason he had not called to greet me. So when I returned to St. Louis in March, 1869, the good citizens of that place gave me a banquet and a most cordial welcome, in which all participated, save one, of those who had seemed to be my most bitter enemies in 1862 and 1863. It was especially noteworthy that the Hon. Charles D. Drake, who had been chairman of the large delegation which went to Washington, and one of the recognized leaders in the movement, to obtain my removal from the command in Missouri, was among the most cordial in his expressions of esteem and regard from March, 1869, up to the time of his death, at which time I was in command of the army. But his principal associate, the Hon. Henry T. Blow, could not forgive me, for what thing especially I do not know, unless for my offense in arresting a "loyal" editor, for which he denounced me in a telegram to the President. That was, no doubt, a very grave offense, but a natural one for a young soldier. Indeed, old as I am now, and much sad experience as I have had with the press, I would probably do the same thing again. That "loyal" editor, professing the greatest zeal for the Union cause and devotion to the National Government, had published, in a city under martial law, a confidential letter from the President, the commander-in-chief of the army, to the commanding general of that department. The ever kind and indulgent President was only too willing to overlook such an offense on the part of one who professed to be a friend of the Union. But a soldier could not overlook such an outrage as that upon his commander-in-chief, and upon the cause he was sworn to defend. Though his respect for a free press be profound, there are some kinds of freedom which must, in time of war, be crushed, even though the soldier himself may also be crushed. A soldier who is not ready to meet his fate in that way, as well as in battle, is not fit to command.

In President Grant's order of March, 1869, assigning the general officers to commands, the Department of the Missouri again fell to my lot. I relieved Lieutenant-General Sheridan, who took command of the Division of the Missouri, and removed his headquarters from St. Louis to Chicago, which then became for the first time the principal military center of all the Western country. These arrangements were intended to be as nearly permanent as practicable, so that all might have a period of comparative rest after the eight years of war and strife. I then reverted, for the first time in those eight years, to the thoughts and ambitions of my youth and young manhood, for I had grown much older in that time. First was the ambition, inherited from my grandfather McAllister, to acquire a farm big enough to keep all the neighbors at a respectful distance. In company with my brother and another officer, I bought in Colorado a ranch about ten miles square, and projected some farming and stock-raising on a large scale. My dream was to prepare a place where I could, ere long, retire from public life and pass the remainder of my days in peace and in the enjoyment of all those out-of-door sports which were always so congenial to me. But events " over which I had no control" soon defeated that scheme. That, like all the other plans of my own invention, came to naught. The ranch was sold, and I got out of it, as I always tried to do, about as much as I had put in.

Upon a suggestion from General Henry J. Hunt, the famous chief of artillery, when I was in the War Department, I ordered a light-artillery school to be established at Fort Riley, Kansas. Also, upon his suggestion, I directed that the four batteries which were to compose that school should be supplied with carbines, so that they might serve as cavalry when necessary to protect the neighboring settlements against Indian raids, and thus overcome any objection which might be urged on the ground that the barracks at Fort Riley were needed for cavalry. The school was organized, under Colonel John Hamilton; the batteries did good service as cavalry in the summers of 1869 and 1870; and all was working, as I thought, in a highly satisfactory manner so long as I remained in command of that department. But after I went to California, for some inscrutable reason the school was broken up and the batteries again scattered to separate posts.

When that department again came under my command, as part of the Division of the Missouri, and General Sheridan was in command of the army, a move was made by somebody to get possession of that splendid military reservation of Fort Riley for some other purpose. Hence it became necessary to manifest in some more striking way the importance of that place for military uses. The occasion had again come for carrying out that scheme which Hunt and I had devised for doing what was so much needed for the artillery. Fortunately, General Sheridan wanted also to do something beneficial for the cavalry, in which he felt much the same special interest that I did in the artillery. So a sort of alliance, offensive and defensive, was formed, which included as its most active and influential member Senator Plumb of Kansas, to obtain the necessary funds and build a suitable post and establish at Fort Riley a school of cavalry and light artillery. The result finally attained, when I was in command of the army, is well known, and is an honor to the country.

The department headquarters were removed to St. Louis during the winter of 1869–70 to make room at Fort Leavenworth for the cavalry who had been on the plains during the summer. I then had the pleasure of renewing the intimate friendships which had been formed between 1860 and 1863 in that most hospitable city. Even those ties which had been so rudely severed by war in the spring of 1861 were restored and became as strong as ever. I found that the memory of a little humanity displayed in mitigating somewhat the horrors of war had sufficed to obliterate in those few years the recollection of a bitter sectional enmity; while, on the other hand, a record of some faithful service far enough from their eyes to enable them to see it without the aid of a microscope, and the cooler judgment of a few years of peace, had so far obscured the partizan contests of a period of war that none were more cordial friends in 1869 than those who

had seemed bitterest enemies six years before. Human
nature is not half so bad as it sometimes pretends to be.
As a rule, it would be pretty good all the time if men
could only keep cool. Among all the enjoyments of that
season in St. Louis, that which left the deepest impression
on my memory, as has always been the case with me,
was the sport at Hat Island, under the management of
that most genial of companions, Ben Stickney. We
hunted with hounds before breakfast every morning, and
shot water-fowl from breakfast till supper. What was
done after supper has never been told. What conclusive
evidence of the "reversionary" tendency in civilized
man to a humbler state! He never feels so happy as
when he throws off a large part of his civilization and
reverts to the life of a semi-savage. The only thing that
saves him from total relapse is the fact that he takes
with him those little comforts, both liquid and solid,
which cannot be found in the woods. He thus keeps up
the taste that finally draws him back again to a civilized,
or, more accurately, semi-civilized life. If any sportsman
knows any better reason than that for not living like a
savage when in his hunting-camp, I would like him to
give that reason to me!

We returned to Fort Leavenworth in the spring, and
expected to make that our permanent home. Some necessary improvements had been made in the quarters
during the winter, and no one could have desired a more
comfortable residence, more congenial companionship, or
more agreeable occupation than that of guarding and
protecting the infant settlements of industrious but un-
armed and confiding people rapidly spreading far out
upon the plains. With my cavalry and carbined artillery
encamped in front, I wanted no other occupation in life
than to ward off the savage and kill off his food until
there should no longer be an Indian frontier in our
beautiful country.

But soon after my pickets were put out on the plains, there came the sad news of the sudden death, in San Francisco, of my old commander, General George H. Thomas. His body was brought east to Troy, New York, for interment. All his old companions, including President Grant, assembled to pay the last tribute of respect and honor to that noble old soldier, whose untimely death was deeply mourned by all. It was a most impressive scene. All the high commanders of the vast army which had been disbanded five years before assembled around the grave of one of their number. The hero was buried, as he had lived, honored by all who knew him, and mourned by the nation he had so faithfully served.

Immediately after the funeral of General Thomas there was, if I recollect rightly, a large assembly, in Philadelphia, of the Society of the Army of the Potomac. General Grant and General Sherman were there, and we met at an early dinner at the house of General Meade, who had been designated by General Sherman to succeed General Thomas in command of the Division of the Pacific. After dinner General Meade took me to drive through Fairmount Park, in which he was greatly interested as president of the commission having it in charge. He explained to me the great sacrifice he would make in giving up command of the Division of the Atlantic, and his congenial occupation and pleasant home in Philadelphia, where he was best known and most highly respected, and where, as I could see in driving along, almost everybody recognized and saluted him. I thought he had indeed better reason to feel satisfied with his home than any other man I had ever known. But he, too, great and brave soldier, was given but little longer to enjoy the high honors he had so nobly won in command of the Army of the Potomac. When I had so far recovered from a severe attack of pneumonia as to be permitted to look for the first time at a morning paper, one of the first things that attracted my attention was the death of General Meade, from the same disease, the day before.

Of course the President did not hesitate to accede to General Meade's desire, for he had given him, only a year before, the division of his choice. As is well known, the relations between General Grant and General Hancock were not at that time quite satisfactory. As I knew the exact truth at the time, I think it my duty to state that General Grant believed that General Hancock had not at one time shown that degree of subordination which a soldier ought always to feel. But to the honor of both be it said that their difference was ere long removed, and General Hancock was assigned to command the Division of the Atlantic, according to his rank. In the meantime, it fell to my lot to take the Division of the Pacific, which I had a year before gladly relinquished in favor of General Thomas.

Soon after my arrival in San Francisco, General Sherman met me there, and we went together, by sea, to Oregon, where we met General Canby, then commanding the Department of the Columbia. We ascended the Columbia River to Umatilla, and rode by stage from that place to Kelton, on the Central Pacific Railroad, seven hundred and fifty miles. After a visit to Salt Lake City, we returned to St. Louis, where I had some work to complete as president of a board on tactics and small arms, upon the completion of which I returned to San Francisco.

In the summer of 1871, after the great earthquake of that year, I made a trip across the Sierra to Camp Independence, which had been destroyed, to consider the question of rebuilding that post. Of the buildings, brick or adobe, not one remained in condition to be occupied. Very fortunately, all in the garrison had received timely warning from the first shock, so that none were injured by the second and third shocks, which tumbled everything to the ground. Some thirty people living in small adobe houses in Owens River valley were killed. Sounds like heavy artillery in the distance were still heard at intervals after our arrival. For many miles along the length of the valley a great crevasse had been formed by the upheaval, which must have been many feet in height. In the subsidence one side had fallen several feet lower than the other, and at a place where the crack crossed the wagon-tracks a horizontal motion of several feet had taken place, the road marking its permanent effect.

We ascended Owens River valley to the source of that stream, recrossed the mountains by the "bloody" cañon, and descended through the great Yosemite valley, which from the higher altitude looked like a little "hole in the ground." That was the least interesting of all my four visits to that wonderful work of nature. Our round trip occupied about seven weeks.

At our last camp, in Tuolumne meadows, some time in August, after the temperature had been above eighty degrees in the daytime, it fell below thirty at night. I contracted a cold which developed into pneumonia, from which I did not recover for many months. It was during my convalescence that I went with Colonel B. S. Alexander to the Hawaiian Islands, under an arrangement previously made with the War Department.

It was the year 1872 when I and Colonel Alexander, the senior engineer officer on the Pacific coast, who had applied to the War Department and obtained an order to visit the Hawaiian Islands for the purpose of reporting to the War Department, confidentially, the value of those islands to the United States for military and naval purposes, went to Hawaii with Rear-Admiral Pennock on the flag-ship *California*, and returned, three months later, on the war-steamer *Benicia*. During our stay we visited the largest island of the group,—Hawaii,—and its principal seaport,—Hilo,—and the great crater of Kilauea.

We made a careful examination of the famous harbor of Pearl River, in the island of Oahu, a few miles from Honolulu, including a survey of the entrance to that harbor and an estimate of the cost of cutting a deep ship-channel through the coral reef at the extremity of that entrance toward the sea.

At that time the young king Lunalilo had just ascended the throne made vacant by the death of the last of the ancient reigning house of Hawaii. The policy of the preceding king had been annexation to the United States; but the new sovereign and his advisers were opposed to that policy, although very friendly to Americans, and largely controlled by their influence in governmental affairs. It was manifest that the question of annexation ought not to be discussed at that time, but that action ought to be taken at once to secure to the United States the exclusive right to the use of Pearl River harbor for naval purposes, and to prepare the way to make annexation to the United States sure in due time. This could readily be done by making such concessions in favor of the products of Hawaiian industries as would develop the resources of the islands and increase their wealth, all of which would be to the ultimate benefit of the United States when the islands should become a part of this country.

The continuous and rapid decay of all the ancient families of chiefs, from which alone would the people ever think of electing a king or a queen, and the notorious corruption in blood and character of the few remaining half-castes nominally belonging to those ancient families, made it plain to all that the monarchical government must soon die a natural death, or become so intolerably corrupt as to make its overthrow inevitable. Americans by birth or descent were then, and had been for a long time, the controlling element in the government. While perfectly faithful to that government, they had lost none of their love for their native country, and looked forward with confidence to the time when the islands, like ripe fruit, should fall into the lap of their beloved mother. These American Hawaiians were men of very high character, and much above the average of intelligence even in this country. They had no desire to force the ripening of the fruit, but were perfectly content to bide the course of nature, which must of necessity produce the result in no long time.

It seems to me a very narrow view of the intelligence of the people of this country which suggests any serious difficulty in the government of outlying possessions which are essential military and naval outposts simply because their heterogeneous populations are not yet capable of self-government, or fit for admission to the Union as a State. If the Territorial system to which the country is accustomed is not appropriate in any special case, and the prejudice against a military government is regarded as insurmountable, we have an example in the present government of the District of Columbia,— one of the best and most economical in the world,—which would require very slight modification to make it perfectly applicable to any of the islands of the Atlantic, the Pacific, or the gulf which may be acquired by this country. I do not believe any man worthy of the title of statesman will admit for a moment that the United States cannot govern, and govern well, any national outposts or other possessions which the interests of the country may require it to hold. In fact, it seems an almost self-evident proposition that a government, under exclusive national authority, exercised over comparatively small districts of country and small population, under the constant observation of the people and public press of the entire country, is more likely to be just and pure than any other. Responsibility to a local constituency undoubtedly has great advantages, but responsibility to

28

the government and entire people of the United States has vastly greater.

When it was proposed to me in Virginia, in 1867, that I become a candidate for the United States Senate under the State government which I was trying to "reconstruct," I replied that in my opinion the highest qualification I possessed for the difficult duty I was then required to perform resided in the fact that there was "nothing in the gift of Virginia which I could afford to accept." I believe now that the highest external incentive to honorable conduct anywhere in the world is that of responsibility to the government and the whole people of the United States. There need be no apprehension that any American who has a national reputation at stake will be guilty of any of the crimes which are said to stain the administration of viceroys in some parts of the world. The prejudice which still exists in this country in respect to military government is due solely to the fact that the people do not yet appreciate the legitimate influence which they themselves exercise over their public servants, military no less than civil. Indeed, there is perhaps no other class of citizens so sensitive to public criticism as those in the military service, certainly none who value more highly their reputation for faithful and honorable conduct in the public service. I do not hesitate to give it as my deliberate judgment, based upon the experience of half a century, that the best and most satisfactory government any island of the West Indies can have in the next hundred years will be a military government under an officer of the United States army.

It is only an incident of despotic governments, past or present, that soldiers have been employed to execute despotic orders. The common inference that military government is essentially despotic is absolutely false. On the contrary, military men are, as a rule, the most humane. This has been most notably so in the history of this country. Almost without exception, the soldiers of all grades in the Union army desired to treat the conquered South with all possible kindness and humanity, while the men who inflicted upon the Southern people the worst form of cruelty were men who had never fought a battle. There have been some cruel soldiers in the world, many more cruel men who were not soldiers except perhaps in name. Men of that character generally avoid danger. What mankind has most to dread is the placing of military power in the hands of men who are not real soldiers. They are quite sure to abuse it in one way or the other, by cruelty to their own men, or else to others. The same disregard for human life which induces an ignorant man to take command of troops and send them to useless slaughter may well manifest itself in barbarity toward prisoners of war or non-combatants; but a real soldier is never guilty of either of those crimes, which seem to me alike among the greatest in military experience.

The Modoc Indians were a brave people, and had always been friends of the whites; but their old home in southern Oregon was rich grazing-land, and was much coveted by the ranchmen of that region. Hence the Modocs were induced in some way to leave their homes and go upon the Klamath reservation. There they were starved and generally abused until they could stand it no longer. They went back to their old place, and declared they would die rather than go to live with the Klamaths again. Repeated requests were made by the Indian Bureau to the War Department to force the Modocs to go back to the Klamaths; but this was firmly opposed by General Canby, commanding the department; by me, who then commanded the Division of the Pacific; and by General Sherman, commanding the army. No such order could be obtained in the regular way. Resort was had to an innocent old army regulation which directed department commanders to render such military assistance as might be necessary to enable the Indian superintendents to carry out their orders from Washington. Without the knowledge of the President, or the Secretary of War, or the general of the army, an order was sent from the Indian Bureau in Washington to send the Modocs back to the Klamath reservation, and to call on the department commander for troops to enforce the order. General Canby, honorable and simple-hearted man that he was, never imagined that such an order could come from Washington, after all that had been said about it, unless with the sanction of the highest authority and the knowledge of the War Department. He did not even think it necessary to report to the division commander the requisition which had been made upon him for troops, but loyally obeyed the old regulation. The first information that came to me was that the troops had been beaten with heavy loss, and that many of the surrounding settlers had been killed by the Indians. A long and bloody war ensued, with some results which were deplorable in the extreme. General Canby's confiding nature had led him into a terrible mistake. He had executed an unwise regulation which placed military power in unworthy hands, without waiting to inquire whether that power was not, in fact, about to be unlawfully abused, and thus had become a party to the sacrifice of many innocent lives. The brave and noble-hearted Canby strove in every possible way to make peace with the Modocs without further ·shedding of innocent blood. But the savage red man, who had never been guilty of breaking faith with a civilized white man, would no longer trust any one of the "treacherous race." He paid them back "in their own coin," according to his traditional method. Though warned of the danger, Canby went calmly into the trap they had laid for him, in the hope that his confidence might inspire their respect; but he was the very man whose troops had been ordered to drive them out from their happy homes, and they treacherously killed him. And I doubt not, if more blood must be shed, he preferred to be the first to die. This is the true history of the "Canby massacre."

After a long contest, costing many lives, the Modocs were subdued and made prisoners. Those Indians who had been engaged in the massacre were tried and justly executed according to the laws of civilized war, while those white men who, in no less flagrant disregard of the laws of civilization, brought on the war were not called to any account for their crime. But President Grant, when I called his attention to the abuse of that old regulation, promptly abolished it. Since that time, as I understand it, no man but the head of the nation can order the army to kill unless necessary in defense, nor determine for what purposes the army may be employed. The people of the United States are advancing, though slowly, in civilization. Their fundamental law has very wisely always provided that Congress alone should have power to "declare war"; but for many years any Indian agent, or any bloodthirsty white man on the frontier, who chose to kill an Indian in cold blood, could inaugurate a war without waiting for anybody to declare it, and that without the slightest danger of punishment. A little military justice, in the absence of any possible civil government, in what was so long called the "Indian country" would have saved many hundreds of millions of dollars and many thousands of lives. But the inherited prejudice against "military despotism" has hardly yet been eradicated from the minds of the millions of freemen who inhabit this country—as if seventy or fifty, or even thirty, millions of people could not defend their liberties against a little standing army! A white murderer was long regarded as so much better than an honest Indian that the murderer must go free because there was no judge or jury to try him, while the Indian must be shot by the soldiers, without trial, for trying to protect himself from murder. If the innocent could be separated from the guilty, "plague, pestilence, and famine" would not be an unjust punishment for the crimes committed in this country against the original occupants of the soil. And it should be remembered that when retribution comes, though we may not understand why, the innocent often share the fate of the guilty. The law under which nations suffer for their crimes does not seem to differ much from the law of retribution which governs the savage Indian.

No possible plea of the demands of civilization, or of the interests of a superior race, can be held to justify such a policy as that long pursued by the people of this country. The natural law of the "survival of the fittest" may doubtless be pleaded in explanation of all that has happened; but that is not a law of Christianity, nor of civilization, nor of wisdom. It is the law of greed and cruelty, which generally works in the end the destruction of its devotees. In their greedy and blind pursuit of their own prey, they lose sight of the shark that is waiting to devour them. It is still the "fittest" that survives. It were wiser to remember that the shark is always well armed, and if you would survive him you must be fitter than he. If the benign law of civilization could be relied upon always to govern, then all would be well. But so long as the sharks still live, the cruel law of nature cannot be ignored. The highest principles and the highest wisdom, combined, would seem to suggest the higher law as the rule of action toward the weaker, and the natural law as the rule for defense against the stronger. This country has, happily, already made some progress in both directions. If that is continued a few more years, then all, strong as well as weak, will be glad to "arbitrate" if we ask them to.

CHAPTER XXIV

SUPERINTENDENT AT WEST POINT — GENERAL SHERMAN'S
ULTERIOR REASONS FOR THE APPOINTMENT — ORIGIN
OF THE "DEPARTMENT OF WEST POINT" — CASE OF
THE COLORED CADET WHITTAKER — A PROPOSED RE-
MOVAL FOR POLITICAL EFFECT — GENERAL TERRY'S
FRIENDLY ATTITUDE — A MUDDLE OF NEW COMMANDS
— WAITING ORDERS, AND A VISIT TO EUROPE — AGAIN
IN COMMAND IN THE WEST — THE ESTABLISHMENT OF
FORT SHERIDAN AT CHICAGO.

IN the centennial year, 1876, I committed the mistake
of my life by consenting, in deference to the opinions
and wishes of my superiors and in opposition to my own
judgment and interests, to give up the command of a
military division appropriate to my rank of major-
general, and accept a position which by law and custom
was appropriate to the rank of colonel. The following
extracts from correspondence will sufficiently explain
the reasons for this extraordinary action, and the assur-
ances which induced it:

(Telegram.)

WASHINGTON, D. C., March 28, 1876.

GENERAL JOHN M. SCHOFIELD, San Francisco, California:

Will you accept the superintendency of the military academy
at West Point? I advise it. Your rank and history will elevate it and solve all trouble. Admiral Porter's example at
Annapolis is suggested as precedent. The President, Secretary
Taft, and I are unanimous on the wisdom and propriety of it.

Advise me of your decision as early as you can — certainly this week. You will be subject to no supervision except by the usual board of visitors and the general commanding the army.

W. T. SHERMAN, General.

(Telegram.)

SAN FRANCISCO, CAL., March 29, 1876.

GENERAL SHERMAN, Washington, D. C.:

I appreciate the importance of the superintendency of the academy, and the compliment paid me by the President, Secretary of War, and yourself in desiring me to accept it. Under the circumstances I cannot decline. . . .

J. M. SCHOFIELD, Major-General.

(Telegram.)

HEADQUARTERS OF THE ARMY,
WASHINGTON, D. C., March 30, 1876.

GENERAL J. M. SCHOFIELD, San Francisco, California:

Despatch received, and am much pleased; think you can add new luster to the old academy. It has always needed a head with rank and experience, and now I am sure that the whole country will be satisfied. . . . I am not yet resolved on my own course of action, but will be governed by events to occur in this week.

W. T. SHERMAN, General.

HEADQUARTERS MIL. DIV. OF THE PACIFIC,
SAN FRANCISCO, CAL., March 30, 1876.

GENERAL SHERMAN, etc., Washington, D. C.

MY DEAR GENERAL: I was not taken entirely by surprise by your despatch relative to the West Point superintendency. General Grant mentioned the subject to me soon after the war, and army officers since that time have spoken of it often enough to keep me in mind of the fact that I might some time be called upon to assume that responsibility. Yet it is with a strong feeling of reluctance that I have brought myself to regard it as a thing to be done. This feeling results from several causes, which I desire to explain to you, while I know you will give me credit for a desire to do what appears best for the public service, and satisfactory to all concerned, without too much concern for my own personal preferences.

In the first place, I have no little doubt of the possession of any special fitness for that position, and have pretty strong appreciation of its difficulties and importance. I do not feel at all confident that the flattering expectations of my friends will be realized from my management of the academy.

I have been there enough to know pretty well how difficult a post that of superintendent is, and how varied the good qualities a man ought to possess to fit him in all respects for it.

Rank and reputation will of course be of some assistance, but their good effect will be greatly impaired without the dignity of command belonging to them. To transfer an officer of rank from a high command and post of great responsibility and trust to one heretofore regarded as appropriate to an inferior grade, may be regarded as elevating the dignity of the new command, but looks much more like degrading the officer, and to that extent impairs the good effect desired to be produced. Besides, it is impossible for any officer not to *feel* that in taking such inferior command, although it is even for the avowed purpose of raising its dignity, that he is stooping to do so. Especially must both these effects be produced when the assignment is only an executive act. If it was done in pursuance of law, the case would be materially different. . . .

We were all delighted at the news of your return to Washington and the prospect of your restoration to the proper duties and authority of general of the army; and I sincerely hope the events to occur this week, alluded to in your telegram to-day, may be such as to justify you in taking the course universally desired by the army. We want our general where he can best look after all the interests of the military service, with power to command the army in fact as well as in name.

I have read with the greatest pleasure your capital speech to the Knights of St. Patrick.

Please present my respectful compliments to the Secretary of War, and my kindest regards to the President.

I am, dear General, as ever, truly yours,

J. M. SCHOFIELD.

During the Civil War the demand for the services in the field of the most capable officers had, as was generally understood, been prejudicial to the interests of the military academy; and this continued some time after the close of the war, in consequence of the unusual increase of rank of those officers who were known to be fitted in all respects for the head of that institution. This difficulty was increased by the very unreasonable notion that because the law had opened the academy to the line of the army, the superintendent must necessarily be taken from the line, and not from the corps of engineers, although the latter contained many officers of appropriate rank who had then added to their high scientific ability and attainments distinguished services in the field. Even in the line, officers were not wanting of appropriate rank, character, ability, education, and experience to qualify them for the duties of superintendent. For example, my immediate predecessor, Major-General Thomas H. Ruger, then a colonel of infantry, was in all respects highly qualified for that office; and when I relieved him I found the academy in about the same state of efficiency which had characterized it before the war. There was, in fact, at that time little, if any, foundation for the assumption that the interests of the military academy required the assignment of any officer of higher rank than colonel to duty as superintendent of the academy. Of course I did not know this before I went there, and it was a matter for the judgment of my superiors, whose duty, and not mine, it was to know the facts.

But General Sherman had other reasons, some of them very cogent in his own estimation at least, for desiring my presence somewhere in the Eastern States; and the West Point "detail" was the only way in which that could readily be brought about. He had just been restored, or was about to be, to the actual command of the army, after having been practically suspended from command a long time because of his differences with the Secretary of War. He desired especially to bring the military academy under his command, and appears to have been assured of President Grant's support in that regard. General Sherman also wished me to revise the army regulations, so as to incorporate the theory of relation between the administration and the command which he and General Grant had maintained as the true one, but which had generally, if not always, been opposed by the Secretaries of War and by the chiefs of staff departments. These were doubtless the principal reasons for General Sherman's anxiety to have me accept the assignment to West Point. But very soon after my arrival in the East I found that I was also expected to preside over a board of review in the case of General Fitz-John Porter and in that of Surgeon-General William A. Hammond; and that my junior in rank, Major-General Irvin McDowell, could not be given a command appropriate to his rank unless it was the division which I had consented to vacate. Of course I could not but feel complimented by this indication that my superiors thought me capable of doing well so many things at once, nor yet could I fail to see that, after all, my care of West Point had not been considered of so vital importance, since it would not interfere with the all-important revision of the army regulations, and the retrial of Porter and Hammond.

But I had given my consent, though under erroneous impressions as to the reasons and necessity, to what my superiors desired, and hence determined to keep my thoughts to myself so long as the promises made by General Sherman were fulfilled. But I had hardly got settled in the academic chair before I received a great affront from the Secretary of War, through the adjutant-general of the army, in direct violation of General Sher-

man's promise that I should "be subject to no supervision except by the usual board of visitors and the
general commanding the army." This offensive action
arose not simply from ignorance of General Sherman's
promise, of which the adjutant-general and the Secretary of War had evidently not been informed, but from
culpable ignorance of the academic regulations on the
part of the adjutant-general, and still more culpable disregard of the invariable rule of courtesy enjoined by
military law among military men. With no little difficulty I restrained my indignation so far as to write a
calm and respectful letter to the Secretary of War,
inclosing a copy of my correspondence with General
Sherman respecting my command at West Point, and
pointing out the regulation which he or the adjutant-
general had ignored, and requesting him to submit the
whole matter to the President. It is due to the Honorable Secretary, and is a pleasure to me, to say that he did
not wait the slow course of the mail, but telegraphed me
at once that it was all a mistake, and that he made all
the amend that a gentleman could make under the circumstances. He as well as I had been made the victim
of the ignorance and discourtesy of a staff officer, in a
matter about which the Secretary of War could of necessity know nothing unless the staff officer informed
him. But I was determined to guard against any such
outrage in future, and hence insisted that West Point
be erected into a military department. By this means
I would become entitled to the effective intervention
and protection of the general of the army. This is
the origin of that anomaly which must have puzzled
many military men, namely, the "Department of West
Point."

But I discovered in time that even this safeguard was
by no means sufficient. I had some apprehension on
this subject at the start, and telegraphed General Sher-

man about it; but his answer of May 25 was accepted as sufficiently reassuring. Indeed it could hardly have been imagined that a President of the United States would disregard an honorable obligation incurred by his predecessor; but before I got through with that matter I was enlightened on that point.

In the spring of 1880 there arose great public excitement over the case of the one colored cadet then at West Point. This cadet, whose name was Whittaker, had twice been found deficient in studies, and recommended by the academic board for dismissal; but had been saved therefrom by me, in my perhaps too strong desire to give the young colored man all possible chance of ultimate success, however unwise his appointment to the military academy might have been. As was stated by me at the time, in my report of the case to the War Department, that second and unusual indulgence was based upon the fact that he was the only representative of his race then at the academy. Being again, for the third time, in danger of dismissal, that colored cadet, either by his own hands, or by others with his consent (of which he was finally convicted by a general court-martial), was bound hand and foot and mutilated in such manner as, while doing him no material injury, to create a suspicion of foul play on the part of other cadets. An official investigation by the commandant, Colonel Henry M. Lazelle, led him to the conclusion that the other cadets had no knowledge whatever of the outrage, and that the colored cadet himself was guilty. Not being fully satisfied with that conclusion, I appointed a court of inquiry to investigate the matter more thoroughly. The result of that investigation fully sustained the finding of Colonel Lazelle, that the colored cadet himself was the guilty person.

But those judicial conclusions did not suffice to allay the public clamor for protection to the recently emancipated negroes in the enjoyment of privileges in the national institutions for which they had not become either mentally or morally fitted. A presidential election was pending, and the colored vote and that in sympathy with it demanded assurance of the hearty and effective support of the national administration. Nothing less than a radical change at West Point would satisfy that demand, and who could be a more appropriate victim to offer as a sacrifice to that Moloch than one who had already gone beyond the limits of duty, of justice, and of wisdom in his kind treatment of the colored cadet? It was decided in Washington that he, the over-kind superintendent himself, should be sacrificed to that partizan clamor before the coming election. Some rumor of this purpose had reached me, though it had been concealed from General Sherman, who assured me that no such purpose existed.

In General Sherman's absence, General Alfred H. Terry was chosen to succeed me. He came to West Point, August 14, for the purpose of learning from me in person the truth as to the assertion made to him that the proposition to relieve me from duty at West Point was in accord with my own wishes. When informed, as he had suspected, that I could not possibly have expressed any such wish under the circumstances then existing, he positively refused, like the honorable man that he was, to be made a party to any such act of wrong. There was not the slightest foundation in fact for the assumption that my relief from command could be based upon my own request, and no such reason could have been given in an order relieving me. That assumption could have had no other apparent motive than to induce my warm friend General Terry to accept the appointment. As soon as he learned the truth from me, General Terry went to Washington and exposed the falsehood of which he and I together were the intended victims. This action of a true friend, and the correspondence which had passed between General Sherman and me, sufficed to prevent the consummation of the wrong which had been contemplated.

After the presidential election was over, and partizan passion had subsided, I made a formal application, November 12, 1880, to be relieved from duty at West Point on or before the first of May following, and to be permitted to await orders until an appropriate command became vacant. I repeatedly expressed my desire that none of my brother officers should be disturbed in their commands on my account, and that no new command should be created for me. I was entirely content to await the ordinary course of events, in view of pending legislation relative to retirements for age, and of retirements which might be made under the laws then existing.

My relief from West Point was effected earlier than General Sherman or I had anticipated. Before the end of 1880 the following correspondence passed between me and the general of the army:

(Confidential.)

HEADQUARTERS, ARMY OF THE UNITED STATES,
WASHINGTON, D. C., December 13, 1880.

GENERAL J. M. SCHOFIELD, West Point, New York.

DEAR GENERAL: General Drum has just shown me the memorandum for orders. The President has worked out this scheme himself, without asking my help, and I am glad of it, for I would not like to burden my conscience with such a bungle.

He creates a new department out of Louisiana, Arkansas, and the Indian Territory, to be commanded by the senior officer present. . . .

You are to command the Department of Texas and this new department, called a division, of what name I don't know.

Howard is to replace you at West Point. I suppose the order will issue at once.   Yours truly,

W. T. SHERMAN.

WEST POINT, N. Y., December 14, 1880.

GENERAL SHERMAN, Washington, D. C.

MY DEAR GENERAL: I have received your confidential letter of yesterday, informing me of the bungling scheme which has been worked out without your help. I presume it would be fruitless to attempt any opposition to the species of mania which manifests itself in such action. It may be best to let it run its course during the short time which must yet elapse until a reign of reason is again inaugurated with the incoming administration. But it occurs to me that you may be able to save the useless expense to the government and the great inconvenience and expense to staff officers which would necessarily result from the organization of a division which could only last for a few months. To me personally it is a matter of little moment; but not so with the staff officers and the military appropriations. I am not willing to have such a thing done, even apparently, on my account. Please advise what official action, if any, should be taken by me in this matter. Personally I am perfectly ready to obey the President's order, without a word of protest; but I am not willing to be the occasion of manifest injury to the public service, and of useless inconvenience and expense to the officers of the general staff who must be assigned to the headquarters of the new division.

Very truly yours, J. M. SCHOFIELD.

But the public interests, and my desire to make my own entirely subservient thereto, were alike disregarded. A new division was carved out of the three old ones, in violation of the plainest dictates of military principles. The government was subjected to a worse than useless expense of many thousands of dollars, and a number of staff officers to like useless expense and trouble. For all this there was no other apparent motive but to make it appear that there were appropriate commands for all the major-generals then in active service, and hence no reason for placing any one of them on the retired list. As a part of that scheme, one of the most active brigadier-generals, younger than one of the major-generals, was selected instead of the latter to make way for an aspirant having greater "influence." The correspondence of that period shows the indignation felt in the army at such disregard of the just claims of officers and of the interests of the military service. Neither General Sherman nor any of the several higher officers at that time could hope to derive any advantage from the passage of the act of Congress, then pending, to retire all officers at a fixed age. On the contrary, such a law would most probably cut them off when in the full prime of activity and usefulness. But all were more than willing to accept that rather than still be in a position to be arbitrarily cut off to make place for some over-ambitious aspirant possessed of greater influence, of whatever kind. I know perfectly well that General Sherman was governed by a generous desire to give General Sheridan command of the army for a number of years, while the latter was still in the prime of life. But that he could have done, and had announced his intention to do, by requesting to be relieved from the command and permitted to await the President's orders, performing such duties, from time to time, as the President might desire of him. Such a status of high officers of great experience, whose inspections, observations, and advice might be of great value to the President and to the War Department, would manifestly have been far better for the country than that of total retirement, which deprives the President of any right to call upon them for any service whatever, even in an emergency. This was one of the subjects of correspondence between General Sherman and me while I was in Europe in 1881-2. But it was finally agreed by all concerned that it would be best to favor the uniform application of the rule of retirement for age, so that all might be assured, as far as possible, of a time, to which they might look forward with certainty, when they would be relieved from further apprehension of treatment which

29

no soldier can justly characterize without apparent disrespect to his official superior.

Such treatment is indeed uncommon. The conduct of the commander-in-chief of the army toward his subordinates has been generally kind and considerate in this country. But the few opposite examples have been quite enough to cloud the life of every officer of high rank with the constant apprehension of an insult which he could neither submit to nor resent.

Soon after the inauguration of President Garfield, the "Division of the Gulf" was broken up, and I was permitted to visit Europe, as I had requested in the preceding November, until the President should be pleased to assign me to a command according to my rank.

(Telegram.)

WASHINGTON, D. C., May 3, 1881.

GENERAL J. M. SCHOFIELD,
Commanding Division, New Orleans, La.:

In case the President will repeal the orders creating the new division and department, and agree to give you the Division of the Pacific in a year, will you be willing to take your leave to go abroad meantime? Telegraph me fully and frankly for use.

W. T. SHERMAN, General.

(Telegram — 9:30 P. M.)

HEADQRS. MIL. DIV. GULF,
NEW ORLEANS, LA., May 3, 1881.

GENERAL W. T. SHERMAN, Washington, D. C.:

Your telegram of this date just received. I am debarred, by a promise made to General McDowell about two years and a half ago, from making any condition affecting his command of the Division of the Pacific. If I am to displace him, it must be without regard to any wish of mine. If it is the purpose of the President to assign me to that command in a year, I would like to go abroad in the meantime, as it would not be convenient to go afterward, though I would prefer to go next year rather than this. But I cannot afford to go on leave with reduced pay. If it is not found practicable to give me a command according to my rank, and so organized as to benefit rather than injure the military service, I am willing to await orders for a year without reduction of pay.

This is substantially the proposition I made in my application to be relieved from duty at West Point; and I am still willing to abide by it, although my wishes were then disregarded, if it will relieve the present administration from embarrassment. But I would much prefer to have a proper command. . . .

J. M. SCHOFIELD, Maj.-Gen.

(Telegram.)

WASHINGTON, D. C., May 5, 1881.

GENERAL J. M. SCHOFIELD,
  Commanding Division, New Orleans, La.:

Your despatch of the third was duly received, and a copy thereof laid before the Secretary of War, who has received the orders of the President to repeal all parts of General Orders, No. 84, of December 18, 1880, which refer to the Division of the Gulf and Department of Arkansas, restoring the *status quo* before that order was made. You will be placed on waiting orders, with full pay, till further orders of the President. You may take action accordingly.

W. T. SHERMAN, General.

My stay in Europe—from May, 1881, to May, 1882—was marked by only one incident of special military interest. Under orders of the War Department, upon invitation from the government of France, I witnessed the autumn manœuvers of the Twelfth Corps of the French army at and about Limoges. A few other officers of our army, and many from other countries, enjoyed the same privilege. The operations, which were interesting and instructive, culminated in an assault upon and the capture of Limoges. The next day the corps was reviewed in the streets of the city. The general-in-chief and his staff and suite rode along the line at full speed. The head of the cavalcade, consisting of the French and American generals, and a few other officers of high rank, came out in good order. The others were much disordered, and so covered with dust that the uniforms of all nations looked very much alike. The ceremony was terminated at the public square, where the cavalry was formed along one side, and the opposite was occupied by high officials and prominent citizens of the town. The charge of the squadrons across the square, halting at command within a few feet of the reviewing general, was a fine exhibition of discipline and perfect control.

After the review the general-in-chief made a long address to his assembled officers, explaining in much detail the important lessons taught by the manœuvers. He closed with a feeling allusion to his own mental and physical strength and vigor, which had been so fully displayed in the last few days, and which were still at the service of his beloved France. But the gallant old soldier was retired, all the same, at the end of the year. Republics seem to have much the same way of doing things on both sides of the ocean!

A pleasing incident occurred at one time during the manœuvers. At the hour of halt for the midday rest a delicious repast was served at the beautiful home of the prefect of the department, between the two opposing lines. The tables were spread in lovely arbors loaded with grapes. When the déjeuner was ended, speeches were made by the distinguished prefect and the gallant general-in-chief, to which, as senior of the visiting officers from foreign countries, I was called upon to respond. Thus suddenly summoned to an unwonted task, I was much too prudent to address the guests in a language which they all understood. But by a free use of those words and phrases which are so common in the military language of France and of this country, linked together by as little Anglo-Saxon as possible, I made a speech which was warmly received, and which, after careful revision with the aid of a highly accomplished French officer who had been educated in England as well as in France, was made to appear pretty well when printed in both languages.

The charming hospitality of the general-in-chief of the Twelfth Army Corps and of the prefect of Limoges, with all the other incidents of the autumn manœuvers of 1881, are an ever fresh and pleasant memory, with the many other recollections of beautiful France under the empire and under the republic.

According to the understanding expressed in my correspondence with General Sherman of May 3, 1881, I returned from Europe at the end of a year, and reported for duty. But in the meantime President Garfield had been assassinated, and the bill then pending in Congress providing for the retirement of all officers at a fixed age was amended so as to make that age sixty-four years instead of sixty-two. Hence I continued to wait without protest until the retirement of my junior in rank, the next autumn, for the fulfilment of General Sherman's assurance conveyed in his despatch of May 25, 1876: "If any hitch occurs at any future time, you can resume your present or some command due your rank." Although this long suspension from command was very annoying, I had the satisfaction of knowing that none of my brother officers had been disturbed on my account.

In the fall of 1882, I was again assigned to the command of the Division of the Pacific, awaiting the time of General Sherman's retirement under the law and the succession of General Sheridan to the command of the army. Nothing of special interest occurred in that interval. In 1883 I succeeded to the command of the Division of the Missouri, with headquarters at Chicago. One of the first and most important subjects which impressed themselves upon my attention after the generous reception and banquet given by the citizens of that hospitable city, was the necessity for a military post near that place. The location of Chicago makes it the most important strategical center of the entire northern frontier. It is also the most important center of interstate commerce and transportation anywhere in the country. Yet in 1883 there were no troops nearer than St. Paul, Omaha, and Leavenworth. At the time of the railroad strikes in 1877, troops had been brought there in time to render the necessary service, but no thought appears to have been given to the necessity of better provision for the future.

There had been in early times a military reservation at the mouth of the Chicago River, on which old Fort Dearborn was located. But that had become far too valuable to be retained for military use, and no longer suitable for a military post, being in the heart of a great city. Hence it had passed out of the hands of the government. Upon consultation with Senator Logan and a few others, it was not thought possible to obtain from Congress the large sum of money necessary to buy ground for a post near Chicago; but that if the United States owned the ground, the appropriations to build a post could readily be obtained. Hence the subject was mentioned to a few prominent citizens, with the suggestion that a site be purchased by subscription and presented to the United States. I was soon invited to meet the Commercial Club at one of their monthly dinners, where the matter was fully discussed. At another meeting, some time later, it was made the special subject for consideration, and this resulted in the organization of the plan to raise the money and purchase the ground. All the eligible sites were examined, the prices obtained, and the purchase-money pledged. Then the proposition was submitted to the War Department and approved. General Sheridan was sent out to select the best of the sites offered, and his choice fell on that which all, I believe, had esteemed the best, though the most expensive — a beautiful tract of land of about six hundred acres, situated on the shore of Lake Michigan twenty-five miles north of Chicago. The cost was nothing to the broad-minded and far-sighted men of that city. The munificent gift was accepted by Congress, and appropriations were made for the finest military post in the country. It was appropriately named Fort Sheridan, not only in recognition of the great services the general had rendered to the country, but as a special and graceful recognition of the services he had rendered Chicago in the time of her sorest need.

During my brief service — two years and some months — in the Division of the Missouri, I traveled many thousands of miles, and visited nearly all parts of that vast territory, from the Canadian line to the Gulf of Mexico, some of which was then new to me, attending to the ordinary routine duties of a time of comparative peace. Nothing else occurred at all comparable in importance, in my judgment, to the establishment of the post of Fort Sheridan.

CHAPTER XXV

THE DEATH OF GENERAL HANCOCK — ASSIGNED TO THE
DIVISION OF THE ATLANTIC — MEASURES FOR IMPROV-
ING THE SEA-COAST DEFENSE — GENERAL FITZ-JOHN
PORTER'S RESTORATION TO THE ARMY — PRESIDENT OF
THE BOARD APPOINTED TO REVIEW THE ACTION OF THE
COURT-MARTIAL — GENERAL GRANT'S OPINION — SENA-
TOR LOGAN'S EXPLANATION OF HIS HOSTILE ATTITUDE
TOWARD GENERAL PORTER.

IN the spring of 1886 we were again called to meet
around the grave of one of the bravest and best of
our companions. The almost incomparably gallant Hancock, the idol of his soldiers and of a very large part of
the people, so perfectly stainless in life and character that
even political contest could not fan the breath of slander,
had suddenly passed away. We buried him with all
honor at his home in Pennsylvania. Again it fell to my
lot — the lot so common to the soldier — to step into the
place in the ranks where my comrade had suddenly fallen.

The Division of the Missouri was then larger in territory and much larger in number of troops than that of
the Atlantic, and had been far more important. But
Indian wars were, as we hoped, approaching an end,
while we also hoped that the country might soon be
aroused to the necessities of the national defense. The
Division of the Atlantic, including also the greater part
of the Gulf States and those of the northeastern frontier, would then resume its rightful place as by far the
most important of the grand military divisions of the

country. Hence I accepted without hesitation the command of that division. My natural tastes and favorite studies had led me largely in the direction of those modern sciences which have in a few years imparted such enormous strides to the development of the mechanical means of attack and defense, changing in a corresponding degree the great problems of war. The valor of great masses of men, and even the genius of great commanders in the field, have been compelled to yield the first place in importance to the scientific skill and wisdom in finance which are able and willing to prepare in advance the most powerful engines of war. Nations, especially those so happily situated as the United States, may now surely defend their own territory against invasion or damage, and the national honor and the rights of their citizens throughout the world, by the wise scientific use of surplus revenue, derived from high import duties if the people so please, instead of by the former uncivilized method of sacrificing the lives of hundreds of thousands of brave men. Far more, such sacrifice of the brave can no longer avail. As well might it be attempted to return to hand- or ox-power, freight-wagons and country roads, in place of the present steam-locomotives, trains of cars, and steel tracks, for the enormous transportation of the present day, as to rely upon the bravery of troops for the defense of a city.

Science has wrought no greater revolution in any of the arts of peace than it has in the art of war. Indeed, the vast national interests involved all over the world have employed the greatest efforts of genius in developing the most powerful means of attack and defense.

Such were the thoughts with which I entered upon my duties in the Division of the Atlantic, and such guided my action there and in the subsequent command of the army. That not very much was accomplished is too painfully true. Yet a beginning was at once made, and progress, though slow, continued until the hope now seems justified that our country may be ready before it is too late to " command the peace " in a voice which all must heed.

I was ably and zealously assisted in all this work by Major Joseph P. Sanger, one of my aides until his well-merited promotion to inspector-general. Then Captain Tasker H. Bliss took Major Sanger's place, and helped me to carry forward the work with his well-known ability, devotion, and industry. The army owes much to those faithful officers, without whose help little could have been done by me. I quote here from a memorandum, prepared at my request by Major Sanger, showing in detail the measures taken to perfect, so far as possible in advance, the instruction of the artillery of the army in the service of the modern high-power armament, so that every new gun and mortar should have, the moment it was finished and placed in position, thoroughly qualified officers and men to use it :

Major-General J. M. Schofield assumed command of the Division of the Atlantic and Department of the East April 13, 1886; and during the remaining months of that year, as opportunity afforded, gave much attention to the condition of the sea-coast forts and their garrisons from the Canadian line to the Gulf of Mexico.

There were at this time sixty-six posts in the division, of which twenty-seven were garrisoned and thirty-nine ungarrisoned; of the total number, fifty-one were sea-coast forts and the balance barracks, properly speaking. Of the garrisoned forts, fifteen had no armaments, and the armaments of all the others were the old muzzle-loading types of low power. The efficiency of the artillery personnel was far from satisfactory, from lack of proper instruction, due in turn to lack of facilities. Artillery target practice, except at Forts Monroe, Hamilton, and Wadsworth, had practically ceased in the division ; and of the forty-five companies of artillery, comprising seventy-five per cent. of the entire artillery troops of the army, only two batteries continually at Fort Monroe had had annual artillery target practice during the preceding ten years, and some of the batteries had not fired a shot.

To remedy these defects, and at the same time provide a system of fire control applicable to the defense of all our harbors, orders were issued in 1887 for mapping the harbors, establishing base lines, and arranging the extremities for the use of angle-measuring instruments, and graduating traverse circles in azimuth. Systematic artillery instruction and target practice were ordered, and a system of reports suited to the preservation and utilization of all data resulting from the firing.

Thus, for the first time in the history of the country, an effort was made to establish and develop a system of artillery fire control adapted to our fortifications and armament. In 1888 General Schofield succeeded General Sheridan in command of the army, and in December issued "General Orders, No. 108" from the headquarters of the army. This order extended to all the artillery troops of the army the system of artillery instruction and target practice which had been established in the Division of the Atlantic. As it had not been found practicable to equip all the artillery posts with the necessary appliances for carrying out the provisions of the order, the eleven principal posts on the Eastern, Western, and Southern coasts were designated as artillery posts of instruction, and provided with all the guns, implements, and instruments necessary for the instruction and target practice of such of the neighboring garrisons as were unprovided with proper facilities.

To insure the proper execution of the order, there was appropriated March 2, 1889, twenty thousand dollars to be expended under the direct supervision of the Board of Ordnance and Fortifications, which had been created by the Fortification Appropriation Act of September 22, 1888, and of which General Schofield was the president. The Army Regulations of 1889 were published on February 9, and paragraph 382 authorized the commanding general of each geographical division within which were the headquarters of one or more artillery regiments to designate, with the approval of the general commanding the army, a division inspector of artillery target practice, whose duty it was to make inspections with a view to insuring uniform, thorough, and systematic artillery instruction.

On June 11, 1889, "General Orders, No. 49" was issued from

the headquarters of the army, in anticipation of the more complete equipment of the artillery posts with the apparatus necessary for the proper conduct of artillery instruction and target practice. The course of instruction covered the use of plane tables, telescopic and other sights, electrical firing-machines, chronographs, velocimeters, anemometers, and other meteorological instruments, stop-watches, signaling, telegraphy, vessel tracking, judging distances, and, in short, everything essential to the scientific use of the guns. By "General Orders, No. 62, Headquarters of the Army," July 2, 1889, Lieutenant T. H. Bliss, First Artillery, Aide-de-Camp to General Schofield commanding, was announced as inspector of small arms and artillery practice. As an inducement to greater application on the part of the student officers of the Artillery School and of the Infantry and Cavalry School, the distinction of "honor graduate" was conferred on all officers who had graduated, or should graduate, either first or second from the Artillery School, or first, second, or third from the Infantry and Cavalry School: the same to appear with their names in the Army Register as long as such graduates should continue on the active or retired list of the army. . . .

In August, 1886, after the passage of a bill by Congress, General Fitz-John Porter was restored to the army, as colonel, by President Cleveland. When I was in the War Department in 1868, General Porter had come to me with a request that I would present his case to the President, and recommend that he be given a rehearing. I declined to do so, on the ground that, in my opinion, an impartial investigation and disposition of his case, whatever were its merits, could not be made until the passions and prejudices begotten by the war had subsided much further than they had done at that time. In the course of conversation I told him that while I never permitted myself to form an opinion of any case without much more knowledge of it than I then had of his, I presumed, from the finding of the court-martial, that he had at least been guilty of acting upon what he supposed to be his own better judgment under the circumstances he found to exist, instead of in strict obedience to General Pope's orders. He said that that was not the case; that he had not even literally disobeyed orders; that in so far as he had acted upon his own judgment, he had loyally done all that could be done to carry out General Pope's wishes; and that all he wanted was an opportunity to prove such to be the facts. I replied that if he could prove what he stated beyond question, he would of course have a case worthy of consideration — not otherwise. Nothing was said in respect to the facts or the evidence in contravention of the judgment of the court-martial which tried him. Hence, beyond that above stated, I had no knowledge of his case when the board of review, of which I was president, met in 1878 to hear the new evidence; and I believe neither of the other members of the board—Generals A. H. Terry and George W. Getty—was any better informed.

The duty of the board was very different from that of a court-martial appointed to try an original case. The accused had already been tried and convicted. He was not to have a new trial. He could not have any benefit whatever of any doubt that might exist after all the evidence, old and new, had been duly considered. He must prove his innocence positively, by absolutely convincing evidence, or else the original judgment of the court-martial must stand. This view of the issue was fully accepted by General Porter and his counsel. This caused a new and peculiar duty to devolve upon the board—at least it was so to me; that is, to find, if possible, some view of all the evidence, or of all the facts established by the evidence, that could be regarded as consistent with the theory or supposition that Porter was guilty.

When the evidence was all in, the members of the board separated for several weeks to let each examine all the evidence and reach his own conclusion, to be presented in form at the next meeting of the board. I believe I devoted more earnest work to the examination and analysis than I had ever done to any one thing before in my life. I tried in succession every possible combination of the established facts, in the effort to find some one consistent with the theory that Porter had been guilty of disobedience, as charged, or of any other military offense. But I could not find one, except the very patent one that he had sent despatches to Burnside which were by no means respectful to Pope; and the board expressed an opinion in condemnation of that, which Porter's counsel very frankly admitted to be just.

In the course of that long and earnest effort to find Porter guilty,—for that is what the effort was in effect,— the whole story of his conduct and of the operations of the two opposing armies and the actions of other prominent officers became so clear, and his honorable and soldierly conduct so absolutely demonstrated, that it was exceedingly difficult, in view of all the wrong he had suffered, to write a cold judicial statement of the facts. The first draft was toned down in many particulars in the effort to bring it within the strictest rules of judicial decisions. I have sometimes thought since that if the report of the board could have been much colder, it might have been better at first for Porter, though less just. But I do not think he or any of his companions and friends will ever feel like finding fault because the board could not entirely suppress the feelings produced by their discovery of the magnitude of the wrong that had been done to a gallant fellow-soldier.

The first time I met General Grant after the decision of the board was published was very soon after he had published in 1882 the result of his own investigation of the case. He at once introduced the subject, and talked about it for a long time in the most earnest manner that I ever heard him speak on any subject. He would not permit me to utter a single sentence until he had gone all over the case and showed me that he understood all its essential features as thoroughly as I did, and that his judgment was precisely the same as that which the board had reached. He intimated very decidedly that no impartial and intelligent military man could, in his opinion, possibly reach any other conclusion. The general evidently desired to make it perfectly clear that he had not adopted the opinion of the board of which I was a member, nor that of any one else; but that he had thoroughly mastered the case for himself, and formed his own judgment in regard to it. I take pleasure in recording the fact that he unquestionably had done it, and I never knew a man who could form more positive opinions, or one who could express them more convincingly, than General Grant.

The board was not called upon to express any opinion respecting the action of the court-martial upon the evidence before it, and it would have been manifestly improper to do so. Speaking for myself, and not for any other member of the board, I do not now hesitate to say that the finding and sentence of the general court-martial which tried General Fitz-John Porter were not justified by the evidence before that court. In my judgment, formed from long observation and much experience, the passions of war often render the administration of justice impossible. A suggestion once made to me by a man in very high military authority, that a finding and sentence of court-martial rendered in time of war should be regarded as *res adjudicata*, produced in my mind the painful impression that a very great man did not find the word "justice" anywhere in his vocabulary; and I watched for many years the conversation and writings and public speeches of that man without finding that he ever made use of that word, or ever gave as a reason for doing or not doing anything that it would be just or unjust. In his mind, whatever might have happened to any person was simply a matter of good or bad fortune which did not concern him. He refused even to consider the question whether injustice had or had not been done, or whether the operation of a law was not relatively unjust to some as compared to others. When to such natural character and habits of thought are added the stern necessities of war as viewed by a commander and many other officers, what possible chance of justice can be left to an *unfortunate* man ?

It is true that even if the life of an innocent man may have been sacrificed under the stern necessities of discipline, that is no more than thousands of his fellow-soldiers have suffered because of the crimes and follies of politicians who brought on the war. But that is no reason why his memory as well as those of his comrades should not be finally honored, if it can be proved that, after all, he also was innocent and brave.

In my opinion, no government can be regarded as just to its army unless it provides, under appropriate conditions, for the rehearing of cases that may be tried by court-martial in time of war. Perhaps it may most wisely be left for the President and Congress to institute appropriate action in each individual case. That is a matter for mature consideration. My only desire is to suggest the necessity for some such action, whenever reasonable grounds for it may be presented. I have no respect for the suggestions sometimes urged that labor and expense are sufficient grounds for failure to secure justice to every citizen or soldier of the republic, whether at home or abroad.

Soon after General Logan's last election to the Senate, I had a very interesting and unreserved conversation with him, at his house in Chicago, in respect to his action in the Porter case. He spoke of it with evident candor, acknowledged that his view of the case was probably wrong, and as if to excuse his mistake, volunteered an explanation as to how he came to take that view of it.

He told me that when he found that the case might probably come before Congress, he wanted to prepare himself in advance as far as possible to deal with it justly, and to defend the right effectively. Hence he went to General Grant to obtain the best possible view of the military questions involved. General Grant gave him the theory of the military situation and of the operations of the opposing armies, as well as that of Porter's own conduct, which had been presented to, and evidently accepted by, the court-martial, as presenting the true merits of the case. General Logan accepted that theory as unquestionably correct, and bent all his energies to the construction of unanswerable arguments in support of Porter's condemnation.

At that time neither General Grant nor General Logan knew anything of the new evidence which was afterward submitted to the board of review. Logan's powerful arguments in the Senate were based upon his preconceived opinion of the case, supported by such part of the new evidence, as well as of the old, as could be made to support that view. In reply to my statement that he had unquestionably been led astray, he said that that was quite probable, but that Grant was responsible, and it was then too late to change. I do not think that anybody will now hesitate to say that General Grant's view of his duty in respect to this last point was the more to be commended. But the fact I wish to record is that of Logan's sincerity in the great efforts he had made to convict Porter on the floor of the Senate, and his explanation of the way in which he had been led into the greatest possible error. It suggests the reflection that even a senator of the United States might better form his own opinions rather than adopt those even of the highest authority, when the only question involved is one of justice, and not one of public policy, in which latter case differences of opinion must of ne-

30

cessity be reconciled for the purpose of securing unity of action.

As an illustration of the necessity for an absolutely impartial review of cases which have involved the passions of war, reference must be made to the action of one member of the Porter court-martial who made it generally understood that his individual opinion supported the finding of that court. He went so far as to make inquiries whether precedents could be found in American or English history to sustain a member of a court-martial in publicly defending the finding of that court, notwithstanding the oath of secrecy imposed by law upon every member. And this same member of the court was furnished by a very able lawyer with an argument in support of the findings of the court, based upon a review of the evidence submitted to the subsequent board, as if that member of the court might make public use of that argument as his own.

CHAPTER XXVI

THE DEATH OF GENERAL SHERIDAN — HIS SUCCESSOR IN
COMMAND OF THE ARMY — DEPLORABLE CONDITION OF
THE WAR DEPARTMENT AT THE TIME — A BETTER
UNDERSTANDING BETWEEN THE DEPARTMENT AND THE
ARMY COMMANDER — GENERAL SHERIDAN'S HUMILIATING
EXPERIENCE — THE GRANTING OF MEDALS — THE SEC-
RETARY'S CALL-BELL — THE RELATIONS OF SECRETARY
AND GENERAL — VIEWS SUBMITTED TO PRESIDENT
CLEVELAND — THE LAW FIXING RETIREMENT FOR AGE
— AN ANECDOTE OF GENERAL GRANT.

AGAIN, in 1888, only two years after Hancock's death,
another of our most gallant companions, the matchless Sheridan, was suddenly stricken down, and soon
passed away, before the expiration of half the term
allotted for his command of the army. As next in rank,
upon the request of the general's family and upon the
order of the Secretary of War it became my duty to arrange and conduct the military ceremonies at the funeral.

We buried our companion in beautiful Arlington, the
choicest spot in America for the last resting-place of a
soldier. It was a bright summer's day, and the funeral
ceremonies, both religious and military, were the most
impressive I have ever seen. As a special tribute of
respect to my brother soldier, a staff officer in uniform
was sent to meet and escort the archbishop who came
to celebrate the funeral mass.

The death of General Sheridan placed me in a position
which I had never anticipated — that of senior officer on

the active list of the army. The President had known little of me either officially or personally, and I had had some grave differences with the Secretary of War upon subjects of great importance in my estimation, though doubtless less in his. I had defended as well as I could, and with some persistence, what I then believed and now know was the right, but had been worsted, as a matter of course. It is due to the Honorable Secretary to say that he disclaimed, many months later, ever having knowingly given his sanction to the document announcing one of the military doctrines which I had so persistently but ineffectually combated. But I did not know that in August, 1888, and he did not then know that he had been thus betrayed. Hence I thought it quite improbable that a general holding opinions so radically opposed to those of the Secretary of War would be called to the command of the army. But I quietly waited in Washington for the President's orders, neither seeking nor receiving any opportunity for explanation of the supposed irreconcilable difference with the Secretary of War. What occurred in that secret council-chamber of the commander-in-chief, where the fate of so many anxious soldiers has been sealed, I have never known or inquired; but in no great length of time came the President's order assigning me to the command of the army,— six or seven hours, as I afterward learned, after it was received in the War Department and given to the press.

It is not too much to say that the condition of the War Department at that time was deplorable. It was the culmination of the controversy respecting the relations between the administration and the command which had lasted, with slight intermissions, for forty years. It is not my purpose to go into the history of that long controversy, but only to state briefly its final result, part of which was perhaps due to General Sheridan's extreme illness for some time before his death, and his retention in nominal command and in the nominal administration of military justice long after it had become impossible for him to discharge such duties intelligently. But that result had been practically reached a long time before General Sheridan became seriously ill. He had long ceased, as General Sherman and General Scott had before him, not only to command, but to exercise any appreciable influence in respect to either the command or the administration. The only difference was that General Scott went to New York and General Sherman to St. Louis, while General Sheridan stayed in Washington.

I have always understood, but do not know the fact, that in former times the Secretary of War had exercised some intelligent control over military affairs, so that there was at least unity in the exercise of military authority. But in 1888 even that had ceased, and it had been boldly announced some time before that each departmental chief of staff, in his own sphere, was clothed with all the authority of the Secretary of War. All that a major-general as well as an officer of lower grade had to do was to execute such orders as he might receive from the brigadiers at the head of the several bureaus in Washington. It was not even necessary for those mighty chiefs to say that their mandates had the sanction of any higher authority. Their own fiat was all-sufficient for a mere soldier of the line or for his commanding general, of whatever grade of rank or of command. It is not strange that the Secretary was finally unable to admit that he, great lawyer as he was, could possibly have given his sanction to such an interpretation of the law as that; but the decision was given by his order, and it governed the army for a long time. Of course the adjutant-general became by far the chiefest of those many chiefs; for it is his function to issue to the army all the orders of both the Secretary of War and the commanding general. Be it said to his credit that he did not assume to issue any orders in his own name, after the manner of the other chiefs. Like a sensible man, he was content with the actual exercise of power, without caring to let the army know that he did it. He had only to use the name of the Secretary or the general, as he pleased; either would answer with the army. Of course I knew something of this before I went to Washington, for the evidence of it was sometimes too plain to be ignored. Yet it did seem to me passing strange to sit in my office about noon, where I had been all the day before, and learn from the New York papers what orders I had issued on that previous day! Upon inquiry I was told that that was only a matter of routine, and a rule of long standing. But I mildly indicated that such a practice did not meet my approval, and that I wished it changed, which was finally done, as explained in a previous chapter. But even then I had no means of knowing whether an order sent to me in the name of the Secretary of War had ever been seen by him, or whether it was the work of the adjutant-general, or the product of some joint operation of two or more of the several chiefs, each of whom had the Secretary's authority to do such things. At length the Secretary, though with evidently serious misgivings respecting some deep ulterior purpose of mine, consented that I might have an officer of the adjutant-general's department, whom I knew, in my own office, to keep me informed of what I was to do, and, if possible, what orders I might actually receive from the Secretary himself, and what from the several other heads of that hydra called the War Department.

After that change things went on much better; but it was at best only an armed truce, with everybody on guard, until the end of that administration, and then it came very near culminating in a pitched battle at the very beginning of the next. By what seemed at the time a very sharp trick, but which may possibly have been only the natural working of the vicious system, I was made to appear to the new Secretary of War as having failed promptly to give effect to an order authorized by his predecessor, but on which no authentic marks of *his* authority appeared, only such as might indicate that it came from another source. But if it was a trick, it signally failed. A few candid words from one soldier to another, even if that other had not been a soldier all his life, were quite sufficient to dissipate that little cloud which at first had threatened a storm. Then sunlight began to appear; and when, in due time, by the operation of some natural laws, and some others happily enacted by Congress, certain necessary changes came about, the sky over the War Department became almost cloudless, and I trust it may never again be darkened as it had been nearly all the time for forty years.

General Sheridan had entered upon his duties with all the soldierly courage and confidence of his nature, declaring his purpose to regain the ground lost by General Sherman when, to use Sheridan's own expressive words, "Sherman threw up the sponge." He announced his interpretation of the President's order assigning him to the "command of the army" as necessarily including *all* the army, not excepting the chiefs of the staff departments; and he soon gave evidence of his faith by ordering one of those chiefs on an inspecting tour, or something of that kind, without the knowledge of the Secretary of War. Thus the Secretary found the chief of one of the bureaus of his department gone without his authority, he knew not where. It was not difficult for the Secretary to point out to the general, as he did in writing, in a firm, though kind and confidential way, that such could not possibly be the true meaning of the President's order. No attempt appears to have been made to discuss the subject further, or to find any ground broad enough for both Secretary and general to stand upon. Nothing further appears to have been said or done on that subject during that administration. But upon the inauguration of the next, the Secretary of War sent out to all the commanding generals of the army copies of that letter of his predecessor, in which the general-in-chief had been so mildly and respectfully, yet so thoroughly, beaten. The army was thus given to understand that on that occasion their senior in command had not even been given a chance to "throw up the sponge," as his predecessor had done, but had been "knocked out" by the first blow.

As if that was not humiliation enough for a great soldier to bear, whenever the Secretary went away one of the same chiefs of bureaus that the general thought he had a right to command acted as Secretary of War, to dominate over him! But the loyal, subordinate soldier who had commanded great armies and achieved magnificent victories in the field while those bureau chiefs were purveying powder and balls, or pork and beans, submitted even to that without a murmur, for a great lawyer had told him such was the law, and how could he know any better? It was only when the adjutant-general, his own staff-officer, so made by the regulations which the general knew, was thus appointed over him, that his soldierly spirit rebelled. The humblest soldier of a republic could not endure that. All this was based upon the theory that the general of the army was not an officer of the War Department, and hence could not be appointed acting Secretary of War. What other great department of the government could recognize the standing army as belonging to it, if not the Department of War? Surely the little army had a hard time while it was thus turned out into the cold, not even its chief recognized as belonging to any department of the government of the country which they were all sworn to serve, but subject to the orders of any bureau officer who happened to be the senior in Washington in hot summer weather, when nearly all had gone to the mountains or the sea!

That same great lawyer announced in my hearing, very soon after his accession to power, in response to a suggestion that war service was entitled to weight in appointments and promotions, that in his judgment "that book was closed." Could any one of the million of soldiers still living, and the many more millions of patriots who are always alive in our country, be expected to support such a policy as that? In my opinion, that one short speech cost the national administration more than a million of votes. Soldiers don't say much through the press, but they quietly talk things over around their campfires. And I hope many generations will pass away before they and their sons will cease thus to keep alive the fires of patriotism kindled by the great struggle for American Union.

Thank God, that "law" did not last many years. There was great rejoicing throughout the little army when it was again recognized as belonging to the Department of War. But that cause of rejoicing was soon beclouded. By another of those inscrutable dispensations of Providence, another superior, under the title of Assistant Secretary of War, was interposed between the commander-in-chief of the army and the general appointed to assist him in the command. It had been thought, and so stated in writing, that the major-general commanding, and the ten heads of staff departments and bureaus, with their many assistants, all educated men of long experience in the several departments of military affairs, and some of them tried in war, might give the Secretary all the assistance he needed, if they were permitted to do it. But no; it appears to have been thought that some other, who had had no education or experience in the affairs of the War

Department, could better assist a Secretary who to similar acquired qualifications for his office added far greater natural endowments and the just confidence of his country. Thus the major-general was treated as much worse than the lieutenant-general had been, as he was inferior to him in rank. But I also submitted without a word, because it was this time unquestionably the law as well as the will of my lawful superiors in office. I waited as patiently as I could, as the lieutenant-general had done, the time when by operation of law, human or divine, welcome relief from a burdensome duty would come, upon the official declaration that I had done, as best I could, all the duty that God and my country required of me.

One illustration will suffice to show the working of this new invention by which the general-in-chief was still further removed from the commander-in-chief, whose chief military adviser he was supposed to be. An act of Congress authorized the President to confer medals of honor upon soldiers of all grades who might be most distinguished for bravery in action. It is the most highly prized of all military rewards because given to the *soldier*, without regard to rank, for that service which every true soldier regards as of the greatest merit. The standard of merit deserving that reward is essentially the same in all the armies of the civilized world, and the medal is made of iron or bronze, instead of anything more glittering or precious, to indicate the character of the deed it commemorates. That standard of merit is the most heroic devotion in the discharge of *soldierly duty* in the face of the enemy, that conduct which brings victory, honor, and glory to the country for which a brave man has devoted his life in obedience to the orders which have come down to him from the head of the nation, which spirit of obedience and devotion creates armies and saves nations from defeat, disaster, or domestic convulsion. These highest tokens of a nation's honor had for many years been given with the greatest care, after most rigid scrutiny of the official records and all other evidence presented, laboriously reviewed by the general-in-chief in person, recommended by him under the universal rule of civilized nations, and approved by the Secretary of War, whose approval is considered equivalent to the order of the President, by which alone, under the law, a medal of honor can be granted. But at length these carefully considered recommendations were disapproved by the Assistant Secretary of War, on the ground that the soldier had only done his duty! He had only done, or heroically tried to do until stricken down by the enemy's fire, what his commander had ordered! Some other standard of soldierly honor was set up, not involving obedience to orders nor discharge of duty, but instead of that some act of each soldier's own volition, as if what a nation most highly honored was independent action of each one of its million of soldiers, without any special regard to the orders of the commander-in-chief or any of his subordinate commanders! Thus the most dearly bought honor of a citizen of this great republic, intrusted by Congress to the commander-in-chief of the army, to be duly awarded to his subordinates, passed into the hands of an Assistant Secretary of War, to be awarded by him under his own newly invented theory of soldierly merit! After a laborious but vain attempt to obtain recognition of the time-honored standard of soldierly honor and merit, the general-in-chief was forced to admit that the new standard set up by the Assistant Secretary of War did not afford him any intelligible guide by which he could be governed in making his recommendations, and hence he requested to be relieved *by the Secretary of War* from consideration of such cases in future, presuming that the vital question would thus, as a matter of course, receive the *personal* consideration of the *Secretary*. The formal action of the " Secretary of War," relieving the general from that important duty involving the honor of those under his command, was very promptly made known to him. But now there is very good reason for the belief that the honorable and very worthy *Secretary* knew nothing at all of the whole transaction! It was my good fortune to have had, by close personal association, exact knowledge of the difficulties which my predecessors had encountered, as well as, perhaps, a more modest ambition, and hence to avoid some of those difficulties. Yet in view of the past experience of all commanders of the army, from that of George Washington with the Continental Congress down to the present time, I advise all my young brother soldiers to limit their ambition to the command of the Division of the Atlantic or Department of the East. But since some of them must in all probability be required to discharge the duties of the higher position, I trust the varied experiences of their predecessors may serve as some help to them in the discharge of those duties, which are vastly more difficult and far less agreeable than any other duties of an American soldier. They are the duties which most closely concern the subordinate relation of the military to the civil power in a republic. In that relation I had the great good fortune to enjoy most cordial and considerate personal treatment on the part of my distinguished associates representing the civil power. Hence my advice to my young military friends may be fairly regarded as based upon the most favorable view of what any of them may reasonably expect. It is the one position of all in the army which most severely tries the spirit of subordination which is so indispensable in a soldier of a republic. I have not thought it surprising that none of my great predecessors were quite able to endure the trial.

It is there where the polished surfaces of military etiquette and military methods come in contact with the

THE SECRETARY'S CALL-BELL

rough cast-iron of those which often prevail in civil administration, and the former get badly scratched. Military rules are invariable, with rare exceptions understood and observed by all, while civil practice varies according to the character and habits of the chief in authority, from those of the illustrious Stanton, now well known in history,[1] to the opposite extreme of refined courtesy. Long observation and experience have led to the belief that such rasping of feelings, too sensitive perhaps, even more than substantial difference, has often been the cause of discord. A single example may suffice to illustrate what is meant. In the arrangements of the room especially designed for the office of the Secretary of War in the splendid new State, War, and Navy Departments building, was a great table-desk on which was a complete system of electric buttons connected with wires leading to bells in all the principal offices in the department, the buttons bearing the titles of the officers at the head of the several bureaus, etc., so that the Secretary could "ring up" any colonel, brigadier-general, or major-general whom he wanted to see, just as a gentleman in private life does his coachman, butler, or valet. To an army officer who had for many years, in lower grades, been accustomed to the invariable formula, delivered by a well-dressed soldier standing at "attention" and respectfully saluting, "The commanding officer sends his compliments to Captain B——, and wishes to see the captain at headquarters," the tinkling of that soft little bell must have sounded harsh indeed after he had attained the rank of brigadier-general. Twice only, I believe, my own old soldier messenger who attended in the room where the telephone and bells were located, came to my room, with an indescribable expression on his face, and said, "The bell from the Secretary's office is ringing!" I replied, "Indeed? Go up and inquire what it means." Presently the Secre-

---

[1] Sherman's "Memoirs," second edition, Vol. II, p. 422.

tary's own messenger appeared, and delivered a message in courteous terms—whether the same the Secretary had given to him I did not know, but had reason to doubt, for I had seen and heard the Secretary violently ring a certain bell several times, and then say with great emphasis to his messenger, "Go and tell M—— to come here," not even using the high military title by which "M——" was habitually addressed in the War Department. But those uncivil methods of an imperfect civilization are gradually passing away, and the more refined courtesies, taught, I believe, in all our great schools as well as in the military and naval service, are taking their place. It is now a long time since that reform was practically complete in the War Department.

Thus it appeared, when I went into the office in 1888, that of my predecessors in command of the army, Scott and Sherman had given up the contest, Sheridan had been quickly put *hors de combat*, while Grant alone had won the fight, and that after a long contest, involving several issues, in which a Secretary of War was finally removed from office with the consent of his own personal and political friends, a President was impeached and escaped removal from office by only one vote, and the country was brought to the verge of another civil war. As I had helped Evarts, Seward, and some others whose names I never knew, to "pour oil on the troubled waters" in the time of Grant and Stanton, and to get everybody into the humor to respond heartily to that great aspiration, "Let us have peace," I thought perhaps I might do something in the same direction in later years. Be that as it might, I had no desire to try again what so many others had failed to accomplish, but thought it better to make an experiment with a less ambitious plan of my own, which I had worked out while trying to champion the ideas entertained by all my predecessors. At the request of General Grant and General Sherman, when the one was

President and the other general of the army, I studied the subject as thoroughly as I was capable of doing, and formulated a regulation intended to define the relations between the Secretary of War, the general of the army, and the staff departments.   I still think that plan of my great superiors, only formulated by me, would have worked quite satisfactorily if it could have had general and cordial support.   Yet I do not think it was based upon the soundest view of the constitutional obligations of the President as commander-in-chief of the army, nor at all consistent with the practice in this country of giving the command of the army to the officer happening to be senior in rank, without regard to the "special trust and confidence" reposed in him by the President for the time being.   It was based too much upon the special conditions then existing, wherein the general of the army, no less than the Secretary of War, enjoyed the confidence of the President in the highest degree.   The plan proposed to give far too great authority to the general, if he did not, for whatever reason, enjoy the full confidence of the President.   It also trusted too much to the ability and disinterested fidelity of the several chiefs of the staff departments.   In short, it was based upon a supposed higher degree of administrative virtue than always exists even in this country.

However all this may be, the proposed regulation did not meet with cordial support, so far as I know, from any but General Grant, General Sherman, and General M. C. Meigs, then quartermaster-general.   The other bureau chiefs earnestly opposed it.   It was near the end of General Grant's second term, and no effort was made, so far as I know, to adopt any regulation on the subject in the next or any succeeding administration.   The personal controversy between General Scott and the Secretary of War many years before had resulted in the repeal, through revision, of the old and quite satisfactory regulation on the subject, and no other worthy of the name has ever been adopted in its place.

Soon after I was assigned to the command of the army I submitted, in writing, to President Cleveland my own mature views on the subject. They received some favorable consideration, but no formal action, in view of the near approach of the end of his first term. From that time till near the present the paper was in the personal custody of the Secretary of War. What consideration, if any, it ever received, I was never informed. But it was the guide of my own action, at least, while I was in command of the army. It is now on file in the War Department. It is to be hoped that some future military and administrative geniuses, superior to any of the last hundred years, may be able to solve that difficult problem. I can only say that my own plan worked well enough so long as I helped to work it. How it may be with anybody else, either under my plan or some other, only the future can determine. I so far succeeded that the most intelligent staff officers used to say, "For the first time the general actually does command the army." They saw only the results, without exactly perceiving the nature of the motive-power.

The way to success in rendering efficient public service does not lie through any assumption of the authority which the nation may have given to another, even if not most wisely, but rather in zealous, faithful, and subordinate efforts to assist that other in doing what the country has imposed upon him.

A soldier may honorably crave, as the dearest object of his life, recognition of his *past services* by promotion to a higher grade. That is his one reward for all he may have done. But the desire for higher command, greater power, and more unrestrained authority exhibits ambition inconsistent with due military subordination and good citizenship. It is a dangerous ambition in a re-

public. The highest examples of patriotism ever shown
in this country have been in the voluntary surrender of
power into the hands of the people or of their chosen
representatives, not in efforts to increase or prolong that
power. Following those highest examples, in the year
1882 all the senior officers of the army, including Sherman, Sheridan, and Hancock, united in advocating the
measure then pending in Congress, to fix a limit of age
when every officer should relinquish command and return
to the ranks of private citizenship. In doing so, nearly
all of those seniors, especially Hancock, relinquished forever all hope of rising to the command of the army.
My case was not so strong as that of Hancock, because I
was younger. But Sheridan was only six months older
than I, and his " expectation of life " was far beyond the
time when I should become sixty-four years old. Hence
I cheerfully relinquished in 1882 any reasonable ambition I may ever have had to command the army. My
ultimate succession to that command in 1888 was, like all
other important events in my personal career, unsought
and unexpected. Hence whatever I did from 1888 to 1895
was only a little " extra duty," and I have had no reason
to find fault on account of the " extra-duty pay " which I
received, though none of it was in money. I am inclined
to think it a pretty good rule for a soldier to wait until
he is "detailed," and not to try to put himself "on guard."
I do not know any case in American history where the
opposite course has not resulted in irretrievable injury
to him who adopted it. Temporary success in gaining
high position, before education and experience have given
the necessary qualifications, necessarily results finally in
failure ; while slower advancement, giving full opportunities for education and experience in the duties of each
grade, insures full qualification for the next higher.
American history is full of such examples, as it is — alas !
too truly — of those cases where the highest qualifica-

31

tions and most becoming modesty have not met with any appropriate advancement or other recognition.

In the official intercourse of a soldier with the great departments of government, he often finds useful those maxims which have served him as commander of an army in the field. The most important of these is, not to enter a combat where he is sure to be beaten, as, for instance, where his opponent is the judge who is to decide the issue. As in war, so in administration, battle once joined, questions of right become obscured. The most powerful guns and battalions are sure to win. It is much wiser to seek an ally who carries a heavier armament. Some subordinates of mine — clerks and messengers, I believe—were once required to refund some money which had been paid them on my interpretation of the law and regulations. My careful explanation of the ground of my action was promptly disapproved. I then requested that the money be charged to me and the whole matter referred to Congress, in reply to which request I was informed that the accounts had been settled. In another case I requested that my appeal from adverse action be submitted to President Grant, who had had occasion to know something about me. I was requested by telegraph, in cipher, to withdraw that appeal, as it was liable to cause trouble. Being a lover of peace rather than war, I complied. In that perhaps I made a mistake. If I had adhered to my appeal, it might have saved a public impeachment. Again, I was called upon by one of the Treasury bureaus to refund some money which had been paid me for mileage by order of the Secretary of War, on the alleged ground that the Secretary could not lawfully give me such an order. I referred the matter to the Secretary, as one that did not concern me personally, but which involved the dignity of the head of the War Department as compared with that of a subordinate bureau of another department. The Treasury official soon notified me that the account had been allowed. To illustrate the application of the same principle under opposite conditions, I must relate the story told of President Grant. When informed by a Treasury officer that he could not find any law to justify what the President had desired to be done, he replied, " Then I will see if I can find a Treasury officer who can find that law." Of course no change in the incumbent of that office proved to be necessary. I have thought in several cases in later years that Grant's military method might have been tried to advantage.

" Be ye wise as a serpent and harmless as a dove " is the only rule of action I have ever heard of that can steer a soldier clear of trouble with the civil powers of this great republic. Yet he must sometimes, when his honor or the rights of his subordinates are involved, make the fight, though he knows he must be beaten. A soldier must then stand by his guns as long as he can, and it has happened that such a fight, apparently hopeless at the time, has given victory to a future generation.

CHAPTER XXVII

EVEN as late as the year 1882, very high military authority in this country advocated with great earnest-
ness the proposition that our old brick and stone forts, with
their smooth-bore guns, could make a successful defense
against a modern iron-clad fleet! At the same time, and
even much later, high naval authority maintained that the
United States navy should be relied upon for the defense
of our many thousands of miles of sea-coast! In view of
such counsel, it does not seem strange that Congress, after the old ships had nearly all rotted away, began to
give some attention to a new navy, but thought little or
nothing of land defenses. The old brick and stone parapets and the cast-iron guns were still there; none of them
had become rotten, though the wooden carriages had gone
to decay, and the guns were lying on the ground! Yet,
after a long dream of security, the Great National Council
announced the decision that *something* ought probably to
be done for sea-coast defense. Provision was made by
law for a very high board, with the Secretary of War
presiding, to report to Congress what was required — a
thing which, if Congress had only known it, the Engineer
Bureau of the War Department could have reported just

as well in far less time.   But at length a very able report
was submitted, which inspired the confidence of Congress.

In the meantime there had arisen a condition which
can best be expressed as "want of confidence" in the
chief of the Ordnance Department of the army on the
part of committees of Congress.   From this it resulted
that no appropriations were made for several years for
any new armament, and hence none for fortifications.
Thus by a trifle were the wheels of a great government
blocked for a long time!   Yet that government still survives!   Finally, in the year 1888 an act was passed creating a Board of Ordnance and Fortification, of which
the commanding general of the army should be president, and appropriating quite a large sum of money to be
expended, under the direct supervision of that board, to
commence the work of fortification and armament of the
sea-coast.   After very careful examination and full consideration and discussion, the board adopted the plans
prepared by the Bureaus of Engineering and Ordnance,
and the work was begun and carried forward substantially the same as if the expenditure of the appropriation
had been intrusted to the two bureaus concerned and the
Secretary of War.

The board did perform, and still continues to perform,
a very important and essential duty, and one which cannot
be satisfactorily intrusted to any one man, namely, that
of deciding the delicate and difficult questions constantly
arising in respect to the practical utility and economy of
new inventions having reference to works of defense or
of attack.   But these questions had no immediate bearing
whatever upon the all-important problem of the day — to
place the sea-coasts of the United States in a satisfactory
state of defense according to the best scientific methods
then known to the world.   And that problem had already
been solved, in all respects save one, namely, how to get
out of Congress the necessary money to do the work!

Genius will never cease to invent something better. If we wait for the best, the next war will be over long before we shall begin to prepare for it. All great military nations had been engaged for many years in elaborate and costly experiments, to develop the best possible means of attack and defense, and our Engineer and Ordnance departments had not failed to profit thereby to the fullest extent. They were ready, without any such costly experiments, to make our defenses as good as any in the world. Yet that work of so vital importance must be delayed until American genius could also be assured of a chance, at government expense, of developing something better than anybody else in the world had done! An end was finally, in 1888, put to that dangerous delay by the device, so happily invented by somebody in Congress, of a Board of Ordnance and Fortification.

The board has also served, and will doubtless continue to serve, another very important purpose. It brings together, in close consideration and discussion of all details of the system of national defense, representative officers of the engineers, the ordnance, and the artillery, together with a representative civilian who has become, by service in Congress, far better able than any other member to insure that perfect understanding between the board and the committees of Congress which is essential to harmonious action. Above all, it has given to the commanding general an opportunity to become perfectly familiar with all the details of the coast defenses, and to exert a legitimate influence in making preparations for war, which must be of vital importance to him and to the country when he has to bear the great responsibility of command. I used to say that it would not be just to me to deprive me of such opportunities for education, and I doubt not all my successors will share that feeling. Thus, what may prove to be of the greatest benefit to the military service has finally come out of that evil of "want of confidence" in an ordnance chief.

When in command of the Division of the Atlantic, in 1886-7, I made a careful estimate of the aggregate strength of the war garrisons required for the fortifications and armament recommended by the Endicott board, and of the peace garrisons which would be absolutely required for the care of the new works and for the instruction of the militia artillery reserves. It was found that the addition of two regiments to the present artillery strength of the army would provide the requisite force. Hence a measure was formulated and submitted to Congress to convert the present five regiments into seven, with some proportionate reduction in the number of officers, intended to promote efficiency and economy. That measure has appeared to meet with the approval of nearly all concerned, but is still pending in Congress. It is probably the most important military measure now awaiting favorable action. The measure which accompanies it for the reorganization of the infantry, though not of so pressing necessity, is based upon sound military principles, and is worthy of prompt and favorable action.

The first introduction of the policy of confining the warlike tribes of Indians upon very restricted reservations necessarily caused great discontent, especially among the young men, who were thus cut off from the sports of the chase and the still greater sport of occasional forays into frontier settlements, which were the only means known in Indian custom by which a young warrior could gain a name and a position of honor in his tribe. Either through too limited appropriations or bad management, or both, the provisions furnished for the support of the Indians, in lieu of those to which they had been accustomed, proved inadequate. This caused the spirit of discontent to increase and to become general among all ages. The natural result was such a threat of war from the great Sioux nation in the winter of 1890–91 as to necessitate the concentration of quite a large army to meet the danger of a general outbreak. In the course of military operations, accidents rather than design on either side occasioned some serious collisions between the troops and the Indians, especially at Wounded Knee, resulting in desperate conflict and in much loss of life. But by very careful management on the part of the commanding general in the field, Major-General Miles, a general conflict was averted, and the Sioux made their submission. They had had no general intention to go to war, if they could avoid it without starvation. After a large sum of money had been expended by the War Department in this way, the deficiencies in food were supplied at about the same cost as would, if made in advance, have removed the cause of war. The Indians gained their point of getting as much food as they needed, and the War Department paid the extra bills, but out of the same public treasury which has so often been bled in that way.

It was quite beyond the power of the War Department to guard against a recurrence of that greatest danger of Indian wars — starvation of the Indians. But long experience and accurate knowledge of Indian character had suggested a method by which the other cause of discontent among the young Indian warriors might be, at least in a great measure, removed. That was by providing a legitimate method by which their irrepressible love of military life and exploits might be largely gratified, and, at the same time, those ambitious young men transferred from the ranks of more or less probable savage enemies to the ranks of friends and practically civilized allies. Fortunately, the strongest trait of the Indian character, namely, fidelity to the war chief, lent itself to this project. Long experience had shown the existence of this Indian trait. In only one solitary instance had the Indian scouts so long employed by the army ever proved unfaithful, though often employed in hostilities against their own tribes. Hence, if the ardent young warriors could be induced to enlist for three years in the army, they would, at least for that time, be converted from enemies into allies, even against such of their own tribes as might refuse to enlist. Of course the army must suffer somewhat, in its effective strength for all purposes, during this experiment; for it is evident that a company or troop of Indians would not be quite as valuable for general service as the same number of white men. Yet the transfer of a few hundred of the best Sioux warriors from the Sioux side to our side would much more than compensate for the loss of the same number of white troops. The result of that experiment seemed to be entirely satisfactory. At all events, there has been no great Indian war, nor any threat of one, since that experiment was begun. It has served to tide over the time during which the young men, who had from earliest childhood listened to stories of the Custer massacre and other great Indian achievements, were undergoing transformation from the life and character of savage warriors to those of civilized husbandmen, under the system of allotments in severalty. When the short warlike part of the life of one generation is past, the danger will no longer exist.

In June, 1891, at Keokuk, Iowa, I married Miss Georgia Kilbourne, daughter of Mrs. George E. Kilbourne of that city. Then a host of old soldiers of the Union army reassembled to greet their comrade.

In 1892 this country seemed on the verge of war with the little republic of Chile. So confident were some officials of the administration that war was inevitable, that I was asked to make an estimate of the military force which would be necessary to occupy and hold a vital point in Chilean territory until the demands of the United States were complied with. It was assumed, of course, that the navy could easily do all the rest. Pending the consideration of this subject, so disagreeable to me, I had a dream which I repeated at the time to a few intimate friends. I saw in the public street a man holding a mangy-looking dog by the neck, and beating him with a great club, while a crowd of people assembled to witness the "sport." Some one asked the man why he was beating the poor dog. He replied: "Oh, just to make him yelp." But the dog did not "yelp." He bore his cruel punishment without a whine. Then he was transformed into a splendid animal, one of the noblest of his species, and the entire crowd of bystanders, with one accord, rushed in and compelled the man to desist from beating him.

CHAPTER XXVIII

IN 1894 the vast development of railroad communication between the Mississippi valley and the Pacific Ocean, and the similar building of new cities and founding of industrial enterprises in the region between the Rocky Mountains and the Pacific, both in anticipation of the future development of the country rather than in response to any demand then existing, having been substantially completed, or suspended for an indefinite time, a large amount of capital so invested was found for the time unproductive, and a great number of laborers were left in the Pacific States without any possible employment. The great majority of these laborers were, as usual, without any accumulated means to pay their transportation to any other part of the country, and hence were left to drift as they might toward the East, subsisting by whatever means they could find during their long tramp of many hundreds of miles. Similar and other causes had produced at the same time industrial depression throughout the country, so that the unfortunate laborers drifting eastward were only an additional burden upon communities already overloaded with unemployed labor. Thus the borrowing of foreign capital to put into unprofitable investments, and the employment of great numbers of laborers in making premature developments, met with the consequences which are sure to follow disregard of natural laws. The management of the Pacific railroads did not appear to appreciate the wisdom of mitigating, so far as was in their power, the evil which had resulted from their own policy, by giving free transportation to the laborers who had been stranded on the Pacific coast. Hence all the transcontinental roads were soon blocked by lawless seizures of trains, and suffered losses far greater than they saved in transportation. Indeed, the requisite transportation of destitute laborers eastward would have cost the roads practically nothing, while their losses resulting from not providing it were very great. Every possible effort was made for a long time to deal effectively with this evil by the ordinary course of judicial proceedings; but such methods proved entirely inadequate. The government was finally compelled, in consequence of the almost total interruption of interstate commerce and of the transportation of the United States mails and troops, to assume military control along the lines of all the Pacific roads, and direct the department commanders to restore and maintain, by military force, traffic and transportation over those roads.

For some time these lawless acts did not seem to result from any general organization. But they gradually developed into the formidable character of a wide-spread conspiracy and combination, with recognized general leaders, to obstruct and prevent the due execution of the laws of the United States respecting transportation and interstate commerce. The principal center of this conspiracy, and by far the most formidable combination, was in Chicago, where the greatest material interests, both public and private, were at stake, though many other important railroad centers and many thousand miles of road were involved. There the insurrection was so great in numbers and so violent in its acts as to require the most prompt and energetic action of a very large force to suppress disorder, protect property, and execute the laws. The city police were utterly powerless in such an emergency, and deputy United States marshals, though employed without limit as to numbers, were no more effective. The State militia were not called out in time to meet the emergency. Hence nothing remained but for the National Government to exercise the military power conferred upon it by the Constitution and laws, so far as the same were applicable.[1] Fortunately, the acts of Congress passed in pursuance of the Constitution, although never before made effective in a similar case, were found to give ample authority for the action then required. Fortunately, also, the wise foresight of the government in establishing a large military post at Fort Sheridan, near Chicago, made a regiment of infantry, a squadron of cavalry, and a battery of artillery immediately available for service in that city. But, unfortunately, the commanding general of that department was absent from his command, where superior military capacity was so much needed at that time. Although the troops west of the Mississippi had been engaged for a long time, under the President's orders, in overcoming the unlawful obstruction of railroad traffic above referred to, the general appears not to have anticipated any emergency which would in his judgment require or justify such use of the troops in his own department, and hence remained in the Eastern States, where he had gone some time before. From this it resulted that when the troops at Fort Sheridan were ordered into Chicago,

[1] See the report of Attorney-General Olney, December 1, 1894, p. 31.

the execution of the order devolved on subordinate officers, and the troops were so dispersed as to be unable to
act with the necessary effect.

It having become apparent that the services of troops
would probably be required in the city of Chicago, and
in anticipation of orders from the President, instructions
were telegraphed on July 2 to the commanding general
of the Department of the Missouri to make preparations
to move the garrison of Fort Sheridan to the Lake Front
Park in the city. The reply of his staff-officer, Colonel
Martin, showed that the department commander, Major-
General Miles, was not in Chicago, and the adjutant-
general of the army did not know where he was, but,
after several inquiries by telegraph, learned that the general had started that afternoon from Long Island for
Washington instead of for Chicago. The next day (July
3), in the President's room at the Executive Mansion, in
reply to my suggestion that his presence was needed
with his command, General Miles said he was subject to
orders, but that in his opinion the United States troops
ought not to be employed in the city of Chicago at that
time. No reply was made by the President or the Secretary of War, who was also present, to that expression of
opinion, but the President approved my further suggestion that General Miles should return at once to his command. The general started by the first train, but could
not reach Chicago in time to meet the emergency. It
became necessary in the judgment of the President to
order the Fort Sheridan garrison into the city in the
afternoon of the same day (July 3).

The instructions given the day before about moving
the troops to Lake Front Park were not complied with.
From that point they could most readily have protected
the sub-treasury, custom-house, post-office, and other
United States property, and also have acted in a formidable body at any other point where their services

might properly have been required. But instead of that, the troops were so dispersed that they could not act with much effect anywhere, and could give no protection whatever to the vast amount of United States property exposed to destruction. This error appears to have resulted in some measure from the too great deference paid by commanding officers to the advice or wishes of civil officers to whom they were referred for information, and much more from lack of knowledge of the lawful relations existing between the national troops and the civil authorities in this country, although those relations had been plainly defined in an order dated May 25, quoted below. Like ignorance in respect to the proper tactical methods of dealing with insurrection against the authority of the United States caused halting and ineffective action of the troops. To correct this error and make known to all the rules which must govern United States troops in all like emergencies, the subjoined order, dated July 9, was issued. The extracts from correspondence quoted below indicate the nature of the errors above referred to, and their correction some time after the arrival of General Miles in Chicago.

The garrison of Fort Sheridan proved sufficient, notwithstanding the first faulty disposition and action of the troops, to hold the mob in check until reinforcements arrived from distant stations and the State troops were brought into effective action. Finally, the proclamation of the President of the United States, quoted below, which was issued at the moment when ample military forces had been placed in position to enforce his constitutional mandates, very quickly terminated all forcible resistance to the execution of the laws of the United States. The same result, though perhaps with greater destruction of life and far less destruction of property, would probably have been accomplished in a single day by the Fort Sheridan garrison alone, acting in one compact body, according to the tactics prescribed for such service. If a like occasion ever again occurs, the action of the troops will doubtless be governed by such tactics. Delay is too dangerous in such cases.

(Telegram.)

HEADQUARTERS OF THE ARMY,
WASHINGTON, D. C., July 2, 1894.

To the Commanding General, Department of the Missouri, Chicago, Illinois.

You will please make all necessary arrangements, confidentially, for the transportation of the entire garrison of Fort Sheridan — infantry, cavalry, and artillery — to the Lake Front Park in the city of Chicago. To avoid possible interruption of the movement by rail and by marching through a part of the city, it may be advisable to bring them by steamboat. Please consider this matter, and have the arrangements perfected without delay. You may expect orders at any time for the movement. Acknowledge receipt, and report in what manner the movement is to be made.

J. M. SCHOFIELD, Major-General Commanding.

(Telegram.)

CHICAGO, ILLINOIS, July 2, 1894.

Adjutant-General U. S. Army, Washington, D. C. :

Confidential despatch this date received at three-thirty P. M. Arrangements can be made to bring troops from Sheridan to Lake Front Park by steamer, but there would be difficulty in disembarking them there, as the Van Buren street viaduct has been torn down; and, besides, transportation from barracks to pier at Sheridan would necessarily be slow. They can be brought from Sheridan to Lake Front direct by rail, and disembark on grounds, thus avoiding marching through city. Suggest the latter plan as best, especially as rail transportation is now at the post sufficient to bring the whole command — infantry, artillery, and cavalry — as soon as they can be loaded on cars at that point.

MARTIN, Asst. Adjt.-Genl.
(in absence of Major-Genl. Comdg.).

(Telegram.)

WASHINGTON, D. C., July 3, 1894, four o'clock P. M.

To MARTIN, Adjutant-General, Hdqrs. Dept. of the Missouri, Chicago, Ills.

It having become impracticable, in the judgment of the President, to enforce, by ordinary course of judicial proceedings, the laws of the United States, you will direct Colonel Crofton to move his entire command at once to the city of Chicago, leaving the necessary guard at Fort Sheridan, there to execute the orders and processes of the United States Court, to prevent the obstruction of the United States mails, and generally to enforce the faithful execution of the laws of the United States. He will confer with the United States marshal, the United States district attorney, and Edwin Walker, special counsel. Acknowledge receipt, and report action promptly.

By order of the President:

J. M. SCHOFIELD, Major-General.

(Telegram.)

CHICAGO, ILLS., July 4, 1894.

Adjutant-General U. S. Army, Washington, D. C.:

At ten-fifteen this morning Colonel Crofton reports his command in the city; located, infantry at Blue Island and Grand Crossing, cavalry and artillery at stock-yards; cannot learn that anything definite has been accomplished, but there has been no active trouble. People appear to feel easier since arrival of troops. General Miles is expected to arrive in city within an hour or at twelve.

MARTIN, Asst. Adjt.-Genl.

(Telegram.)

CHICAGO, ILLS., July 4, 1894.

Adjt. Genl. U. S. Army, Washington, D. C.:

Returned at eleven-thirty this morning.

MILES, Maj.-Genl. Commanding.

32

(Telegram.)

CHICAGO, ILLS., July 4, 1894.

Adjutant-General U. S. Army, Washington, D. C.:

Cavalry and artillery moving to the stock-yards were delayed by obstructions placed upon the track, also cars being overturned on track and the threatening mob in the vicinity. A report is received that a mob of about two thousand men has gathered near Blue Island and threatened to take that place at four o'clock this afternoon. It is occupied by four companies of infantry. At the request of U. S. Marshal Arnold, troops had been located at Blue Island, the stock-yards, and the crossing at Forty-seventh street of the Lake Shore and Rock Island railroads before my arrival, and others are desired at South Chicago. I have directed all commanding officers not to allow crowds or mobs to congregate about the commands in a menacing or threatening manner, and to keep out pickets and guards; and, after due warning, if the mobs approach the commands in a threatening manner, they must be dispersed, even if firearms have to be used. A large number of men in the city are wearing white ribbon, the color ordered by Debs to indicate their allegiance to his orders. Owing to the feeling of feverish excitement in the city, and the large number of unoccupied, the condition to-day is more critical than at any other time. Most of the roads are moving mail and passenger trains. All of the roads will attempt to move their trains to-morrow morning. Sufficient number of men are available and anxious to work to take the place of all the strikers, provided proper protection can be given them. Seven roads have moved a few cars of perishable freight. All the troops from Sheridan are occupied, and I renew my recommendation that that garrison be very largely increased at once to meet any emergency that may arise. The effect of moving troops through the country, especially from Kansas to Chicago, at this time would be desirable.

NELSON A. MILES, Major-General Commanding.

Additional troops were concentrated in Chicago as rapidly as they could be transported, until the force there aggregated about two thousand men. More were in readiness to move if necessary.

(Telegram.)

CHICAGO, ILLS., July 5, 1894.

Adjutant-General U. S. A., Washington, D. C.:

Owing to the excellent discipline and great forbearance of officers and men, serious hostilities were avoided yesterday; several small fights and affrays occurred. Matters look more favorable to-day, although interference exists on five roads. All railroads are endeavoring to move freight and mail trains.

MILES, Major-General Commanding.

(Telegram.)

CHICAGO, ILLS., July 5, 1894.

Adjutant-General U. S. Army, Washington, D. C.:

The mob of several thousand are moving east along Rock Island nearer center of city, overturning cars, burning station-houses, and destroying property. There is a report that the mob intend sacking some of the principal buildings near Rookery Building to-night. The riot will soon embrace all the criminals of the city and vicinity. Unless very positive measures are taken, the riot will be beyond the control of any small force. Has the government any additional instructions?

NELSON A. MILES, Major-General Commanding.

(Telegram — Confidential.)

CHICAGO, ILLS., July 5, 1894.

Adjutant-General U. S. Army, Washington, D. C.:

While most of the roads are moving passenger and mail trains, nearly all the freight-trains are interfered with, and but very few are moving. This morning a mob of over two thousand men gathered at the stock-yards, crowded among the troops, obstructed the movement of trains, knocked down a railroad official, and overturned some twenty freight-cars on the track, which obstructs all freight and passenger traffic in the vicinity of the stock-yards, and thereby the transit of meat-trains to different parts of the country, as well as the passenger traffic of the Rock Island Railroad. The mob also derailed a passenger-train coming into the city on the Pittsburg, Fort Wayne, and

Chicago Railroad, and burned switches, which destroys track. The injunction of the United States Court is openly defied, and unless the mobs are dispersed by the action of the police, or they are fired upon by United States troops, more serious trouble may be expected, as the mob is increasing and becoming more defiant. Shall I give the order for troops to fire on mob obstructing trains?

MILES, Major-General Commanding.

The following extracts from correspondence and orders, and the proclamation of the President, with the foregoing explanation, sufficiently indicate the methods by which the unlawful combination in Chicago was suppressed:

(Telegram.)

HEADQUARTERS OF THE ARMY,
WASHINGTON, D. C., July 5, 1894, 10:15 P. M.

To MAJOR-GENERAL MILES, Headquarters Department of the Missouri, United States Army, Chicago, Illinois.

In view of the situation in Chicago, as reported in your despatches to the adjutant-general this evening, it is your duty to concentrate your troops so as to enable them to act effectively either in execution of the orders heretofore given, or in protecting the property of the United States, as in your judgment may be necessary. In any event, the troops should not be scattered or divided into small detachments, nor should they attempt to do service in several places at the same time, which their numbers will not enable them to do effectively.

The mere preservation of peace and good order in the city is, of course, the province of the city and State authorities.

J. M. SCHOFIELD, Major-General Commanding.

(Telegram.)

CHICAGO, ILLS., July 6, 1894.

Adjutant-General, U. S. A., Washington, D. C.:

In accordance with the orders of the War Department, the troops were sent to Blue Island, stock-yards, Grand Crossing, and Forty-ninth street, at the request of the U. S. marshal. This disposition was made before my arrival yesterday. The roads were obstructed in several places by mobs; the largest and most violent gathered near. the stock-yards at noon, and gradually moved east along the line of the Rock Island road, overturning cars, burning station-house, roundhouse, and other property. The mob was estimated at ten thousand men, three miles long and a half a mile wide; it moved steadily north until after dark, destroying property and setting fires, and the cry of the mob was "To hell with the government!" It reached Eighteenth street after dark, and then dispersed. While this threatening movement was in action I withdrew some of the troops on the outskirts of the city, and in the evening the battery and one troop of cavalry, to the Lake Front Park, for the purpose of attacking the mob should it reach the vicinity of the government building between Adams and Jackson sts. During the afternoon, night, and this morning I have concentrated nine (9) companies infantry, troop cavalry, and the battery of artillery on the Lake Front Park. This includes troops from Leavenworth and Brady. During last night a proclamation was issued by the mayor directing the police to disperse mobs and prevent the lawless from interfering with railroads. If this order is executed there will be no further trouble. One engineer has been stoned to death. During the night a dozen fires were started in different places, but destroying very little property, except the principal buildings of the World's Fair and more than a hundred cars; this morning a mob has gathered near the stock-yards in as large numbers as yesterday at this time; they threatened to hang U. S. marshals and policemen. The law-breakers constitute a very small percentage of the people. The mass of the people desire the maintenance of law and order. The action of the Chief Executive has given universal satisfaction.

MILES, Major-General Commanding.

BY THE PRESIDENT OF THE UNITED STATES OF AMERICA.

A PROCLAMATION.

Whereas, by reason of unlawful obstructions, combinations, and assemblages of persons, it has become impracticable, in the judgment of the President, to enforce, by the ordinary course of judicial proceedings, the laws of the United States within the State of Illinois, and especially in the city of Chicago, within said State:

And whereas, for the purpose of enforcing the faithful execution of the laws of the United States and protecting its property, and removing obstructions to the United States mails, in the State and city aforesaid, the President has employed a part of the military forces of the United States:

Now, therefore, I, Grover Cleveland, President of the United States, do hereby admonish all good citizens and all persons who may be, or may come, within the city and State aforesaid, against aiding, countenancing, encouraging, or taking any part in such unlawful obstructions, combinations, and assemblages; and I hereby warn all persons engaged in, or in any way connected with, such unlawful obstructions, combinations, and assemblages, to disperse and retire peaceably to their respective abodes on or before twelve o'clock noon on the ninth day of July instant.

Those who disregard this warning and persist in taking part with a riotous mob in forcibly resisting and obstructing the execution of the laws of the United States, or interfering with the functions of the government, or destroying or attempting to destroy the property belonging to the United States or under its protection, cannot be regarded otherwise than as public enemies.

Troops employed against such a riotous mob will act with all the moderation and forbearance consistent with the accomplishment of the desired end; but the stern necessities that confront them will not with certainty permit discrimination between guilty participants and those who are mingled with them from curiosity and without criminal intent. The only safe course, therefore, for those not actually unlawfully participating is to abide at their homes, or at least not to be found in the neighborhood of riotous assemblages.

While there will be no hesitation or vacillation in the decisive treatment of the guilty, this warning is especially intended to protect and save the innocent.

In testimony whereof, I have hereunto set my hand and caused the seal of the United States to be hereto affixed.

Done at the city of Washington, this eighth day of July, in the year of our Lord one thousand eight hundred and ninety-four, and of the independence of the United States the one hundred and nineteenth.

By the President:

GROVER CLEVELAND.

W. Q. GRESHAM, Secretary of State.

(General Orders, No. 6.)

HEADQUARTERS DEPARTMENT OF THE MISSOURI,
CHICAGO, ILLINOIS, July 9, 1894.

To all United States troops serving in the Department of the Missouri.

The acts of violence committed during the past few days in obstructing the mail-trains and post-roads; the blocking of the interstate commerce; the open defiance and violation of the injunction of the United States Court; the assaults upon the Federal forces in the lawful discharge of their duties; the destruction, pillage, and looting of the inland commerce property belonging to citizens of the different States, and other acts of rebellion and lawlessness, have been of such a serious character that the duties of the military authorities are now clearly defined.

The proclamation of the President, the commander-in-chief of the land and navy forces and the State militia when called into service, is understood by the military to be in the interests of humanity and to avoid the useless waste of life, if possible. *It is an executive order for all law-abiding citizens to separate themselves from the law-breakers and those in actual hostility to the action of the United States Court and the laws of the National Government.* He has defined the attitude of these law-breakers to be that of enemies of the government, and hence it is the duty of the military forces to aid the United States marshals to disperse, capture, or destroy all bodies of men obstructing the mail-routes and in actual hostility to the injunction of the United States Court and the laws of the United States.

This does not change the relations of the Federal officials with those of the local authority, as it is expected that the State and municipal governments will maintain peace and good order within the territory of their jurisdiction. Should they fail or be overpowered, the military forces will assist them, but not to the extent of leaving unprotected property belonging to or under the protection of the United States.

The officer in the immediate command of troops must be the judge as to what use to make of the forces of his command in executing his orders, and in case serious action be required and there be time, he will communicate with his next superior for his instructions.

The earnest efforts of the law-abiding citizens have done much to improve the condition of affairs during the last few days, and I earnestly request all law-abiding citizens to do whatever is possible to assist in maintaining the civil government and the authority of the municipal, State, and Federal governments in preserving peace and good order.

By command of Major-General Miles:

J. P. MARTIN, Assistant Adjutant-General.

(General Orders, No. 23.)

HEADQUARTERS OF THE ARMY,
ADJUTANT-GENERAL'S OFFICE,
WASHINGTON, July 9, 1894.

The following instructions are published for the government of the army:

A mob forcibly resisting or obstructing the execution of the laws of the United States, or attempting to destroy property belonging to or under the protection of the United States, is a public enemy.

Troops called into action against such a mob are governed by the general regulations of the army and military tactics in respect to the manner in which they shall act to accomplish the desired end. It is purely a tactical question in what manner they shall use the weapons with which they are armed — whether by the fire of musketry and artillery, or by use of the bayonet and saber, or by both, and at what stage of the operations each or either mode of attack shall be employed.

This tactical question must necessarily be decided by the immediate commander of the troops, according to his best judgment of the situation and the authorized drill regulations.

In the first stage of an insurrection lawless mobs are frequently commingled with great crowds of comparatively innocent people drawn there by curiosity and excitement, and ignorant of the great danger to which they are exposed. Under such circumstances the commanding officer should withhold the fire of his troops, if possible, until timely warning has been given to the innocent to separate themselves from the guilty.

Under no circumstances are the troops to fire into a crowd without the order of the commanding officer, except that single sharp-shooters, selected by the commanding officer, may shoot down individual rioters who have fired upon or thrown missiles at the troops.

As a general rule, the bayonet alone should be used against mixed crowds in the first stages of a revolt. But as soon as sufficient warning has been given to enable the innocent to separate themselves from the guilty, the action of the troops should be governed solely by the tactical considerations involved in the duty they are ordered to perform. They are not called upon to consider how great may be the losses inflicted upon the public enemy, except to make their blows so effective as to promptly suppress all resistance to lawful authority, and to stop the destruction of life the moment lawless resistance has ceased. Punishment belongs not to the troops, but to the courts of justice.

By command of Major-General Schofield:

GEO. D. RUGGLES, Adjutant-General.

(General Orders, No. 15.)

HEADQUARTERS OF THE ARMY,
ADJUTANT-GENERAL'S OFFICE,
WASHINGTON, May 25, 1894.

The following instructions are issued for the government of department commanders:

Whenever the troops may be lawfully employed, under the orders of the President, to suppress "insurrection in any State against the government thereof," as provided in section 5297 of the Revised Statutes; or to "enforce the execution of the laws of the United States" when "by reason of unlawful obstructions, combinations, or assemblages of persons" it has "become impracticable, in the judgment of the President, to enforce, by the ordinary course of judicial proceedings, the laws of the

United States," as provided in section 5298 of the Revised Statutes, the troops are employed as a part of the military power of the United States, and act under the orders of the President, as commander-in-chief, and his military subordinates. They cannot be directed to act under the orders of any civil officer. The commanding officers of the troops so employed are directly responsible to their military superiors. Any unlawful or unauthorized act on their part would not be excusable on the ground of any order or request received by them from a marshal or any other civil officer.

By command of Major-General Schofield:

GEO. D. RUGGLES, Adjutant-General.

It appears to have been thought in Chicago that " the request of the United States marshal," with whom the commanding officer of the troops had been directed to " confer," was equivalent to " orders of the War Department," notwithstanding the order of May 25, above quoted, strictly prohibiting any such use of troops. Hence the faulty disposition of the troops which was corrected when the mob was approaching the heart of the city. Then " some of the troops on the outskirts of the city" were withdrawn, and " in the evening the battery and one troop of cavalry" were moved " to the Lake Front Park, for the purpose of attacking the mob should it reach the vicinity of the government building between Adams and Jackson sts." And during the afternoon and night of the 5th and morning of the 6th an effective force was concentrated on the Lake Front Park, forty-eight hours after the time when the orders from Washington indicated that the Fort Sheridan garrison should be at that place.

On July 9, the day after the President had issued his proclamation, it appeared in Chicago that " the duties of the military authorities are now clearly defined." The President's proclamation was "understood by the military to be in the interests of humanity," and to concern, in some way, " the State militia," as if they had been "called into service" of the United States. It was "the duty of the military forces to aid the United States marshals." Again, "it is expected the State and municipal governments will maintain peace and good order. . . . Should they fail or be overpowered, the military forces will assist them . . . " — and this notwithstanding the well-known law on that subject to which allusion was made in the despatch of July 5 from the headquarters of the army.

The President's proclamation was strictly limited to "the purpose of enforcing the faithful execution of the laws of the United States, and protecting its property, and removing obstructions to the United States mails," for which purpose the proclamation stated "the President has employed a part of the military forces of the United States" — not *is about to employ*, but *has employed*, under specific orders, which were telegraphed to Colonel Martin on July 3, to do certain things which were precisely the things specified in the proclamation of July 8, and not "to aid the United States marshals" in doing those things or any others. Yet it was not until July 9, six days after the order to Colonel Martin, that those duties became "clearly defined," and then they were misunderstood in the very essential particulars above specified.

The lawless interruptions of traffic on the Pacific roads had continued from the latter part of April till early in July, — two months and a half, — in spite of all the efforts to enforce the laws, in each special case, by the ordinary course of judicial proceedings. Yet as soon as full discretionary authority was given to the several department commanders to act promptly as each emergency might require, all obstruction to the operations of the Pacific railroads rapidly disappeared.

The ordinary course of judicial proceedings is generally far too slow to produce satisfactory results when military force is required. Fortunately the Constitution and laws of the United States do not require such ineffective mixture of civil and military methods. When the civil power ceases to be effective and the President is required to exercise his authority as commander-in-chief of the army, his acts become purely military, untrammeled by any civil authority whatever. This is perhaps one of the strongest and most valuable provisions of the Constitution and laws — one which, if generally known, is most likely to deter the lawless from any attempt to act in defiance of the judicial authority of the United States. The General Order No. 15, issued at the time herein referred to (May 25, 1894), was based upon the foregoing interpretation of the Constitution and laws.

Under the Constitution and existing statutes of the United States it is not proper to use the troops, either in large or small numbers, to "aid the United States marshals." When the civil officers, with their civil posse, are no longer able to enforce the laws, they stand aside, and the military power, under the orders of the commander-in-chief, steps in and overcomes the lawless resistance to authority. Then the civil officers resume their functions, to make arrests of individuals, hold them in custody, and deliver them to the courts for trial. It is not the duty of the troops in such cases to guard prisoners who are in the custody of civil officers; but it is the duty of the troops, if necessary, to repel by force of arms any unlawful attempt to rescue such prisoners. This distinction should be clearly understood by all army officers, and it is of universal application. The duty of the army is, when so ordered by the President, to overcome and suppress lawless resistance to civil authority. There military duty ends, and the civil officers resume their functions.

The distinction between the authority of the United States and that of the several States is so clearly defined that there can be no possible excuse for ignorance on that subject on the part of any officer of the army. But the relation between the civil and the military authorities of the United States had not been clearly defined, after the passage of the "Posse Comitatus Act," until the order of May 25, 1894, was issued. But that can hardly excuse continued ignorance of the law a month or more after that order was issued; and it is worthy of note that at least one department commander showed himself familiar with the law before the order was issued, by correcting the mistake of a subordinate, which called attention to the necessity of issuing some such order.

Of course that order had the sanction of the President, after consideration and approval by the Attorney-General, before it was issued.

The acts of Congress creating the Pacific railroads and making them military roads justify and require that the government give them military protection whenever, in the judgment of the President, such protection is needed. It is not incumbent on the commander-in-chief of the army of the United States to call on civil courts and marshals to protect the military roads over which he proposes to move his troops, whether on foot or on horseback or in cars. It appears to have been almost forgotten that the transcontinental railroads were built, at great expense to the national treasury, *mainly as a military bond* between the Atlantic States and the Pacific States, and that this is by far their most important service, and this explains the meaning of the language employed in the acts of Congress creating them.

At the time of the massacre of Chinese laborers at Rock Springs, Wyoming, during President Cleveland's first administration, I was ordered by the President to go to that place from Chicago and suppress that violation of the treaty obligations between this country and China. On my arrival at Omaha, I was informed by press reporters that a grand conclave at Denver that night was to consider a proposition to order out all the train-men on the Union Pacific Railroad the next morning, for the purpose, as I understood, of preventing the passage of my train. I told the reporters they might telegraph those people in Denver, but not for publication, that I was traveling over a military road, on military duty, under orders from the commander-in-chief of the army; that interference with that journey would be regarded by me as an act of war, and would be so treated. I heard no more on that subject. That interpretation of the Pacific Railroad acts was suggested several times, but never officially accepted until 1894.

The following are in substance the orders sent on July 6 and 7, by the President's direction, to all the department commanders in the country traversed by the Pacific railroads, and the President's proclamation which followed two days later, under the operation of which traffic was resumed throughout all that vast region of country as rapidly as trains conveying troops could be moved. No serious opposition or resistance was offered anywhere.

(Telegram.)

HEADQUARTERS OF THE ARMY,
WASHINGTON, July 7, 1894.

BRIGADIER-GENERAL OTIS, Commanding Department of the Columbia, Vancouver Barracks, Washington:

In view of the fact, as substantiated by communications received from the Department of Justice, from military official reports, and from other reliable sources, that by reason of unlawful obstructions, and combinations or assemblages of persons, it has become impracticable, in the judgment of the President, to enforce, by the ordinary course of judicial proceedings, the laws of the United States, and to prevent obstructions of the United States mails, and interruptions to commerce between the States, on the line of the Northern Pacific Railroad, and to secure to the United States the right guaranteed by section 11 of the act approved July 2, 1864, constituting the Northern Pacific Railroad " a post route and military road subject to the use of the United States for postal, military, naval, and all other government service," you are directed by the President to employ the military force under your command to remove obstructions to the mails, and to execute any orders of the United States courts for the protection of property in the hands of receivers appointed by such courts, and for preventing interruption of interstate commerce, and to give such protection to said railroad as will prevent any unlawful and forcible obstruction to the regular and orderly operation of said road "for postal, military, naval, and all other government service."

J. M. SCHOFIELD, Major-General Commanding.

(Telegram.)

HEADQUARTERS OF THE ARMY,
WASHINGTON, July 7, 1894.

BRIGADIER-GENERAL OTIS, Commanding Department of the Columbia, Vancouver Barracks, Washington:

The order of the President sent you this morning by telegraph is the same in substance as one sent last night to General Merritt, the purpose being to extend military protection over the entire line of the Northern Pacific Railroad from St. Paul to Puget Sound. In the movement of the troop-trains along the line of the road in the execution of this order, the Department of Justice will furnish a sufficient force of marshals to make arrests and hold prisoners subject to the orders of the United States courts. You will please concert with General Merritt by direct correspondence the necessary exchanges of guards upon moving trains at the military posts in your department and in his, nearest to each other, so that the troops may return to their proper stations without unnecessary delay.

J. M. SCHOFIELD, Major-General Commanding.

BY THE PRESIDENT OF THE UNITED STATES OF AMERICA.

A PROCLAMATION.

Whereas, by reason of unlawful obstructions, combinations, and assemblages of persons, it has become impracticable, in the judgment of the President, to enforce, by the ordinary course of judicial proceedings, the laws of the United States at certain points and places within the States of North Dakota, Montana, Idaho, Washington, Wyoming, Colorado, and California, and the Territories of Utah and New Mexico, and especially along the lines of such railways traversing said States and Territories as are military roads and post routes, and are engaged in interstate commerce and in carrying United States mails;

And whereas, for the purpose of enforcing the faithful execution of the laws of the United States, and protecting property belonging to the United States or under its protection, and of preventing obstructions of the United States mails and of commerce between the States and Territories, and of securing to the United States the right guaranteed by law to the use of such roads for postal, military, naval, and other government service, the President has employed a part of the military forces of the United States:

Now, therefore, I, Grover Cleveland, President of the United States, do hereby command all persons engaged in, or in any way connected with, such unlawful obstructions, combinations, and assemblages, to disperse and retire peaceably to their respective abodes on or before three o'clock in the afternoon on the tenth day of July instant.

In witness whereof, I have hereunto set my hand, and caused the seal of the United States to be hereto affixed.

Done at the city of Washington, this ninth day of July, in the year of our Lord one thousand eight hundred and ninety-four, and of the independence of the United States the one hundred and nineteenth.

GROVER CLEVELAND.

By the President:

W. Q. GRESHAM, Secretary of State.

CHAPTER XXIX

LESSONS OF THE CIVIL WAR — WEAKNESS OF THE MILITARY
POLICY AT THE OUTBREAK OF THE REBELLION — A
POOR USE OF THE EDUCATED SOLDIERS OF THE ARMY
— MILITARY WISDOM SHOWN BY THE CONFEDERATE AU-
THORITIES — TERRITORIAL STRATEGY — GENERAL MILI-
TARY EDUCATION INDISPENSABLE TO GOOD CITIZENSHIP
— ORGANIZATION OF THE NATIONAL GUARD — GENERAL
GRANT WITHOUT MILITARY BOOKS — MEASURES NECES-
SARY TO THE NATIONAL DEFENSE.

IN my opinion, the most important of all the lessons
taught by the Civil War is the necessity of using in
the most effective manner the means at the disposal of
the government when war breaks out. The necessity
for adequate preparation is a different question, which
has been much discussed, and in regard to which some
progress has been made toward a satisfactory solution.
Whatever the outcome may be in respect to preparation
for war, certainly the government and the people ought
to adopt such a policy as will lead to the best practicable
use of the preparations which have actually been made.

In this respect the policy adopted by the National Government in 1861 was about as weak as possible, while that
of the Confederates was comparatively strong. It is said
that this weak policy was due largely to General Scott,
and grew out of his distrust of volunteer troops; he
having thought it necessary to have a considerable body
of regular troops to give steadiness and confidence to the
volunteers or militia. This is a very good theory, no

doubt, provided the regulars could be provided in advance in such numbers as to produce the desired effect. But if that theory had been relied upon in 1861, the "Confederate States" would have established their independence long before the regular army could be organized and made effective. What was demanded by the necessities of the country in 1861 was the best large army that could be made in the shortest possible time, not a better small army to be made in a much longer time.

The United States government actually had at hand the means of creating in a very short time a far larger efficient army than the South could possibly have raised in the same time. This means had been provided, with great care and at great expense, through a long term of years, by the education of young men at the Military Academy, and their practical training in the small regular army in all kinds of actual service, including one foreign war and almost constant campaigns against the Indians. Nowhere in the world could have been found a better corps of officers to organize, instruct, and discipline new troops. Yet those officers were hardly employed at all in that service at first, when it was of supreme importance. Some time later, when the necessity was not so great, a few officers of the army were permitted to accept commands in the volunteers. Even then it often required great "influence" to secure such "indulgences." Scores of young officers, qualified in every way to do such service in the first six months of the war, sought in vain for opportunities to render the valuable services for which the government had educated them, and were compelled to drag along four years in the discharge of duties several grades below their qualifications.

In the regular army in 1861 there were, exclusive of those who went South, at least 600 officers who, after graduating at West Point, had served several years with their regiments, and were well qualified to drill a regiment and to command it in battle. A large proportion of them were fitted to command brigades, and some of them divisions, and even army corps. The three years' volunteers first called out could have been fully supplied with brigade, division, and corps commanders from graduates of West Point who were thoroughly qualified by theoretical education and established character, and many of them by practical experience in the Mexican war and Indian campaigns, for the instruction, discipline, and command of troops, still leaving a sufficient number with the regulars for efficient service. The old sergeants of the army in 1861 were relatively competent company commanders. One commissioned officer to four companies of those veteran Indian-fighters made as reliable a battalion as any general could wish for in the conditions then existing.

Experience demonstrated that a volunteer regiment could in a very few weeks be converted into an efficient and thoroughly reliable force in battle by a single young officer of the regular army. In other words, by a judicious use of the small body of officers whom the country had educated at so great expense, a fine army of 500,000 men, or more, could have been called into service, organized, disciplined, and put into the field by August 1, 1861; and that without interfering in any way with the three months' militia called out to meet the first emergency, which militia ought, of course, to have acted strictly on the defensive until the more permanent force could take the field. In a few months more, certainly by the spring of 1862, the instruction, discipline, and field experience of the first levy would have given good officers enough to organize and command a million more men. It required, in short, only a wise use of the national resources to overwhelm the South before the spring of 1863.

The supply of arms, it is true, was deplorably deficient in 1861. But the South was only a little better off than the North in that regard. Besides, the National Government had command of all the markets of the world, and of the means of ocean transportation. It could have bought at once all the available arms everywhere, and thus fully equipped its own troops, while preventing the South from doing the same. Hence the excuse given at the time—namely, want of muskets—was no excuse whatever for delay in the organization of armies.

The rebellion made some progress at first, and offered effective resistance for a long time, simply because the Southern authorities manifested greater military wisdom than the Northern. The difference in preparation and in military training in advance was quite insignificant. The North had many more educated and competent military men than the South. The difference was that the South used the few they had to the best advantage, while the North so used only a very few of their many.

The lesson next in importance taught by our experience is the necessity of general military education in a country having a popular government. No man can be fully qualified for the duties of a statesman until he has made a thorough study of the science of war in its broadest sense. He need not go to a military school, much less serve in the army or in the militia. But unless he makes himself thoroughly acquainted with the methods and conditions requisite to success in war, he is liable to do almost infinite damage to his country. For example, the very first success of the Union armies—the capture of Fort Donelson—was quickly followed by a proclamation of thanksgiving and an order to stop recruiting. That one act of "statesmanship" cost the country untold millions of dollars and many thousands of lives. It was necessary only to take the ordinary military advantage of the popular enthusiasm throughout the country after Grant's first victory to have made the Union armies absolutely irresistible by any force the South could raise and arm at that time.

There has been much irrelevant discussion about the ability or inability of commanders in the North and South. The fact is that political instead of military ideas controlled in very large degree the selection of commanders in the Union armies; while for three whole years the authorities in Washington could not see the necessity of unity of action in all the armies under one military leader. It required three years of costly experience to teach the government that simple lesson, taught in the military text-books! As experience finally proved, there was no lack of men capable of leading even large armies to victory; but, with few exceptions, they were not put in command until many others had been tried. Information as to military fitness was not sought from military sources. If a lawyer is wanted for the supreme bench, or an engineer to construct a great bridge, information is sought from the best men of the profession concerned; but the opinions of politicians were thought sufficient in determining the selection of major-generals!

Again, the policy of the government required the capture and occupation of all the important seaports and other places in the South, and the permanent occupation and protection of all the territory gained in military operations. Until near the close of the war, neither the public nor the government seemed to have the remotest conception of the fundamental fact that Confederate armies, wherever they might go, instead of places and States, were the only real objectives. Even some of the best Union generals were constrained to act upon this popular heresy, contrary to their own sound military judgment and education. Yet while this erroneous " territorial" strategy was insisted on, no adequate conception was formed of the vastly greater force required to hold all the territory gained, and to push aggressive operations still further into the heart of the South. Very rarely indeed were the Union armies large enough, until near the end of the war, to assure success. The end finally came through a long succession of desperate battles between forces so nearly equal that decisive victory was impossible until the weaker side finally became exhausted. Thus the aggregate loss in men as well as in money was vastly greater than it would have been if the Union had put forth its full strength and ended the rebellion in two years instead of four.

It is true that some of the worst of these " blind guides " were men supposed to have a very high military education. But if sound military education had been at all general in the country, statesmen would have known by what standard to judge of any one man's fitness for high command.

It is true that no amount of military education can supply the place of military genius or create a great commander. It may possibly happen at any time that there may not be among all the living graduates of West Point one Grant or Sherman or Sheridan, or one Lee or Johnston or Jackson. So much greater the need of a well-educated staff and a well-disciplined army. Nobody is wise enough to predict who will prove best able to command a great army. But it is the easiest thing in the world to tell who can best create such an army and command its subdivisions, and this is the work to be done instantly upon the outbreak of war. The selection of commanders for the several armies, and, above all, of a general-in-chief, must of course be the most difficult; for it is not probable that any man young enough will have had any experience in such commands in this country. But even this difficulty will disappear in a very great measure if statesmen will make the study of the art and science of war, instead of far less important subjects, a part of their pastime. They will thus acquire the ability to judge, from personal acquaintance with military men and conversation with others best informed, of the relative fitness of officers for the highest commands.

There is no possible remedy for such evils as this country has suffered except general military education. In my opinion, no man is fit for a seat in Congress unless he has such an education. The first thing he ought to learn is the old and trite military maxim that the only way to carry on war economically is to make it "short, sharp, and decisive." To dole out military appropriations in driblets is to invite disaster and ultimate bankruptcy. So it is in respect to the necessary preparations for war in time of peace. No man is wise enough to tell when war will come. Preparations are made upon the theory that it may come at any time. If a hundred millions are necessary for adequate preparation for defense, and you have spent only fifty when war comes, you might as well have thrown your fifty millions into the sea. There is no such thing as partial defense in modern war. If there are weak points in your defenses, your enemy is sure to find them. Indeed, he knows about them all the time, and will strike them at once. Then your whole costly system will be worthless.

What would be thought of the business capacity of a man who would not insure his house or his store or his stock of goods against fire because he did not happen to have money enough in bank to pay the premium, but would have to borrow it at three per cent.? Or of a man who would wait until he had realized the expected profit on a commercial venture before insuring the goods? If preparation for defense is the policy of a country, it would be little short of blindness to delay it on account of a temporary deficiency in the current revenues.

All now admit that universal education is an indispensable requisite to fitness for universal suffrage. The most serious questions upon which a free people can be called to vote are: a question of war, a question of preparation for war, and a question of approval and support, or disapproval and condemnation, of an administration on account of the mode in which war has been conducted. Can this highest duty of the citizen be intelligently performed without military education ? A sovereign *individual* regards this as demanding the highest education and the ablest counsel he can possibly obtain. Can sovereign *millions* do it wisely without any education whatever ? I believe no proposition could possibly be plainer than that general military education is indispensable to good citizenship in this country, and especially to all who may be intrusted with high responsibilities in the legislative and executive departments of the National Government. What would be thought of a general of the army who tried to shield himself from censure or punishment behind his ignorance of the law ? Can a legislator be excused because he knows nothing of the art and science of war? If there is any one offense in this country which ought never, under any circumstances, to be pardoned, it is ignorance in those who are trusted by the people to manage the affairs of their government. As in the military, so in the civil departments of government, there are few greater crimes than that of seeking and assuming the responsibilities of an office for which the man himself knows he is not fit. It is nearly as great as that committed by the appointing power under similar circumstances.

A system of general military education should of course include elementary training in all the schools, public and private, so that every boy, before he is sixteen years old, would know how to use the rifled musket in ranks, and be familiar with the simple evolutions of a company and battalion. Young men never forget such training received when they are boys. The country would have in a few years several millions of fairly well-trained young soldiers, requiring only competent officers and a few days' drill in regimental tactics to make a reliable army for any service this country will probably ever require of her volunteer soldiery. If it were a question of the invasion of a foreign country against a modern veteran army, the case would be different. But for defense against any possible landing of a hostile army on our shores, our available force ought to be so overwhelming in numbers as to far more than compensate for lack of experience. Yet it must not be forgotten that some training is *indispensable*. No possible advantage in numbers can overcome the disadvantage resulting from total ignorance of tactics and of the use of the modern long-range rifle. Good parents who apprehend evil effects from giving their boys military training ought to reflect that the boys will go, all the same, whether trained or not, when the country is threatened with invasion. Then, if ignorant, they will simply be doomed to fall the victims of skilled marksmen to whose shots they know not how to reply. Possibly the most cruel fate which American parents could prepare for their sons would be to keep them in ignorance of the highest duty their country may call upon them to perform, so that, unable to offer any effective resistance to invasion, they could only die in a hopeless effort to do their duty as citizen soldiers and patriots—or, worse, live only to be driven in disgrace from a field which a little education would have enabled them gloriously to win.

There should be, under State authority, a general enrolment and organization of all the young men who have received military training, and places of rendezvous fixed at convenient centers at or near railway-stations. Officers of all grades up to that of colonel should be appointed in advance, and occasional musters held under State laws, even if military exercises were not attempted.

Our colleges and high schools, besides the military academies of the country, are even now educating a fair percentage of young men to be officers of such an organization of enrolled regiments as that here suggested. This percentage could easily be increased in accordance with the demand. Besides, the retired men of the regiments of the National Guard in the several States might furnish some officers for the enrolled militia. But those well-trained and fully equipped regiments would be required to move with full ranks at once to the place of danger. Hence their active members would not be available in the great expansion of the army in the first period of war. The organization of the first reserve must, for this reason, be entirely independent of the National Guard.

A great and very important advance has already been made in bringing the regular army into close relations with the National Guard of the several States, and in the employment of regular officers in disseminating military education, both theoretical and practical, throughout the country. These are among the most valuable services the regular army can render in time of peace, and they should be extended, if practicable, still further. Especially in the State artillery, which must soon be organized for war service in the new fortifications, instruction by regular officers will be indispensable, and this can best be given in conjunction with the regular garrisons, the same as in war service. It would also be well to perfect an arrangement by which the new infantry regiments, when first taking the field upon the breaking out of war, might be accompanied by small bodies of regulars, to lead the way and indicate by example what is to be done. Experience has shown that under such example the rawest volunteers will be almost as stanch in battle as the regulars themselves. The beneficial effect upon new troops of the example of men who have before been in battle is very great. Hence it is that old regiments should always be kept full by the addition of recruits, rather than that the casualties of service be replaced by new regiments.

What constitutes valuable education, military no less than civil, is often greatly misunderstood. Elementary education and practical training are indispensable to everybody, while higher education may be rather injuri-

ous than beneficial, unless it is so regulated as to cultivate the reasoning faculties and independence of thought,
rather than mere acquisition of knowledge. Some notable examples of this have appeared in the military annals
of this country, and no doubt in the civil also. Men who
had become famous military scholars were total failures
in war, not only as commanders in the field, for which no
amount of theoretical education alone can qualify a man,
but also as military advisers. This was apparently because their elaborate studies had made them mere imi-
tators or copyists. Whatever originality of thought or
power of invention they ever possessed had ceased to
exist from disuse. They could plan and direct a campaign with absolute accuracy, according to the teachings
of the great masters, for the well-defined purpose upon
which those teachings had been based. But when a
wholly new problem was presented to them, they had no
conception of the right mode of solving it. The plan of
one great campaign was based absolutely upon the best-
approved method of capturing a certain place, without
any reference to what damage might or might not be
done to the opposing army in that operation. The plan
of another great campaign had for its sole object the conquest and permanent occupation of a great territory, and
was so conducted as to avoid the possibility of seriously
hurting the enemy in that operation. Yet the theory upon
which this last plan was based, as well as the first, governed the policy of the government more than two years.

It was not until Grant took command of "all the armies" that the true strategic principle governed the general military policy. In this connection, the story told by
Grant himself about his military studies is very instructive. When asked by the representative of some friends
who wished to present him a library for his new house in
Washington, what military books he then had, so that
they might not duplicate them, he replied that he did not

have any military books, and never had any, except the West Point text-books. No doubt Grant might have profited by some additional study, but none at all was far better than so much as to have dwarfed his mind into that of an imitator of former commanders.

The development of great military ability in Grant, as the result of his own experience and independent thought, — that is, the independent development of his own native military genius, — is by far the most interesting part of his history.

In short, the great lesson taught by our own experience is that elementary military training should be universal, because every young man may be called upon to perform the duties of a soldier; that general military reading, and habits of independent thought upon all great military subjects, should be cultivated by all who aspire to any high place in life, because they may be called upon to discharge the highest possible duties of good citizens in peace or in war, namely, those connected with the national defense; that due preparation for defense ought to be made without delay, and the requisite means kept always ready; and, above all, that the best method of making the quickest possible effective use of those means ought to be fully matured and understood by all who may be called upon to execute the orders of the government.

It now seems to me amazing that the affairs of an enlightened nation could have been so badly managed as to leave the secession issue in doubt almost to the last moment of a four years' contest, as it is now well known it was. Probably the one saving fact in all those years was that the young soldiers of the republic — and they were nearly all young then — knew little and cared less about the wrangling of self-seeking politicians and visionary doctrinaires in the rear, but fought steadily on to the end, never doubting for a moment the final triumph. I have never been able to recall a single instance of doubt manifested by any soldier in the field, though I did know a very few cases of officers of considerable rank, who thought they ought to have had more rank, who went to the rear and said something about failure in the field.

I believe now that it required only some *real* emergency, such, for instance, as the capture of Washington in July, 1863, to call forth the power of the North and crush the rebellion in six months. If any man thinks a great disaster would have disheartened the North, he knows nothing of the people of our country. It was the slow waste of enormous resources and of latent military strength that at length made many even of the stoutest hearts begin to feel despondent. I do not believe there was any time when the people would not have responded with unanimity and enthusiasm to an appeal to put forth all their strength and end the rebellion at a single blow.

The one lesson of reason and experience that I would impress upon my countrymen in every possible way is, when war or insurrection comes or is threatened, do not trifle with it. Do not invoke judicial proceedings, or call for 75,000 men; but call for *men*, and let them come as many as will! If some of them do not get there in time, before it is all over, it will not cost much to send them home again! The services of the Pennsylvania reserve, though ready for the field, were actually, positively refused until after the disaster of Bull Run! The greatest wonder in the history of this wonderful republic is that the government actually survived such a military policy as that!

In this connection, it ought to be distinctly understood that the great object of education at West Point and other military schools is not to make high commanders, but to make thorough soldiers, men capable of creating effective armies in the shortest possible time, and of commanding comparatively small bodies of men. If great commanders are ever again required in this country, they will come to the front in due time. They cannot be selected in advance of actual trial in war. Even West Point, though one of the best schools in the world, can at the most only lay the foundation of a military education. Each individual must build for himself upon that foundation the superstructure which is to mark his place in the world. If he does not build, his monument will hardly appear above the surface of the ground, and will soon be covered out of sight.

It is of vital importance that the necessity of providing for calling into active service a very large army in the shortest possible time be fully understood. It is assumed that every important seaport will in time be so fortified as to be safe against any *unsupported* naval attack. Modern science has rendered this easy and certain. Hence a naval attack must necessarily be supported by the landing of a military force upon the open coast, to attack the land defenses in reverse; and such defenses are now far more vulnerable to attack in rear than those of former times.

The sea-coasts of the United States are many thousand miles in extent, and an attack may be made at any one or several of the many important seaports in these long lines of coast. No one can anticipate where the blow or blows may fall. Hence it is necessary to be prepared to resist an attempt to land at any one of those many points which are of such importance as to tempt an enemy to attack them. The railroad facilities of the country are such that the necessary armies can be moved to all exposed points in time to meet any emergency. But the armies must be ready to move almost at a moment's notice. There will be no time to organize, much less to drill, new troops. Before that could be done, any one or two or three of our largest seaport cities could be captured and destroyed, and the invading forces get back again on their transports, and under the protection of the guns of their own fleet. And even if we had a navy more powerful than that of our enemy, it alone could give us no adequate protection; for the enemy would be sure to select a point of attack where our navy was not at the time, and which it could not reach until too late. Indispensable as a navy is to this country, it cannot act any very important part in the defense of so extended a sea-coast unless it is many times more powerful than any fleet which an enemy may send to attack us. The enemy being free to choose his point of attack, we would require at or near every one of the exposed points a fleet at least as large as his, or in the aggregate at least five times as large. No one, it is presumed, contemplates the creation of any such navy as that in this country.

Indeed, it would be the height of folly to require the navy to take part in the defense. In a country having the situation of the United States, the navy is the *aggressive* arm of the national military power. Its function is to punish an enemy until he is willing to submit to the national demands. For this purpose entire freedom of action is essential; also secure depots whence supplies may be drawn and where necessary repairs may be made, and harbors where cruisers or other vessels may seek safety if temporarily overpowered. Hence arises one of the most important functions of the land defense: to give the aggressive arm secure bases of operation at all the great seaports where navy-yards or depots are located. It may be that in special cases military forces may be needed to act in support of naval operations, or to hold for a time important points in a foreign country; but such service must be only auxiliary, not a primary object. Foreign conquest and permanent occupation are not a part of the policy of this country. There is no division of opinion among standard naval and military authorities on this great subject; such standard authors as Rear-Admiral Walker and Captain Mahan have clearly set forth the relative functions of the army and the navy in enforcing the military policy of the United States. The military problem which this country must solve is to provide such means of aggressive and defensive action as to be able to enforce a due observance of American public law on this continent, and, while doing this, to defend itself against insult and spoliation. The land defenses, including torpedoes and in a few cases floating batteries, should be entirely independent of the active navy, so that the latter may be free to act in one compact mass against any enemy which may anywhere oppose it.

There will be another important necessity for very large forces of infantry and light artillery,—that is, large in the aggregate,—in the event of war with even a second- or third-class naval power: to protect our long lines of open coast and small unfortified harbors from destruction by the guns and landing-parties of the enemy's light-draft cruisers. This would require a " picket-line " with considerable "reserves," several thousand miles in length. The national pride, if not the material interests involved, would not permit the government to submit to such destruction or spoliation without making every possible effort to prevent it. In short, unless the government and the people of the United States are willing to prepare in advance for putting into the field at a moment's notice a very large and effective army, as well as to fortify all important seaports, they may as well make up their minds to submit, at least for a time, to whatever indignity any considerable naval power may see fit to inflict upon them. No half-way measures will do any good. Fortifications without an army would be worth no more, against any country having a considerable army and navy, than an army without fortifications.

CHAPTER XXX

ANOTHER great lesson taught by our Civil War, perhaps even more important than any other, is the
financial lesson. An established government which has a
place to maintain among the commercial nations of the
world must maintain its credit. It must purchase its supplies and munitions of war and pay its troops *in money*.
In a great and prolonged war it is not possible for the
people to contribute all the means required at the time.
The amount of taxation would be greater than any people
could bear. Hence the government must borrow the
necessary money. This cannot be done without national
credit. If credit declines, rates of interest and discount
on securities increase until the national debt reaches its
limit and no more money can be borrowed. In short, the
nation becomes bankrupt. This was the condition of
the United States before the close of the late Civil War.
With a million of men on the muster- and pay-rolls, including several great armies of veteran troops in the field,

while the Confederate army was reduced to a very small fraction of that number, the Union cause was on the very verge of failure, because the government could no longer raise money to pay its troops, purchase supplies, or make any further use of its magnificent armies. This astounding fact was confided to the generals of the army in the winter of 1864–5 by the Secretary of War, who then said the rebellion must be suppressed in the coming spring campaign, or the effort abandoned, because the resources of the treasury were exhausted. In corroboration of my recollection on this subject, I now find the following in a private letter written by me at that time:

WASHINGTON, February 3, 1865.

There is much excitement here over the peace rumors, and it would seem there must be good foundation for it. The President has actually gone to Fort Monroe to meet the rebel commissioners. I do not, however, indulge much faith in the result of these negotiations. We will probably have to beat Lee's army before we can have peace. There is much commotion among politicians, and there will be a storm of some kind on the political sea if peace is made now. On the other hand, if the war continues long, the treasury will most likely become bankrupt. It has got far behind already. There is no money to pay the army, and no one can tell where it is to come from. I have succeeded in getting enough to pay my troops, which was obtained by special arrangement with the treasury, and as a special reward for their distinguished services. No other troops in the country have been paid for five months, and there is no money to pay them.

The reasons for this deplorable condition of the United States treasury are understood by all financiers. Yet a very large proportion of the voting population do not appear to understand it, or do not know the fact. People engaged in an effort to throw off their dependency or political connection, and establish their own independence, or a country defending itself against a powerful adversary, may be compelled to resort to forced loans, in the absence of national credit, to carry on the war. But in a great country with unlimited resources, like the United States, resort to forced loans would seem to be entirely unnecessary. However this may be, and whatever may be the necessity in any case, a forced loan, *without interest*, is simple robbery to the extent of unpaid interest, even if the principal is paid. And a robber cannot expect to have much credit left after his character becomes known to the world.

The issue of legal-tender notes during the Civil War was of this character. The country received a deadly blow to its financial credit when that policy was adopted. Nations or peoples cannot, any more than individuals, violate the established rules of honest dealing without suffering the just penalty. If money is needed beyond current revenues, there is no other honest way to get it but by borrowing it at such rate of interest and upon such security as can be agreed upon. Besides, to leave any room for doubt or cavil about the conditions of a loan, or about the standard of money in which principal and interest are to be paid, necessarily arouses suspicion of bad faith, and hence destroys or seriously injures national credit. It is now perfectly well known to all who have taken the pains to study the subject that this false and practically dishonest policy, however innocently it may have been conceived, cost the United States many hundreds of millions of dollars, and came very near bringing disaster upon the Union cause. One of the most astounding spectacles ever presented in the history of the world was that presented by this country. It went into the war practically free from debt, and came out of it with a debt which seemed very large, to be sure, and was in fact nearly twice as large as it ought to have been, yet so small in comparison with the country's resources that it could be paid off in a few years. It went into the war practically without an army, and came out of the war

with its military strength not even yet fully developed.
It had more than a million of men, nearly all veterans, in
the ranks, and could have raised a million more, if necessary, without seriously interfering with the industries of
the country. Yet in four short years a false financial
policy destroyed the national credit, brought its treasury to bankruptcy, and thus reduced a great people to
a condition in which they could no longer make any
use of their enormous military strength! This lesson
ought to be taught in every school-house in the United
States, until every child is made to understand that there
is no such thing in the world as paper money; that the
only real money in the world is standard gold and silver;
that paper can be used in the place of money only when
it represents the real gold or silver in which it can at any
time be redeemed; that even gold and silver can be used
together as standard money only under their real intrinsic
values as recognized by all the world; that any attempt
to force either gold or silver into unlimited circulation,
under any arbitrary ratio different from their real ratio,
is not honest; and that dishonesty is the worst of all financial policies, as well as the most unworthy of a civilized
people.

The laws of finance, like the laws of military strategy,
were never invented by anybody, any more than the law
of gravitation or the law of electrical attraction and re-
pulsion. They have all been learned by the experience
and study of mankind since the dawn of civilization.
All alike are parts of the great laws of nature. They
should be carefully and diligently studied and taught in all
the schools, until the rising generation understand that
all the affairs of mankind are governed by the uniform
laws established by the great Creator and Ruler of the
universe; and that self-appointed "leaders of the people"
who would entice them to follow their own inventions
cannot save them from the penalties which naturally

follow the violation of any of the laws of the universe. In short, education,—wisely directed education,—both in science and in morals, is the one indispensable foundation of good popular government. The relative importance to be attached to the many branches of popular education demands the careful consideration of all educators, and still more the *purity* of the doctrines taught in all the schools. There is good reason to believe that this last duty has been much neglected, especially in respect to financial theories.

In this connection, it is worthy of serious consideration whether one of the teachings of a corrupt age has not found its way into that almost sacred writing, the Constitution of the United States. What right has Congress, or any other department of government, or any government on earth, to "regulate the value" of money, any more than that of wheat or corn? Is not the real value of money, like that of everything else, regulated by the general law of supply and demand throughout the world? Ought not the value of money, and what shall constitute money, be left, without governmental interference, to be determined by the common consent of mankind? Must not commercial intercourse among all the countries of the world necessarily regulate all this, in spite of the decrees of government? Ought not the function of government in this regard to be limited to the coining of money and stamping on its face its real value—that is, in effect, the amount of gold or silver it actually contains? In short, is not the attempt of government to make a certain weight of one thing equal to a certain weight of another thing a plain violation of a natural law, and hence necessarily vicious? Is not all our serious monetary controversy in this country the result of vicious teaching to be found in our own Constitution, inherited from a corrupt age, when the fiat of a prince was thought sufficient to make a coin worth more than it was in fact? Where did so many of the people of the United States learn the heretical doctrine of fiat money? Is it not taught in the Constitution of the United States? It so seems to me, and hence it seems to me that the people should at once strike at the very root of the evil, and eradicate from their fundamental law the theory that the value of anything can be regulated by arbitrary fiat, in violation of natural law. Let the people restore to themselves their inalienable right to liberty of trade, so that they can deal with each other in gold, or in silver, or in cotton, or in corn, as they please, and pay in what they have agreed to pay in, without impertinent interference from legislators or anybody else. Then, and only then, can the monetary system of this country be placed on a sound foundation, and all the gold and silver of our mines, as well as all other products of human industry, and the people who produce or own them, become truly free.

Another important lesson taught by our experience since the Civil War, no less than at the commencement of that period, is that prompt and vigorous action, in accordance with established military methods, whenever military force must be employed, necessarily presupposes such knowledge of the laws on the part of department and army commanders as will justify the President in intrusting them with discretionary authority to act without specific orders in each case. Such emergencies as that of 1894, for example, give striking proof of the necessity for the higher education to fit men for high command in the army. It is not mainly a question of *military* education. Early deficiencies in that respect may soon be overcome by the constant practice afforded by active service. The indispensable necessity is for *education in general*, and especially in those things which army officers are not habitually required to know, but which are of vital importance to those who must, in great emergencies, be intrusted with great responsibilities and with discretionary authority. That very emergency of 1894 gave examples of officers, not educated at West Point nor at any other military school, distinguished for gallant and efficient military service in the field, who proved to be perfectly familiar with the principles of constitutional and military law which ought to govern the action of troops under circumstances like those of 1894; while others, distinguished as commanders in the field, seemed strangely ignorant of both constitutional and military laws. It is also worthy of remark that such necessary legal education did not appear to be universal among the West Point graduates at that time. Some men who are not graduates of West Point are much better qualified for high command than some who are.

Much has been said about a supposed prejudice in the army against officers who have not enjoyed the advantages of education at the military academy. I aver, emphatically, that I have never seen any evidence of any such feeling, and I do not believe it has ever existed to any appreciable extent. On the contrary, the general feeling has been that of just and generous consideration for officers who were at first laboring under that disadvantage. Some of the most popular men in the army have been among those appointed from civil life or from the volunteers. General Alfred H. Terry was a fair example of this. He was a ripe scholar, a thorough lawyer, a very laborious student of the art and science of war,— more so than most West Point graduates,— and so modest that he hesitated to accept the appointment of brigadier-general in the regular army, although it had been given for so distinguished a service as the capture of Fort Fisher, on the ground that older officers who had devoted their whole lives to the military service were better entitled to it.

The general feeling in the army has no special reference to West Point. It is a feeling, and a very strong one, in favor of *education*, of qualification in all respects for the service which may be required, of that dignified self-respect and becoming modesty which prevent an officer from desiring a position for which he is not fully qualified, and, above all, that manly delicacy which makes it impossible for an officer to *seek* a position which ought to be left to *seek him.* As well might a maiden ask a man to marry her, or get some one else to do it for her, as a soldier to seek in the same way a position on the staff of a general or of the President.

This is especially true in respect to the position of the "commanding general," or general-in-chief, of the army. The President being, by the Constitution, commander-in-chief of the army and navy, no law of Congress, even with his own consent, could relieve him from that responsibility. There is no law, and there could not constitutionally be any law passed, establishing any such office as that of commanding general of the army, and defining the duties and authority attached to it. Such a law would be a clear encroachment upon the constitutional prerogatives of the President. The only constitutional relation in which the so-called "commanding general," or "general-in-chief," of the army can occupy is that usually called "chief of the staff"—the chief military adviser and executive officer of the commander-in-chief. He cannot exercise any command whatever independently of the President, and the latter must of necessity define and limit his duties. No other authority can possibly do it. In this regard the President's power and discretion are limited only by his constitutional obligation to exercise the chief command himself. He can give his general-in-chief as much authority as he pleases consistently with that obligation. Hence it is entirely in the discretion of the President to define and fix the relations which should exist between the general and the Secretary of War—a very difficult thing to do, no doubt,—at least one which seems never to have been satisfactorily done by any President. The Secretary and the general appear to have been left to arrange that as best they could, or to leave it unarranged. However this may be, the relations of the general to the President are, or ought to be, of the most confidential character, no less so than those of any member of the cabinet. And the necessity of that confidential relation is far more important than in the case of any cabinet officer, for the reason that it is brought into prominence in times of great emergency, when questions of peace and war are involved, and when the President is required to act upon momentous military questions about which he cannot, in general, have much knowledge, and hence must trust to the ability, judgment, discretion, and scientific military knowledge of the general-in-chief. In such cases the general becomes, as it were, the "keeper of the President's conscience" in respect to the most momentous questions he can ever have to decide.

It is necessarily extremely embarrassing to the President to be compelled to place or retain in that close, confidential, and important relation to himself an officer in whom he has not entire confidence in all respects; or else, as the only alternative, by selecting another, to cast a reflection upon the senior in rank, whose soldierly character and services may have entitled him to the highest distinction. The situation is no less embarrassing, under the existing law and custom, to the officer who may at any time happen to be the senior in commission. He may be compelled to submit to the humiliation of being superseded by some junior in rank, or else to occupy a confidential position of great importance in the absence of that confidence which is necessary to make such a position even tolerable to himself or to the army, which must inevitably be deprived of his legitimate influence for good if he does not enjoy the confidence of the President and the Secretary of War. There can be no relief from this dilemma, so embarrassing to both the President and the general, except by appropriate legislation.

The most important military reform now required in this country is a law authorizing the President, "by and with the advice and consent of the Senate," to appoint, not a commander of the army, but a "general-in-chief," or "chief of staff," to aid him (the commander-in-chief) in the discharge of his military duties. The President ought to have the power to retire such officer at any time, with due regard for his rank and services, and to appoint another in the same manner. The title "commanding general of the army" is inappropriate and misleading. There never has been any such office in this country, except that created especially for General Grant in 1864. The old title of "general-in-chief," given to the officer at the head of the army before the Civil War, is the appropriate title in this country. That officer is, in fact, the chief general, but does not command the army.

If it be considered the best policy to reserve the two highest military grades,—those of general and lieutenant-general,—to be conferred only by special act of Congress for distinguished services, appropriate distinction may be given to the officer at the head of the army at any time by the title of general-in-chief, with such additional compensation as is necessary to defray his living expenses in Washington. Neither the rank nor the pay of an officer in a subordinate position can possibly be regarded as appropriate to one in a higher grade of duty. Every grade of public service should have an officer of appropriate rank and compensation, certainly the highest in any department even more than any other. The government of this country has not been duly regardful even of its own dignity and self-respect, in denying to its chief military officer appropriate rank, and in requiring him to expend all the savings of a lifetime to maintain his official position for a few years at the seat of government.

Not by any means the least benefit to be expected from a law authorizing each President to select his chief general, would be the education thus given to officers of the army in respect to the relation in which they stand to the commander-in-chief, and in respect to the reasonable limits of military ambition in a republic where the President is and must be commander-in-chief, whether he is a man of military education and experience or not.

So strongly were these views impressed upon my mind by my studies of the subject, made at the request of General Grant and General Sherman many years ago, that when I became the senior officer of the army I refrained scrupulously from suggesting to the President or the Secretary of War or anybody else that I had any expectation of being assigned to the command, or regarded myself as having any claim to it. It seemed to me solely a question for the President himself to decide whether or not he wanted me as his chief military adviser and assistant, and it would have been impossible for me to consent that anybody should try to influence his decision in my favor.

The duties of patriotic citizenship in time of war have not always been duly appreciated, even by those most zealous in their loyalty to the government. I would not detract one iota from the honor and fame of the wise, brave, and patriotic statesmen who upheld the hands of the great Lincoln in his struggle against the avowed foes of the Union, and his still harder struggle with professed patriots who wielded national influence only for evil, though under the guise of friends of the Union. But if many thousands of those zealous and "truly loyal Union men," many of whom I knew, could have managed in some way to get into the ranks and get killed in battle the first year, I firmly believe the Union would have been restored much sooner than it was.

When the people have chosen their chief to lead them

through the fierce storms of civil war, he alone must guide the ship, or else all must perish. After the storm has burst upon them it is too late to select another pilot. Then partizan opposition, impairing the popular strength and confidence of the leader and embarrassing his military operations or public policy, becomes treason, and a far more dangerous treason than any which the open sympathizers with the public enemy could possibly commit. Those powerful leaders of public opinion who hounded Lincoln on to measures which his far greater wisdom and his supreme sense of responsibility told him were unwise, deserved to be hanged, or at least to be imprisoned until the war was over. That some of them died in shame and disgrace upon the failure of their own selfish schemes for personal or political aggrandizement, was only a mild measure of righteous retribution.

In the calm atmosphere of these later years I still think that the course of the young soldier who had not learned any of the arts or of the ambitions of partizan leaders, but whose only motto was " the President's policy is my policy; his orders my rule of action," was much more in accord with the plain duty of every citizen of the republic. I can find in my mind or heart only contempt for that theory of patriotic duty which sends one citizen to the front, freely to give his life, without question, to enforce the orders of the chosen leader of the nation, and permits another to stay at home and bend all his efforts toward forcing the substitution of his own egotistical views upon the country, in lieu of those which the great leader has decided to be most wise.

Let the names of the great war governors, and of the statesmen in Congress and cabinet who gave all of their strength to the support of the measures of Lincoln, stand by the side of the foremost commanders of armies on the roll of national honor. Let the others be covered by the mantle of charity, and quietly pass into oblivion.

CHAPTER XXXI

GENERAL SHERMAN'S FRIENDSHIP — HIS DEATH — GENERAL
GRANT'S RECOGNITION OF SERVICES — HIS GREAT TRAIT,
MORAL AND INTELLECTUAL HONESTY — HIS CONFIDENCE
IN HIMSELF — GRANT, LIKE LINCOLN, A TYPICAL AMERICAN
— ON THE RETIRED LIST OF THE ARMY — CONCLUSION.

GENERAL SHERMAN never failed to manifest his
generous appreciation of my services as one of his
trusted lieutenants, from the time we met in the field
until he retired from command of the army. Our long-
standing friendship increased till the time of his death.
While I was in command of the army, General Sherman
never came to Washington without coming very promptly
to see me at headquarters, not waiting for a first visit
from his junior in rank. Of course this great and cordial
courtesy was very promptly returned. Upon the occasions of these visits at the office, the general would sit a
long time, talking in his inimitably charming manner
with me and the staff officers who came in with their
morning business. Then he would insist upon my going
with him to call upon the President, a formality which
was demanded by his high sense of the respect due from
him and me together, as past and present commanding
generals, to the commander-in-chief. This high regard
for military courtesy which was a characteristic of General Sherman, though he seemed comparatively indifferent to any lack of it toward himself, well merits the
imitation of all military men.

The last of those visits occurred a very short time before the general's death. He was then well aware of the weakness which so soon proved fatal to him, and submitted like a child while I wrapped him up before going over to the White House. Upon my suggestion of the necessity of caution, he said, " Yes," and gripping his hand near his chest, added, " It will catch me like that some time, and I will be gone." Yet General Sherman preferred the life in New York which was so congenial to him, rather than seek to prolong his days in a milder climate.

We laid him by the side of his wife, that highest type of the Christian woman, wife, and mother. Who can ever forget that touching scene by the grave in St. Louis? The brave young priest, the very image in character, even more than in face, of his great father, standing alone, without another of all the priests of his church, and daring, without ecclesiastical sanction or support, to perform the service for the dead prescribed by his church for those who " die in the Lord." " Worthy son of a noble sire!" What man dares to pass judgment upon him who so mightily helped to save his country from ruin, and to strike the shackles from millions of slaves, or to say that he was not worthy to be numbered among those to whom the Divine Master has said, "Inasmuch as ye have done it unto one of the least of these my brethren, ye have done it unto me"?

The subject of this volume being limited to events of which I have had personal knowledge, and it never having been my good fortune to serve in the field with General Grant, it would be inappropriate to make herein any general comments upon his military operations. But I cannot close this account of events so closely connected with my own official life without making acknowledgment of my obligations to that great-hearted man for the justice, kindness, and generosity which he invariably manifested toward me whenever occasion offered.

It was General Grant whose voluntary application, in the winter of 1863-4, relieved me from the disagreeable controversy with partizan politicians in Missouri, and gave me command of an army in the field. It was upon his recommendation that my services in that command were recognized by promotion from the grade of captain to that of brigadier-general in the regular army and brevet major-general for services in the battle of Franklin. It was Grant who, upon my suggestion, ordered me, with the Twenty-third Corps, from Tennessee to North Carolina, to take part in the closing operations of the war, instead of leaving me where nothing important remained to be done. It was he who paid me the high compliment of selecting me to conduct the operations which might be necessary to enforce the Monroe doctrine against the French army which had invaded Mexico. It was he who firmly sustained me in saving the people of Virginia from the worst effects of the congressional reconstruction laws. It was he who greeted me most cordially as Secretary of War in 1868, and expressed a desire that I might hold that office under his own administration. And, finally, it was he who promoted me to the rank of major-general in the regular army, the next day after his inauguration as President.

It was a great disappointment to me to find only casual mention of my name in General Grant's " Memoirs." But I was not only consoled, but moved to deep emotion when told by his worthy son, Colonel Frederick Dent Grant, that his father had not ceased up to the last day of his life to cherish the same kind feeling he had always manifested toward me, and that one of his last fruitless efforts, when he could no longer speak, was to put on paper some legible words mentioning my name.

General Sherman wrote that he could not understand Grant, and doubted if Grant understood himself. A very distinguished statesman, whose name I need not mention, said to me that, in his opinion, there was nothing special in Grant to understand. Others have varied widely in their estimates of that extraordinary character. Yet I believe its most extraordinary quality was its extreme simplicity — so extreme that many have entirely overlooked it in their search for some deeply hidden secret to account for so great a character, unmindful of the general fact that simplicity is one of the most prominent attributes of greatness.

The greatest of all the traits of Grant's character was that which lay always on the surface, visible to all who had eyes to see it. That was his moral and intellectual integrity, sincerity, veracity, and justice. He was incapable of any attempt to deceive anybody, except for a legitimate purpose, as in military strategy; and, above all, he was incapable of deceiving himself. He possessed that rarest of all human faculties, the power of a perfectly accurate estimate of himself, uninfluenced by pride, ambition, flattery, or self-interest. Grant was very far from being a modest man, as the word modest is generally understood. His just self-esteem was as far above modesty as it was above flattery. The highest encomiums were accepted for what he believed them to be worth. They did not disturb his equilibrium in the slightest degree.

While Grant knew his own merits as well as anybody did, he also knew his own imperfections, and estimated them at their real value. For example, his inability to speak in public, which produced the impression of extreme modesty or diffidence, he accepted simply as a fact in his nature which was of little or no consequence, and which he did not even care to conceal. He would not for many years even take the trouble to jot down a few words in advance, so as to be able to say something when called upon. Indeed, I believe he would have regarded it as an unworthy attempt to appear in a false light if he had made preparations in advance for an "extemporaneous" speech. Even when he did in later years write some notes on the back of a dinner-card, he would take care to let everybody see that he had done so by holding the card in plain view while he read his little speech. After telling a story in which the facts had been modified somewhat to give the greater effect, which no one could enjoy more than he did, Grant would take care to explain exactly in what respects he had altered the facts for the purpose of increasing the interest in his story, so that he might not leave any wrong impression.

When Grant's attention was called to any mistake he had committed, he would see and admit it as quickly and unreservedly as if it had been made by anybody else, and with a smile which expressed the exact opposite of that feeling which most men are apt to show under like circumstances. His love of truth and justice was so far above all personal considerations that he showed unmistakable evidence of gratification when any error into which he might have fallen was corrected. The fact that he had made a mistake and that it was plainly pointed out to him did not produce the slightest unpleasant impression, while the further fact that no harm had resulted from his mistake gave him real pleasure. In Grant's judgment, no case in which any wrong had been done could possibly be regarded as finally settled until that wrong was righted; and if he himself had been, in any sense, a party to that wrong, he was the more earnest in his desire to see justice done. While he thus showed a total absence of any false pride of opinion or of knowledge, no man could be firmer than he in adherence to his mature judgment, or more earnest in his determination, on proper occasions, to make it understood that his opinion was his own, and not borrowed from anybody else. His pride in his own mature opinion was very great; in that he was as far as possible from being a modest man. This absolute confidence in his own judg-

35

ment upon any subject which he had mastered, and the moral courage to take upon himself alone the highest responsibility, and to demand full authority and freedom to act according to his own judgment, without interference from anybody, added to his accurate estimate of his own ability and his clear perception of the necessity for undivided authority and responsibility in the conduct of military operations, and in all that concerns the efficiency of armies in time of war, constituted the foundation of that very great character.

When summoned to Washington to take command of all the armies, with the rank of lieutenant-general, he determined, before he reached the capital, that he would not accept the command under any other conditions than those above stated. His sense of honor and of loyalty to the country would not permit him to consent to be placed in a false position,—one in which he could not perform the service which the country had been led to expect from him, —and he had the courage to say so in unqualified terms.

These are the traits of character which made Grant a very great man—the only man of our time, so far as can be known, who possessed both the character and the military ability which were, under the circumstances, indispensable in the commander of the armies which were to suppress the great rebellion.

It has been said that Grant, like Lincoln, was a typical American, and for that reason was most beloved and respected by the people. That is true of the statesman and of the soldier, as well as of the people, if it is meant that they were the highest type, that ideal which commands the respect and admiration of the highest and best in a man's nature, however far he may know it to be above himself. The soldiers and the people saw in Grant or in Lincoln, not one of themselves, not a plain man of the people, nor yet some superior being whom they could not understand, but the personification of their highest ideal of a citizen, soldier, or statesman, a man whose greatness they could see and understand as plainly as they could anything else under the sun. And there was no more mystery about it all in fact than there was in the popular mind.

Matchless courage and composure in the midst of the most trying events of battle, magnanimity in the hour of victory, and moral courage to compel all others to respect his plighted faith toward those who had surrendered to him, were the crowning glories of Grant's great and noble character.

On September 29, 1895, came the hour when I had done, however imperfectly, all the duty my country required of me, and I was placed on the retired list of the army. Having been, at appropriate periods in my official career, by the unsolicited action of my official superiors, justly and generously rewarded for all my public services, and having been at the head of the army several years, near the close of the period fixed by law for active military service I was made the grateful recipient of the highest honor which the government of my country can confer upon a soldier, namely, that of appointment to a higher grade under a special act of Congress. My public life was, in the main, a stormy one, as this volume has, perhaps too fully, shown. Many times I felt keenly the injustice of those who did not appreciate the sincerity of my purpose to do, to the best of my ability, what the government desired of me, with little or no regard for my own personal opinions or ambitions. But I can now concede to nearly all those who so bitterly opposed me the same patriotic motives which I know inspired my own conduct; and I would be unworthy of my birthright as an American citizen if I did not feel grateful to my countrymen and to our government for all the kindness they have shown me.

THE END.

INDEX

549

36